Bethsaida

BETHSAIDA

A CITY BY THE NORTH SHORE
OF THE SEA OF GALILEE

EDITED BY
RAMI ARAV AND
RICHARD A. FREUND

VOLUME THREE
BETHSAIDA EXCAVATIONS PROJECT
REPORTS & CONTEXTUAL STUDIES

TRUMAN STATE UNIVERSITY

© 2004 Truman State University Press
All Rights Reserved
Published 2004 by Truman State University Press, Kirksville, Missouri 63501
tsup.truman.edu

Cover designer: Teresa Wheeler
Body type: ITC Stone Serif
Printed by Thomson-Shore, Inc., Dexter, Michigan USA

Library of Congress Cataloging-in-Publication Data

Bethsaida Excavations Project Reports and Contextual Studies
        p. cm.
    Includes bibliographical references and indexes.
    Contents: v. 3. Bethsaida : A city by the north shore of the Sea of Galilee / edited by Rami
Arav and Richard A. Freund
    ISBN 1-931112-38-X (casebound) ISBN 1-931112-39-8 (paperback)
    1. Bethsaida (Extinct city). 2. Excavations (Archaeology)—Israel—Bethsaida (Extinct
city). 3. Bible—Antiquities. 4. Rabbinical literature—History and criticism. I. Arav, Rami.
II. Freund, Richard A. III. Bethsaida Excavations Project Reports and Contextual Studies.

Contents

vi   *Contents*

Figures and Tables

Foreword

TZER, BETHSAIDA, AND JULIAS

I have lived here in the Holy Land intermittently since 1968. Like many others, I feel something special about this land. I especially receive inspiration from the famous biblical sites in Lower Galilee, the focus of Jesus' ministry. I like to walk by the Kennereth (the Sea of Galilee) and feel the early morning breeze (or stormy wind) long before the orange sun pops up from behind the Golan Heights. Somehow I feel at home here in the Galilee. Perhaps some of this feeling might be shared by reflecting on the continuing power of scriptural traditions that are now enriched by archaeological discoveries and insights.

During the past year, when I completed my tenure as Lady Davis Professor in the Hebrew University in Jerusalem, I went three times to et-Tell. The first time I came here, in November, a severe drought had affected the Kennereth. Near Magdala, the end of a dock—from which I once dove into the water—was about one hundred yards from the receding and brackish water. The second and third times, in late spring and summer, the abundant rains had colored the Kennereth a light green and the water was now at least two hundred yards closer to the old shoreline. Again, the dock was a good spot from which to dive safely into the sea. Sixty thousand years ago, one freshwater lake stretched from the slopes of Mount Hermon to the end of the sea now called the Dead Sea, and rivers once flowed further southward.

Even though et-Tell is now about a mile and a half from the shore of the Kennereth, I realized that the Jordan River is not now so far away from the site. The heavy rains and snow this year moved the Jordan River closer to the site; the roaring water was only a short distance from the western slope of et-Tell. It is likely that the Beteiha Plain has shifted over the past two thousand years and a quiet cove has silted up, separating et-Tell from the Kennereth.

At et-Tell I pondered the black basalt stones of Bethsaida. Sitting in the shade of a tree I contemplated the three names that have made this elevated hill famous: Geshur in the tenth century BCE, Bethsaida in the first century CE until 30, and then Julias.

Sitting outside the gates of et-Tell, I tried to imagine people entering and exiting the Iron Age city of Tzer, capital of the kingdom of Geshur. Surely one who passed this way was David's wife Maacah the daughter of King Talmai. David's third son, Absalom, spent three years here before traveling to Hebron from which he organized a rebellion against his father. Absalom too must have frequently entered and exited the wide gate to my left.

Three independent and important accounts tell us of Bethsaida in the first century: the Evangelists, Josephus, and Pliny the Elder. Is et-Tell the Bethsaida famous from the New Testament accounts of Jesus' ministry? Is et-Tell the location in which Jesus met Bartholomew and where the "Feeding of the Gentiles" is traditionally located? Were Andrew, Peter, Philip, and perhaps also James and John, the sons of Zebedee, from et-Tell?

Josephus informs us that he was injured during some unreported battle in or near Bethsaida and that the city was on the main road from Capernaum to Gamla. Pliny, who may have used Agrippa's lost *Geography* as one of his sources, tells us that Bethsaida is on the eastern portion of the Kennereth. About 530 CE, Theodosius informs us that as one moves northward from Tiberias, one travels two miles from Tabga to Capernaum and then another six miles to Bethsaida. In about 725 CE, Saint Willibald reported that in Bethsaida there was a church commemorating the house of Peter and Andrew.

After Jesus' death, the village called Bethsaida became a city and was renamed Julias. Philip built two new cities: Caesarea about thirty miles north of et-Tell and Julias at this site. Both cities honored the emperor Tiberius. One bore his name, Caesar, and the other Julia, Livia, or Julias. Josephus, who wrote from the seventies to a little after 100 CE, calls the site not only Bethsaida but also Julias. Ptolemy and Pliny also use the name Julia or Julias. The Evangelists, who wrote from the sixties to the nineties, never call this site Julia. The only name they use is Bethsaida.

The archaeologists of the Bethsaida Excavations Project may well have discovered the village cursed by Jesus because the inhabitants did not appreciate the mighty works he had performed there even though it was the home of at least three disciples. Scientific research may help us answer some questions, but often it brings into focus more challenging questions: Did the Evangelists stress Jesus' cures in Capernaum and Bethsaida because the towns were known to have physicians? Is the large "Fisherman's House" the house of Zebedee? If et-Tell is Bethsaida, did Jesus and his disciples not see the majestic walls and gates of ancient Geshur? Could Jesus have been thinking about Bethsaida, which is built on basalt, when he spoke about a city built on rock?

Archaeologists and biblical scholars are indebted to Rami Arav and his team of distinguished archaeologists for their labors at et-Tell and their focus on traditions related to Tzer, Bethsaida, and Julias. They certainly have found the remains of a tenth-century city, which is probably the Geshurite city of Tzer. It is notable that the walls and gates of this Iron Age city are exposed, but no wall or gate of the contemporary City of David (Jerusalem) has yet been discovered.

Historical and religious research is enriched by the years of archaeological excavations at Bethsaida/et-Tell. Fortunately for archaeologists, historians, and sociologists, Bethsaida was depopulated in the third century CE. No longer can it be said that Bethsaida's "name and all memory of its site have perished," hence "no positive identification can be made of it."*

James H. Charlesworth
Princeton Theological Seminary
Hebrew University
Jerusalem, Summer 2003

*Sir William Smith. 1893. *Dictionary of the Bible*. 2d ed. (London: William Clowes & Sons), 1:1:417.

Father Bargil Pixner, O.S.B. (1921–2002)

"The Spiritual Father of Bethsaida"

When the history of Bethsaida will finally be concluded, one person will stand out as a person who made it possible for the rest of us to write that history: Father Bargil Pixner. We called him the "Spiritual Father of Bethsaida" because he encouraged Rami Arav to excavate it fully back in the mid-1980s and he continued to provide the inspiration for volunteers, guides, pilgrims, and researchers to come to Bethsaida.

In the period following the Six Day War, Father Pixner visited many of the sites around the Golan and the Sea of Galilee which he was not able to visit before 1967 and began to draw his own conclusions about the religious importance of these sites. At the solitary mound of et-Tell, ringed by land mines and used by the Syrian military as an outpost until 1967, he came and began his own investigations of the area.

Father Pixner risked life and limb (according to him by "following cows grazing in the field around the mound") to climb to the top of the hill, and began to collect shards that indicated to him that a Greco-Roman site lay at his feet. Its panoramic view of the Sea of Galilee and its proximity to a spur of the Jordan River and an expanse of the Beteiha Plain made his insights more compelling. He identified architecture and walls near the surface, and he felt sure that et-Tell was indeed Bethsaida, even before the systematic excavations were launched.

He established a single basalt stone under a tree near the mound as the site of the miracle of the healing of the blind man (Mark 8:22–26). When I asked him how he knew that this was the site of the healing of the blind man, he said it occurred to him one day as he read the text and walked along the natural road from the archaeological site. He would peer at you with his piercing eyes and wonderful beard and take you by the hand and show you how he came to his conclusions. He never forced you to agree with him, just to experience the exhilaration of discovery that he had known. I saw many nuns, priests, and pilgrims who came with him and then brought other groups to sit by that rock under that tree. I often wondered whether he had created a religious experience or whether he had simply tapped into a well-spring of religious experience and given it expression. It was the power that one person of faith had to influence others.

Father Pixner was instrumental in the establishment of two open-air chapels at Bethsaida, both generous gifts from the Roman Catholic Church. One was established by the Archdiocese of Omaha and another by the Holy See in Jerusalem (of the Vatican). Both chapels are used by visitors of all religions when they visit the site.

He single-handedly developed two distinctly religious pilgrimage sites at Bethsaida that are found on most new pilgrim maps: one at the rock where the blind man was healed just outside the village of Bethsaida and the other at the pool of Bethsaida, a natural spring located at the base of the mound. The basalt rock, which is incised with an "open" eye, today rests under the shade of one of the ubiquitous eucalyptus trees and has become a place of reflection and rest for many weary travelers and pilgrims. For Father Pixner, it represented a real manifestation of the teachings of Mark 8:22–26; most of us bring our students to this spot and tell the story told to us by Bargil. Regarding the "pool of Bethsaida," I remember the first time I showed him the natural spring and the small, round basalt "port," and the enormous enjoyment he got from "discovering" another piece of the ancient history of Bethsaida. He told me it was here that the young Peter (the founder of the Western church) and the young Andrew (the founder of the Eastern church) would play in the water together. In his mind there was a simpler, more ecumenical time symbolized by Bethsaida before rabbinic Judaism and Christianity even existed as separate religions.

One of the most important parts of our work at Bethsaida has been creating connections between the different groups that visit Bethsaida on religious pilgrimage, for scientific information-gathering, and for the archaeological excavations. Father Bargil Pixner was a link between all of these diverse groups and his presence will be missed by all of our Bethsaida Excavations Project consortium members. He appeared in two documentaries that featured Bethsaida, "The Lost City of Bethsaida" and "The Fifth Gospel." He chaired sessions on Bethsaida held at many of the different national and international academic conferences in Italy, Switzerland, Germany, and the United States. For Rami and me, the most distinctive moments were his visits to the University of Nebraska at Omaha and the University of Hartford campuses as well as many of the other consortium universities, to lecture on the importance of Bethsaida for Jews and Christians.

Among the most memorable, however, was our meeting with Pope John Paul II during his visit to Israel in March 2000. It was Father Pixner who arranged for us to meet the pope at Tabgha. When the papal representative asked us to present the pope with a copy of one of the artifacts found at Bethsaida, a Roman key (first century) from the Fisherman's House, we knew it was Father Pixner who has initiated the pope's interest in the artifact. On the day of the presentation, we all waited at Tabgha for Father Pixner to return from the mass held on top of the "Mount of the Beatitudes" nearby. We had chosen not to go to the mass, because of the traffic and related difficulty of travel (to get to the Tabgha monastery after the ceremony). When we heard about an overturned car that was blocking passage for buses on the narrow path down the mountain to Tabgha, we feared that Father Pixner would not make it back for the ceremony. As we waited, the helicopter carrying the pope arrived. Then, Father Pixner (as if on cue) mystically appeared and was seen walking down the Mount of the Beatitudes in front of the massive security detail assigned to the pope's visit that ringed the Tabgha monastery. He knew all of the back roads and byways and was surprised at how concerned we were for his safety. The crowds of security guards parted for him as he walked between them into our waiting group.

As we offered the artifact on behalf of our member universities, we explained to the pope that it had come from the Fisherman's House at Bethsaida, home of Peter. Father Pixner looked at the pope and said: "It is the key of Peter." As we looked at Father Pixner, his face beamed and he went on to explain the history of the Bethsaida excavations as the pope quietly listened. And then we watched as the cardinals and bishops in the pope's entourage all began to kiss the outside of the glass case in which the key was framed. Father Pixner, a master of capturing the spirit of the moment, transported those present back almost two thousand years through his description of one simple artifact from the dig at Bethsaida.

When he last visited me in Hartford, Connecticut, in September 2000, we had an evening dedicated to Jewish-Christian unity and honored him by showing a short documentary on our visit with the pope. I introduced him with what he felt was the highest compliment. He was honored that I, as a rabbi, scholar of Judaic Studies, and director of the Bethsaida Excavations Project, wanted to introduce him by reading something from one of his books. I asked him to choose something that was meaningful from his books to read and was surprised by his choice. I thought he would choose something about the important archaeological discoveries he had made in Galilee and Jerusalem. He did not. He gave me a section to read from the preface of his book, *With Jesus in Jerusalem*. This is what I read:

> In the fall of 1944, when Hitler's engine of war was retreating on all fronts, there still remained in Southern Tirol some Italian subjects of German tongue, who had not yet been called up for service in the German army. But in the fall, their turn came, as the "final mobilization." I, too, was one of them, when in the fall of 1944, the Regiment of Brixen was called up for army service. In January 1945, the swearing-in ceremony was to take place. However, our entire regiment refused to take an oath to the Führer. We were disarmed and sent to the eastern front under SS-guard. I worked as a medical orderly of our company. On the Silesian front, the rifles were returned to us. Many fellow soldiers had already fallen, when I was ordered in April to find out who the soldier was who had been killed during the night, and was lying over there in the barn.

> When I lifted the blanket, I realized with dismay that it was my good friend, the eighteen-year-old Andreatta from Kaltern. In the room where I made the report, the SS officers of the regiment were assembled. They noticed how greatly I was affected by the death of this young friend.

> The captain, who knew that I was preparing myself for the priesthood, said sneeringly: "Now you may love your enemies; isn't that what you were told by this Jew Jesus?"

> "Yes, Jesus was a Jew, and he was the Son of God, as well."

> "Don't you see how stupid this is? How can the Son of God belong to this inferior people! They are the enemies of the German people. Tell me, do you love the Jews as well?"

> I gave him a bold retort, under these circumstances: "Yes, I love the Jews, after all, they are the people of Jesus."

> To this the SS-man screamed: "Pixner, leave this room immediately; anybody who speaks in such a way is not worthy of being a German soldier."

An SS-man who liked me whispered in my ear: "Pixner, you shouldn't have done that!" During those last desperate days of the war, people were shot or hanged for less than this. But I was not afraid; I had been straightforward and had expressed my sincere conviction."

It was this sincere conviction and love of all people that drew others to him. It was a rare and very profound characteristic and we will miss our "spiritual father" in more ways than one as we continue his work at Bethsaida and elsewhere.

Rabbi Dr. Professor Richard Freund
Director, Bethsaida Excavations Project
Director, Maurice Greenberg Center for Judaic Studies,
    University of Hartford

Acknowledgments

There have been many developments in the five years since the publication of the second volume of *Bethsaida: A City by the North Shore of the Sea of Galilee.*

The Bethsaida Excavations Project has added a number of new institutions and staff. We welcome into the consortium the University of Hartford (Connecticut), Creighton University (Nebraska), Iowa State University, Messiah College (Pennsylvania), the University of Wisconsin–Eau Claire, the University of Wisconsin–La Crosse, University of South Florida, and Komex International, Ltd. (Calgary, Alberta, Canada).

Numerous research projects have been launched and completed, thanks to the ongoing commitment of Bethsaida staff and faculty. In particular, this volume owes a great debt to the work of Wendi Chiarbos Jensen, Coordinator of the Bethsaida Excavations Project; Stephen Reynolds, Archivist; DreAnna Hadash, Staff Artist; Christine Dalenta, Chief Photographer; Charleen Green, Restorer; Carl Savage and Sandra Fortner, assistants to the Director of Excavations and Research; and the other staff involved in the ongoing research projects.

John F. Shroder Jr. of the University of Nebraska at Omaha continues as the overall Chief Geologist and participates in ongoing research in the Beteiha Plain with geographer Philip Reeder of the University of South Florida, ground penetrating radar specialist Harry Jol of the University of Wisconsin–Eau Claire, and geophysicist Paul Bauman of Komex International. Their ongoing research projects will be featured in the next volume of *Bethsaida: A City by the North Shore of the Sea of Galilee* and involve the subsequent study of the Beteiha Plain as well as the new techniques we have employed at Bethsaida to decide where to excavate in the future.

Zooarchaeologist Toni Fisher continues her work on the thousands of animal bones uncovered in the excavations. Conservation at the site continues under the direction of Orna Cohen. Arieh Kindler continues to work diligently on coin finds, while Donald Ariel of the Israel Antiquities Authority has begun work on associated inscribed pottery handles. Baruch Brandl of the Israel Antiquities Authority continues to work on seals. Andrea Rottloff's research on glass finds proceeds, and Monika Bernett has contributed important research on a variety of other areas. We note with great sadness the loss of our esteemed colleagues Father Bargil Pixner and staff member Pinchas Porat. Their presence at conferences and on-site, as well as their friendship, will be missed.

This volume contains some chapters originally presented in regional, national, and international meetings of the Society of Biblical Literature (SBL), the American Academy of Religion (AAR), and the American Schools of Oriental Research (ASOR) among many different academic societies. In particular, we would like to thank the SBL for allowing us to organize two sessions (one complete day of the conference) at the international SBL conferences in Cambridge (2003), Berlin (2002), Rome (2001), Lausanne (1997), and Budapest (1995). National and regional conferences of ASOR, AAR, and SBL also allowed us to gather and pursue research presented here and forthcoming in volume 4 of *Bethsaida: A City by the North Shore of the Sea of Galilee.*

Many articles and books too numerous to list have appeared on topics related to Bethsaida research over the past four years. We are gratified that the discoveries made at Bethsaida and our publication of data have contributed to developments in archaeology and literature of the Iron Age, as well as the Hellenistic and Roman periods.

Many of our directors have presented new research at conferences sponsored by the University of Nebraska at Omaha (UNO), under the auspices of International Studies and Programs, sponsor of the excavations and home of the Bethsaida Excavations Project. Our thanks to Thomas E. Gouttierre, UNO Dean of International Studies and Programs, who, from the very beginning of the UNO-Bethsaida relationship, has been a strong supporter of the research and its subprojects. Since 1999, UNO has hosted its own annual research conference in Biblical Archaeology, which is now known as the Clifton Batchelder Conference in Biblical Archaeology. Scholars of biblical archaeology, Bethsaida dig "alumni," students, and community members gather in Omaha for a conference featuring updates on the Bethsaida Project and other associated archaeological projects, including the John and Carol Merrill Cave of Letters Project, the John and Carol

Merrill Qumran Excavations Project, the Mary's Well and Bathhouse of Nazareth Archaeological Excavations Project, and the Yavne Excavations Project. In addition, many other archaeological and geological projects from other parts of the Mediterranean and Middle East have been presented at the Batchelder Conference, which has developed into a highly respected venue for scholarly exchange. In the summer of 2000, together with the University of Hartford, the Bethsaida Excavations Project and the Shrine of the Book at the Israel Museum in Jerusalem sponsored an international conference entitled "The Millennium Conference on the Sea of Galilee and Jerusalem" featuring some of the research presented in this book. Over seventy-five scholars participated in the three-day conference held at Kibbutz Ginosar and at the Israel Museum in Jerusalem.

The Bethsaida Project is proud of the many new developments and exhibitions associated with the site that have taken place since the publication of volume 2 in 1999. These include two new exhibitions, "In the Footsteps of David Roberts: A Redocumentation and 160th Anniversary Exhibition of the Watercolors of David Roberts" (1999) and "Bethsaida Excavations: Life Revealed in the Layers" (2002). The "David Roberts" exhibit was seen in several locations around the United States. The "Layers" exhibit was in Omaha through the end of 2003 and is scheduled to show in the several other American venues, including Billings, Montana, and Hartford, Connecticut. We are pleased to offer this glimpse into the past to audiences in Omaha, Billings, and Hartford.

In March 2000, the Bethsaida Project sponsored a special trip to Israel led by Rami Arav and Richard Freund. During this special trip, which coincided with the visit of Pope John Paul II to Israel, a small delegation met the pope and presented him with a replica of an artifact found at Bethsaida—an iron key from the Fisherman's House (discussed and shown in volume 2 of this series). The delegation included Dean Thomas Gouttierre; University of Nebraska Regent Nancy O'Brien; President Walter Harrison and Regent Chair Arnold Greenberg, from the University of Hartford; and President Jack Magruder of Truman State University. Following the presentation, the pope was given an aerial tour of the Bethsaida site.

Our thanks to our neighbors and friends in our "Israel home" at Beit Yigal Allon Museum on Kibbutz Ginosar. Special thanks to Katy Bar-Noff, Bill Scheinmann, Katrin Nakar, and Nitza Kaplan, whose support for Bethsaida over the past ten years has aided our work in innumerable ways. The gift shop at the museum now sells a "Bethsaida" wine made by the Golan Winery and markets it throughout the world with a label that bears the story of Bethsaida that we have carefully researched in these volumes. Maintaining an office and laboratory space at Beit Allon has enabled the Bethsaida scholars to pursue their research with constancy and have access to the multitudes of archived data from the excavations. Over the years, Kibbutz Ginosar has made the pottery restorers and staff members who have stayed for extended periods feel like a part of the kibbutz family and makes our foreign visitors comfortable at the Ginosar Hotel. It has become a much appreciated hospitality.

This third volume of Bethsaida research is unlike the previous two in which archaeology and literature were "halves" of the whole book. This volume instead features the literature-related articles; the next volume will focus on archaeology and geology. We look forward to completing the fourth volume.

Finally, thanks go to the thousands of past participants at Bethsaida, our dig alumni, who volunteered their time, energy, creativity, and enthusiasm. Without them, none of the results disseminated here and through other media would be possible. Thanks to all who have shared space and friendship with us as we enter our seventeenth year of excavations.

Rami Arav, Editor
University of Nebraska at Omaha

Richard A. Freund, Editor
University of Hartford

June 2004

Abbreviations

ANET	Pritchard, J. B., ed. 1969. *Ancient Near Eastern Texts relating to the Old Testament.* 3d ed. Princeton: Princeton University Press.
AT	*Annales theologici*
BCE	Before the Common Era; equivalent to BC dates
BMCRE	Mattingly, Harold. 1975. *Coins of the Roman Empire in the British Museum.* London: British Museum
BT	Babylonian Talmud
CE	Common Era; equivalent to AD dates
CIG	Broeckh, August, et al. 1828. *Corpus Inscriptionum Graecarum.* 13 vols. Berlin: Berolini
EA	El Amarna letters
GCS	Die griechische christliche Schriftsteller der ersten [drei] Jahrhunderte
IG	*Inscriptiones Graecae.* 1873. Berlin: W. de Gruyter
MPG	Migne, Jacques-Paul. 1857–87. *Patrologiae cursus completes.* Bibliotheca universalis, series graeca. Paris: P. Geuthner
PT	Palestinian Talmud
RIC	Mattingly, Harold, et al. 1923. *Roman Imperial Coinage.* 9 vols. London: Spink
RPC	Crawford, M. H. 1974. *Roman Republican Coinage.* 2 vols. NewYork: Cambridge University Press
SEG	*Supplementum Epigraphicum Graecum.* 1923. Leiden

Rami Arav

Toward a Comprehensive History of Geshur

Why have I come from Geshur? It would be better for me to be there still.

2 Samuel 14:32

ETHSAIDA IS LOCATED on a basalt extension that descends from the Golan plateau to the Sea of Galilee. It is approximately two kilometers from the seashore and a few hundred meters from the Jordan River. Bethsaida is one of the largest mounds in Israel; its ruins occupy an area of eight hectares, situated thirty meters above the Beteiha Plain. On a clear day, a magnificent view of the entire lake is seen from the summit of the mound (fig. 1).

Fourteen seasons of excavation at Bethsaida have revealed that the city was founded at about the middle of the tenth century BCE.[1] At this time, there was a thriving kingdom known as Geshur on the east side of the Sea of Galilee.[2] Bethsaida most likely served as the capital of the kingdom of Geshur. If one reads the enigmatic verse in Joshua 19:35 correctly, the city was called Tzer or Tzed.[3]

THE HISTORY OF GESHUR

The name Geshur appears before the foundation of the city. The curtain of history is lifted for Geshur in the fourteenth century BCE, when it appears—for the first time—in a letter addressed to a certain

1

Rami Arav

Fig. 1. Aerial photograph of Bethsaida looking to the south

Yanhamu, a governor of the province of Canaan, on behalf of the Egyptian king Akhenaton. The letter, which is perhaps a copy of the original, is one of many others written in Akkadian and known as the El Amarna (EA) letters, dating from the first half of the fourteenth century BCE (EA number 254). It reads:

> To Yanhamu, my lord, say:[4] Thus Mut-ba'lu, thy servant. At the two feet of my lord I fall. How is it said before thee, "Mut-ba'lu has fled, Ayab has hidden himself? How can the prince of Pella flee from the face of the commissioner of the king, his lord? As the king my lord lives, as the king my lord lives, Ayab is not in Pella. Behold, he has not been [here] for two months [?]. Indeed, ask Ben-Ilima, ask Taduwa, ask Yashua. Again, at the instance of the house of Shulum-Marduk, the city of Ashtartu came to my help, when all the cities of the land of Gari were hostile, (namely) Udumu, Aduru, Aruru, Meshqu, Magdalu, Eni-anabu and Zarqu, and when Hayanu and Yabilima were captured.
>
> Further, behold—after thy writing a tablet to me, I wrote to him. Before thou dost arrive with thy caravan, behold, he will have reached Pella, and he will hear thy words. (*ANET* 486)

This letter was sent by Mut-ba'lu, the "prince of Pella" (town also called Pehel opposite of Beth She'an in Transjordan, about forty kilometers south of Bethsaida),[5] who complains about a report, saying that he has fled his city, and Ayab, ruler of Ashtaroth (the capital of the region of Bashan located about thirty-five kilometers east of Bethsaida), is hidden away. He states that he is still in his own town and calls for three people as witness: Ben-Ilima, Taduwa, and Yashuya (Hebrew Joshua?). Then he explains the situation, which perhaps led to this report, and accordingly, he was attacked by the Garites, which are listed by seven different cities. Two of his towns, Hayanu and Yabilima (perhaps Abel/Abila), fell to the hands of the Garites when he requested help. Apparently, Ayab from the dynasty of Shulum-Marduk of Ashtaroth came to his aid, and perhaps together they restored his dominion in Pella. It has been quite reasonably suggested that the land of Ga-ri is located between the land of Pella and the land of Ashtaroth. The Bible states frequently that this area is the land of Geshur (fig. 2). This is why Benjamin Mazar suggested that the name "Ga-ri" is a scribal mistake and should have been "Ga-shu-ri." Mazar has shown that scribal mistakes were not rare among the El Amarna scribes.[6] If

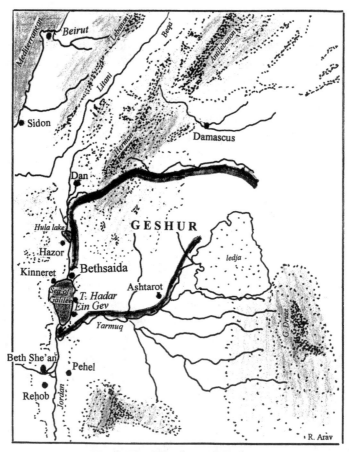

Fig. 2. The Kingdom of Geshur

this is correct, then the territory of Geshur was fairly large. It occupied seven hundred square kilometers, which is the size of the kingdom of Judah[7] with the boundaries of the land of Geshur at the Yarmuq River in the south. This river marks the northern borders of the hinterland of Pehel; the Jordan River marks the western borders of the Geshurites and the eastern border of the hinterland of the city of Hazor. Only a few settlements dating to the Iron Age period were discovered at the central and northern Golan, and it seems that the Hermon range (Arav 1992) would mark the northern borders of the Geshurites and the southern border of the Maachites. At the east, the Geshurites border the region of Bashan and their capital, Ashtaroth.

There are several reasons to believe that the Geshurites may have had a certain affiliation with the Maachites, who were situated in the northern Golan and the valley of Abel. First, the composition Geshur and Maacah appear together in the Bible as one phrase more than once (see, for example, Josh. 13:11,13; Deut. 3:14). Second, the name Maacah was used by the Geshurites[8] as the name of the daughter of the Geshurite king Talmai, as well as the name of the daughter of Absalom, the son of David. Third, the Maachites are related, according to the biblical account, to the sons of Nahor, who was Abraham's brother. The biblical view assigns them a derogatory origin, born from Nahor's concubine, whose name was Reumah. The names of the children of Reumah are Tebah, Gaham, Tahash, and Maacah. Mazar (1975, 190–202) has suggested that the list of these children indicates a tribal confederation in the middle Euphrates and northwest Mesopotamia. The religious center of this confederation was the city of Haran, which was a major center for the moon-god worshippers. There are also examples of moon-god worship at Bethsaida. It can be posited, therefore, that the Geshurites and the Maachites shared a common worship.

Unlike the accounts describing Geshur's neighbors, Pehel and Ashtaroth, no single ruler or capital is mentioned for the Geshurites. It seems that their sociopolitical structure looked more like a federation of small city-states than a petty kingdom. This type of sociopolitical organization may also indicate that unlike Ashtaroth and Pehel, Geshur's arrival in the region was relatively recent.

In the long-fought struggle over the area, Pehel finally lost. During the twelfth century BCE, Pehel declined, and rose up as a city only during the Hellenistic period, while Geshur enjoyed a period of prosperity during the Iron Age.

If the language of the Geshurites was not changed drastically in the next few centuries, then one can infer, based on the inscriptions from the Iron Age, that the language of the Geshurites would have been a certain dialect of Aramaic with Hebrew influence.[9] It was perhaps somewhere between Aramaic, represented in the Dan inscription[10] forty kilometers north of Bethsaida, and the Hebrew—with a strong Aramaic influence—represented in the inscription of the Tell Deir-Alla (Ahituv 1992, 256–86) eighty kilometers south of Bethsaida. The Luwian hieroglyph on the decorated stele of the high place at the gate of Bethsaida may suggest that Luwian (the language of the Hurrians) was familiar to certain strata of the population (Bernett and Keel 1998).

Claire Epstein suggested that the seven Geshurite cities mentioned in the El Amarna letter should be identified with sites dating to the Late Bronze Age she located in the southeast of the Sea of Galilee (Epstein 1993, 83–90).[11] If her identifications are correct, then the main body of the Geshurite inhabitation would have been in the western sections of the Golan plateau. This would indicate that their main socio- economic and political orientation would have been toward the Sea of Galilee, and their main interaction during the Iron Age would have been with the Israelite kingdom, which occupied, in this region, the western half of the Sea of Galilee.[12]

It seems that toward the end of the eleventh century BCE, the Geshurite city-states undertook a process of consolidation and developed into a kingdom (Maoz 1992, 996; Hess 2004.) If the Hurrian name Talmai, the king of Geshur (2 Sam. 3:3), indicates a Hurrian origin and not only the choice of his parents,[13] and if the Hurrian military elite, known as Marianu, was still in power in the end of the eleventh century as it was in the middle of the second millennium BCE in the western and southern Levant, then it is reasonable to assume that this process was led by an elite Hurrian dynasty[14] (Alt 1954, 81; 1956, 181–85, Aharoni 1962, 130; Yon 2000, 200). The Hurrians (Morrison 1992) were a unique non-Semitic and non-Indo-European ethnic group that originated in northern Mesopotamia and constituted the kingdom of Mittanni. In the sixteenth century BCE, the kingdom of Mittanni was defeated by the Egyptians and the Hittites, and as a result, the Hurrians' remnants spread throughout the Near East and particularly among the Syrian and Canaanite city-states, forming the majority of the known Marianu. The Marianu's main reputation and business derived from owning and operating military chariots pulled by horses. The name Talmai is the latest-recorded Hurrian name in ancient writings.

The formation of the Geshurite kingdom was followed by the foundation of their capital city. The excavations at Tel Hadar have demonstrated that the Geshurites reached a high level of prosperity during the eleventh century BCE that could support a kingdom (Kokhavi 1996, 184–201), and in the end of that century, the new kingdom was stable enough to erect a capital city. Although there is not yet enough evidence to date precisely the foundation of the earliest stratum at Bethsaida, the monumentality of the Bethsaida remains indicates that this was Geshur's permanent capital city from at least as early as the mid-tenth century BCE.[15] Red slip and burnished pottery, in addition to tenth-century Syro-Phoenician pottery and Philistine monochrome shards of pottery found on the floor of Stratum 6b, testify that the city was destroyed sometime before 925 BCE. The city must have been founded, therefore, no later than 950 BCE. There is no evidence of inhabitation before then.[16] The city was founded on an extension formed on a basalt hill that descended from the Golan Heights to the Sea of Galilee. At the time the city was founded, the Sea of Galilee reached the foot of the extension (Shroder and Inbar 1995; Shroder et al. 1999, 115–76). Instead of attempting to level the rocks down, the builders preferred to build series of terraces around the city, fill them up, bury the rocks inside, and build the structures on top. Remains of four terraces have been discerned at the eastern side of the mound. The northeastern side of the hill was lifted higher than the rest of the hill, and the upper city was built on top of it. On the same side was also the monumental city gate, situated approximately twenty meters above the bottom of the ravine. The foundations of the floors were established eight meters above the bedrock on an immense, filled-in area. Thus far, the excavated structures of the upper city have revealed only monumental buildings, such as a four-meter-wide road leading to a city gate, a plaza, and a palace, in the fashion of the Neo-Hittite/Aramean type known as *bit hilani*. This is Stratum 6 at Bethsaida; a destruction layer followed by a new construction phase on the outline of the older structure divide the strata into 6a (the later phase) and 6b (the earlier phase).

The Bible is still the only source of information about the political history of Geshur, and therefore, every historical reconstruction of the politics of Geshur relies on a critical reading of the Bible. According to the biblical narrative, the Geshurites and the Davidic dynasty had an interesting and close relationship. Each had an interest in the other's country. As a result of this mutual interest, the two dynasties signed a peace treaty, which was reinforced by a political marriage. King David married Maacah, the daughter of Talmai (2 Sam. 3:3), at the onset of his reign. King David needed this treaty to secure his northeastern borders, which the kingdom of Geshur was able to provide. The Geshurites needed this treaty presumably to defend their territory from threats of the Arameans of Tzoba, headed by a powerful king Hadadezer, the son of Rehob.[17] Unlike many other coalitions in the ancient Near East, this treaty lasted five generations, so presumably the treaty worked well for both sides. When David waged a war against the Ammonites and besieged their capital city Rabat Ammon, the Ammonites recruited a coalition of Arameans to save their kingdom. The coalition parties included the Arameans of "Beth Rehob, the Arameans of Tzoba, the king of Maacah, and the strong man of Tob" (1 Sam. 10:6; 1 Chron. 19:7). The Geshurites are conspicuously missing. In return for their loyalty, David fought this coalition, which presumably threatened the Geshurites, too.[18] His victory over the coalition is recorded once or twice in the Bible.[19] It seems that as a result, the reign of Hadadezer ended, the kingdom of Tzoba ceased to function as a political entity, and the Geshurite kingdom gained another century of independence. It is hard to believe that David achieved this without the active assistance of the Geshurites.

One way to evaluate the balance of political power in the region during this period is to look at political marriages. Scholars who investigate political marriages in biblical times indicate that the stronger party in such a treaty marries his daughter to the weaker one. The rationale may be to enable the stronger party to establish a loyal branch in the weaker dynasty, which will look after the interests of the stronger party in the generations to come (Spanier 1999, 295–306). If this is the case, the marriage of David and Maacah indicates that the Geshurites had a remarkably strong position in the region, and indeed Bethsaida was much larger than Jerusalem at the time of David, if the City of David was located only on the hill known as the Southeastern Hill. In addition, in a royal marriage such as this, the new bride would bring with her an entourage, which would include her court men, architects, and masons who would build her new palace and the court. If Maacah was not different from this model, she might have transported the Aramean architectural tradition with her to Hebron and later to Jerusalem, the architectural and historical significance of which cannot be exaggerated.

The Geshurite involvement in the Davidic dynasty did not end there. The son of David and Maacah was the famous Absalom, David's third son. David's first son and the crown prince was Amnon, whose mother was Ahinoam the Jezreelite. The second son was Kilab, the son of Abigail, the former wife of Nabal of Carmel. Kilab was presumably a weak personality for his name never appears again in the Bible. Absalom must have felt superior to his brothers, because he was "the son of Maacah, the daughter of Talmai, the king of Geshur" (2 Sam.

3:3), which means that he was royal from both parents and more fit to the crown. Against this political background, the ambitions of Absalom are perhaps better understood. Absalom waited for the proper time, and when it arrived, he ruthlessly murdered his half brother, the crown prince, and became the crown prince himself. David presumably did not accept this manner of appointment, and Absalom fled to his grandparents at Geshur where he stayed for three years and perhaps married.

After Absalom's return to Jerusalem, his father David still did not want to see him for four years, and he finally turned to Joab in complaint: "Why have I come from Geshur? It would be better for me to be there still" (2 Sam. 14:32). In light of the Bethsaida excavations, this is understood as not merely a complaint but an observation of the surroundings. Bethsaida enjoyed better advantages than Jerusalem: it was near a lake, Jerusalem was not. It is located near international routes and a fertile area, while Jerusalem is far from international routes and is situated on the fringe of the desert. Compared to Jerusalem in the time of David, Bethsaida was much larger and more magnificently adorned, with lavish and great public buildings. Absalom died attempting to seize power and left a daughter whose name was also Maacah, just like her grandmother.

A generation later King Rehoboam, the son of King Solomon, married Maacah the daughter of Absalom, and "he loved her more than all his wives and concubines" (2 Chron. 11:21). The reason for this "love" was related, perhaps, to the political connection Maacah could provide—namely the connections to the northern kingdoms of Geshur, Maacah, and their overlordship at that time, the Aramean kingdom of Damascus. Rehoboam needed these links to gain advantage over his rival King Jeroboam of Israel, because "there was a war between Jeroboam and Rehoboam all their life long" (1 Kings 15:6). Absalom's daughter Maacah was the Queen Mother of the next king— King Abiam, the son of Rehoboam—and later the grandmother (or perhaps the mother) of King Asa. According to the Bible, she introduced "foreign worship" to Jerusalem, which may have been the same moon-god worship seen at Bethsaida. King Asa removed the "abomination" she created to Ashera, burnt it in the Kidron Valley, and deposed her from her position (1 Kings 15:13).

Toward the end of the tenth century BCE, drastic political changes occurred in the region. The united monarchy collapsed, and two rival kingdoms, Judah and Israel, were established instead. The

Egyptian king Sosonek (the biblical Shishak) invaded Judah and Israel and caused further deterioration to the power of the Israelites. The Aramean kingdom of Tzoba collapsed earlier, and into this vacuum the Arameans of Damascus entered and erected the kingdom of Aram Damascus. Having no other testimony, one may presume that the founder of this kingdom was Razon, the son of Eliyada, perhaps identified with Hezion (1 Kings 11:23–26, 15:18), who, most probably, was also skillful enough to turn the kingdoms of Geshur and Maacah into his vassal kingdoms. From the late tenth century or early ninth, the region of Golan, in which Geshur was located, was integrated into the Aramean kingdom of Damascus. It seems possible that the biblical phrase that relates an invasion of Aram and Geshur into the Israelite, Menessite regions of the Bashan, east of Geshur (1 Chron. 2:23), belongs to this period.[20] If this verse indeed dates to this particular period, then it is the last witness to Geshur in the narratives of kings of Judah and Israel.

During this period the Israelite kings were still engaged in rivalry, but there were attempts to reunite the kingdoms of David and Solomon. The Judahite king Asa was the son or grandson of Maacah (the daughter of Absalom). Asa clashed with the king of Israel, Ba'asha. Around 879 BCE, King Ba'asha of Israel took the upper hand and managed to lay siege to Jerusalem and fortified the city of Mitzpah against the kingdom of Judah. King Asa could not leave the city and perhaps was close to defeat, which most probably would have terminated the Davidic dynasty. It seems that he was left with no other choice but to use his old connection and urge the king of Damascus, whose name is preserved in the Bible as Ben Hadad the son of Tabrimon, the son of Hezion (known in scholarship as Ben Hadad I), to harass Ba'asha to force him to release the pressure from Jerusalem (1 Kings 15:17–21). King Asa mentioned the treaty that their forefathers had made, and perhaps he meant the treaty between King David and Talmai. After all, Asa's grandmother or great-grandmother was Geshurite. Ben Hadad I, the patron of the Geshurite kingdom, willingly took the opportunity to intervene, and he launched a campaign on the western side of the Jordan River and conquered the area between Dan (at the north) and the Sea of Galilee. The campaign was successful from King Asa's point of view, and the Davidic dynasty was saved. It is noteworthy that the itinerary of the campaign as mentioned in the Bible (1 Kings 15:20) does not mention the eastern side of the Jordan River, which, obviously, was already in the hands of the Arameans of Damascus. During the next decades, the Arameans would clash with the Israelites—mostly in regions south of Golan and Geshur, namely the region of Gilead.

The excavators of Tel Kinorot did not associate any stratum to the campaign of Ben Hadad I, but it is possible that Stratum 4 in Kinorot, which is defined as "secondary settlement on the entire mound" and dates from the tenth century BCE, came to its end in this campaign. The next stratum (Stratum 3) is defined as "limited settlement on the northern cape of the mound" and dates from the ninth century BCE. It was destroyed, presumably by Shalmaneser III, in 841 BCE (Fritz and Muenger 2002, 2–23).[21]

Ironically, the end of the semi-independent kingdom of Geshur came with the defeat of Geshur's overlord, Ben Hadad II, the king of Damascus, at the gates of Shomron (Samaria) together with "thirty-two kings assisting him" (1 Kings 20:16)[22] in 856 BCE (Mazar 1975, 198). Consequently, Ben Hadad II performed a thorough reformation in his kingdom. "He removed the kings and installed commissioners *(pahvot)* instead" (1 Kings 20:23–25). From this point in history and until the collapse of Aram Damascus, the history of Geshur is intertwined within the history of Aram Damascus. Geshur, situated between two strong local kingdoms—the kingdom of Israel and the kingdom of Aram Damascus—ceased to exist as a buffer state.

The next battle was fought between Aram Damascus and the kingdom of Israel a year later near the town of Aphek, in the territory of Geshur, but Geshur is not mentioned anymore. Ben Hadad II was defeated once more, and Ahab extended his kingdom toward Damascus and established his markets there. It is also possible that the destruction of Stratum 6b at Bethsaida was due to this battle. The destruction was discerned only in the gate area. An accumulation of about 0.4 meter of debris separates Stratum 6a from a clear clay floor embedded to create Stratum 6b. The end of the political independence of Geshur does not mean the obliteration of its culture. Geshur was swallowed by Aram Damascus, but did not cease to exist as an ethnic and cultural entity. Bethsaida and the other Geshurite cities in Tel Hadar and Ein Gev flourished remarkably until the conquest of the Assyrian king Tiglath-pileser III in 732 BCE.

The next clash between the kingdom of Israel and the kingdom of Aram Damascus took place a year after the battle of Qarqar. In 853 BCE, Ahab, Ben Hadad II, and Irhulani, the king of Hamat, fought against Shalmaneser III, the king of Assyria, and tried to block his way to the south (Luckenbill 1926, 223). In this clash (852 BCE), which came after three years of peace between the rival kingdoms, Ben Hadad II managed to defeat a coalition of the two kingdoms of Israel and Judah. The battle took place in Ramot Gilead, which was left under the Arameans. In this period, Geshur acted as a bridge—the meaning of its name—between the northern kingdom of Aram Damascus and the kingdom of Israel at the south/southwest. The armies of Aram Damascus passed through Geshur as if in their own territory. Ahab was severely wounded and died in the battle. Yehoram succeeded him (1 Kings 22:2–40).

The accession of Hazael to power in 842 BCE marked a turning point in the history of Geshur and Bethsaida. In spite of the fact that his accession (and the accession of Jehu to power a short time after in the kingdom of Israel) was accompanied by a divine blessing from the prophets of Israel and presented as a divine choice, this period was one of the lowest periods in the life of the kingdom of Israel. At the onset of his reign, Hazael took advantage of the weakness of the kingdom of Israel, waging war against it. He defeated the coalition of the two kingdoms led by Yoram, the son of Ahab, and Ahaziah, the king of Judah (2 Kings 8:28).[23]

The Aramean pressure was somewhat lessened during the campaign of the Assyrian king Shalmaneser III to Damascus in his eighteenth year of reign (841 BCE). In this campaign, Shalmaneser III defeated Hazael at the "Saniru" mountain (the biblical Senir, another name for Mount Hermon). He laid siege to Damascus but never took it. Then he continued to the southern Hauran regions and from there he turned west. He passed through Geshur and possibly through Bethsaida, crossed the kingdom of Israel, and reached "Mount Ba'li-ra'si, a head[land] on the sea" (Luckenbill 1926, 243; Yamada 2000, 185–95), presumably the Carmel range.[24] While in the kingdom of Israel, he received tribute from "Jehu the son of Omri"[25] and from the Phoenicians, the Sidonians, and the Tyrians. A fragment of his annals of unknown origin (perhaps Calah) reports the following: "countless cities I destroyed, I devastated, I burned with fire. Their spoil, without number, I carried off" (Luckenbill 1926, 243). The destruction layer of Stratum 6a at Bethsaida could have been caused in this campaign.

Shalmaneser III waged another campaign in his twenty-first year of reign (838 BCE) against Hazael (Yamada 2000, 205–9). His attempt to conquer Damascus failed again, but he reported destroying four cities. Following this, in the same campaign, Shalmaneser III recounted that a king by the name of Bai`l "seized" his "feet" and "gave" him "tribute"; then Shalmaneser III placed his "royal image" in the temple of his fortified city of "Laruba." Based on a new reading of the inscription showing that the city name ends with an r, Nadav Na'aman suggests identifying the land of the king Bai`l with Geshur (2002, 205); however, the name Tzer, as has been suggested for Bethsaida in the Iron Age, could also qualify for the identification. If this is correct, then not only Geshur, or Tzer, appears again in an extrabiblical document, but presumably Bethsaida was saved during Shalmaneser III's second campaign.

These campaigns weakened Aram Damascus, but not for too long. Around 814 BCE, Hazael regrouped enough to wage a new campaign against Philistia and Judah. He conquered the city of Gat and turned against Jerusalem, receiving the treasures of the temple and of the palace from Jehoash, the king of Judah.

During the time of Hazael, Bethsaida flourished. The city gate was rebuilt and became one of the largest city gates in the region. It was formed in a magnificent shape known by archaeologists as a four-chamber city gate. Together with the outer city gate and the courtyard in between, the gate extended over an area of 525 square meters with a fifty-meter paved road leading to the city gate. The old *bit hilani* palace was remodeled as an administrative structure. Loom weights found inside indicate that some textile activity took place there.

In the generation after the death of Hazael, the balance of power changed. Ben Hadad III succeeded Hazael, and Joash succeeded Jehoahaz, the son of Jeh, the king of Israel. According to the Bible, Joash defeated the Arameans three times. One of the battles took place near the city of Aphek, near Bethsaida. Did Joash annex the central Golan Heights to the territory of Israel? Without documents, scholars perhaps will never know. Mazar assumed that the end of Stratum 2 in Ein Gev, a few kilometers south of Bethsaida, came as a result of this campaign. If Stratum 5 at Bethsaida was built by Hazael, then there is no indication that this campaign made any change in Bethsaida.

Jeroboam II (786–746 BCE) continued his father's campaigns. According to the Bible, he regained large territories that had previously been lost. The verse, "and the rest of the deeds of Jeroboam and the mighty things he did and the battles that he fought and that he regained Damascus to Israel and Hamath to Judah in Israel, aren't they written in the chronicle book of the kings of Israel?" (2 Kings 14:28), is interpreted as conquest of territories in the Golan Heights, including Damascus (Gal and Oded 1990, 148). Were there any remains at Bethsaida for these "mighty things"? A seal impression on a handle, which was found out of context in Area C at Bethsaida, bears the inscription "to Zechario." An identical seal impression was found in Dan, and its excavator speculates that it may have been the seal of Zechario, the son of Jeroboam II, who reigned for only six months. If he served as a co-regent, maybe this seal belonged to him. If correct, this is evidence for a change of sovereigns in Bethsaida.[26] It is unlikely that there was also a population change in this area and that Israelites entered Bethsaida. There is no historical parallel that population changes occurred as a result of a local, sporadic military campaign before the Assyrians began their deportation policy. In addition, it is very difficult to identify changes of population in archaeological contexts.[27] If the worship of the moon-god, which took place at Bethsaida in Stratum 5, and the consumption of pork are not ethnic indicatives and do not testify that there were no Israelites in Geshur in Stratum 5, then there are no other indications for an identification of ethnic groups at Bethsaida; however, high quality pottery bowls known as "Samarian ware" that were discovered at Bethsaida could indicate interaction with the kingdom of Israel, which could have happened during the conquest of Jeroboam II.

From the death of Jeroboam II until 734/2 BCE, the stability of the kingdom of Israel declined rapidly, but the kingdom of Aram Damascus, on the other hand, experienced a quick recovery. The strong person in the region became Rezin, the king of Aram Damascus. He probably was behind the enthroning of Pekah, the son of Remaliahu from the Gilead, over the kingdom of Israel, with whose assistance he tried to depose the Davidic dynasty and to impose Ben Tabel from Transjordan (Isa. 7:6) (Gal and Oded 1990, 152–53). Ahaz, the son of Uziah, the king of Judah, felt threatened and turned to Assyrian King Tiglath-pileser III for help. The king of Assyria accepted this plea, although he never mentioned it in his records (Tadmor 1994). According to his accounts, he launched a campaign against Hanun the king of Gaza in 734 BCE and against "the house of Hazael" in Damascus in 733 and again in 732 BCE. Whether these campaigns were invited by the king of Judah or initiated by Tiglath-pileser III, or a combination of both, it was the most significant military campaign since the campaign of the Egyptian king Tutmoses III about seven hundred years earlier.

Not only did it completely change the political situation in the Levant, but it also created an irreversible situation in the region which caused ultimately the destruction of the kingdom of Israel in 720 BCE and the kingdom of Judah in 586 BCE. In this campaign, the kingdom of Aram Damascus was completely destroyed. The kingdom of Israel lost the territory of Galilee and the Gilead. Tiglath-pileser III annexed these territories and Assyria became an empire. He performed administrative changes in his regions. The area was divided into satrapies, with new capital cities erected, and the old centers, which were destroyed in the campaign, either deserted or rebuilt according to completely new plans. Tiglath-pileser III deported the inhabitants and settled new inhabitants in their place. In short, a new order was installed on the ruins of the old order. In this campaign, all the cities at the northern part of the country were destroyed: Ein Gev, Dan, Hazor, Kinneret, Beth She'an, and Megiddo. The destruction of Stratum 5 at Bethsaida was a result of this campaign. The monumental city gate was thoroughly devastated in a fierce conflagration; the upper floors collapsed into the first floor and created a high mound. The palace was partly destroyed and the settlement was abandoned. Thus, the magnificent Geshurite kingdom came to its final end.

SOCIOECONOMIC OBSERVATIONS

Archaeological finds from excavations and research carried out in the land of Geshur shed light also on the economic and social history of this region. In spite of the perpetual turmoil in Geshur from the eleventh to the eight centuries BCE, the economy of the region continued to flourish without major interruption (see table 1). The small settlement at Tel Hadar, a few kilometers south-southeast of Bethsaida, shows statehood traits from the foundation of its eleventh century BCE stratum. Grain surpluses produced on the plains of the Golan were stored in the granaries of the site. After a tenth century BCE gap in occupation, the settlement was not only rebuilt during the ninth century BCE as a granary site, but its size was doubled, and it flourished until the Assyrian conquest in 732 BCE. The settlement in Ein Gev was essentially a settlement of granaries, which suffered destruction a few times during these centuries, but never changed from a granary and storage town. Stratum 6 at Bethsaida also included a granary containing wheat, which dates to the tenth century BCE. This granary was similar

in architecture to the earlier granary of Tel Hadar (Stratum 4). Three of
the four chambers of the city gate at Bethsaida (Stratum 5) contained
grain. One ton of carbonated barley was found in Chamber 3. It was
burnt by the Assyrians during a brief siege. A section that was cut
through the floor of Chamber 1 at Bethsaida shows sequences of layers
containing grain; this means that the custom of storing grain at the
chambers of the gate was in place and was not a swift decision made
during the siege period.

Table 1. A stratigraphic chart of different sites
in the land of Geshur and nearby areas

	Late Bronze I 1550 1400	Late Bronze II 1200	Iron Age I 1200 1000	Iron Age IIa 1000 900	Iron Age IIb 900 372
Ein Gev Area A Area B				5 4	4, 3 3, 2, 1
Tel Hadar	6		5, 4		3, 2, 1
Bethsaida				6b, 6a	5b, 5a
Tel Kinorot	7		6, 5, 4		3, 2, 1
Hazor				10, 9	8, 7, 6, 5b, 5a
Dan				4	3

Import vessels found at the Geshurite sites testify to vibrant
commercial connections among Geshur, the kingdom of Israel, and
the cities of the Phoenician coast. Aramean vessels at Ein Gev show
close connection with the northern Geshurite neighbors.

The city gate was approached, during the tenth century BCE, by
a four-meter-wide dirt road that was partly excavated and discerned
by Ground Penetration Radar to a distance of at least fifty meters outside of the outer city gate. The dirt road was replaced a century later
by a meticulously laid cobble pavement. This wide road clearly
implies that it was built for wheeled vehicles. The existence of
wheeled vehicles, although none has been discovered, is a clear indication that law and order were strictly employed. In recent research
on the medieval Middle East, Bernard Lewis has commented that "a
cart is large and, for a peasant, relatively costly. It is difficult to conceal

and easy to requisition. At a time and place where neither law nor custom restricted the powers of even local authorities, visible and mobile assets were poor investments" (2002, 175–76, 192). A road made for wheeled vehicles may be interpreted, therefore, as a sign of strong and lawful government, which was, during the Iron Age, a hallmark of a kingdom.

Table 2 shows possible contenders for perpetrating the construction and destruction of the different strata of Bethsaida. There are, of course, many possible ways to match the different candidates and the various strata and phases of construction and destruction. Possibility 1 assumes a span of sixty to eighty years for each stratum and about a century for the entire Stratum 5, which is rather reasonable. Possibility 2 assumes a longer time for Stratum 6. Possibility 3 assumes more prominent historical figures for the changing strata, such as Ben Hadad II, Shalmaneser III, and Hazael. The time frame is similar to Possibility II. Possibility 4 assumes almost two hundred years for Stratum 6, which is divided into two separate substrata, and about seventy years for Stratum 5 with one reinforcement stage (5b). It is rather difficult to determine which of all the possibilities is correct

THE RELIGION OF GESHUR

Two decades ago scholars knew very little about the history of Geshur, let alone the Geshurite religion. Since then much has been learned; the excavations at Bethsaida have revealed extensive evidence of the religious practices of the Geshurites. Among the finds there are five high places, with two each of two different forms and seven stelae (of which six were discovered in their original context). One of the stelae is decorated and indicates that the deity worshipped in the high place was the moon-god. Offering vessels were found in Chamber 4 of the gate, which is the closest chamber to the stepped high place. One of these vessels bears a religious dedicatory inscription that helps in reconstructing the religion of the Geshurites. The finds will be discussed in detail in a later volume. Here the finds are presented as they relate to the religion of the Geshurites.

THE HIGH PLACES

All the high places discussed in this report were discovered inside the city. Four of them are located in the courtyard between the inner city gate and the outer city gate and its vicinity,[28] and one was found at

Rami Arav

Table 2. Possible candidates for construction and destruction of strata at Bethsaida

Strata	Phase	Possibility 1	Possibility 2	Possibility 3	Possibility 4
Stratum 6b	Construction	Amihur? (Amihud) Talmai? No later than 950	Amihur? (Amihud) Talmai? No later than 950	Amihur? (Amihud) Talmai? No later than 950	Amihur? (Amihud) Talmai? No later than 950
	Destruction	Hezion c. 920	Ben Hadad I 879	Ben Hadad II 856	Ahab 856
Stratum 6a	Construction	Hezion c. 920	Ben Hadad I 879	Ben Hadad II 856	Ben Hadad II 856 Hazael c. 830
	Destruction	Ben Hadad II 856	Ben Hadad II 856 Hazael 842	Shalmaneser III 841	Joash or Jeroboam II c. 802–746
Stratum 5b	Construction	Ben Hadad II c. 856 Hazael c. 830	Hazael c. 830	Hazael c. 830	Ben Hadad III c. 800
		Was not destroyed			
Stratum 5a	Construction	Ben Hadad III c. 800 Rezin c. 740	Ben Hadad III c. 800 Rezin c. 740	Ben Hadad III c. 800 Rezin c. 740	Ben Hadad III c. 800 Rezin c. 740
	Destruction	Tiglath-pileser III 732	Tiglath-pileser III 732	Tiglath-pileser III 732	Tiglath-pileser III 732

Fig. 3. The stepped high place at the niche of the northern
tower, flanking the entrance to the city gate

the back of the inner city gate. It seems that they were organized sym-
metrically with one of each type in the northern and southern wings
of the inner city gate. There are two high places in a style called here
"the stepped high place." One is located in the niche of the northern
tower of the inner city gate and one at the back of the southern tower.
Two other high places are named here "direct access high places" and
are located in a similar fashion—one in the niche of the southern
tower and the other behind the northern tower. The fifth high place
is the largest, called here "the sacrificial high place," and is located at
the back of the inner gate, inside the city.

THE STEPPED HIGH PLACE

The high place near the entrance and at the northern niche of the
tower consists of two steps leading to an elevated platform (Arav

1999a, 128–36) (fig. 3). In the middle of the platform there is a basalt basin, and behind the basin the decorated stele was posted. Two perforated cups were found inside the basin; their purpose is still not clearly understood. Some scholars suggested that they served as incense burners (Pritchard 1969); however, the absence of ashes in the cups makes this assumption difficult. A more plausible explanation is that they served for libation purposes. They were presumably dipped in the basin full of liquid, and then perhaps were elevated and the liquids (such as water, milk, wine, or oil) would pour out of the perforations, creating a shower.[29]

The decorated stele shows a bull with very large horns on top of a nonfigurative design, which was interpreted as a stele sign in Luwian hieroglyph (Bernett and Keel 1998, 42). The deity was identified as a representation of the moon-god. Without a name on the stele it is impossible to discover the name of the moon-god, but the decorated stele alludes to the fact that the moon-god was one of the most prominent deities of the Geshurites. This is not entirely surprising, as two similar stelae were found in southern Syria, at a distance of about thirty or forty kilometers east of Bethsaida. One was discovered at the site of Tell Ashri and the other at Awas, near the town of Salhad (Bernett and Keel 1998, 8–21). Presumably they belong to the same cultural-religious milieu. It is no wonder that the moon-god was so prominent in the southern Syrian regions; he was commonly worshipped in the ancient Near East as the creator of the universe. A major moon-god worship center was located in the city of Harran (in north Syria) and presumably radiated its influence over a vast territory to the south.

The second stepped high place consists of three shallow steps leading to a shallow and rather symbolic podium. No finds were discovered at this high place. The parallel to the northern high place and the fact that the steps and podium face a wall are crucial indicators, as they identify this structure as a high place (fig. 4).

THE DIRECT ACCESS HIGH PLACE

In the opposite direction of the entryway, in the southern niche, another type of high place was found (fig. 5), which consists of a high shelf, situated about ninety centimeters above the ground (this is also the elevation of the northern stepped high place), located near a bench and an un-iconic stele that flanked the entrance. The shelf is certainly too high for a bench since the benches flanking the high place are

Fig. 4. The stepped high place at the southern tower

Fig. 5. The direct access high place at the niche of the southern tower, flanking the entrance to the inner city gate

about fifteen to twenty centimeters above the ground. No cultic object was found on or near the shelf. The analogy with the niche at the northern corner reinforces the assumption that it is a high place. This is perhaps a high place of the type that may be named a direct access high place, where the worshipper would access the high place directly without having to climb steps.[30] A similar type was found in the corner between the northern tower and the city wall. This one consisted of a shelf about fifty centimeters high, which consisted of a wall of field-stones filled with dirt, and plastered and whitewashed. No religious objects were discovered near or on this high place.

This direct access high place calls to mind the commandment in Exodus 20:25–26, which explains how a high place to Jehovah should be built:

> And if a stone altar you will build for me, do not build it using ashlars since you raised your sword on it and desecrated it, and do not climb on steps of my altar for your nakedness might be disclosed on it.

Although this passage has a long history of interpretations, it seems obvious that the holy ground of the altar, which confines the territory of the divine, consists of the entire structure, not only the podium, but also the steps. Assuming that the divine "can see every-where" (over the entire altar), "nakedness" would be "seen" from the bottom of the first step and not only when approaching the podium at the upper part, where, for instance, the basin would be located. The prohibition against walking naked on sacred ground is not unusual, but what is unusual here is that the prohibition would not apply were the worshipper wearing any clothing. The reason is that nakedness can also be observed from the ground. This prohibition obviously does not refer to the entire religious *temenos*, but only to the altar that was the holy of holies. It would be interesting to see how it was inter-preted and understood in the Iron Age Israelite religion. Obviously, there are no texts interpreting this and very few archaeological remains that would indicate the practice of this command.[31] During the Second Temple Period, however, and also during the Talmudic period, this passage was interpreted in the typically sophisticated manner by which steps were prohibited, but ramparts were permitted. The idea that the steps were included within the holy ground of the altar was suppressed, and the main focus was shifted to the style of the approach. Another interpretation suggests that what matters is the type of the vestment worn, which—it was speculated—might disclose naked-ness while climbing on steps but not on a rampart.[32] On one hand, this interpretation seems rather strange, since it would be easier to change the style of the garment than to change the structure. On the other hand, it seems that this interpretation functions as a rationalization for a situation where a large high place was built, such as the Second Temple in Jerusalem, where there was a need to climb on top of it.

The similarity of the direct access high place at Bethsaida to the biblical passage has a few possible explanations.

1. It was dedicated to the worship of Jehovah.

2. The deity is unknown, but Jehovah favored this type of high place.

3. It is coincidentally the same high place described in the Bible.

Of these, the second explanation seems most plausible. If this is cor-rect, it has significant implications for biblical interpretation and is beyond the scope of this research.

THE SACRIFICIAL HIGH PLACE

A third type of a high place was found at the back of the inner city gate, adjacent to the southern wing (fig. 6). It is the largest high place thus far discovered at Bethsaida and consists of a cobble-paved podium elevated only about forty centimeters above the surrounding floors. A sloped, cobble-paved rampart approaches the podium. Two lower, compact, large shelves of dirt flanked the podium on both sides. The objects found on the altar includes burnt bones, a broken basin with high corners, large flat slabs of stones similar to other altars,[33] and a large boulder with unclear incisions that might repre-sent a bull. Slightly to the north, at the edge of the northern compact dirt shelf, there is a rather deep pit. The pit was filled up with ashes and bones, and it seems clear that the bones and the surpluses of the sacrificial meals were thrown into this pit. Analysis of the animal bones of the pit reveals that all the animals were cows, sheep, goats, and a small percentage of fallow deer.[34] It is most noteworthy that pigs are absent in this collection. This discovery is extremely interest-ing since all these animals are also "purified," "clean," or "kosher" as

Fig. 6. The back of the inner city gate. The structure on the upper right is the sacrificial high place, remains of a horned altar, a flat slab, and a stone with an incision depicting a bull

indicated in Leviticus 11, as being permitted for consumption by Israelites. Fallow deer are the only animals in this collection that are not domesticated and are found as sacrificial animals at Bethsaida. It is also extremely interesting to note that while pigs are absent from the sacrificial pit, preliminary bone analysis in other areas of the site indicates that the Bethsaida population did consume them.

IDENTIFICATION OF THE DEITY WORSHIPPED ON THE SACRIFICIAL HIGH PLACE

The meaning of this discovery can undoubtedly shed light on the question of the origin of the dietary laws that appear in Leviticus 11 and Deuteronomy 13:3–21, a topic with a very long history of exegesis and interpretation. Baruch A. Levine states that these laws are a "prerequisite for attainment of holiness." Levine advocates an anthropological explanation and maintains that the laws have social objectives and are supposed to maintain "a distance between the Israelite and their neighbors" (1989, 244). In other words, the dietary laws were meant to distinguish between Israelites and those living around them. Accordingly, an Israelite could have said, "We do not eat pork, they do, and this is how we differ from them." This interpretation has been suggested by several scholars and is summarized by Levine (1989, 243–48); however, it does not seem persuasive enough, since saying, "We are monotheistic, and they are polytheistic," or using any other demarcation based on more prominent traits would seem a clearer differentiation. The fact that dietary laws were unique to ancient Israelites and not commonly used to define boundaries among other ancient Near Eastern people supports rejecting the boundary explanation.

In a very extensive treatment of the topic, Jacob Milgrom refutes the very common theory that the laws are arbitrary on the ground that obvious patterns can be discerned. He maintains that hygienic reasons, which are another common argument for the laws, are untenable because they were not common knowledge for people of that time. Practical theorists suggest environmental reasons for the dietary laws and in particular laws that pertain to the consumption of swine (Hesse 1990, 195–225). According to this theory, nomadic societies refrained from cultivating pigs; the Hebrews, being originally a nomadic society, continued traditional habits and even sanctified them (Milgrom 1991, 718–36). This claim was refuted because the idea that the Hebrews were originally a nomadic group has yet to be proven and cannot, therefore, be used as an argument. In addition, the Philistines apparently migrated from farther distances, their migration period lasted well over a century, and they raised pigs.

Milgrom developed the theory that taxonomy reflects the values of a society. He developed a structure of parallel sets of concentric circles (1991, 718–36). The first set is the dietary laws structure. The innermost circle consists of the "food of the Lord." This is surrounded by the middle circle, consisting of the food of the Israelites, which expands on the food of the Lord by adding wild animals, fish with fins, and certain birds. The outermost and the largest circle includes the entire animal kingdom, which may be consumed by all humankind. This parallels the second structure called "the holiness structure," also built of three concentric circles. In the innermost and holiest circle are the priests; in the middle circle are the Israelites; and in the third and the outermost circle are the rest of human beings. According to Milgrom, this structure echoes the arrangement of space into three concentric circles, with the sanctuary at the center, surrounded by the promised land of Israel, which is considered to be holy, and surrounding it is the earth, which is the dwelling of the rest of humankind (1991, 722).

This sophisticated structure can be developed further in other tripartite divisions not mentioned by Milgrom, such as the tripartite division of the temple in Jerusalem in an increasing rate of holiness, the *ulam* (porch), *hiekhal* (hall), and *devir* (Holy of Holies). It can be echoed by the three famous covenants made between God and mortals, each representing a more definite divine choice, with Noah representing the broader sense of human, Abraham representing monotheism, and Moses representing the Israelites, the chosen people. The existence of subtle or palpable tripartite divisions in the biblical literature suggests that this type of symbolism is not the reason for the dietary laws but an outcome of them, and that all these tripartite divisions are not necessarily related. Due to difficulties in deconstructing the texts and discerning and isolating historical layers, Milgrom and Levine prefer to ignore historical developments, and to draw conclusions from the final outcome of the redaction process. The result is a formidable structure that historically suits the Second Temple period. It suggests, however, very little about the formation processes of the dietary laws. Levine and Milgrom are familiar with the archaeological material but make little use of it.

The bone finds from Bethsaida are not an isolated case. Similar discoveries and analyses were unearthed at Ugarit on the Syrian coast of the Mediterranean[35] (Herdner 1963, 61:18–29, Milgrom 1991, 723), Dor on the Mediterranean coast (Milgrom 1991, 723), and perhaps Mount Ebal (Zertal 1992; 2000, 67–74).[36] The first locations were not inhabited by Israelites, and in the latter, the excavator Adam Zertal discovered a large high place on the top of the mountain. The high place was surrounded by ash pits filled with content similar to Bethsaida, Dor, and Ugarit, namely bones of sheep, goats, bovines, and a small percentage of fallow deer bones. Zertal associated these finds with the altar built by Joshua on Mount Ebal (Josh. 8:30–35); however, the discovery of fallow deer at the site indicates that it is not an Israelite altar.

Fallow deer are among the animals that were permitted for consumption but were excluded from sacrifice.

Socioreligion scholars and theologians (Anderson 1992), have long explored the meaning of sacrifice, the type of necessity it fulfils, and the essence of this meaning. Few scholars have looked at the recipients of the sacrifices. Who were they and what did they really want? Deities in the ancient world were, by and large, divided into two separate groups: chthonic deities who dwelled below the surface of the earth, and those deities who dwelled on top of the surface of earth, including the skies. Although the residence of the deities was permanent, they interacted with each other. Both Eastern and Western mythologies record elaborate communication between the two groups, which ensured the vitality and the seasonal fertility revival of the world. Although deities who dwelled on the top of the surface did not have a real collective name, the worshippers had the notion that they were "the upper gods." When worshippers offered sacrifice to a god either group, they were very careful to serve each one his preferred diet and never mixed their preferences. Chthonic deities preferred, for one reason or another, pigs and pomegranates (Turner and Coulter 2000, 146), while upper gods preferred bulls, sheep, and goats (Milgrom 1991, 718–36). The fact that Jehovah was an upper god is attested to not only by the story of the creation (Jehovah as the creator of earth and sky), but also by his name "Elion." This name is mentioned thirty times in the Bible and usually translated as "God Most High." Although a more accurate translation would be "an Upper God," as opposed to a chthonic god. The word "most high" is a superlative form and would translate into Hebrew as *ha'elion beyoter*. *Elion* without the preposition *beyoter* is a comparative form, meaning higher or upper. Thus *el Elion* is "Upper God," and would be better translated and understood in the *sitzen im leben* of the dual upper versus chthonic gods.

The bones in the sacrificial high place at Bethsaida indicate that the god worshipped there was an upper god. It could have been Hadad, the chief god of the Arameans, who as a storm god would have been an upper god. The food of an upper god is similar to the food in the Leviticus dietary laws and is what the Israelites chose to consume. The food of Jehovah is a slightly more narrow selection of this food. It lacks only the wild animals.

The process known in the history of religion as *imitatio dei* is one in which the worshippers assume the features of their deity in order to identify with him. By consuming the food of the divine, the worshipper receives the nature of the divine. One sees how this process functioned in the two common systems of the religion of the ancient world: polytheism and monotheism. In a polytheistic system where more than one divinity is worshipped, the process of *imitatio dei* was done usually on an individual basis. The features that were adopted were usually external features, and include parts of the outfits and attributes of the divine. *Imitatio dei* may last the entire life of the individual or may last for a shorter period of time. Historical examples of this phenomenon are numerous. Alexander the Great is seen on his coins wearing the lion's skin of Hercules and having his name written next to the statue of Zeus. Roman emperors who sought to be worshipped in the imperial cult adopted divine features as well.

In a monotheistic system, where the choice of the individual is limited to a single god and where the divinity explicitly prohibits the use of imagery, *imitatio dei* may be assumed not only by individuals but also by the entire community and may take features that do not involve images of consuming the food of the divine. When food of the divine is adopted, however, the problem becomes very complicated. Every meal would turn into a sacred meal, similar to a sacrifice, and daily life would become extremely difficult (Smith 1992). One aspect of the problem would be the question of the leftover food. A sacred leftover food cannot be discarded. When the meal is holy, the holiness does not expire as soon as the meal is over. The leftover would also be regarded as holy, and, therefore, would require special treatment. Archaeological excavations reveal that the leftover food was buried in special pits in the ground. Burial guaranteed that the food would not be defiled or consumed, for instance, by dogs (Smith 2000, 531). It is obvious that this would put restrictions on every meal. A compromise in which one would adopt the divine food but not have the burden of sacred meals could consist of narrowing the food of the divine to fewer items. This is where the holiness nature of the divine will still be extended over the worshipper but without the obligations of the sacred meal. The fact that the content of sacrifices at Bethsaida, Dor, and Ugarit included fallow deer indicates that the alternative of removing items from the diet of the upper gods, for the food of Jehovah, was the one that was selected. The final result would be a tripartite division as Milgrom has suggested, in which the food in the middle tier would be similar to the food of an upper god and holier than the food of the lower tier, but not as holy as the food of Jehovah in the upper tier. Therefore, it would not be treated as a sacred meal.

There is perhaps no better illustration than the explanation given at the end of the biblical verses dealing with the dietary laws in which the worshipper who assumes the laws and consumes the extended divine food would still have holiness extended upon him:

> You shall not make yourself impure therewith and thus become impure, for I the Lord am your God. You shall sanctify yourselves and be holy, for I am holy... you shall be holy for I am holy. (Lev. 11:43–45)

The principle of *imitatio dei* will function once the people of Israel will comply with the laws.

STELAE

Seven stelae were discovered at Bethsaida (figs. 7–13). Four were found at the courtyard of the gate and two were found at the back of the gate. One stele was found in a secondary use at Chamber 2. The stelae of the courtyard were nicely dressed; the one on the stepped high place at the niche of the northern tower was decorated. The stelae were placed near the entrances of the courtyard: one on each side of the entrance to the courtyard and two near the passageway near the threshold of the inner city gate. Two roughly dressed stelae were placed at the back of the inner gate as one leaves the inner gate toward the city.

The stele discovered at the wall of Chamber 2 is of a different type. It is—either naturally or artificially—a very polished stele. It is thicker and taller than the other stelae, and its location suggests that it derives from the previous period, presumably the tenth century BCE (fig. 13).

CHAMBER 4 OFFERING VESSELS

Chamber 4 is the northeastern chamber of the inner city gate and is closest to the stepped high place. Finds from this chamber include vessels (fig. 14) that were offered at the high place; for example, several perforated cups similar to the two found in the basin. There were several cooking pots (one with a lid) and a small number of jars. Most of the pots were jugs, bowls, and shallow plates. The vessels demonstrate a rather unusual religious practice, which thus far has not been

Rami Arav

Fig. 7. A basalt stele found on top of the stepped high place at the northern niche of the inner gate. It depicts the moon-god in the shape of a bull with crescentlike horns placed on top of Luwian hieroglyphs that mean "stele"

Fig. 8. The un-iconic stele near the stepped high place

Fig. 9. The un-iconic stele near the direct access high place

Fig. 10. The un-iconic stele near the outer city gate

Fig. 11. The northern un-iconic stele inside the inner city gate

Fig. 12. The southern un-iconic stele inside the inner city gate

Fig. 13. The un-iconic stele in secondary use inside Chamber 2

Fig. 14. Offering vessels from Chamber 4

observed in other places. Most of the vessels were of extremely poor
quality; some were broken in the past and were mended or repaired,
and some plates cracked during firing. Instead of being discarded, they
were repaired by applying white plaster on the cracks. Scholars who
presumed that gods are offered the prime vessels would be disap-
pointed with this Geshurite practice.

A JUG WITH AN INSCRIPTION

One jug was found with a three-letter inscription on it (fig. 15). It
reads, in Paleo-Hebrew characters, *LShM*, followed by an ankh-like
sign (Arav 1999b, 78–91). The translation would be "to the name of"
or "on behalf of the name." The ankh-like sign is usually associated
with the moon-god, and therefore the inscription would mean "on
behalf of the name of the moon-god." This is the first time that a dedicatory inscription like this has been found, but it recalls the biblical
practice of referring to the name of Jehovah.

Fig. 15. A jug from Chamber 4 with the inscription *Leshem* (to the name of) followed by a moon-god symbol (H.-W. Kuhn)

FIGURINES

Several figurines and statuettes representing deities were discovered at
Bethsaida; some of them were published in the past. None of the figurines was discovered intact, making it difficult to identify the deities or
their original gestures. One of the clay figurines shows the head of a
male wearing an *atef* crown, which is a tall flat crown flanked by two
feathers on both sides and a large knob on the top of the crown (Arav
1995a, 17–18) (fig. 16). This crown is known in the Ammonite culture
and recalls the biblical passage where King David removed the Ammonite crown and placed it on his head. The biblical verse does not clearly
indicate the possessor of the crown. The text has the characters *MLKM*,
which could be read *Milkom* like the Ammonite deity, or *malkam*
meaning "their king." It is suggested here to read the word as *Milkom*,
because figurines usually indicate deities and not kings. Did the Geshurites also worship *Milkom*, did they have a different name for this deity,
or did the Geshurites use the same features for a totally different deity?
In the current stage of scholarship, it is difficult to know the answer.

A
588
1930
IAA: 93-2752

B
453
5519
IAA: 1995-3433

Fig. 16. A clay figurine with *atef*
crown

Fig. 17. A clay figurine with Hathor
hairstyle

E 341
9070

Fig. 18. A clay figurine
holding an object in her
hand

Fig. 19. A Pataekos figurine in faïence

A clay figurine of a female wearing the Egyptian Hathor hair-style (fig. 17) was found at Bethsaida. Only the head is preserved, so it is difficult to identify the deity. The figurine has large, pronounced eyes, which are indicative of those known and produced locally, rather than imported from Egypt.

Another clay figurine shows a female wearing the Hathor hair-style standing and holding something in her hand, which is, unfortunately, not preserved. Inferring from a similar, but intact, figurine found in Transjordan, it is assumed that she was holding a tambourine or a similar object (sun disk?) in her hand (fig. 18).

Among the fine discoveries made at the *bit hilani* palace (Arav and Bernett 2000, 47–81)[37] was a small Egyptian statuette made from faïence, a manifestation of the Egyptian dwarf god known in its Greek name only as *Pataekos* (Arav and Bernett 1997, 198–213), which is the second most common Egyptian amulet found outside of Egypt. This figurine, a protective amulet (fig. 19), shows a naked dwarf wearing the tight cap of the Egyptian god Ptah and a necklace, and holding two knives. The figurine was presumably standing on a crocodile, which is not preserved.

SUMMARY

The recent excavations in the region shed light on the political history, socioeconomic life, and religion of Geshur.[38] Apart from short inscriptions on pottery, no substantial new literary documents were unearthed. The material culture revealed in the excavations bears important implications for the study of history and the Bible. The process that supposes a development from small city-states in the Late Bronze Age into chiefdoms or principalities, and into solid kingdoms during the tenth and ninth centuries BCE is not new and was already suggested by Albrecht Alt (1967, 175–309). The archaeological discoveries made in Geshur and Bethsaida provide the material culture for this textual context[39] (the *sitzen im Leben* of archaeology). The construction of a capital city on bedrock, contrary to a development from an existing town, was undoubtedly a complex undertaking that required a combination of engineering and architectural skills, together with a high quality of constructional capabilities. The impressive remains of this town, which are still visible today, suggest that the construction operation was successfully accomplished. The most important implication for historical and biblical studies is that Bethsaida serves as the best-preserved paradigm for development of statehood in the southern Levant. Its impressive accomplishments testify that kingdoms in this area were able to carry out monumental endeavors successfully.

For two and a half centuries, from the foundation of the city in the tenth century BCE to its final destruction in 732 BCE, the city was destroyed only three times (including the last destruction). There are more historical figures who could be responsible for the destruction of the city than there are layers of destructions. This fact means that although some of the contenders had good reason and opportunity to destroy the city, only three actually managed to do it. In the current stage of the research, and in lack of written evidence, it is impossible to be more precise.

The Geshurite religion suggested by the remains of Iron Age Bethsaida demonstrates strong ties and connection to the northern Mesopotamia regions where the cult of the moon-god was prominent. In addition to this, there was an obvious connection to Egyptian religion. It seems, however, that the Egyptian influence was confined to art, amulets, and popular religion, while the Mesopotamian religion had a much more profound influence. In addition, ties can be observed between the Geshurites and their neighbors, such as the Ammonites. Particularly interesting ties are observed between the Geshurites and the monotheistic Israelite religion, which is observed in the direct access high place and the selection of the sacrificial animals.

CHAPTER NOTES

Unless otherwise indicated, all translations are my own. All biblical translations are my own.

1. At the beginning of the excavations it was thought that the city was first founded during the Early Bronze Age; however, the Early Bronze Age pottery was always found in a mixed context of Early Bronze Age I and II. These finds suggest that there must have been some remains of Early Bronze Age I and II settlements somewhere at the site and that the Iron Age construction workers thoroughly destroyed these settlements and, to level the foundation of their city, brought in dirt containing a mixture of shards. See note 16 below and Arav 1995a, 6; 1999a, 15.

2. Edward Lipinski's arguments (2000, 334–37) that the kingdom of Geshur and Maacah never existed are very difficult to accept. According to Lipinski, Maacah is the name of the founder of the dynasty of Abel Beth Maacah and Geshur is a name of a town that gave its name to the kingdom and was also called Beth Maacah. On the one hand, this suggestion partially solves a minor problem of the appearance of the phrase Abel Beth-Maacah in which Beth-Maacah is understood as a founder of a dynasty. On the other hand, it creates a further more serious problem. Lipinski ignores the possible reading of Geshur in El Amarna letter 254. In addition, his arguments do not agree with archaeological evidence. He totally ignores the evidence from Bethsaida indicating that the city bears features of a capital city containing monumental architecture and *bit hilani* palace.

3. See Arav 1995, 193–201. The verse should be read:"The fortified cities of the fishermen were: Tzer (Tzed?), Hamat, Rakat and Kinneret." The city Tzer (Tzed) is at the top of a list of cities, set in a clockwise direction around the Sea of Galilee. Its position at the top reflects perhaps the significance of the city among the fishermen cities and indeed Bethsaida is the largest of all the Iron Age cities around the Sea of Galilee.

4. The letter is addressed to the scribe who will read the letter to Yanhamu, the governor, who apparently was illiterate. It is not an unusual address since most rulers were illiterate in the pre-alphabetic era. Yanhamu is suggested also to be a Hebrew name (*ANET* 486; EA 256, 266)

5. The name mentioned in the text is Pehel, which was identified in the Hellenistic Roman period as Pella. See Houston-Smith 1992.

6. Mazar has repeated this idea a number of times. See Mazar 1946, 8; 1975, 190–202; 1986, 113–25.

7. It is double the size that Zvi U. Maoz has estimated (1992, 2:996). It is hard to believe that a city like Bethsaida reached the size of a major city equipped with monumental buildings without a strong hinterland. It seems plausible that the Arameans appeared in Geshur concurrent with their general appearance in the Near East during the middle of the second millennium BCE.

8. Eight or nine people in the Bible are known by the name Maacah. Two or perhaps three are males (Schearing 1992).
9. Lipinski (2000, 334–37) argues that the kingdom of Geshur was not Aramaic since the names Talmai and perhaps Maacah are not Aramaic. Out of seven proper names and references in the Geshurite area, only one is not Aramaic. Talmai is indeed a Hurrian name, but his father's name, Amihud (Amihur?), is Aramaic although it bears a suffix mentioning Hurrians. The other names occurring in the archaeology of the lower Golan are all Aramaic, such as Shakaya (found in Ein Gev excavations), Akiba, and Mky (Bethsaida). The jug from Bethsaida with the dedication "*leshem*" meaning "to the name of" is either Hebrew or Aramaic but certainly not Hurrian. David's son Absalom was born to a Geshurite mother and his name occurs in the Aramaic regions. Absalom recalls also the name Shulum from the El Amarna letter 256. The excavators of Tel Hadar reported also on the discovery of Aramaic inscriptions (Kokhavi 1994, 140).
10. For the Dan inscription, see Biran and Naveh 1993, 81–98; 1995, 1–18; Na'aman 2000, 92–104.
11. There was a suggestion to identify Adumu with a site near Har Odem at the southern slopes of Mount Hermon as this name appears also at the Ugarit mythology of Anat (Margalit 1995, 228-30).
12. Moshe Kokhavi has suggested that the trade routes leading from the southern Golan led to the eastern shores of the Sea of Galilee and to the Israelite kingdom (1996, 184–201).
13. The king list of the Ugarit bore Semitic and non-Semitic names interchangeably. This may mean that the distinction between Hurrians and Semites was not very clear (Yon 2000, 201; Singer 1997, 603–733).
14. The Marianu are recorded in sites such as Allalakh and Ugarit and were perhaps present in the southern Levant.
15. There is no historical model to show how a capital city was founded other than the biblical narrative. One example is the foundation of Jerusalem as the capital city of David and the other is the foundation of Shomron (Samaria) by Omri, the king of Israel. In these two examples, the kings worked on establishing their reign first and later selected their capital city. Prior to their accession to the throne, they both administrated their kingdoms from several small capital cities. The kings of Israel reigned during the first fifty years from various capital cities before Omri established a permanent capital city. The kingdom of Judah under Saul and for seven years under David functioned from different capital cities before David established his permanent capital at Jerusalem. Jerusalem was not built on bedrock and although the Bible maintains that Samaria was built on a mountain that was bought from Shemer, "the owner of the mountain" (1 Kings 15:24), archaeological remains indicate that there were some earlier remains there (Avigad 1992, 1497). In addition to this, the fierce conflagration that destroyed Stratum 4 in Tel Hadar may indicate that the formation of the kingdom was associated, very likely, with some local violent actions (Kokhavi 1994, 136–41).

16. Shards of Early Bronze Age I–III pottery were discovered with the fill of the city wall at the northern edge of the mound and may indicate the presence of a small inhabitation of that period. No architecture has been found so far, and apparently the entire Early Bronze settlement was dismantled during the construction of the city.

17. Lipinski (2000, 334–37) suggests that Hadad-Ezer was not a historical figure at all, but was a late biblical invention. Likewise he suggests locating the confrontations with David at the Beth She'an Valley near Bezek Valley. Lipinski's suggestions solve some epigraphic problems, but create many other historical and archaeological problems. For instance, how could a biblical narrator (supposedly living in the seventh century BCE) know anything about Geshur when the kingdom had ceased to exist as an independent kingdom in the ninth century BCE and was totally destroyed by the Assyrian king Tiglath-pileser III in 732 BCE? Without such knowledge, one would expect narration discrepancies.

18. The coalition members were discussed a few times by scholars and there is a wide consensus (Lipinski 2000, 334–37) that it is a dim recollection of historical documents. Beth Rehob is most probably a name of a dynasty. The exact location of Aram-Tzoba is unknown. Maacah was located perhaps on the western slope of the Hermon mountain. Sometimes it is referred to as Abel Beth Maacah, i.e., Maacah is the name of the dynasty ruling at Abel. The location of Tob is also unknown but the words Tob and Tzoba (Tzaba) are almost synonyms in Aramaic and perhaps it is a reference to the same kingdom.

19. David fought against this coalition one time in Madaba (1 Chron. 19:7). It is difficult to assess how many times David fought against the coalition in the north. The verses in 2 Samuel 8:3–8 and 10:16–19 speak of an absolute defeat of the Arameans. It is possible that they were engaged only in one battle (Malamat 1983, 196–97; Gal and Oded 1990, 119).

20. Mazar (1975, 198) associates the beginning of the region Gaulanitis to this period. He asserts that Golan became the major city of the region and its name was given to the entire region. However, more plausible is the suggestion of Arnold Hugh Martin Jones and Michael Avi-Yonah (Avi-Yonah 1984, 29) that the suffix *"itis"* is Ptolemaic Egyptian and therefore the region Gaulanitis dates to the early Hellenistic period when the city Golan was thriving. Excavations at the site of Sahem el Julan, which is identified with the biblical city Golan, will certainly contribute to this question.

21. The excavators relate this stratum to the tenth century BCE but indicate that it is Iron Age I. They do not associate construction and destruction dates to the various strata but it is obvious that each stratum has a construction and destruction date and they are not necessarily close to each other.

22. The *bit hilani* palace was altered, the main room in the palace was bisected, and obviously the building ceased to function as a palace. It is possible that this is connected to the reformations of Ben Hadad II.

23. Most scholars maintain that these are the events referred to in the inscription of Dan.
24. In support of this identification one should consider the fact that a valley descending from Mount Carmel is called Rasmia. The component *ras* (head) survived from the ancient period (Yamada 2000, 191–92).
25. Luckenbill 1926, 243; Yamada 2000, 192–95. Nadav Na'aman speculated that Shalmaneser knew that Jehu was an usurper and wanted to flatter him (2000). Why should it not be assumed that Shalmaneser was not aware that the dynasty had just been replaced? There are many possibilities, such as perhaps Jehu lied to Shalmaneser III fearing that the latter would replace him with the legitimate heir of the Omride dynasty because the Omrides were rivals of Hazael.
26. Finkelstein and Silberman (2001, 207) attribute the destruction of Stratum 5 at Bethsaida to the campaign of Jeroboam II. This is untenable for the following reasons: (1) the destruction pattern of the Bethsaida city gate is similar to the destruction pattern ascribed to Tiglath-pileser III in other places; (2) an Assyrian pottery vessel found on top of the destructions testifies to the connection between the destruction and the Assyrians; and (3) carbon 14 testing of carbonated barley found at Chamber 3 at the gate indicates the date of 732 BCE.
27. Contrary to Finkelstein and Silberman's ideas (2001, 207) that different languages as they appear on ostracons are evidence to changes of population.
28. For further treatment of high places at the city gate, see Bernett and Keel 1998; Blomquist 1999.
29. I wish to thank Ziony Zevit for discussing this issue with me. See Zevit 2001, 149–53.
30. Similar high places were observed in a few places (Bernett and Keel 1998, 45–74; Blomquist 1999, 57–131).
31. The altar at Dan is almost the only altar that can be ascribed to the Israelites. It is not yet clear how much this altar complies with the Jehovistic laws. The altar at Mount Ebal seems to have a large podium and a rampart leading to it. This altar has no parallels yet and its reconstruction and ethnic affiliation are still unclear.
32. This is the view the Mishnah holds for this passage (Midot 3).
33. See for example Tel-Mudayneh in Moab (Daviou and Dion 2002, 42).
34. See forthcoming research by T. Fisher in volume 4 of this series.
35. Ugarit, situated at north Syria, was excavated since the 1920s. Marguerite Yon (2000) summarized the latest finds of the site.
36. No clear ethnicity can derive from the finds represented in Zertal's report. The only ethnic indicators found were two Egyptian scarabs. Zertal's suggestion that the ethnicity of Israelites was created in a onetime ritual on the top of a mountain has, to the best of my knowledge, no parallel in human history.
37. The palace in the Neo-Hittite/Aramean style was discovered at the early stages of the dig. Its construction dates from the tenth century BCE and it

was in fact never thoroughly destroyed. The western wings of it were in use until the Hellenistic period.

38. William Dever asserted that "only as scholars learn to structure questions more appropriate to the archaeological record itself and to socioeconomic history, rather than religious and political history, will archaeology become the powerful interpretive tool that Albright envisioned for reconstructing biblical life and times" (Dever 2001, 73; Albright 1928). However, the premise of this paper is that political history and religion are reflected in archaeological remains and should not be dismissed from the environmental reconstruction that archaeology can provide (Arav 1999c, 75–79).

39. The question of how the Geshurites acquired their land, which is sort of parallel to the famous question of how the Israelites acquired their land, cannot be unequivocally answered. The heavy destruction layers at Tel Hadar Stratum 4 (eleventh century BCE) do suggest violent actions; however, the Geshurites are perhaps recorded in Late Bronze Age documents which indicate that their appearance in this region was prior to these events.

LITERATURE CITED

Aharoni, Yohanan. 1962. *The Land of Israel in Biblical Times, a Historical Geography* (in Hebrew). Jerusalem: Mosad Byalik.

Ahituv, Shmuel. 1992. *Handbook of Ancient Hebrew Inscription, The Biblical Encyclopedia Library* (in Hebrew). Jerusalem: Mosad Byalik.

Albright, W. F. 1928. Among the Canaanite Mounds of Eastern Galilee. *Bulletin of the American Schools of Oriental Research* 29:1–8.

Alt, Albrecht. 1961. *Der Herkunft Der Hyksos in neuer Sicht*. Berlin: Akademie-Verlag.

———. 1956. *Kleine Schriften zur Geschichte des Volkes Israel*. Band 3. Munich: H. Beck.

———. 1967, *Essays on Old Testament History and Religion*. Translated by R. A. Wilson. Garden City, N.Y.: Doubleday & Company, Inc.

Anderson, G. A. 1992. Sacrifice and Sacrificial Offerings in the Old Testament. In *Anchor Bible Dictionar,* edited by D. N. Friedman. New York: Doubleday.

Arav, Rami. 1992. Hermon. In *Anchor Bible Dictionary*, edited by D. N. Friedman. New York: Doubleday.

———. 1995a. Bethsaida Excavations: Preliminary Report 1987–1993. In Arav and Freund 1995.

———. 1995b. Bethsaida, Tzer, and the Fortified Cities of Naphtali. In Arav and Freund 1995.

———. 1999a. Bethsaida Excavations: Preliminary Report 1994–1996. In Arav and Freund 1999.

———. 1999b. Bethsaida (in Hebrew). *Qadmoniot* 32 (118): 78–91.

———. 1999c. New Testament Archaeology and the Case of Bethsaida. In *Das Ende der Tage & die Gegenwart des Heils, Begegnungen mit dem Neuen Testament und seiner Umwelt*, edited by M. Becker and W. Fenske. Leiden: Brill.

Arav, Rami, and Monika Bernett. 1997. An Egyptian Figurine of Pataekos at Bethsaida. *Israel Exploration Journal* 47 (3–4): 198–213.

———. 2000. The Bit Hilani Palace at Bethsaida: Its Place in Aramean/Neo-Hittite and Israelite Palace Architecture in Iron Age II. *Israel Exploration Journal* 50:47–81.

Arav, Rami, and Richard Freund, eds. 1995. *Bethsaida: A City by the North Shore of the Sea of Gailiee*. Vol. 1. Kirksville, Mo.: Thomas Jefferson University Press.

———. 1999. *Bethsaida: A City by the North Shore of the Sea of Gailiee*. Vol. 2. Kirksville, Mo.: Truman State University Press.

Avigad, Nahman. 1992. Samaria. In *The New Encyclopedia of Archaeological Excavations in the Holy Land* (in Hebrew), edited by Ephraim Stern. Jerusalem: Israel Exploration Society and Carta.

Avi-Yonah, Michael. 1984. *Geographical History of the Land of Israel from the Persian Period to the Muslim Conquest* (in Hebrew). Jerusalem: Mosad Byalik.

Bernett, Monika, and Othmar Keel. 1998. *Mond, Stier und Kult am Stadttor, Die Stele con Bethsaida (et-Tell)*. Orbis Biblicus et Orientalis 161. Freiburg: Universitätsverlag; Göttingen: Vanderhoeck & Ruprecht.

Biran, Abraham, and Joseph Naveh. 1993. An Aramaic Stele Fragment from Tel Dan. *Israel Exploration Journal* 43 (2–3): 81–98.

Blomquist, Tina Haettner. 1999. *Gates and Gods: Cults in the City Gates of Iron Age Palestine: An Investigation of the Archaeological and Biblical Sources.* Stockholm: Almqvist & Wiksel International.

Daviou, Michelle, and Paul-Eugene Dion. 2002. Moab Comes to Life. *Biblical Archaeology Review* 28 (1): 38–49.

Dever, William G. 2001. *What Did the Biblical Writers Know, and When Did They Know It? What Archaeology Can Tell Us about the Reality of Ancient Israel.* Grand Rapids, Mich.: Eerdmans.

Epstein, Claire. 1993. The Cities of the Land of Ga-ru Geshur Mentioned in EA 256 Reconsidered. In *Studies in the Archaeology and History of Ancient Israel in Honor of Moshe Dothan* (in Hebrew), edited by Michael Heltzer, Arthur Segal, and Daniel Kaufman. Haifa: Haifa University Press.

Finkelstein, Israel, and Neil Asher Silberman. 2001. *The Bible Unearthed.* New York: The Free Press.

Fisher, Toni. Forthcoming. Bone Analysis at Bethsaida. In *Bethsaida: A City by the North Shore of the Sea of Galilee*, vol. 4, edited by Rami Arav and Richard A. Freund. Kirksville, Mo.: Truman State University Press.

Fritz, Volkmar, and Stephen Muenger. 2002. Vorbericht ueber die zweite Phase der Ausgrabungen in Kinneret (Tell el-'Oreme) am See Gennesaret, 1994–1999. *Zeitschrift des Deutschen Palaestina Vereins* 118 (1): 3–32.

Gal, Zvi, and Bustanai Oded. 1990. The Kingdom of Israel and Judah (circa 1020 until 586 BCE). In *The History of Eretz Israel, Israel and Judah in the Biblical Period* (in Hebrew), rdited by Israel Eph'al. Jerusalem: Keter, Yad Ben-Zvi.

Herdner, Andree. 1963. *Corpus des tablettes en cunéiforme alphabétique découvertes à Ras Shamra—Ugrit de 1929 à 1939.* 2 vols. Paris: Nationale; P. Geuthner.

Hess, Richard. 2004. Geshurite Onomastica of the Bronze and Iron Ages. In *Bethsaida: A City by the North Shore of the Sea of Galilee*, vol. 3, edited by Rami Arav and Richard A. Freund. Kirksville, Mo.: Truman State University Press.

Hesse, B. 1990. Pig Lovers and Pig Haters: Patterns of Palestinian Pork Production. *Journal of Ethnobiology* 10 (2): 195–225.

Houston-Smith, R. 1992. Pella. In *Anchor Bible Dictionary*, edited by D. N. Friedman. New York: Doubleday.

Kokhavi, Moshe. 1989. The Land of Geshur Project: Regional Archaeology of the Southern Golan (1987–1988 Seasons). *Israel Exploration Journal* 39 (1–2): 1–17.

———. 1994. The Land of Geshur Project 1993. *Israel Exploration Journal* 44 (1–2): 136–41.

———. 1996. Land of Geshur Project (in Hebrew). *Eretz Israel* 25:184–201.

Levine, Baruch A. 1989. *Leviticus—Va-yikra: The Traditional Hebrew Text with the New JPS Translation, Commentary by Baruch A. Levine.* Philadelphia: Jewish Publication Society.

Lewis, Bernard. 2002. *What Went Wrong? Western Impact and Middle Eastern Response.* Oxford: Oxford University Press.

Lipinski, Edward. 2000. *The Arameans: Their Ancient History Culture, Religion.* Orientalia Louvaniensia Analecta 100. Sterling, Va.: Peeters.

Luckenbill, David Daniel. 1926. *Ancient Records of Assyria and Babylonia.* Vol. 1, *Historical Records of Assyria from the Earliest Times of Sargon.* Chicago: University of Chicago Press.

Malamat, Abraham.1983. *Israel in the Biblical Times* (in Hebrew). Jerusalem: Mosad Byalik.

Maoz, Zvi U. 1992. Geshur. In *Anchor Bible Dictionary*, edited by D. N. Friedman. New York: Doubleday.

Margalit, Baruch. 1996. K-R-T Studies. In *Ugarit Forschungen.* Internationales Jahrbuch für die Altertumskunde Syrien-Palästinas. Edited by M. Dietrich and O. Loretz. Vol. 27, 215-315.

Mazar, Benjamin. 1959–59. Geshur and Maacah. *Zion* 23-24.

———. 1975. Geshur and Maacha. In *Cities and Districts in Eretz Israel* (in Hebrew). Jerusalem: Israel Exploration Society.

———. 1986. Geshur and Maacah. In *The Early Biblical Period*, edited by Shmuel Ahituv and Baruch A. Levine. Jerusalem: Israel Exploration Society.

Milgrom, Jacob. 1991. *Leviticus 1–16, A New Translation with Introduction and Commentary.* The Anchor Bible, vol. 3. New York: Doubleday.

Morrison, M. A. 1992. Hurrians. In *Anchor Bible Dictionary*, edited by D. N. Friedman. New York: Doubleday.

Na'aman, Nadav. 2000. Three Notes on the Aramaic Inscription from Tel Dan. *Israel Exploration Journal* 50:92–104.

———. 2002. In Search of Reality behind the Accounts of David's Wars with Israel's Neighbors. *Israel Exploration Journal* 52:200–24.

Pritchard, James B., ed. 1950. *Ancient Near East Texts relating to the Old Testament.* Princeton: Princeton University Press.

———. 1969. On Use of the Tripod Cup. In *Ugaritica VI*, edited by C.F.A. Schaeffer. Mission de Ras Shamra, Paris: P. Geuthner.

Schearing, L. S. 1992. Maacah. In *Anchor Bible Dictionary*, edited by D. N. Friedman. New York: Doubleday.

Shroder, John F., Jr., and Moshe Inbar. 1995. Geologic and Geographic Background to the Bethsaida Excavations. In Arav and Freund 1995.

Shroder, John F., Jr., M. P. Bishop, K. J. Cornwell, and M. Inbar. 1999. Catastrophic Geomorphic Processes and the Bethsaida Archaeology, Israel. In Arav and Freund 1999.

Singer, Ithamar. 1997. A Political History of Ugarit. In *Handbook of Ugaritic Studies.* Edited by W. Watson and N. Wyatt. Leiden: Brill.

Smith, D. E. 1992. Greco-Roman Sacred Meals. In *Anchor Bible Dictionary*, edited by D. N. Friedman. New York: Doubleday.

———. 2000. Meals. In *Encyclopedia of the Dead Sea Scrolls*, edited by Lawrence H. Schiffman and James C. VanderKam. New York: Oxford University Press.

Spanier, Ketziah. 1999. The Two Maacahs. In Arav and Freund 1999.

Tadmor, Haim. 1994. *The Inscriptions of Tiglath Pileser III, King of Assyria, Critical Edition with Introductions.* Jerusalem: Israel Exploration Society.

Turner, Patricia, and Charles Russell Coulter. 2000. *Dictionary of Ancient Deities.* New York: Oxford University Press.

Yon, Marguerite. 2000. Daily Life. *Near Eastern Archaeology* 63 (4): 200-24.

Zertal, Adam. 1992. Har Ebal. In *The New Encyclopedia of Archaeological Excavations in the Holy Land,* edited by Ephraim Stern. Jerusalem: Israel Exploration Society.

———. 2000. *Am Nolad* (in Hebrew). Tel Aviv: Yedioth.

Zevit, Ziony. 2001. *The Religions of Ancient Israel: A Synthesis of Parallactic Approaches.* London and New York: Continuum.

Yamada, Shigeo. 2000. *The Construction of the Assyrian Empire: A Historical Study of the Inscriptions of Shalmaneser III (859–824 B.C.) relating to His Campaigns to the West.* Vol. 3 of *Culture and History of the Ancient Near East,* edited by B. Halpern, M. H. E. Weipert, Th. P. J. Van den Hout, and I. Winter. Boston: Brill.

Richard S. Hess

"Geshurite" Onomastica
of the Bronze and Iron Ages

T HIS STUDY WILL REVIEW personal names associated with the land
of Geshur during the Bronze and Iron Ages based on available
evidence from textual sources. Methodologically, there are two problematic areas: first, the identification of the land of Geshur; second,
the actual texts to be used as legitimate sources for onomastica according to the parameters defined.

The territory defined by the name Geshur is attested solely in
biblical sources. No other ancient source, and specifically no Bronze
Age or Iron Age source, designates the region by this name. However,
the proposal of William F. Albright to identify the land of Gari
described in the Late Bronze Age Amarna texts with that of Geshur
seems logical and has enjoyed general favor (Albright 1943, 14 n. 35;
Maisler 1954; Mazar 1986; Ma'oz 1992; Galil 1998, 374). The location
of this land between the cities of Ashtaroth to the south and Hazor to
the northwest accords nicely with the biblical evidence associating
this site with the region east and immediately north of the Sea of Kinnereth. This area is mentioned in El Amarna letter 256 on line 23 as
KUR *ga-ri*, using the determinative for a land or region (Hess 1984,
471). This may imply a scribal omission of the *šu* sign between the *ga*
and *ri*, as Benjamin Mazar has suggested. Such omissions are known
elsewhere in the Amarna correspondence. Thus the reading would be
KUR *ga-<šu>-ri*, the Late Bronze Age equivalent of Geshur.

If this is accepted, there remains the question of which texts can be regarded as legitimate sources for Geshur onomastica. There is no text identified as being from Geshur in the Bronze Age. However, it seems from the above-cited Amarna letter, EA 256, and from another letter, EA 364, that the land of Geshur was disputed between the city states of Hazor and of Ashtaroth. If so, then Middle and Late Bronze Age cuneiform texts from these sites may preserve personal names associated with Geshur or with adjacent territories. Several Iron Age texts from the site of Bethsaida have been discovered and these provide three personal names.

Finally, there is the question of the Bible as a source for names from Geshur. The kingdom of Geshur is referred to eight times: six times in 2 Samuel (3:3; 13:37, 38; 14:23, 32; 15:8) and twice in 1 Chronicles (2:23, 3:2). In addition, the gentilic, Geshurite, occurs once in Deuteronomy (3:14) and four times in Joshua (12:5; 13:11, 13 [twice]). Two other occurrences (Josh. 13:2; 1 Sam. 27:8) refer to a people south of the land of Israel. However, the isolation of the personal names associated with these references raises questions about authenticity. Is there any historical value to these texts and, specifically, do the names of Geshurites reflect an authentic early Iron Age tradition? It is impossible to answer this here on the basis of the present evidence. However, this study will consider the earlier Bronze Age onomastica of the region as well as the Iron Age names attested from Bethsaida and discuss the degree to which the names found in the biblical tradition relate to the onomastica from this region.

BRONZE AGE NAMES

Because there are no texts from the area of Geshur itself, it is necessary to compare information from texts of adjacent areas. The Amarna texts that mention *ga-<šu>-ri* and Ashtaroth are sources for possible names, as are those from the city of Hazor. Among the former, there are the texts of EA 256 and EA 364. The following names may be associated with Ashtaroth and the region bordering Geshur to the south:

mu-ut-ba-aḫ-lum
a-ia-ab
bi-in₄-e-lí-ma
ta-du-a
ya-šu-ia
SILIM-ᵈMARDUK

EA 364 adds no additional names from this region. As for Hazor, the site is mentioned in EA 364 as well as once in a letter from the leader of Tyre (EA 148.41) and four times in two letters from the king of Hazor (EA 227.3, 21; EA 228.4, 15. See Hess 1984, 491). Only one name from Hazor is preserved in these letters, that of the king, ˓Abdi-Tirši (EA 228.3). Of these seven personal names, five are West Semitic (see Hess 1993, 491). SILIM-MARDUK may be Akkadian but no certain linguistic affiliation can be made at present due to the logographic spelling (Hess 1993, 177). Only one name, *Tadua*, is Hurrian as reflected in the *tad* element (Hess 1993, 151–52). The same name occurs in Late Bronze Age Level 4 at Alalakh, spelled as *ta-du-wa* (*AT* 210.4; Wiseman 1953, 148).

In addition to the personal names found in the Amarna letters, several cuneiform tablets from Hazor have been discovered in excavations. These include a lawsuit (Hallo and Tadmor 1977), an administrative tablet, two letters, and a multiplication table (Horowitz and Shaffer 1992a; 1992b; 1993; Horowitz 1997; Horowitz and Wasserman 2000), as well as epistolary and administrative fragments and an inscribed stone bowl (Horowitz 1996; 2000; Horowitz and Oshima 2002). The mathematical fragments contain no personal names, nor do the more recently published letter, administrative fragment, and stone bowl inscription (Horowitz and Wasserman 2000; Horowitz and Oshima 2002). The administrative text, the lawsuit, and the other letter date from the Old Babylonian period and contain more than twenty personal names. The three names in the letter are all broken and only partially preserved:

ib-ni-[ ]
¹ir-p[a]
¹a-b[a]

In every case, these can be identified as Amorite formations. The same is true for all six names in the lawsuit:

DUMU-*ḫa-nu-ta*
ir-pa-a-du (related to the second name in the letter?)
su-um-ḫa-nu-ta
su-mu-la-ilu(DINGIR*ᶦᵘ*)
ya-aḫ-zi-ra-da
ab-di-ḫa-da

Nineteen names can be identified in the administrative tablet:

> *i-lu-ka-a-nu[m]*
> *iš-me-ilum*(DINGIR)
> *ya-aḫ-tuk-addu*(^{d}IM)
> *ḫi-in-ni-ilum*(DINGIR)
> *iš -ni-du*
> *si$_{2}$-ib-li-du*
> *iš-pu-uṭ-addu*(^{d}IM)
> *ḫa-ab-da-du*
> *a-bi-ra-pi$_{2}$*
> *ya-an-ṣur*(!)*-addu*(^{d}IM)
> *in-te-du*
> *in-te-du-addu*(^{d}IM)
> *ib-lu-ṭa$_{3}$-du*
> *a-bi-eraḫ(30)*
> *šu-mu-pa-aḫ*
> *ib-lu-uṭ-ilum*(DINGIR)
> *bu-nu-ma-nu*
> *ya-da-d[a]*
> *ḫa-ba-du*

Of these nineteen names, there is no reason to identify any of them as other than Semitic. Most of the names are Amorite. A name such as *bu-nu-ma-nu* may have been Amorite or Akkadian (Horowitz and Shaffer 1992a, 22 n. 4). However, the Akkadian derivation is less likely because the second element, *ma-nu*, normally occurs as the first element in Akkadian personal names (see further Hess 2002, 2003).

From the Late Bronze Age a letter and an administrative fragment each contain three personal names (Horowitz 2000). The names from the letter are:

> ^{I}*pu-ra-at-pur-ta*
> ^{I}*ad-du-ap-*⸢*di*⸣$^{?}$
> ^{I}*i-ia-ri-ma*

The first name is not Semitic, but may be Kassite or Hurrian (Hess 2003). The remaining two names are West Semitic. The origin of the letter is not known.

From the admininstrative fragment there are three names, with the following provisional readings:

> ^{I}⸢*da*⸣*-ni-bé-li*
> ^{I}*ba-*⸢*ʾ*⸣*-li-ia$_{5}$*
> ^{I}*pu[r]-ri-i-di*

The first two of these names are West Semitic. The third name may contain Hurrian or Kassite elements (Hess 2003).

Thus the Bronze Age in and around Geshur is dominated by West Semitic onomastica. In the Middle Bronze period, there is a preponderance of Amorite names with a possible Akkadian name. In the Late Bronze Age, the evidence suggests the appearance of Hurrian names among the largely West Semitic onomastica. In fact, Hurrian names are exactly what might be expected at this time, given the traditional strength of the northern cultural influence, as attested both by the onomastica and in the archaeology (Hess 1989, 1997). The Bekaa and Jordan Valleys shared this influence with citizens and town leaders of many of the sites in this region bearing Hurrian or other northern names, as attested in the Amarna correspondence and other cuneiform evidence. For example, note the following Hurrian or Indo-Aryan personal names in the region:

i-tag-ga$_{14}$-ma at Kadesh
ti$_4$-wa-te at Lapana
a-ra-wa-na at Kumidi
ma-ya-ar-za-na at Ḫasi
ya-mi-ú-ta at Guddashuna
a-ki-iz-zi at Qatna
a-ki-Teššub at Tunip
bir$_5$-ia-wa-za at Damascus
ar-ta-ma-an-ya at Ziri-Bashan
bi-ri-da-aš-wa at Ashtaroth
da-ša as a shortened form of or equivalent name for *bi-ri-da-aš-wa*?

This influence extended westward through the Jezreel Valley where it reached Megiddo, Achshaph, and Acco. These sites are associated with the names, *bi-ri-di-ya* and *in$_4$-tar-ú-ta* at Megiddo and Achshaph respectively, and the names *sà-ta-at-na* and *sú-ra-ta* at Acco. This is to be contrasted with the remaining towns along the coast, from Byblos to Ashkelon, where the leaders possessed West Semitic personal names in the fourteenth century BCE.

IRON AGE NAMES

As the smaller Akkadian influence of the Middle Bronze Age recedes in the Late Bronze Age, so the Hurrian and other northern influences of that period disappear in the Iron Age, with no clear attestations after the tenth century. The evidence from Geshur is small, limited to a few personal names preserved in inscriptions excavated from Bethsaida.[1]

A precise dating for these names has not been established; however, the published excavations suggest that the site's Iron Age occupation was primarily in Iron Age II instead of Iron Age I. Therefore, these personal names should be examined with the recognition that they probably date from the first millennium and should be studied within the context of the onomastica of that period.

The first published Iron Age name appears as four letters on an Iron Age ostracon, עקבא (Arav 1995, 17–18, with photo). It has been dated to the eighth century (Arav, Freund, and Shroder 2000, 54). In the original publication, Rami Arav referred to the epigraphist Joseph Naveh and his identification of this as an Aramaic form of the name, Akiba. The עקב root is productive of West Semitic personal names throughout the second and first millennia, particularly Amorite, Aramaic (Hatra and Nabatean), and Arabic (Maraqten 1988, 200–1). The hypocoristic suffix א is common among Aramaic personal names, but also found in Phoenician names (Zadok 1988, 155). As an Aramaic personal name, עקבא fits well with the onomastica of a region bordering the Aramean city-states and powers of the area. The name contains a root, perhaps with the meaning "to guard." With the hypocoristic suffix, it is likely a confessional name referring to the protection of an unnamed deity.

A second name occurs as an inscription on a jar handle from the palace at Bethsaida. It is מכי (photos have been published in Arav, Freund, and Shroder 2000, 56; Arav 1999, 88). There is a *ma-ki* or *me-gi* that may be a title of a ruler or a personal name. This occurs as early as Ebla and Middle Bronze Age Mari and continues in usage into the Late Bronze Age in West Semitic sites such as Ugarit and Alalakh (Kühne 1998). In addition, there are Late Bronze Age attestations from Alalakh of a title [lú]*ma-ki-šu* (*AT* 198.40) and a personal name [I]*me-eg-gi* (*AT* 493.14). However, the precise relationship of these occurrences to each other, let alone their relation to מכי of the Iron Age, is not certain.

In the first millennium, the name מכי appears in Punic and Aramaic inscriptions as well as in the biblical description of a Gadite in Numbers 13:15 (Koehler, Baumgartner, et al. 1995, 2:579). Martin Noth identified the biblical name as a shortened form of Machir (1928, 232). Frank L. Benz makes a similar suggestion for the Punic name, but with reference to a different original name (1972, 342–43). An alternative analysis of this name is to recognize a West Semitic *mwk* root meaning "low, poor quality" (Hoftijzer and Jongeling 1995, 623). The same analysis occurs for the personal name *ma-ku-ya* from Ugarit (Sivan 1984, 250). However, is that the best interpretation of the Bethsaida personal name? What is clear is that the final *y* is a common indication of a shortened form of a name, that is, a hypocoristic suffix.

It is possible to find in the name מכי a shortened form of the Israelite name Mikayahu, "Who is like Yahweh" (Arav, Freund, and Shroder 2000, 54). Further, the occurrences of this name in three seventh and sixth century texts from Arad, Horvat Uza, and a Judean(?) seal (Davies 1991, 38, 114, 139) should be compared with fourteen occurrences of מכיהו in Iron Age Hebrew inscriptions (Davies 1991, 422–23). This suggests that the latter name frequently occurs in ancient Israel and that the most likely explanation for מכי is as a shortened form of this more frequent longer name, either with Yahweh as the chief deity or another god, perhaps an Aramean deity. In any case, it is clearly a name known in Israelite, Phoenician, and Aramean contexts.

A third name at Bethsaida has been found stamped on a jar handle (Arav, Freund, and Shroder 2000, 54–55) in what is described as an Iron Age context. No photograph, drawing, or transliteration of the inscription has been published. Arav has stated that the reading is זכריו. This is a name known in the surrounding regions. A form without the final *waw* occurs at Ugarit (with the phonemic equivalence *ḏkry*), in Aramaic inscriptions, and in at least one Hebrew seal from the end of Iron Age II or the beginning of Iron Age III (Gröndahl 1967, 196; Maraqten 1988, 160–61; Davies 1991, 159, inscription 100.309). Spelled with the final *waw*, this form occurs in two Hebrew seals of unknown provenance, of which one is dated from about 700 BCE (Davies 1991, 141, inscription 100.167) and the other is of unknown date (Davies 1991, 161, inscription 100.323). A third occurrence appears on a jar stamp from Tel Dan and is dated to the eighth century (Davies 1991, 243, inscription 100.882; Biran 1989; 1994, 255). The form is that of the verbal root זכר "to remember," followed by a shortened form of the divine name Yahweh. It is a confessional or thanksgiving name that describes how a deity has remembered. Examples of other divine names compounded with זכר occur in the languages of the surrounding states, Aramaic and Ammonite (Aufrecht 1989, 363) as well as Hebrew.

NAMES FROM THE HEBREW BIBLE

Biblical names can be found that are close or identical to those from the inscriptions at Bethsaida. There is no form identical to עקבא; however, there is the name עֲקוּב with either an active meaning (protector) or a passive one (protected one). This name is late, occurring only in post-exilic texts with reference either to a family of gatekeepers (Ezra 2:42; Neh. 7:45, 11:19, 12:25; 1 Chron. 9:17), or to an individual who may be a temple slave (Ezra 2:45), a Levite (Neh. 8:7), or a member of Zerubbabel's line (1 Chron. 3:24). Thus, insofar as the Bethsaida inscription is correctly dated to the eighth century, it remains an early attestation of this root as a personal name in an alphabetic script. It bridges the gap between the second millennium occurrences of the root in West Semitic personal names and those of the later first millennium.

The personal name מכי occurs as מִכִּי מ (Machi), a Gadite who appears in Numbers 13:15, as already noted. If the מכי at Bethsaida is a shortened form of a longer name, it would fit with suggestions for the biblical name and for many other occurrences of this name in the second and first millennia. Forms of the name occur over a long period of time and provide little guidance as to the dating of the biblical occurrence.

The name זכריו does not occur in the Bible with this spelling. However, Avraham Biran (1989; 1994, 255) has related it to זְכַרְיָה, which refers to an eighth century northern king of Israel, Zechariah (2 Kings 14:29, 15:11, 18:2). The same spelling of the Bethsaida name also appears at Dan in the eighth century. It is not possible to say whether the name bearer at Bethsaida is the same as the others, because both inscriptions omit any patronymic or other identifying feature.

Several names occur in the Hebrew Bible that are associated with the kingdom of Geshur. These cluster around the period of the United Monarchy. David's marriage to a daughter of the king of Geshur provides three personal names that originated in Geshur: עַמִּיהוּד, his son תַּלְמַי, and his daughter מַעֲכָה, whom David married (2 Sam. 3:3, 13:37). David and Maacah (מַעֲכָה) had two children, Absalom (אַבְשָׁלוֹם) and Tamar (תָּמָר). Both of these have West Semitic names. However, it is the previous three generations that are of interest, since each of these was presumably born in the kingdom of Geshur.

The feminine name מַעֲכָה occurs throughout the Hebrew Bible. It is given to a son or daughter of Nahor (Gen. 22:24), a wife of the

Israelite Machir (1 Chron. 7:16), a concubine of Caleb (1 Chron. 2:48–
49), the father of Achish, king of Gath (1 Kings 2:39), and at least four
other figures (three women and one man) associated with the early
Israelite monarchy (1 Kings 2:39, 11:21; 1 Chron. 8:29, 11:43, 27:16;
Shearing 1992). This name does not have clear attestation outside of
the Bible. Its etymology has been related to a *m'k* root. In Hebrew this
root carries the meaning "to squeeze, thrust"; however, it is not productive of personal names. An Arabic root using the same consonants
produces words related to "stupid." This etymology was popularized
by Noth (1926, 250) and remains to this day; however, Ran Zadok
rejects it as unlikely. His suggestion (Zadok 1988, 83) of the Arabic
root 'wk (to attack) remains a possibility at best. Nevertheless, a West
Semitic derivation for this name is most likely.

The king of Geshur is identified as תַּלְמַי (Talmai). He is presumably the figure with whom David arranges his diplomatic marriage in
order to guarantee friendly relations between the two states. He is also
the king to whom David's grandson Absalom flees after avenging the
rape of his sister Tamar. The name תַּלְמַי occurs elsewhere in the Bible as
one of the sons of Anak (Josh. 15:14). In the ancient Near East, this
name occurs in Late Bronze Age cuneiform archives (Hess 1996, 211–
12): at Nuzi in the forms *tal-mu-ia* and *da-al-mu*; at Ugarit in the forms
tlmyn, tlmyn, and *tal-mi-ya*; and at Late Bronze Age Alalakh (Level 4) in
forms such as *tal-ma* and *tal-mi-ia*. These names are all related to the
Hurrian *talmi* meaning "great." This Hurrian form occurs in personal
names as well as common nouns. Thus the name of the Geshurite king
is Hurrian.

Finally, there is עַמִּיהוּד (Ammihud) the father of תַּלְמַי. As a figure
associated with Geshur this name occurs only in 2 Samuel 13:37. There
is a textual problem because the *kᵉtîb* of the Masoretic Text has עַמִּיחוּר.
However, the *qᵉrê,* as well as all the versions read עַמִּיהוּד. This latter reading has the most support and is followed here. עַמִּיהוּד is a name ascribed
to at least four Israelites from traditions that claim to describe Israel's
earliest times and those that reflect the exilic period: the father of
Elishama and great-grandfather of Joshua (Num. 1:10; 1 Chron. 7:26),
the father of Samuel (Num. 34:20), a father of a member of the wilderness generation (Num. 34:28), and the father of a returnee from the
exile (1 Chron. 9:4). Otherwise, the name is not attested.

The name is composed of two West Semitic elements that are
productive of personal names in Hebrew and other West Semitic

58 — Richard S. Hess

languages. עַמִּיהוּד means "the/my divine uncle is glorious." The first element, עַמִּי, is composed of a root that is a kinship term that, along with terms for "brother" and "father," is used in West Semitic names to designate a deity.

CONCLUSION

The three biblical names of royalty from Geshur reflect three generations that, following conventional biblical chronology, may be ascribed to the eleventh and tenth centuries. The youngest and oldest generations possess West Semitic names while the middle generation, that of תַּלְמַי, possesses a Hurrian name. These names fit well into the onomastic profile of Geshur and its neighbors in the transition from the Late Bronze Age through Iron Age I and into Iron Age II. Although the evidence from the Bronze Age suggests that the name bearers in the region of Geshur possessed largely West Semitic names, there is evidence of Hurrian and other northern names in the Late Bronze Age.

Such northern names may have been remembered and continued in use into Iron Age I. There is evidence for it in Jerusalem as well. There the Jebusite Araunah sells his threshing floor to David (2 Sam. 24:16). This name is either Hurrian or Hittite in origin (inter alia, McCarter 1984, 512). The Hebrew Bible ascribes this figure to the same period as תִּלְמִי. However, this is the last period in which the Bible or any other source preserves such northern names. Their influence is on the wane and disappears altogether. It is replaced by entirely West Semitic names throughout Iron Age II. This is not only true of the named descendants of תַּלְמַי; it is also the case with the three personal names that are preserved from Iron Age Bethsaida. They all possess West Semitic names whose roots are used in the personal names of Israelites, Arameans, and other peoples in the neighboring regions of Geshur.

Thus, despite the fragmentary nature of the evidence, the Bronze Age cuneiform texts, the biblical witness, and the Iron Age alphabetic inscriptions from Bethsaida preserve a coherent picture of the change of cultural influence in the region of Geshur.

CHAPTER NOTE

1. The Aramaic inscription on a storage jar at 'En Gev should also be mentioned here. It is dated paleographically to the early ninth century and
   reads לשקיא. It may be translated as a title, "Belonging to the cupbearer,"
   rather than a personal name. Cf. Mazar 1993, 410.

LITERATURE CITED

Albright, William F. 1943. Two Little Understood Amarna Letters from the Middle Jordan Valley. *Bulletin of the American Schools of Oriental Research* 89:7–19.

Arav, Rami. 1995. Bethsaida Excavations: Preliminary Report, 1987–1993. In Arav and Freund 1995.

———. 1999. Bethsaida (in Hebrew). *Qadmoniot* 32/2 (118): 78–91.

Arav, Rami, and Richard A. Freund, eds. 1995. *Bethsaida: A City by the North Shore of the Sea of Galilee.* Vol. 1. Kirksville, Mo.: Thomas Jefferson University Press.

Arav, Rami, Richard A. Freund, and John F. Shroder, Jr. 2000. Bethsaida Rediscovered. *Biblical Archaeology Review* 26/1 (Jan./Feb.): 44–56.

Aufrecht, Walter E. 1989. *A Corpus of Ammonite Inscriptions.* Ancient Near Eastern Texts & Studies, vol. 4. Lewiston: Edwin Mellen.

Benz, Frank L. 1972. *Personal Names in the Phoenician and Punic Inscriptions.* Studia Pohl 8. Rome: Biblical Institute Press.

Biran, Avraham. 1989. Tel Dan 1987, 1988. *Israel Exploration Journal* 39:93.

———. 1994. *Biblical Dan.* Jerusalem: Israel Exploration Society.

Davies, Graham I. 1991. *Ancient Hebrew Inscriptions: Corpus and Concordance.* Cambridge: Cambridge University Press.

Galil, Gershon. 1998. Ashtaroth in the Amarna Period. *Israel Oriental Studies* 18:373–85.

Gröndahl, Frauke. 1967. *Die Personennamen der Texte aus Ugarit.* Studia Pohl 1. Rome: Pontifical Bible Institute.

Hallo, William W., and Hayim Tadmor. 1977. A Lawsuit from Hazor. *Israel Exploration Journal* 27:1–11.

Hess, Richard S. 1984. *Amarna Proper Names.* Ph.D. diss., Hebrew Union College–Jewish Institute of Religion, Cincinnati.

———. 1989. Cultural Aspects of Onomastic Distribution in the Amarna Texts. *Ugarit Forschungen* 21:209–16.

———. 1993. *Amarna Personal Names.* ASOR Dissertation Series 9. Winona Lake: Eisenbrauns.

———. 1996. Non-Israelite Personal Names in the Book of Joshua. *Catholic Biblical Quarterly* 58:205–14.

———. 1997. Hurrians and Other Inhabitants of Late Bronze Age Palestine. *Levant* 29:153–56.

———. 2002. Omonastics and Culture in Cunieform Texts from Middle Bronze Age Palestine. Paper persented at the American oriental Society Annual Meeting, Houston, March 25, 2002.

———. 2003. Preliminary Perspectives on Late Bronze Age Culture from the Personal Names in Palestinian Cuneiform Texts. *Dutch Studies on Near Eastern Languages and Literatures* 5/1–2:35–57.

Hoftijzer, J., and K. Jongeling. 1995. *Dictionary of North-West Semitic Inscriptions.* 2 vols. Handbook of Oriental Studies: The Near and Middle East Band 21. Leiden: Brill.

Horowitz, Wayne. 1996. The Cuneiform Tablets at Tel Hazor, 1996. *Israel Exploration Journal* 46:268–69.

———. 1997. A Combined Multiplication Table on a Prism Fragment from Hazor. *Israel Exploration Journal* 47:190–97.

———. 2000. Two Late Bronze Age Tablets from Hazor. *Israel Exploration Journal* 50:16–28.

Horowitz, Wayne, and Aaron Shaffer. 1992a. An Administrative Tablet from Hazor: A Preliminary Edition. *Israel Exploration Journal* 42:21–33.

———. 1992b. A Fragment of a Letter from Hazor. *Israel Exploration Journal* 42:165–66.

———. 1993. Additions and Corrections to "An Administrative Tablet from Hazor: A Preliminary Edition." *Israel Exploration Journal* 42:167.

Horowitz, Wayne, and Nathan Wasserman. 2000. An Old Babylonian Letter from Hazor with Mention of Mari and Ekallātum. *Israel Exploration Journal* 50:169–74.

Horowitz, Wayne, and Takayoshi Oshima. 2002. Two More Cuneiform Finds from Hazor. *Israel Exploration Journal* 52:179–86.

Koehler, Ludwig, Walter Baumgartner, et al. 1995. *The Hebrew and Aramaic Lexicon of the Old Testament*. Vol. 2. Leiden: Brill.

Kühne, Cord. 1998. Meki, Megum und Mekum/Mekim. *Israel Oriental Studies* 18:311–22.

Maisler (Mazar), Benjamin. 1954. Canaan on the Threshold of the Patriarchs (in Hebrew). *Eretz-Israel* 3:18–22.

Ma'oz, Zvi U. 1992. Geshur. In *Anchor Bible Dictionary*, edited by D. N. Friedman. New York: Doubleday.

Maraqten, Mohammed. 1988. *Die semitischen Personennamen in den alt- und reichsaramäischen Inschriften aus Vorderasien*. Text und Studien zur Orientalistik 5. Hildesheim: Georg Olms.

Mazar, Benjamin. 1986. Geshur and Maacah. In *The Early Biblical Period: Historical Studies*, edited by S. Ahituv and B. Levine. Jerusalem: Israel Exploration Society.

———. 1993. 'En Gev. In *The New Encyclopedia of Archaeological Excavations in the Holy Land*, edited by E. Stern. Jersalem: Israel Exploration Society and Carta.

McCarter, P. Kyle, Jr. 1984. *II Samuel: A New Translation with Introduction and Commentary*. Anchor Bible 9. Garden City, N.Y.: Doubleday.

Noth, Martin. 1928. *Die israelitischen Personennamen im Rahmen der gemeinsemitischen Namengebung*. Stuttgart: W. Kohlhammer.

Shearing, Linda S. 1992. Maacah (Person). In *Anchor Bible Dictionary*, edited by D. N. Friedman. New York: Doubleday.

Sivan, Daniel. 1984. *Grammatical Analysis and Glossary of the Northwest Semitic Vocables in Akkadian Texts of the 15th–13th C.B.C. from Canaan and Syria*. Alter Orient und Altes Testament 214. Kevelaer: Butzon & Bercker; Neukirchen-Vluyn: Neukirchener.

Wiseman, Donald J. 1953. *The Alalakh Tablets*. London: British Institute of Archaeology at Ankara.

Zadok, Ran. 1988. *The Pre-Hellenistic Israelite Anthroponymy and Prosopography.* Orientalia Lovaniensia Analecta 28. Leuven: Peeters.

John T. Greene

Tiglath-pileser III's War Against the City of Tzer

URING THE FIRST SEASON of the Bethsaida Archaeological Research Project in 1988, Iron Age IIB material and structures became evident immediately.[1] Until the 1997 season, the most impressive discovery had been a multiphase structure used for various religious purposes over a protracted period: a well-preserved basalt stone plaza and a large public building reminiscent of the *bit hilani* type.[2] Entering the twenty-two-acre mound from the north, one immediately encounters a huge defense wall with massive tower, revetment, and glacis that occlude any further movement southward. This wall is about thirty feet wide at the point of a defense/observation tower, with an average width of about twenty feet. In 1996, while excavations revealed the public building, a probe on the eastern slope of the tell revealed a twenty to twenty-five foot wide defense wall oriented north/south. Pottery and other artifacts show that all these structures are related and belong to Iron Age I and II (about 1100 to 700 BCE). A five-by-five-meter square probe was sunk in the eastern center section of the southernmost area of excavations (Area A) to a depth of about ten feet. The probe revealed a perfectly preserved cobblestone surface; however, this discovery occurred at the end of that season's work, and further research had to wait until the following season.

Excavations were resumed in late spring of 1997 and traced the cobbled surface in an easterly direction to one of the largest four-chambered city-gate complexes from Iron Age IIB discovered to date in the region. These four chambers were about nine to ten feet deep, thirty feet long, and twelve feet wide. Eight baskets of restorable Iron Age IIB vessels as well as a large number of (possibly) spearheads and (definitely) arrowheads were found in the northeast chamber (Chamber 4). The finds were well preserved, though smashed due to the sudden violence of a roof having caved in, as evidenced by large deposits of ash distributed over the entire chamber. Burned mud bricks and clinkers[3] just outside the threshold of the four chambers; more arrowheads found on the cobbled passageway running in front of the four chambers; another arrowhead discovered in Chamber 1; a large mass of melted, red, mud-brick plaster just inside the northern side of the city-gate door threshold; white plaster at the city-gate threshold and high place steps and offering(s) shelf on the southern side of the city-gate ramp opposite that high place; and two toppled, rectangular towers located on either side of the cobbled/ramped entranceway into the city by its main thoroughfare are evidence that this complex structure was destroyed by purposeful and planned violence.

The Iron Age IIB destruction debris evident in numerous excavations in the area of Syria and Palestine, including Transjordan and northern Arabia, has often been attributed to campaigns by the neo-Assyrian conqueror Tiglath-pileser III. Tiglath-pileser III's activities in the area of Syria, Palestine, and Philistia belong to the continuum of neo-Assyrian conquerors who expanded westward and southwestward during the second half of the eighth century BCE. In his 734–732 BCE campaign, Tiglath-pileser III was not only attempting to conquer Egypt, but was also chastising rebelling vassals who had sued for independence since his first campaign there in 739/8 BCE. He secured the eastern Mediterranean coast, and conquered Philistia and many Transjordanian Arabian tribes during his 734/3 BCE and later campaigns to retrieve Elath/Ezion Geber for Ahaz, vassal king of Judah. Based on reports of his army's movements and reported appearances, it seems likely that the conqueror split his forces into two great columns heading northward on both sides of the Jordan Valley in 732 BCE. The western column was directed at parts of Israel not already under Assyrian control, while the eastern column pursued the forces of Pekah and Rezin northward, back into their homelands. Syria would soon fall, but Samaria would stand until 722/1 BCE. The account in 2 Kings 15 provides only a portion of the Naphtali section of Tiglath-pileser III's itinerary, but none of the cities mentioned are located around the Sea of

Galilee, especially in the region known as Geshur. It seems probable that the western Assyrian column executed its itinerary in reverse order. Even with this reversed order, some cities known to have been conquered by Tiglath-pileser III, such as Dan and Megiddo, are not mentioned at all, showing that the biblical list of conquered cities is incomplete. Scientific analysis of the Iron Age IIB ruins at et-Tell show violence having been visited upon this city during the 732 BCE neo-Assyrian sweep northward. Although, from an archaeological point of view, the city enshrined in the ruins of et-Tell remains unnamed and anonymous, Rami Arav, Director of the Bethsaida Archaeological Research Project, identifies the Iron Age city as Tzer. Tzer does not appear in the *Annals* of Tiglath-pileser III; however, Arav links the Iron Age IIB destruction at et-Tell to the 2 Kings 15 itinerary of Tiglath-pileser III through mention of the territory of Naphtali. This contribution will examine whether the ruins of et-Tell's Iron Age IIB city are the handiwork of Tiglath-pileser III during his second campaign in the west and whether the destruction was caused by the western column or the eastern column. It will also explore the reasons why the walled, Iron Age city at Bethsaida site was involved in the overall campaign of Tiglath-pileser III and his forces.

A SEARCH FOR TZER

Bethsaida, as the acknowledged name of the city enshrined in the Late Hellenistic and Early Roman Era strata of et-Tell, appears in the New Testament Gospels, Josephus (*Ant.* 8:2), Pliny the Elder's *Natural History* (books 5, 6, and 7), and rabbinic literature (Freund 1995), but is nowhere to be found in known literature from earlier periods. In literature of the Iron Age, the name Geshur refers to either the general region or kingdom where et-Tell is located,[4] but does not identify the city occupying this mound by name. Arav (1995, 193–201) argues that one name of the city during the Late Bronze period was Tzer; therefore this study will refer to this site as Tzer. Even the name Tzer does not appear in any of the neo-Assyrian literature, especially between 745 and 727 BCE. These dates bracket the reign of the neo-Assyrian conqueror Tiglath-pileser III, considered the founder of the last Assyrian empire. His empire stretched from present-day Iran to the border of Egypt, but he was not the first Assyrian monarch to campaign there (that is, in the "west"). According to

2 Kings 15, ancient Syria (Aram) and the territory of Israel-the-Kingdom as well as all of Transjordan were subjected to his overlordship. The Aram/Israel region includes Tzer.

Assyrian kings traveled far from their capitals to hunt and to wage war. By 1100 BCE, Tiglath-pileser I had campaigned as far west as the Land of the Hatti and Mount Lebanon. He also campaigned against several cities in Aram. Ashur-nasir-pal II (859–833 BCE) seized the Land of the Amorites and the Lebanon mountains, and reached the Mediterranean. His successor, Shalmaneser III (838–824 BCE), is famous for having fought against an Aramean coalition that had been joined by Ahab king of Israel. This was the first significant encounter between Israelite and Assyrian forces, but it was not fought on Israelite soil. Following Shalmaneser, Adad-nirari III (810–783 BCE) fought campaigns in the "Land of Omri" (Israel) and in Philistia, "as far as the shore of the Great Sea of the Setting Sun..." (the Mediterranean). Many of these kings recorded their deeds in annals that still exist, albeit in a fragmentary form. In some cases, a king chose not to record details of a campaign, perhaps because he thought the place insignificant and/or ancillary to his main purpose(s) for being in a region.

Many annals and inscriptions contain formulaic accounts of military activities (Rost 1893; Budge and King 1902; Tadmor 1994). In an inscription from the city of Kurkh, Ashur-nasir-pal boasts formulaically, "Into the city of _____ I entered. I did _____. From the city of _____ I departed." Texts often record that, before departing, the conqueror imposed "tribute, and taxes, and overseers..." (Budge and King 1902, 227). Another frequently used formula reads, "many of their fighting men I overthrew, their spoil I carried off, and their cities I burned with fire" (Budge and King 1902, 228). Regarding the city of Madara, Ashur-nasir-pal records that "the city was exceedingly strong and was girt about with four walls" (Budge and King 1902, 230). Whenever a walled city was encountered, it was "stormed, destroyed and laid waste and turned into mounds and heaps of ruins" (Budge and King 1902, 231). One account records the inhabitants destroying their own walls as a sign of surrender: "At my royal splendor...the walls of their (that is, the Arbakis') strongly fenced cities they cast down..." (Budge and King 1902, 335). City gates figure prominently when a walled city is mentioned—"a pile of the living and the heads over against the city-gate I set and seven hundred men I impaled on stakes over against their city-gate" (Budge and King 1902, 234).

Although the formula states repeatedly that this monarch and his immediate predecessors reached Lebanon and the Mediterranean, Ashur-nasir-pal states specifically that he also campaigned in Aram (Budge and King 1902, 240). Later Assyrian monarchs and conquerors would follow this same pattern.

Assyrian campaigns began as raids to secure booty and tribute, and to defend Assyrian borders. By the late tenth century BCE, Assyrian rulers began to incorporate conquered lands into their domain and gradually extended Assyrian rule. Shalmaneser III (ruled 859–824 BCE) fought many campaigns in Aram and Tiglath-pileser III (ruled 744–727 BCE) began a campaign aimed at annexing enemy territory. He "gathered new armies, reconquered Armenia, overran Syria and Babylonia, made vassal cities of Damascus, Samaria, and Babylon, extended the rule of Assyria from the Caucasus to Egypt, tired of war, became an excellent administrator, built many temples and places, held his empire together with an iron hand and died peacefully in bed" (Durant 1954, 267).

Many military policies that neo-Assyria developed to use in dealing with its enemies, captives, and vassals are traceable to Tiglath-pileser III. He "established the characteristic policy of deporting conquered populations to alien habitats, where, mingling with the natives, they might lose their unity and identity, and have less opportunity to rebel.... Revolts came nevertheless..." (Durant 1954, 270). While it is clear that Tiglath-pileser III and his successors campaigned in the area of Geshur, there is no written historical evidence that he was responsible for the destruction of Tzer.

One of the most important cities located in the northern portion of the plain of Ginosar, Kinneret/Ginosar, was most certainly destroyed by the neo-Assyrian conqueror Tiglath-pileser III in 732 BCE during his second western campaigns (Josh. 19:35). His attack would have been from the south. Less than twelve kilometers east of Kinneret lie the ruins of an impressive Iron Age II walled city that shows signs of having also been destroyed by Tiglath-pileser III. Although it is not mentioned in his *Annals*, the scientific dating of material and cultural objects recovered from Kinneret's ruins puts Tiglath-pileser III not only in the neighborhood, but at this site also. Literature mentions his presence at other large and strategically placed cities in the region (Dan, Hazor, and Megiddo), and given the potential threats from walled or fortified cities in the region, it seems unlikely that

Tiglath-pileser III would have left his flanks exposed as he moved through the area. Thus it is reasonable to suppose that the Iron Age IIB damage and consequent changes to the layout of some of the buildings at Tzer were due to the movement of (and later rebuilding by) Tiglath-pileser III and his forces in 732 BCE.

A reasonable itinerary for Tiglath-pileser III's campaigns in Syria/Palestine and Transjordania/Arabia may be cobbled together from his *Annals*,[5] 2 Kings 15:29, and Deuteronomy 1:4. According to 2 Kings 15:29, Tiglath-pileser III conquered "Ijon, Abel-beth-ma'acah, Jano'ach, Kedesh, Hazor, Gilead and Galilee, all the land of Naphtali; and he carried the people captive to Assyria." Damascus was also besieged in the days of Pekah, king of Israel (736–732 BCE).

The itinerary provided by the 2 Kings chronicler, though perhaps correct in naming the cities involved, is nevertheless misleading. One might assume that Tiglath-pileser III attacked from the north to south on both sides of the Jordan/Sea of Galilee/Dead Sea waterway system simultaneously. That would appear to have been a reasonable and thorough way to proceed, coming from Assyria, but this order of the itinerary cannot be demonstrated. All of the dates acquired by comparing events with itinerary suggest that the attacks on Israel, Gilead, and Damascus—all dated to 732 BCE—were mounted from a southerly direction, that is, they were attacked and subdued on Tiglath-pileser III's return trip home.

Before the end of the Assyrian empire in the seventh century BCE, its influence had been felt as far as Egypt on the southwest and the Caucasus on the north. Assyria aspired to control the giant forests located to its northwest and any seaports located on the eastern Mediterranean shore. Because of this, Aram/Damascus (which sat astride the seaward route and controlled much of this giant forest and many important seaports) and Assyria became antagonists. Located between Israel and Assyria, Aram often attacked Israel. When Assyria was not busy with internal problems, she usually attacked Aram and other weaker nations. Although other Assyrian rulers who preceded Tiglath-pileser III are known to have been connected to some of Israel's leaders, the first direct biblical reference to an Assyrian ruler is to Pul (that is, Tiglath-pileser III) in 2 Kings 15:19.[6]

In 743 BCE, a Syrian-led coalition under King Rezin of Damascus and supported vigorously by the assassin of King Pekahiah—now king of Israel, Pekah—opposed Assyrian overlordship. On his return visit to the region, Tiglath-pileser III was sidetracked by his old enemy of the north, Sarduris, the king of Urartu (Ararat/Armenia). During the delay, Rezin and Pekah formed a coalition to resist the Assyrians. They invited Judah's King Ahaz to join the coalition to strengthen their southern flank. Rezin and Pekah also coveted Ahaz's territory and southern seaport. Ahaz refused, although he was beset on his own southern flank by the Edomites, who by this time had taken his southern port of Elath, and on his western flank by the Philistines, who had annexed the Negev (2 Chron. 28:18) and the Lower Hill Country (Shephelah). After Tiglath-pileser III settled matters in Urartu/Ararat/Armenia, and was on his way down the Mediterranean toward Egypt, he received an embassy from Ahaz, who offered tribute in exchange for protection from his enemies. Although Tiglath-pileser III already had plans to subdue Ahaz's enemies, he accepted the tribute (2 Kings 16:7 ff.). His move down the coast was designed to cut off communication between Israel and its hoped-for ally, Egypt. Egypt had recently been conquered by Ethiopia, and a new pharaoh was considering the possibility of further expansions into Asia Minor. Tiglath-pileser III quickly captured Gaza and Ashkelon in Philistia on the border of Egypt. Having secured the territory southwest, and with Gezer, that of southern Israel, he waged war against the Arab queen Samsi, who he considered an ally of the Philistines. The campaign against her and the insertion of an anti-Samsi tribe between her influence and the region south of the Dead Sea secured an Assyrian-controlled flank starting at Gaza on the Mediterranean and extending eastward to southern Gilead, effectively cutting off Israel and northern Transjordania/Arabia. This campaign occupied 734/3 BCE. With his southern, southwestern, and southeastern flanks secure, Tiglath-pileser III turned his attention to central and northern Israel and northern Transjordania/Arabia through which he also pushed the forces of Israel and Aram which had joined their ally, Edom, to besiege Judah.

Tiglath-pileser III returned up the Mediterranean coast to a point where he entered Israel through the Plain of Jezreel (Esdraelon), already under Assyrian control from earlier campaigns there against Menachem. He may have followed the northern bank of the Kishon River until he was able to turn northward with one column. With a second column, he may have continued into the Jezreel Valley, then crossed the Jordan near Bethshean, south of the Sea of Galilee, into Transjordania/northern Arabia, for his forces were certainly active in Bashan and northern Arabia.

ASSYRIAN ACTIVITIES WEST OF THE JORDAN

Tiglath-pileser III's western column would have encountered Ijon, at the foot of Mount Lebanon, as one of the last cities in what might have been northern Israelite territory. Before this, his western column would have conquered the city of Abel (also known as Abel-beth-maacah or Abel-maim). Dan would have been the final Israelite city to be attacked by the western column of Tiglath-pileser III's forces as they left Yanoam/Janoah. Excavations at Dan (Tel el-Qadi) revealed a city wall closely resembling those recently excavated at et-Tell. Keith Schoville explains that "the gate was destroyed in the first half of the ninth century BC, perhaps by Ben-Hadad of Aram.... Later constructions at Dan show evidence of an occupation in the eighth century, no doubt brought to an end by Assyrians in 732 BC" (1978, 152). Thus, while the 2 Kings itinerary does not mention the destruction of Dan by Tiglath-pileser III, many changes in the city date from this time. Archaeological evidence suggests that the forces of Tiglath-pileser III visited this city and subjected it to military control. He could not have ignored such a well-fortified city on Israel's northern border.

Slightly northwest of Dan, the western column would have encountered Kedesh, then moved to take the city of Yanoam/Janoah to its northeast. This fits the 2 Kings 15 itinerary, only reversed. Control of Ijon, Abel, Dan, Janoah, and Kedesh were merely necessary, preparatory strategic steps to be taken before taking on the important, fortified city of Damascus.

The city enshrined in Tel el-Qedah in the Upper Galilee has been identified as Hazor. Its main function was to guard the Hulah Valley through which one gained access to the Upper Galilee. Archaeological evidence suggests that "in the period before this destruction [to the eighth-century stratum], the inhabitants of Hazor tried desperately to alter their city to be able to meet the enemy. Many changes in the city date from this time" (Schoville 1978, 377). Nevertheless, according to Kathleen Kenyon, the end of Stratum 5 was due to destruction "by Tiglath-pileser in 732" (1970, 282). Hazor's Iron Age II Stratum 5A consisted of a broadened fortification wall like that of et-Tell's Iron Age II city wall. But even this wall was penetrated by Tiglath-pileser III. Following this destruction wrought by the Assyrians, which was said to have been terrible, "only poor squatters [Stratum 4] occupied Hazor" (Mazar 1990, 414). Although this city is the last one to be mentioned on the list in 2 Kings 15, it was probably the second major fortified city in Israel to be besieged by Tiglath-pileser III during this northward sweep; the first, because of location, would have been Megiddo.

Tell el-Mutesellim houses the impressive ruins of ancient Megiddo. Situated on a spur of the Carmel Mountain Range, it commanded a view of almost the entire Esdraelon Valley. Because of its location adjacent to the Wadi 'Arah, which allowed passage between the Plain of Esdraelon and the Plain of Sharon, it occupied an extremely important strategic position from the fourth millennium until the fourth century BCE. Schoville states that "Megiddo maintained its importance as an Israelite fortified city until it was occupied by Tiglath-pileser III in 733. The Assyrians rebuilt the city according to a new plan containing several large buildings with a central court, a common feature of the Assyrian style. Megiddo became an important military-administrative center" (1978, 444).

Samaria, the capital of the kingdom of Israel, is not mentioned in the list of cities visited by Tiglath-pileser III. Beginning in the ninth year of the reign of the Israelite ruler Menachem (c. 752–742 BCE), Israel became a tributary to Assyria. He levied a special tax on his subjects to raise the tribute.[7] Samaria was still honoring its vassal status in 732 BCE and thus escaped the terrible wrath of Tiglath-pileser III. Ten years later, however, under the reign of Sargon II (722 BCE), Samaria fell after a three-year siege. Excavations show that the city was burned at that time.

The account in 2 Kings 15 does not mention by name any cities south of an east-west line running from the Mediterranean, south of Samaria, to the regions of Bashan and Ammon east of the Jordan River; however, archaeological evidence suggests that Tiglath-pileser III's forces were active and destructive in that area. A relief from the palace of Tiglath-pileser III depicts the capture of a city called Gazru. If this is a reference to the city of Gezer in the Shephelah northwest of Jerusalem, it would mark the southern boundary of the Kingdom of Israel, a place where the Assyrians garrisoned troops before 722 BCE. Numerous documents have been found on the site (Schoville 1978, 351; Dever 1970, 110; Macalister 1912; Lance 1967, 34–47).

The evidence from Gezer should not be surprising, for Tiglath-pileser III's expansionist goals included the occupation of Egypt. In this he failed, and by 734 BCE he had to be content with controlling Philistia on Egypt's northeastern border and frontier.

Even there, he did not occupy the territory, but allowed the subject leaders to administer their own territories through autonomous rule (Schoville 1978, 293–301).

The eastern Assyrian column may have split from the western column near Beth She'an and crossed the Jordan to enter northern Gilead. Once there, it would have proceeded to join Assyrian elements already operating in southern Transjordania/northern Arabia. There is archaeological evidence of the eastern column's advance. It is known that one of Tiglath-pileser III's goals in the area was to subdue Bashan, Manasseh, Gad, Ammon, Reuben, Moab, and Edom. Tiglath-pileser III (or at the least elements of his eastern column) had reason and opportunity to visit the city now enshrined in et-Tell. According to the Israeli archaeologist Amihai Mazar:

> After Tiglath-pileser III's conquests in 732 BCE, northern Transjordan was annexed to the Assyrian empire, and Ammon, Moab, and Edom again became vassal states.... At the site of biblical Ramot Gilead *[Tell er-Rumeith]* in the territory of Gilead, a casemate wall was destroyed by the Assyrians in 732 BCE. At Tell es Sa'idiyeh in the Jordan Valley a well-planned residential quarter was destroyed, probably at the same time. The most fascinating discovery in this region is the ink inscriptions on a plastered wall of a large building at Tell Deir 'Alla. This structure was destroyed by fire, perhaps also during the Assyrian conquest, though a later date cannot be ruled out. (Mazar 1990, 532)

The difficulties in exact dating of conflagrations and destruction make it impossible to be certain that destruction of a city resulted from Tiglath-pileser III's campaigns as opposed to those of his Assyrian successors or predecessors, or aggressions of Aram and Israel during the Syro-Ephriamitic War. Tiglath-pileser III's itinerary may assist in determining his eastern column's activities in Transjordan/north Arabia.

A cuneiform inscription (Pritchard 1958, 150) provides information about Tiglath-pileser III's deporting of people from a city identified as Astartu (called Ashtaroth in Deut. 1:4), a fortified city twenty-five miles east of Lake Kinneret. This puts him close to the Iron Age IIB city at Tzer and provides a plausible reason for his having been there. This passage states that Ashtaroth was in Bashan, the territory between Gilead and Syria/Aram. In other terms, Astartu and vicinity were understood as belonging to southern Aram/Syria. Astartu's fate, therefore, would have been linked to the fate of Aram, even when Hamath, not Damascus, was the capital of Aram. Astartu was located on one of the Yarmuk River's tributaries just southwest of the city of Karnaim, both due east of Lake Kinneret, and therefore slightly southeast of et-Tell. Nelson Glueck identified Ashtaroth and Karnaim as being in southern Syria (1940; cf. Harding 1899f) and the prophet Amos (6:13) identifies Hamath on the Orontes River as the capital of Syria during a time when LoDebar and Karnaim were chief cities in the Aramean territory. Thus, as part of either northern Bashan or southern Syria/Aram, these closely allied cities would have been natural targets for Tiglath-pileser III's forces. With Gilead as an important target in Transjordan/northern Arabia, Ashtaroth apparently could not be bypassed without exposing the eastern column's extreme right flank to hostile opposition.

According to the Book of Jubilees (29:11), Ashtaroth and Karnaim were located in the territory that stretched from the land of Ammon to Mount Hermon. Karnaim, Ashtaroth, Edrei, Misur, and Beon were their major seats. Ashtaroth means "Ashtart of the two horns." Ashtart was a cow divinity worshipped throughout the ancient Near East. Artifacts connecting the worship of Ashtart with two horns have been discovered at numerous sites, including En-Gedi (mentioned in Ezekiel 47:10 as "the spring of the two calves") Ashtaroth–Karnaim, and Tzer. Excavations at et-Tell uncovered at least seven basalt stelae, one of which has a low-relief image of "a bull standing upright on his hind legs, with a moon-like eight-sliced circle between his horns, and a sword stretching down diagonally from beneath his right foreleg" (Bernett and Keel 1998). This one was discovered broken at the northern side of the inner entrance to the city near a ritual center or high place. Another was discovered during excavations near Ashtaroth–Karnaim at Tell el-Asari. A third was discovered being used in a Roman-era tomb in the territory of Aram.

Archaeological evidence from near Ashtaroth–Karnaim and at et-Tell has revealed enigmatic figures in ceremonial contexts. These figures are girded with swords, suggesting warfare as one of their prominent responsibilities. The figures are almost identical, and thus show a connection between the cities. Perhaps it was that connection that caused both cities, a mere twenty-five miles apart and on either flank of the northward-advancing eastern Assyrian column, to be assaulted successfully. It may be pointed out with some certainty, therefore, that the damage to the city of Tzer and to Ashtaroth and Karnaim was due to their membership in the same or similar cultic observance of a criocephalic, lunar deity-plus which caused them to oppose even the might of Tiglath-pileser III's sweep northward through the territory of Gilead on its way to vanquishing Damascus. Although religious difference was probably not the sole reason for opposing Tiglath-pileser III, it may provide plausible evidence of why Tzer met the same fate as Ashtaroth and Karnaim.

The location and strategic significance of Tzer strongly suggest that forces from this same column of Tiglath-pileser III's forces were responsible for the destruction discovered in the Iron Age II level, apparently attempting to secure their western flank from another fortified hilltop city. Evidence of destruction from et-Tell's Iron Age II level is similar to that found at other cities visited by Tiglath-pileser III's forces. The city-gate complex and towers at et-Tell certainly show signs of having been toppled by battering rams.

CRITICAL ANALYSIS OF THE DATA BEARING ON ET-TELL/TZER

Accounts of Tiglath-pileser III and other Assyrian kings describe their techniques and strategies of conquest, especially how they treated fortified cities. One of the most frequent boasts these conquerors are supposed to have made was, "I stormed the city's walls, destroyed and laid waste, and turned [the city] into mounds and heaps of ruins." Yet upon continued reading of the same formulaic accounts, one learns that tribute was exacted, taxes were levied, and that frequently overseers (sometimes the same, formerly independent, kings or rulers) were appointed. This could not have been the follow-up in a city that had been "laid waste" and made a "mound of ruins." While some cities probably held out to their death and destruction, appointment of a vassal ruler whose duty it was to collect and send tribute annually to the conqueror was much more common. Resettlement of the city's former leadership and a sizable amount of its population to the fringes of the empire appears to have been a far more practical solution than total annihilation of the city. Tiglath-pileser III is credited with introducing this practice.[8]

Archaeological evidence supplies the most reliable evidence of whether a city was destroyed or crippled. The major problem remains reliable identification of a city not mentioned in Tiglath-pileser III's

Annals, but nevertheless having been visited by him. King Ashurnasir-pal boasted that he rendered judgment at the gate of a city in the form of stacked bodies and/or body parts, as well as by having impaled many other rebels on stakes (Budge and King 1902, 1:234).

After conquering Megiddo, Tiglath-pileser III had portions rebuilt in Assyrian architectural style and it served subsequently as a military-administrative center (Mazar 1990, 444). The city of Samaria was spared because of King Menachem's capitulation and suit for vassalage, and because it was in territory already under Assyrian control (2 Kings 17:24).

While cities lying astride the route of either the western or eastern columns, and ascertainable from other sources such as inscriptions and/or biblical references are not in doubt, what is disputed is the veracity and seeming prima facie evidence of the *Annals* accounts. While it is clear that cities along the eastern and western Assyrian column's routes would have been natural targets for destruction, it seems doubtful that, as the *Annals* state, all cities were "turned into mounds and heaps of ruins" (Budge and King 1902, 231).

A comparison of the *Annals* accounts with actual archaeological evidence suggests that certain buildings or areas were targeted once the city's defenses had been breached. These would include palaces, religious centers or structures, independent granaries, defensive city walls and towers, and city-wall or city-gate complexes. This assumption is supported by evidence found at Iron Age IIB et-Tell and similar evidence at other fortified cities along Tiglath-pileser III's eastern and western routes.

THE EVIDENCE OF TZER/ET-TELL

The largest Iron Age II structure unearthed at et-Tell thus far is a multi-room *bit hilani* building. Both substantial damage and alterations were evident; the large rectangular hall had been divided later into two smaller rectangular rooms. Mud-brick benches located on both sides of the east entrance to the southernmost of the two rectangular rooms were relatively intact when excavated, suggesting that they had been added during the reuse phase of this chamber. No burnt objects were evident and a large number of large clay vessels dating from the Iron Age IIB were found intact in a square room on the northeastern side.

Their condition suggests they were covered due to a sudden action against the *bit hilani* structure.

In the north central section of Area A of et-Tell, a building was uncovered whose floor plan suggests a structure employed for religious purposes. It, too, showed signs of having been damaged then repaired, altered both by expansions internally and by external additions later reused during the second half of the eighth century BCE. It is located on the southern side of the plaza across from the *bit hilani* structure.

The massive city walls also show signs of destruction. Portions of the southward-running east wall were toppled. The eastern city-gate complex includes a series of massive defense towers. To the west of the northern defense tower, the city wall continues intact for about twenty feet or more; thereafter one discovers thousands of huge toppled stones, the remains of the northern wall defending what is thought to have been the western or "lower city," where ordinary citizens lived and worked. It is speculated that this section was toppled by Tiglath-pileser III's forces or by the city citizens on their orders. Pottery in the toppled "lower city" wall dates to Iron Age II, as does pottery discovered at the base level along uncovered sections of the "upper city" wall. From the tower westward, the wall dissolves into a cascade of huge basalt stones toppled down the northwestern portion of the northern slope. The chief archaeologist speculates that the toppled mass was caused by the Assyrian conquerors of the city, and not by the defenders (Arav 1999).

The city-gate complexes included religious or cultic structures and objects. The northern gate complex contained stelae, one inscribed with a low-relief image. The low-relief stele, though broken into several pieces, was found draped over a carved-out offering site. It appears to have been toppled deliberately (Bernett and Keel 1998).

Immediately beyond the gate entrance are four large rectangular chambers, two on either side of the cobbled street leading westward beyond the second gate. Covering the entire floor surface of Chamber 3 (the northwesternmost) was a thick, charred layer of grain. Flotation and lab analyses revealed that the grain was barley. Such an extensive amount suggests that this chamber was used exclusively as a granary, and that this use was considered worthwhile and profitable. Its presence adds another dimension to the activity that took place at city gates, or at least at this city gate. Charred remains of grain were also discovered in Chamber 2, which was sealed and filled with grain from above. Both Chambers 2 and 3 represented important currency for the rulers of the city, and both show signs of having been burned purposely.

CONCLUSIONS

There are two main reasons for attributing the considerable damage done to the Iron Age II city of et-Tell to Tiglath-pileser III. Firstly, the destruction can be dated to a period coinciding with his 734–732 BCE campaign in the area of Palestine, Philistia, the Negev, Transjordania/ Arabia, and Aram/Syria. A low-relief stele was found near the cities of Ashtaroth and Karnaim and another at the entrance to the city of Tzer. The Tzer low-relief was, unlike the low-relief stele near Ashtaroth and Karnaim, found in situ, a large portion of its demolished three sections lying across a ceremonial, basalt basin in the city's "high place," and thus sealing two incense burners dating to Iron Age IIB. Carbon 14 dating of barley samples taken from one of the two grana-ries located in the city-gate complex suggests a date of 732 BCE. More-over, the discovery of a clay figurine wearing an *'atef* crown depicting an anthropomorphic figure wearing horns suggests veneration of a moon (and perhaps solar) deity and religious practice similar to that in the Transjordan/north Arabian kingdom of Ammon.

Examination of the itinerary of Tiglath-pileser III demonstrates that his forces had been active in the area of et-Tell, which was along a route his eastern column would have followed on his second west-ern campaign. Et-Tell's location and its extensive defenses posed a threat to Tiglath-pileser III's domination of the region. In addition, shared and related iconography, as well as the Geshur region's known associations with and probably membership in the kingdom of Aram/ Syria sealed its general fate with that of Syria/Aram whose capital, Damascus, fell in the same year of 732 BCE.

Although it seems plausible that it was Tiglath-pileser III who destroyed et-Tell's Iron Age IIB city, he did not completely destroy it. There was major structural damage to many parts of the related ruins, but archaeological investigation shows continued, though limited, use after the 743–732 BCE campaign. There is also literary evidence of destruction to a city's defenses by fainthearted defenders attempting to avoid the wrath of a conqueror.

Et-Tell's damaged Iron Age IIB city suggests a city wounded but not slain. Certain portions were made unusable, such as the city-gate complex. The high place, the arrowheads and numerous ceramic vessels strewn on the floor of Chamber 4, the scorched, plastered floor and evidence of burned grain in the granary which was Chamber 2, the burned barley covering all of the floor of Chamber 3, the toppled towers flanking the inner city gate, the toppled tower of the north city wall, and the toppled western portion of what had been designed to protect the northern portion of the lower city, all still evident, attest to having been damaged in the 732 BCE northward sweep of Tiglath-pileser III's forces.

Other portions of the city remained habitable and show continued use. It is known that the cities of Megiddo and Samaria were used for administrative purposes after having been conquered by Tiglath-pileser III's forces during his earlier campaign in the region. An examination of alterations to et-Tell's *bit hilani* structure suggests that this city too continued to function after Tiglath-pileser III's departure.

CHAPTER NOTES

Unless otherwise indicated, all translations are my own. All biblical citations are taken from the Revised Standard Version.

1. Scholars debate the length, beginning, end, and characteristics of each period. According to the dating scheme of Amiahi Mazar (1990, 363), the Iron Age IIB lasted from 721 to 605 BCE. Each dating scheme attempts to clarify material-cultural phases within the periods, and assigns further delineating characteristics and nomenclatures to each period and subperiod. It is generally acknowledged, however, that Tiglath-pileser III's campaigns occurred during the Iron Age IIA period (930–721 BCE). Yet many archaeologists argue that Tiglath-pileser III's campaigns fall well within the Iron Age IIB period.
2. There are several types of Iron Age architecture that contained columns or pillars. Private dwellings were frequently of a type known as the "pillared house," generally a four-room structure with pillars holding up a shed or covered area where much family activity occurred. The royal *bit hilani* structure was a large residence with a pillared portico, a central court, and numerous rooms surrounding the court. The large Iron Age II structure in Area B at et-Tell may be such a structure. A third type of pillared building has been identified as warehouses, granaries, and stables. See Lamon and Shipton 1939, 1948, 32–47; Geraty and Herr 1987, 103–65.
3. Clinkers are slugs of basalt, mud-brick or plaster, pottery, and even metal fused together by the intense heat of a fire with a temperature of at least 1,000 to 1,200 degrees Fahrenheit. Clinkers, therefore, are not the result of ordinary cooking fires or campfires, and serve as excellent indicators of disaster.
4. Greene 1995, 224. This district is alluded to several times in literature. According to 2 Samuel 3:3, David's father-in-law was Talmai, king of Geshur. David's commander Joab returned Prince Absalom to Jerusalem from his grandfather's estates in Geshur (2 Sam. 14:21–23). Prince Absalom complained that he made a sacred vow while in Geshur (2 Sam. 15:8). Two places in 1 Chronicles corroborate the Samuel testimony: 1 Chronicles 3:2 identifies the mother of Absalom as the daughter of Geshur's king, while 1 Chronicles 2:23 shows that Geshur, along with Aram, was instrumental in capturing some Calebite territory. The reader then is in a much better position to notice and appreciate the enigmatic character of the 1 Samuel 27:8 text. A much later, apocryphal text concerning John the Baptist as risen-savior-figure adds interesting geographical information about the relationship between Bethsaida and Geshur (Mazar 1958, 115–23; 1961, 16–28).
   01: "...we entered into Bethsaida and into the country of the Geshurians,..."
   02: "...there met us out of the mountains of Bethsaida, a man...who had his dwelling in the caves of Geshur."

      11: "And they began to beseech me, that I would depart from
their country of Geshur."

      16: "And immediately I obliged my disciples to take care of the
boat, and then to go up the inland strait of Geshur, whilst
they awaited my arrival by the sea of Hula."

5. In the *Annals* of the Assyrian conqueror Adad-nirari III (810–783 BCE), his
scribe wrote: "He conquered other lands…marched after them, but these
deeds of his hand he did not record." Thus not all destructions or engage-
ments were recorded. This may explain why Tzer is not mentioned by
name in the *Annals*. Because of the fragmentary nature of Tiglath-pileser
III's *Annals*, as well as the poor condition of those available, some accounts
are not designated by year of his reign. Daniel Luckenbill's text number
777 (1926, 279), however, mentions people and events that, when compared with the biblical record, allow for a dating by other reliable chronol-
ogies. He mentions Rezin of Aram, and text 778 (Luckenbill 1929, 280)
alludes to Samsi, queen of Arabia. She was most likely the successor (and
daughter) of Queen Zabibe who paid tribute to Tiglath-pileser III prior to
his ninth year.

6. King Ahab fought against Shalmaneser III at Qarqar on the Orontes River
in 853 BCE with a coalition of kings, and Adad-nirari is probably alluded to
in 2 Kings 13:5 as a "savior."

7. King Menachem paid 1,000 talents of silver as tribute to Tiglath-pileser III
(2 Kings 15:19ff.; Schoville 1978, 204).

8. His other great contribution was the introduction of decentralized rule by
his deputies. Cf. Rogers 1901, 110, 122.

LITERATURE CITED

Arav, Rami. 1995. Bethsaida, Tzer, and the Fortified Cities of Napthali. In Arav and Freund 1995.

———. 1999. Bethsaida Excavations: Preliminary Report, 1994–1996. In Arav and Freund 1999.

Arav, Rami, and Richard Freund, eds. 1995. *Bethsaida: A City by the North Shore of the Sea of Galilee.* Vol. 1. Kirksville, Mo.: Thomas Jefferson University Press.

———. 1999. *Bethsaida: A City by the North Shore of the Sea of Galilee.* Vol. 2. Kirksville, Mo.: Thomas Jefferson University Press.

Bernett, Monika, and Othmar Keel. 1998. *Mond, Stier und Kult am Stadttor. Die Stele von Bethsaida (et Tell).* Orbis Biblicus et Orientalis 161. Goettingen: Vandenhoeck & Ruprecht/ Universitaetsverlag Freiburg, Schweitz.

Budge, Ernest A. Wallis, and L. W. King, eds. 1902. *Annals of the Kings of Assyria, The Cuneiform Texts with Translations, Transliterations, etc., from the Oriental Documents.* Vol. 1. London: Harrison and Sons.

Dever, William G., et al. 1970. *Gezer I: Preliminary Report of the 1964–66 Seasons. Hebrew Union College Biblical and Archaeological School Annual.* Vol. 1. Jerusalem: Keter.

Durant, Will. 1954. *Our Oriental Heritage. The Story of Civilization.* Part 1. New York: Simon and Schuster.

Freund, Richard A. 1995. The Search for Bethsaida in Rabbinic Literature. In Arav and Freund 1995.

Geraty, Laurence T., and L. G. Herr, eds. 1987. *The Archaeology of Jordan and Other Studies.* Berrien Springs, Mich.: Andrews University.

Glueck, Nelson. 1940. *The Other Side of the Jordan.* New Haven: American Schools of Oriental Research.

Greene, John T. 1995. Bethsaida-Julias in Roman and Jewish Military Strategies. In Arav and Freund 1995.

Harding, Gerald Lankestar. 1899. Antiquities of Jordan. Cambridge: James Clarke & Co.

Kenyon, Kathleen. 1970. *Archaeology in the Holy Land.* 3rd ed. New York: Praeger Publishers.

Lamon, Robert, and G. Shipton. 1939. *Megiddo I.* Chicago: University of Chicago Press.

———. 1948. *Megiddo I–II.* Chicago: University of Chicago Press.

Lance, Hubert Darrel. 1967. Gezer in the Land and in History. *Biblical Archaeologist* 30:34–47.

Luckenbill, Daniel D. 1926. *Ancient Records of Assyria and Babylonia.* 2 vols. Chicago: The University of Chicago Press.

Macalister, Robert A. S. 1912. *The Excavation of Gezer, 1902–1905 and 1907, 1909.* 3 vols. London: Palestine Exploration Fund.

Mazar, Amihai. 1990. *Archaeology of the Land of the Bible: 10,000–586 B.C.E.* New York: Doubleday.

————. 1992. The Iron Age Period. In *The Archaeology of Ancient Israel*, ed. Amnon Ben-Tor. New Haven, Conn.: Yale University Press.

Mazar, Benjamin. 1958. Geshur and Maacah. *Zion* 23/4:115–23.

————. 1961. Geshur and Maacah. *Journal of Biblical Literature* 80:16–28.

Pritchard, James B., ed. 1958. *The Ancient Near East: An Anthology of Texts and Pictures*. Princeton: Princeton University Press.

Rogers, Robert W. 1901. *A History of Babylonia and Assyria*. 2 vols. New York: Eaton and Mains.

Rost, Paul. 1893. *Die Keilschrifttexte Tiglat-Pilesers III*. 2 vols. Leipzig: Eduard Pfeiffer.

Schoville, Keith. 1978. *Biblical Archaeology in Focus*. Grand Rapids: Baker Book House.

Tadmor, Hayim. 1994. *The Inscriptions of Tiglath-Pileser III King of Assyria: Critical Edition, with Introductions, Translations and Commentary. Fontes ad res Judaicas spectantes*. Jerusalem: Israel Academy of Sciences and Humanities.

Mark D. Smith

Bethsaida in the *Natural History* of Pliny the Elder

O NE OF THE EARLIEST REFERENCES to Bethsaida/Julias appears in Pliny the Elder's *Natural History*,[1] an eclectic collection of "facts," borne of observation and culled from written sources, ranging from descriptions of the universe, to the geography of the earth, to the nature of human beings, plants, animals, and minerals (Locher 1986, 21). Within his geographical section (books 3 through 6) Pliny devotes a brief passage to the description of Judea and Syria, in the midst of which he makes mention of Bethsaida, which he calls Julias:

> The Jordan River...widens out into a lake which many call Genesar. This is sixteen [Roman] miles long and six broad, and it is surrounded by the pleasant towns of Julias and Hippos on the east, Tarichea (by which name some call the lake) on the south, and on the west, Tiberias, with its salubrious hot springs.[2]

At first glance, this passage bears many marks of an eyewitness account, especially when one considers the surrounding context, which includes references to the Dead Sea: its dimensions, how bodies of animals float in it, and the problems it poses for local water supplies. In addition, Pliny includes an intriguing note about the sect of the Essenes who, although they renounce women and sexual intercourse, continue to maintain a stable population, "so advantageous for them is others' weariness of life" (*Nat.* 5.72–73). Despite such vivid elements in the account, when one considers the relatively well-documented career

83

of Pliny, there is no evidence that he spent any time in the eastern Mediterranean.

Pliny was born in Transpadane Gaul in 23/24 CE of Equestrian stock. By the 30s, he was in Rome undertaking the rudiments of a gentleman's education. Beginning about 47 CE, he was involved in several military campaigns along the Rhine where, during the later 50s, he was a fellow officer with Titus, the future emperor. In 58 or 59 CE, he returned to Rome where he launched a short-lived and insignificant career as a lawyer, which he supplemented by writing, and generally avoided the volatile political atmosphere of the later years of Nero's reign. After Vespasian emerged victorious in 69 CE, Pliny resumed his public career under the patronage of the emperor and his son Titus. After this time Pliny held a number of procuratorships in rapid succession, perhaps including Gallia Narbonensis (70 CE?), Africa (c. 70–72 CE), Hispania Tarraconensis (c. 72–74 CE), and Gallia Belgica (c. 74–76 CE?). By 77 CE, he had been appointed prefect of the Roman fleet stationed at Misenum in the Bay of Naples, a post that eventually cost him his life.[3] When Mount Vesuvius erupted in August of 79 CE, Pliny, drawn by his innate curiosity, sailed into the Bay to take notes on his observations and to help with evacuation efforts. Ultimately he stayed too close for too long, eventually succumbing to what may have been a heart attack, brought on by the combined effects of a chronically weak constitution, the stress of the day's activities, and perhaps the sulphurous fumes spewing from the volcano.[4] Throughout his active life, Pliny spent considerable time writing.[5] Of his many works, the only one that survives is the *Natural History*, which he completed in 77 CE and dedicated to Titus.

If there is no evidence that Pliny ever traveled to Judea, what may have been the source of his vivid account of Judea and Syria, including his reference to Julias?[6] One intriguing possibility is Josephus, who arrived in Rome, along with Titus, not long after the sack of Jerusalem in 70 CE, thenceforth living on the patronage of the imperial family and residing in one of their villas. Both Josephus and Pliny, then, took up residence as eminent literati among the clients of the Flavians in the early 70s (though Pliny's official duties often took him abroad). What would be more natural than for Pliny, when he undertook his research on the region around Judea, to seek out information from the local expert? As plausible as this reconstruction may sound, and as intriguing as may have been a meeting between these two men, there is no evidence that Pliny ever used Josephus as a source. In book 1, where Pliny provides the reader with a sort of table of contents and a list of sources, Josephus does not appear among the authorities cited. In addition, when the two treat the same issues, they do so quite differently. For example, in his discussion of the Essenes, Pliny focuses on their celibacy and marvels at the poverty of human existence that would continue to swell their ranks with those abandoning normal walks of life. Josephus, although he does note many Essenes' renunciation of passions and marriage, clarifies that they keep up their population by adopting other people's children.[7] He also mentions a group of Essenes who do in fact marry (though only after the prospective wives fulfill a three-year trial period!) and produce a worthy crop of future Essenes (*J.W.* 2.8.13). But, beyond any note of their methods of propagation, Josephus, unlike Pliny, is concerned to emphasize the purity, piety, and virtue of the Essenes. Josephus was, therefore, probably not Pliny's source.

Where, then, did Pliny get his geographical and cultural knowledge of Judea and Syria? The first source Pliny lists for book 5 is Agrippa (and the sources are not listed in alphabetical order). It is well known that Agrippa wrote a *Geography* of the Roman world,[8] and that he spent two stints in the eastern Mediterranean, as proconsul and co-regent of the empire.[9] There he made the acquaintance of Herod the Great with whom he became close friends—so close that, according to Josephus, Herod held none closer, and Herod's grandson was named after Agrippa.[10] Is it possible that Agrippa was Pliny's primary source for this region? That depends on what can be reconstructed of the *Geography* of Agrippa, for it survives only in fragments quoted by later authors. Scholars can learn a good deal about Agrippa's *Geography* from the work of Pliny alone. Although Pliny does not always mention his sources by name, he does so often enough to reveal some significant patterns. Agrippa's name appears as Pliny's source no fewer than thirty times throughout books 3 through 6 (Reinhold 1986, 145). In *Natural History* 3.8, 16–17, Pliny cites Agrippa as his source for the dimensions of the Hispanic region of Baetica. Agrippa's measurement of the dimensions of Gallia Narbonensis appears in *Natural History* 3.37. Pliny includes Agrippa's figures for circumference of Sicily (*Nat.* 3.86), of Britain (*Nat.* 4.102), and of the Black Sea (*Nat.* 4.45, 77–78, 83; cf. 6.3). Agrippa provides Pliny with the raw data for the dimensions of the land of the Scythians (*Nat.* 4.81); Magna Graecia *(Nat.*

3.96); the coastline of the Adriatic (*Nat.* 3.150); the size of Crete (*Nat.* 4.60); the area inhabited by Scythians, Sarmatians, and Taurians (*Nat.* 4.91); the size of the borders of Germania (*Nat.* 4.98); the length of the Gallic coastline (*Nat.* 4.105); the land of Lusitania, Asturia, and Gallaecia (*Nat.* 4.118); the distance between rivers in Africa (*Nat.* 5.9); the length of the African coast (*Nat.* 5.40, 65; 6.209); the dimensions of Lycaonia and Phrygia (*Nat.* 5.102); the size of the region surrounding the Caspian Sea (*Nat.* 6.37) and the length of some of its coastal cliffs (*Nat.* 6.39); the length of the coastline of India (*Nat.* 6.57); the dimensions of Mesopotamia (*Nat.* 6.136–37); the length of the Red Sea coast (*Nat.* 6.164); the size of Ethiopia (*Nat.* 6.196); and the distance of sailing routes from the Straits of Gibraltar (*Nat.* 6.207). In short, Pliny, in the geographical portion of his *Natural History*, makes constant use of Agrippa's work, far more than of any other geographer of antiquity.[11] And, in twenty-nine of the thirty instances where Pliny names Agrippa as his source, he does so with reference to the measurements the latter provided of land masses and bodies of water.[12] This is important because, in the brief section on Judea and its environs, Pliny includes measurements of both the Sea of Galilee and of the Dead Sea.[13] This is just the sort of information one should expect to find in Agrippa's work.[14]

Scholars cannot, of course, be certain whether Agrippa was the only source of Pliny's discussion of Palestine, but it is quite probable that Agrippa's *Geography* was at least one of the sources Pliny utilized in compiling his account. If that is true, and the reference to Julias appears within the immediate context of the note of the dimensions of the Sea of Galilee, there is some probability that it was Agrippa who was the primary witness to Julias. If this inference is correct, it would mean that Pliny's information on Julias must date from before the death of Agrippa in 12 BCE, and probably from before his return to Rome in 13 BCE.

This reconstruction poses a chronological problem, however, since Philip did not change the name of Bethsaida to Julias until considerably later (30 CE) and, similarly, Tiberias was not founded until between 19 and 23 CE.[15] Yet Pliny uses both of these later place-names. As a result, even if Pliny's description of the Galilee region depends largely on Agrippa, he must have derived his knowledge of the names of Tiberias and Julias from another source. There was, indeed, a source near to hand for Pliny: his patrons Vespasian and

Titus. It is difficult to imagine that there was never an occasion for Pliny to have heard the emperors' reminiscences of their campaign in Palestine which early on focused on the Galilee region. It is also possible that Pliny had access to written memoirs of Vespasian and/or Titus.[16]

After evaluating the most promising sources available to Pliny, it is most probable that Pliny based his account of the Judean/Syrian landscape on Agrippa, but added place-names and perhaps some of those vivid images based either upon his conversations with Vespasian and Titus or written accounts of their campaigns. Pliny therefore provides evidence that Julias was a significant town in the mid-first century, to the east of the Jordan, on the Sea of Galilee. That Pliny makes no mention of the fate of Julias is curious, but then again, neither does Josephus. Perhaps he has nothing to tell. Whether Bethsaida-Julias was razed by angry legionaries, merely abandoned, suffered the ravages of an earthquake, or some combination thereof, cannot be determined by an analysis of Pliny.[17]

CHAPTER NOTES

All translations are my own unless otherwise indicated.

1. Pliny's text can be firmly dated to 77 CE, based on its dedication. According to the common assumptions about the date of the Gospels, it would appear to have been composed later than Mark and Q and, perhaps, shortly before the writing of Matthew, Luke, and John, though there is considerable room for disagreement concerning each of these. In addition, Josephus' *Jewish War* (*J.W.*) may have appeared about the same time as Pliny's *Natural History* for, according to most scholars, the first edition of the former work appeared somewhere between 75 and 79 CE, though some would push the date up to the reign of Titus. For fuller discussion, see Cohen 1979, 84ff.; Thackeray 1926, xii; Stern 1987, 72; Hadas-Lebel 1993, 213.

2. Iordanes...in lacum se fundit quem plures Genesaram vocant, XVI p. longitudinis, VI latitudinis, amoenis circumsaeptum oppidis, ab oriente Iuliade et Hippo, a meridie Tarichea, quo nomine aliqui et lacum appellant, ab occidente Tiberiade aquis calidis salubri (Pliny the Elder *Nat.* 5.71). According to John Rousseau and Rami Arav, the Sea of Galilee is now thirteen miles long and eight wide at the broadest point (1995, 246). Josephus says it was in his time 240 x 40 stadia = 15.6 x 4.5 miles (*J.W.* 3.506). Although Pliny's dimensions accord fairly well with Josephus', and recent geographical studies indicate that the dimensions of the lake have changed since antiquity, it would be unwise to take Pliny's measurements too seriously. At times he can be wildly inaccurate, as in the case of his discussion of the Dead Sea a few sentences later.

3. For Pliny's career, see Syme 1969; cf. Reynolds 1986, 1–10.

4. On Pliny's death see Pliny the Younger *Epistula* VI.16, 20. Cf. Zirkle 1967, 553–59; Bessone 1969, 166–79.

5. For a list of his works, see Pliny the Younger *Epistula* III.5.

6. For fuller discussion of Pliny's sources, see Müntzer 1988.

7. Josephus *J.W.* 2.8.2ff.; other references to Essenes include *Ant.* 13.5.9, 15.10.5, 17.13.3, 18.1.5.

8. Herbert Rose considers Agrippa's *Geography* to be one of the primary sources of Pliny's work (1949, 439–40). For a collection of the extant fragments, see Klotz 1931.

9. According to Meyer Reinhold, Pliny was in the eastern Mediterranean from 23 to 21 BCE and again, from 17/16 to 13 BCE (1965, 84–85, 107ff., 167). During the latter period, Agrippa paid a visit to Herod's realm, visiting at least Sebaste, Caesarea, Alexandreion, Herodeion, Hyrcania, and Jerusalem (Josephus *Ant.* 16.13).

10. Josephus *Ant.* 15.350, 16.12ff.; *J.W.* 1.400. The two seem to have spent much of the spring of 14 BCE together around the Aegean (Josephus *Ant.* 16.15ff.; cf. Reinhold 1986, 117–21; cf. Grant 1971, 145, 175ff.).

11. Only Eratosthenes comes close: Pliny refers to him nine times in the same books, at times alongside Agrippa, especially when the two differ in their calculations.
12. For his measurements, Agrippa relied, at least in part, on the work of earlier Greek geographers (Klotz 1931, 464; Reinhold 1986, 145).
13. Whereas his measurements for the Sea of Galilee are at least in the right ballpark, his calculations fly far afield when he claims that the Dead Sea is one hundred miles long, seventy-five wide at its widest point, and six miles wide at its narrowest (*Nat.* 5.72).
14. For further discussion of Pliny's use of his sources, including Agrippa and official lists, see Jones 1937, 491–99.
15. John Greene suggests that Bethsaida was renamed in 27 CE (1995, 211); however, Arie Kindler, based upon the earliest appearance of the portrait and name of Julia on a coin of Philip, together with a coin inscribed ΚΤΙΣ, both of which date from 30 CE, suggests that the latter is a more probable date (1999). See also Strickert 1995, 67; Meshorer 1982, 42ff. For the date of the founding of Tiberias, based on numismatic evidence, see Meshorer 1982, 36. Compare Harold Hoehner, who dates it to 23 (1972, 93–95).
16. Feldman and Hata 1987, 24; see also Greene 1995, 204. Josephus mentions his use of such documents in *Vita* (342, 358) and *Contra Apionem* (1.56).
17. The most promising place to look for evidence of the fate of Bethsaida is in the works of Eusebius of Caesarea. For further discussion, see my "Eusebius of Caesarea and the Fate of Bethsaida" included in this volume. The archaeological evidence offers little to support the thesis that Bethsaida was sacked by the Romans. According to Arav, the excavated houses were largely empty and not burnt. There is no ash layer, and the number of coins found thus far seems to diminish in the years leading up to the war.

90   *Mark D. Smith*

LITERATURE CITED

90   *Mark D. Smith*

LITERATURE CITED

LITERATURE CITED

Arav, Rami, and Richard Freund, eds. 1995. *Bethsaida: A City by the North Shore of the Sea of Galilee.* Vol. 1. Kirksville, Mo.: Thomas Jefferson University Press.

————. 1999. *Bethsaida: A City by the North Shore of the Sea of Galilee.* Vol. 2. Kirksville, Mo.: Truman State University Press.

Bessone, Luigi. 1969. Sulla morte di Plinio il vecchio. *Rivista di studi classici* 17:166–79.

Boissonade, Jean Francois. [1819] 1963. *Herodiani partitiones.* Amsterdam: Hakkert.

Cohen, Shaye. 1979. *Josephus in Galilee and Rome: His Vita and Development as a Historian.* Leiden: E. J. Brill.

Feldman, Louis, and Gohei Hata. 1987. *Josephus, Judaism, and Christianity.* Detroit: Wayne State University Press.

Grant, Michael. 1971. *Herod the Great.* New York: McGraw-Hill.

Greene, John. 1995. *Bethsaida-Julias in Roman and Jewish Military Strategies, 66–73 CE.* In Arav and Freund 1995.

Hadas-Lebel, Mireille. 1993. *Flavius Josephus: Eyewitness to Rome's First-Century Conquest of Judea.* New York: Macmillan.

Hoehner, Harold. 1972. *Herod Antipas.* Grand Rapids: Zondervan.

Hunt, E. D. 1982. *Holy Land Pilgrimage in the Later Roman Empire A.D. 312–460.* Oxford: Clarendon.

Jones, Arnold Hugh Martin. 1937. *The Cities of the Eastern Roman Provinces.* Oxford: Clarendon.

Josephus. 2003. *De Bello Judaico.* Edited by H. Leeming and K. Leeming. Leiden: Brill.

Kindler, Arie. 1999. The Coins of the Tetrarch Philip and Bethsaida. In Arav and Freund 1999.

Klotz, A. 1931. Die geographischen commentarii des Agrippa und ihre Überreste. *Klio,* n.s. 6 (24): 38–58, 386–466.

Locher, A. 1986. The Structure of Pliny the Elder's Natural History. In *Science in the Early Roman Empire: Pliny the Elder, His Sources and Influence,* edited by R. French and F. Greenaway. Totowa, N.J.: Barnes & Noble.

Meshorer, Yaakov. 1982. *Ancient Jewish Coinage.* Vol. 2, *Herod the Great through Bar Cochba.* Dix Hills, N.Y.: Amphora Books.

Müntzer, Friedrich. [1897] 1988. *Beiträge zur Quellenkritik der Natugeschichte des Plinius.* Hildesheim: Weidmann.

Pliny the Elder. 1905. *Plinii Naturalis Historia.* Edited by K. Mayhoff. Leipzig: Teubner.

Pliny the Younger. 1915. *Epistulae.* New York: W. Heinemann.

Reinhold, Meyer. [1933] 1965. *Marcus Agrippa: A Biography.* Studia Historica 16. Roma: "L'Erma" di Bretschneider.

Reynolds, J. 1986. The Elder Pliny and His Times. In *Science in the Early Roman Empire: Pliny the Elder, His Sources and Influence,* edited by R. French and F. Greenaway. Totowa, N.J.: Barnes & Noble

Rose, Herbert Jennings. 1949. *A Handbook of Latin Literature*. London: Methuen.

Rousseau, John J., and Rami Arav. 1995. *Jesus and His World*. Minneapolis: Fortress.

Stern, M. 1987. Josephus and the Roman Empire as Reflected in the Jewish War. In *Josephus, Judaism, and Christianity*, edited by Louis Feldman and Gohei Hata. Detroit: Wayne State University Press.

Strickert, Fred. 1995. The Coins of Philip. In Arav and Freund 1995.

Syme, Ronald. 1969. Pliny the Procurator. *Harvard Studies in Classical Philology* 73:201–36.

Thackeray, Herbert St. J. 1926–27. *Introduction to Josephus*. Loeb Classical Library. Cambridge: Harvard University Press.

Zirkle, C. 1967. The Death of Gaius Plinius Secundus (23–79 AD). *Isis* 58:553–55.

Fred Strickert

The Renaming of Bethsaida in Honor of Livia, a.k.a. Julia, the Daughter of Caesar, in Josephus, *Jewish Antiquities* 18.27–28

I N HIS DESCRIPTIONS of the Herodian family, Josephus several times mentions their work in founding new cities.[1] Such is the case with the village of Bethsaida renamed Julias:

καὶ Ἡρώδης Σεπφωριν τειχίσας πρόσχημα τοῦ Γαλιλαίου παντὸς ἠγόρευεν αὐτὴν Αὐτοκρατορίδα· Βηθαραμφθᾶ δέ, πόλις καὶ αὐτὴ τυγχάνει, τείχει περιλαβὼν Ἰουλιάδα ἀπὸ τοῦ αὐτοκράτορος προσαγορεύει τῆς γυναικός· Φίλιππος δὲ Πανεάδα τὴν πρὸς ταῖς πηγαῖς τοῦ Ἰορδάνου κατασκευάσας ὀνομάζει Καισάρειαν, κώμην δὲ Βηθσαϊδὰ πρὸς λίμη τῇ Γεννησαρίτιδι πόλεως παρασχὼν ἀξίωμα πλήθει τε οἰκητόρων καὶ τῇ ἄλλῃ δυνάμει Ἰουλίᾳ θυγατρὶ τῇ Καίσαρος ὁμώνυμον ἐκάλεσεν· (Josephus *Ant.* 18.27–28)

[Meanwhile Herod and Philip received and were taking in hand their respective tetrarchies. Herod fortified Sepphoris to be the ornament of all Galilee, and he called it Autocratoris. He also threw a wall about another city, Betharamphtha, which he called Julias, after the name of the emperor's wife. Philip too made improvements at Paneas, the city near the sources of the Jordan, and called it Caesarea. He also raised the village Bethsaida on Lake Gennesaritis to the status of city by

93

adding residents and strengthening the fortifications. He
named it after Julia, the emperor's daughter.]

The name of Julias for this city is confirmed by Pliny the Elder (*Nat.*
5.15.71) and Ptolemy (*Geog.* 5.16.4), in addition to six other passages
in Josephus, while the name Bethsaida is restricted in the first century
to the Gospels and this single occasion in Josephus.

The difficulty, however, is what to make of the reference to
Julia, the daughter of Caesar. The demise of Julia, the only daughter of
Augustus and his first wife, Scribonia, is well known (Ferrill 1980).
After a succession of three husbands including Tiberius, Julia became
infamous for her adulterous affairs in Rome and was banished by
Augustus in 2 BCE, first to the island of Pandateria, then to the town of
Rhegium on the strait opposite Sicily, where she wasted away until her
death in 14 CE.[2] How does one reconcile the discrepancy between the
honor of having a city named after Julia and the dishonor of her
becoming a public embarrassment to her father the emperor?

TRADITIONAL SOLUTION—
BETHSAIDA NAMED BEFORE JULIA'S DEMISE

The traditional solution for this perplexing question represented by
Emil Schürer[3] a century ago is that the renaming of Bethsaida to Julias
must have taken place prior to Julia's banishment in 2 BCE. Since
Herod died in 4 BCE, there is still a window of two years for his successor Philip (4 BCE–34 CE) to have carried out the name change as a first
order of business in his thirty-eight-year rule. This, in fact, occurred
with Caesarea Philippi, the other city founded by Philip, corroborated
by the coins of Philip minted in 1 CE with images of both Caesar and
Philip (Meshorer 1982, 45; Kindler, 1971, 162). Thus Ya'akov
Meshorer explained the abbreviation KTIΣ for κτιστης [founder] on a
coin of Philip in 30 CE as a celebration of the thirtieth anniversary of
the founding of Caesarea Philippi (1982, 49).

The traditional solution is not without problems. It assumes that
Philip would have engaged in the construction of two cities simultaneously rather than stagger the building as in the case of his brother
Antipas, who began with Sepphoris from 4 BCE to 8 CE, then built Livia
in Perea from 8 CE to 13 CE, and completed his construction activities
with Tiberias (13 CE to 20 CE). Even if this assumption is correct, the
construction of Julias would have been completed by 2 BCE, an

extremely short period by first-century standards of city construction projects. Lastly, even if the first two assumptions are true, it seems unlikely that the name Julias would have been retained after Julia's banishment. Interestingly, the earliest sources, Mark and Q, as well as the entire gospel tradition (Matt. 11:20–24 = Luke 10:13–15; Mark 6:45, 8:22–26; Luke 9:10–11; John 1:43–44, 12:20–22), employ the name Bethsaida in the context of Jesus' ministry from 27 to 30 CE, while the name Julias occurs in later sources: Ptolemy, Pliny, and Josephus, including a description of a battle outside Julias in 67 CE. The literary data do not mesh.

MODERN PROPOSAL— JOSEPHUS IN ERROR, BETHSAIDA NAMED FOR CAESAR'S WIFE

The modern interpretation, proposed since the beginning of archaeological research into the city of Bethsaida/Julias by Rami Arav in 1987, is that Josephus' mention of "Julia, the daughter of Caesar" is simply incorrect. The city was named after Livia, the wife of Augustus, who was also given the honorary name Julia. Here coin evidence has been formidable. The discovery of two Philip coins bearing the image of Livia demonstrates her prominent standing in the eyes of the Herodians. The fact that one of these bearing the inscription ΙΟΥΛΙΑ ΣΕΒ-ΑΣΤΗ [Julia Sebaste] was minted in 30 CE (Strickert 2002b), the same year as the ΚΤΙΣ coin inscription, is overwhelming evidence that Philip founded the city and renamed it Julias in the year 30 CE (Strickert 1995, 165–89; Kindler 1999, 245–49). Citing these recent works, Meshorer has revised his interpretation of the ΚΤΙΣ inscription as referring to the founding of Bethsaida/Julias (Meshorer 2001, 88). This then is consistent with gospel usage of the name Bethsaida describing events up to the year 30 CE. The archaeological evidence, including the discovery of a Roman-style temple, figurines, and implements of the imperial cult, confirm this solution.

What then accounted for the erroneous notation in Josephus? One explanation is that Josephus is simply wrong (Strickert 1995). He was writing at the end of the first century, and this is certainly not the first time that Josephus had included incorrect information. This is supported by the fact that a parallel passage he wrote several decades earlier in the *Jewish War* does not mention the daughter of Caesar at all.

On the death of Augustus, who had directed the state for fifty-seven years, six months, and two days, the empire of the Romans passed to Tiberius, son of Julia. On his accession, Herod Antipas and Philip continued to hold their tetrarchies and respectively founded cities: Philip built Caesarea near the sources of the Jordan in the district of Paneas, and Julias in lower Gaulanitis; Herod built Tiberias in Galilee and a city which also took the name Julia in Perea (2.168).

One can even make a strong argument that this paragraph implies that the city Julias and the city Julia in Perea are both named for Livia/Julia, the wife of Augustus, since she is mentioned in this paragraph and in the previous one.[4] One could argue that the material in Josephus' *Jewish War* came from his sources, while he took a freer editorial hand in embellishing material in *Antiquities* and simply got it wrong.

A second explanation attributes the "daughter of Caesar" reference to scribal error. With the repetition of the name Julia or Julias in this account, one can see where a scribe's eye might jump ahead. Thus H.W. Kuhn and Rami Arav (1991) proposed that this is a case of *homoioteleuton* in which the scribe omitted a phrase that occurred between two like endings. John Greene produces a reconfigured reading as follows:

Philip built a wall around Betharamptha...
and called it Julias,
from the name of the emperor's wife...
he also advanced the village of Bethsaida...
and called it Julias by the name of Julias [*Caesar's wife, and Julias is*], the same name with Caesar's daughter.[5]

The assumption is that Josephus recognized that two cities Betharamptha and Bethsaida were named for Livia/Julia, Augustus' wife, and that he then added the coincidental detail that this was "the same name with Caesar's daughter."

This proposal is not without difficulties. Foremost is the complete absence of manuscript variants. Also, one would have to explain Josephus' motive in mentioning the infamous Julia since her name occurs only one other time in *Antiquities* (17.229; Smith 1999, 336–37). A more likely scribal alteration would be the intentional substitution of θυγατρί for γυναίκᾳ. Again manuscript evidence and motive are lacking. The suggestion that the current reading is the result of a scribal change, though appealing, is not totally convincing.

Mark Smith suggests that Josephus is responsible for the reference to the younger Julia; however, he did not intend to say that the city was named for her. Here the argument revolves around the verb ὁμώνυμον ἐκάλεσεν, which he translates as *"he called it the same name as Julia, the daughter of the emperor"* (Smith 1999, 336). Thus it does not necessarily mean "to be named after," but rather that two persons or places share the same name.[6] Smith recognizes the difficulty with this solution, since Josephus does use this expression elsewhere to designate that something is in fact named after someone. More importantly, it fails to explain adequately why Josephus would even want to call attention to the infamous Julia.

A NEW PROPOSAL—BETHSAIDA NAMED FOR LIVIA AS CAESAR'S DAUGHTER

Is it possible that Josephus intended to say what he actually wrote, yet it is merely a question of misunderstanding? The adulterous Julia was not the only daughter of Caesar. Livia, Augustus' own wife, was officially adopted as daughter by decree of the Roman Senate and granted the names Julia and Augusta.[7] Tacitus describes the events following Augustus' death in 14 CE:

> On the first day of the Senate he [Tiberius] allowed nothing to be discussed but the funeral of Augustus, whose will was brought by the Vestal Virgins. He named as his heirs Tiberius and Livia. The latter was admitted into the Julia *familia* with the name of Augusta. (*Ann.* 1.8)

Livia Drusilla, from the noble Claudii and Livii families, married Octavian (Augustus) in 38 BCE, while pregnant with Drusus, bringing with her a son, Tiberius, from her previous marriage. Octavian's daughter Julia likewise had been from his previous marriage to Scribonia. Livia and Augustus never had children of their own, so the issue of succession had always been one of intrigue. Following the deaths (sometimes mysterious) of a series of potential heirs, Tiberius was adopted as Augustus' son in 4 CE and fell into succession when confirmed by the Senate at the death of Augustus.

The deposition of Augustus' will and the decree of the Senate was more than an honorary declaration for Livia. Adopting her into the Julian clan helped to legitimize the selection of Tiberius as heir, established the continuation of the Julian dynasty, and raised Livia to the status of co-regent (Ritter 1972, 313–38; Perkounig 1995). As later developments attest, she became a powerful figure throughout both Rome and the empire. The frequent use of the name Julia in subsequent years was a subtle way of declaring her role, not only as Augustus' wife, but also as Augustus' daughter.

Subtle allusion is one thing; the actual use of the expression "daughter of Caesar" is another. However, several cases can be documented. Velleius Paterculus in his *History of Rome* describes Livia as follows:

> Livia, nobilissimi et fortissimi viri Drusi Claudiani filia, genere, probitate, forma Romanarum eminentissima, quam postea coniugem Augusti vidimus, quam transgressi ad deos sacerdotem ac filiam (2.75.3).

> [Take for example Livia. She, the daughter of the brave and noble Drusus Claudianus, most eminent of Roman women in birth, in sincerity, and in beauty, she, whom we later saw as the wife of Augustus, and as his priestess and daughter after his deification.]

Velleius wrote this as an army officer to commemorate the elevation to consulship of his friend Marcus Vinicius—his writing in this case is most significant because it is dated to the year 30 CE, the same year that Bethsaida was renamed in honor of Julia. In this short description admiring her virtues, Velleius does refer to Livia as the daughter [*filia*] of the Claudian Drusus. However, he then recognizes her three roles in relationship to Augustus. She is wife [*coniugem*], priestess [*sacerdotem*], and daughter [*filiam*], the latter two being conferred following Augustus' death and deification. At the very end of his book, Velleius notes Livia's own death in 29 CE, stating that she "in all things resembled the gods more than mankind" [per omnia deis quam hominibus similior] (2.130.5).

The extent of appreciation for Livia has been long attested by the number of sculptures and inscriptions from throughout the Roman Empire. One such statue (fig. 1) was discovered in 1761 at Velleia, as part of thirteen portraits from a Julio-Claudian dynastic group in an imperial-cult building. Dated to the Caligulan period (37–41 CE) because of the group's dynastic politics,[8] the larger-than-life (2.13

Fig. 1. "Velleia Livia." Madrid Archaeological Museum

meters) statue of Livia towers over the three other women figures—
Drusilla, Agrippina 1, and Agrippina 2. Garbed in a sleeved tunic and
mantle, her melon-styled hair and youthful appearance are typical of
this period.[9] Two attributes are consistent with the comments of Velleius. Her veil represents Livia's role as priestess of Augustus. The
diadem is a mark of divinity, an attribute technically "illegal" prior to
her deification by Claudius in 42 CE.

It is the inscription on a marble plaque accompanying this
statue that is of special interest:

[Iulia]e Divi	[To Julia Augusta,
A[ugusti] f. Augustae	daughter of Divus Augustus,
matri Ti. Caesaris	mother of Tiberius Caesar
[Di]v[i Au]gusti f.	the son of Divus Augustus
Aug[usti e]t Neronis	and of Nero
[C]lau[di] Dru[si][10]	Claudius Drusus]

Although broken, there is no doubt that this inscription is dedicated
to Livia. She is identified as "Augusta" and the "daughter of the deified
Augustus" (*Divi A*[ ] *f.*). The reconstructed Julia makes perfect sense so
that her name "Julia Augusta" parallels numerous Latin inscriptions,
as well as the occurrence of the equivalent Ιουλια Σεβαστη [Julia
Sebaste] on numerous Greek inscriptions—including the legend on
the 30 CE coin of Philip (Meshorer 1982, 148). Her dual role here is
that of daughter of Augustus and mother of Tiberius.

A second statue base from the Caligulan era has been discovered
at Aphrodisias. Once again it was part of a statue group along with
Agrippina, Germanicus, and M. Aemilius Lepidus, the husband of
Drusilla (Bartman 1999, 123, 139 n. 17; Rose 1997, 164, cat. 104). However, the statue of Livia has not survived. The slightly damaged marble
base includes the following inscription:

[Ἰο]υλίαν Σεβαστή[ν]	[To Julia Augusta,
Σεβαστοῦ Θυγατέ[ρα]	daughter of Augustus,
Ἡραν [11]	the new Hera]

Again the name Julia Sebaste—established with confidence through
restoration—is consistent with the Velleia inscription and Philip's

coin of 30 CE. Here she is identified with the goddess Hera (Hahn 1994, 42–47), while the coin gives her attributes of Demeter, again conforming to the citations listed above.

The three examples of the use of "daughter of Augustus" for Livia—the Velleius Paterculus passage, the Velleia inscription, and the Aphrodisias inscription—do have a number of significant points in common. All three come from the period following Livia's death. In one way or another, they recognize Livia as having divine characteristics, perhaps contributing in some way to the movement toward her eventual deification under Claudius in 42 CE.[12]

Another way to understand the significance of these two inscriptions is to analyze the various relationship terms used to describe Livia at different stages of her life. In her comprehensive study of the portraiture of Livia, Elizabeth Bartman has catalogued seventy-six epigraphic references to her from statue bases and plaques (1999, 198–211). By using this kind of epigraphic evidence, one can see the development of certain patterns in a chronological framework. Of the seventy-six total, twenty-seven can be dated to the Augustan era, from the battle of Actium in 31 BCE until Augustus' death in 14 CE, and forty-one (the largest number) can be dated to the Tiberian era, from 14 CE until Livia's death in 29 CE. Only eight can be dated posthumously to the remainder of Tiberius' life (29–37 CE), to the rule of Caligula (37–41 CE), and to the rule of Claudius (41–54 CE).

Table 1. Relationship terms in epigraphic references to Livia

	AUGUSTAN ERA 31 BCE–14 CE	TIBERIAN ERA 14–29 CE	POSTHUMOUS AFTER 29 CE
Wife of Augustus	14	3	—
Wife of Augustus reconstructed	3	1	—
Livia Augusti	4	3	1
Daughter of Drusus	3	5	—
Mother of Tiberius	1	7	1
Grandmother of Claudius	—	—	1
Daughter of Augustus	—	—	2
Livia or Julia	2	22	3
Total number of statues	27	41	8

As was common for women in the ancient world, Livia was often described in relationship to one of the male figures in her life. The most frequent relationship term was wife, occurring in twenty-nine of these inscriptions, or one third of them. While the Latin term *uxor* or the Greek γυνη was typical, there are also eight occurrences of *Livia Augusti* or *Julia Augusti* (the woman's name with the genitive), meaning Livia of Augustus. Perhaps the most significant trend is that the use of the expression "wife of Augustus" markedly decreases following the death of Augustus. During Augustus' lifetime, this relationship is expressed in nearly 70 percent of the inscriptions. Following the death of Augustus, "wife of Augustus" [*Livia Augusti*] decreases to 16 percent of inscriptions. The only occurrence of this designation following the death of Livia is dated to the Claudian period from Haluntium (Bartman 1999, epig. cat. 73).

Along with a decrease in the use of "wife of Augustus" following 14 CE, there is a higher tendency to mention Liva/Julia on her own merits without noting any relationship to a male figure. During the Tiberian era, there is also an increase in "mother of Tiberius" and "daughter of Drusus."

The total number of examples from the era following Livia's death is probably too small to draw many sweeping conclusions; however, one trend is quite clear. The relationship expressions used most frequently during her lifetime—"wife of Augustus," "mother of Tiberius," and "daughter of Drusus"—drop out of use almost entirely. With this background, the two examples of "daughter of Augustus" are not insignificant.

How does all this relate to Josephus' reference to Bethsaida/Julias in *Antiquities*? It may be surprising at first glance, but Josephus is quite consistent with the usage displayed in this survey of inscriptions. He notes that the rebuilt Betharamphtha was called Julias for the wife of the emperor and that the rebuilt Bethsaida was called Julias for the daughter of the Caesar. The general interpretation is that the work on Betharamphtha was completed during the Augustan era and quite possibly dedicated in 13 CE (Jones 1937, 237–77). As noted above, the work on this city would likely have begun following the completion of Sepphoris, which was dedicated in 8 CE, and it would likely have been complete well before Antipas undertook construction of the new city of Tiberias, dedicated in 20 CE. The tradition that Betharamphtha also went by the name Livia (Eusebius *Onom.* 12, 16,

44, 48, 168), has led to the general assumption that it was built and renamed Livia prior to the death of Augustus, and then renamed again as Julias when Livia was adopted into the Julian *familia* (Jones 1937). The likely year for the dedication of this city was 13 CE in honor of Livia's seventieth birthday and her fiftieth anniversary of marriage with Augustus. Thus, when Josephus mentions that Betharamphtha was renamed in honor of the wife of the emperor, this was the most fitting designation for Livia during the Augustan period and especially appropriate to this jubilee year of their marriage. The only complicating factor is the renaming from Livia to Julias, but Josephus has kept it simple.

Likewise, when Josephus mentions that Bethsaida was renamed in honor of Julia the daughter of the emperor, this was fitting for that period following Livia's death. This was that crucial time leading up to her deification by Claudius in 42 CE, a time when individuals like Velleius Paterculus described her as more like the gods than humans. Thus the recent archaeological evidence from Bethsaida points to a Roman-style temple likely in her honor, and the coins minted by Philip in 30 CE identify her as the goddess Demeter/Ceres and designate her with the epithet Καρποφορος [karpophoros/fruit bearing] as continuing benefactress (Grether 1946, 222–52; Strickert 2002b, 65–91). At this point in her recognition, contemporaries were less likely to speak of her as "wife of Caesar" and more as "daughter of Caesar." This designation places her in the most prominent position, perched between past and present emperors and the bridge to future successors in the Julio-Claudian dynasty.

Perhaps one might argue from a stylistic standpoint that this change by Josephus in a matter of lines from "wife of the emperor" to "daughter of the emperor" is unnecessarily confusing; however, a closer look at this section demonstrates that Josephus has knit things together rather carefully. The following table illustrates the balanced structure of *Antiquities* 18.27–28. When the literary structure is outlined, it is evident that Josephus has written a balanced account concerning two rulers and four cities. For each city, both the old name and the new name are given with a short description of the building activity. In two cases, the location is mentioned and twice the reader is told explicitly who is being honored.

More precisely, it is interesting to note that each ruler has dedicated two cities, the first one for Augustus, the second for Julia—and

Table 2. Literary structure of *Antiquities* 18.27–28

Builder	Old Name	Building Process	New Name	Person Honored
Herod Antipas	Sepphoris	made it the ornament of Galilee	Autocratoris	
Herod Antipas	Betharamptha	threw a wall around	Julias	for the wife of Autocrator [the emperor]
Philip	Paneas at the source of the Jordan	made improvements	Caesarea	
Philip	Bethsaida on Lake Gennesaret	added residents and strength	Julias	for the daughter of Caesar

each pair is presented in correct chronological order. What is glaring in this description is the omission of the city of Tiberias—a third city built by Herod Antipas included by Josephus in the parallel passage in *Jewish War*—yet this would disrupt the parallelism. The balance strongly suggests that both women are the same person, Livia/Julia.

As a skillful writer, Josephus has produced a highly parallel structure, yet he has taken pains to use a variety of expressions so that he does not repeat himself. For example, he uses ἠγόρευεν, προσαγορεύει, ὀνομάζεί, and ὁμώνυμον ἐκάλεσεν respectively for the naming of the cities—again the first two are linked linguistically, as are the last two. Likewise, he takes care to describe the building process in four distinct ways.

Some of the credit for the varied language is of course due to the builders themselves. Herod Antipas and Philip both named a city for Augustus, yet each employed a different one of his titles in naming a city—Herod used *Autocrator* and Philip used *Caesar*.[13] Josephus, realizing this, cleverly repeated that same title in reference to the second city in each pair. Herod built a city named *Autocratoris*, so he constructed a second city named for "Julia…of *Autocrator*." Philip built a city named *Caesarea*, so he constructed a second city named for "Julia…of *Caesar*." Josephus has done a masterful job.

Our modern reading has misunderstood Josephus by calling for parallelism in expression (or rather identical expressions) rather than noticing the parallelism in structure. From a historical point of view, there is no question that both cities called Julias were named for the same person, both the wife of Augustus. Yet the last thing one should expect in the last line of this section would be "he named it after Julia, the Caesar's wife." Josephus seems to have gone out of the way not to repeat himself. Two different titles for Augustus are used. Why should not two different titles be used for Julia? The use of both *Autocrator* and *Caesar* helps to give a better understanding of Augustus' role. To speak of Livia/Julia as both "wife of the *autocrator*" and "daughter of *Caesar*" is to enhance her standing.

The epigraphic evidence shows that Livia/Julia was referred to as "daughter of Caesar" in the decade of the 30s CE and that Josephus' description of the founding of Bethsaida/Julias is consistent with that pattern. Yet a critical question is whether one would expect Josephus to be familiar with the expression "daughter of Caesar" for Livia/Julia when he wrote *Antiquities* in the mid-90s CE. There are two possible explanations: Josephus was already familiar with the expression from his younger days in Galilee; or Josephus became familiar with this expression later in Rome during the twenty years between writing *Jewish War* and *Antiquities*. The fact that the only other documentation for the expression "daughter of Caesar"—one literary text and two inscriptions—are found outside of Palestine would support the second option. One might argue that a comparison of the parallel passages between *Jewish War* 2.168 and *Antiquities* 18.27–28 would support the idea that, in the latter, Josephus has merely added these new data about Julia into the description of newly built cities from the former work. At closer analysis, however, the *Jewish War* passage is a totally different account. The only agreement is that Herod and Philip were responsible for the construction of four cities. While the latter work mentions Sepphoris, Julias, Caesarea, and Julias, the earlier work has Caesarea, Julias, Tiberias, and Julias, following a geographical order from north to south along the Jordan River valley (Sepphoris is thus omitted). The style of the earlier description is short and to the point. A single verb κτίζει [founded] commands the construction of all four cities. Former names are not related, nor is there any mention of the naming process itself in the *Jewish War* text. It is clear that Josephus has at his disposal in *Antiquities* 18.27–28 much more information than simply the explanation that Julias was named for "the daughter of Caesar"—including his only reference to the biblical name Bethsaida.

This leads to an alternate explanation. Was Josephus familiar with traditions about Bethsaida/Julias and its naming after the "daughter of Caesar" from his earlier experience in Galilee? From *Jewish War* by itself, one would have to answer in the negative. There are three different occasions when Julias is mentioned (*J.W.* 2.168, 3.57, 3.515), yet in each case the passage has the tenor of a geographical listing of cities (with no depth of information) like the references in Pliny and Ptolemy. In one respect, this is clearly part of his stated goal not to delve too far in the past (*J.W.* 1.17). Yet there is something more. It is Josephus' even later work, *Life*, which leads one to think that he has not been totally forthcoming in his description in the *Jewish War*. According to his autobiographical work, one of the major battles of the Galilean campaign took place just outside the city of Julias (*Life* 398–406). His own personal reminiscences of his leadership role in battle, of his horse stumbling, of his injury breaking his wrist, and his detailed topographical descriptions consistent with current archaeological surveys of the area, all leave no doubt concerning his familiarity with Julias. The character of this later work as a defense of his own leadership certainly has something to do with his eventual recording of this episode. Yet, it is still enigmatic why this too was not included in the *Jewish War*, as well as more detailed descriptions of Julias. The surprise may be that *Antiquities* only mentions the city Julias twice, although the more detailed description of its founding (18.28) and a report about the death of Philip in Julias (18.106–8) imply early knowledge about the city. There is no reason to think that they do not present a relatively accurate picture of the founding of the city based on material familiar to Josephus from his Galilean days.

The description of the founding of Julias, of course, is still of a different character from the personal reminiscing in *Life*. Born in Jerusalem in the first year of Caligula's rule, 37 CE, Josephus had no firsthand knowledge of those early years following the dedication of Julias and apparently was without any Galilean experience prior to the Jewish revolt, when he was chosen as leader of the Galilean forces. Presumably, this is where he began to gather information about the cities of Galilee and Gaulanitis from local histories and military intelligence reports. The description of cities in *Antiquities* 18.27–28 does exhibit this kind of character: Herod "fortified" Sepphoris and "threw a wall around" the Perean Julias. When he rebuilt Bethsaida/Julias, Philip added πλήθει τε οἰκητόρων καί τῇ ἄλλῃ δυνάμει, which Louis Feldman renders as "by adding residents and strengthening the fortifications." In a very careful word study, Smith has noted that Josephus most often uses the word δύναμις to refer to military forces.[14] He concludes that "it is probably best to interpret this phrase as a reference to the stationing of an additional military contingent, perhaps a garrison, at Julias" (1999, 339).

The one piece that doesn't fit as intelligence gathering is the explanation of the name Julias in terms of "daughter of Caesar." It could be the result of a creative hand, an allusion to an obscure reference about Livia tucked in the recesses of the mind. It could also be the character of personal reminiscence from a visit to Julias. Prominent in that first-century city was a temple to Livia/Julia.

In recent archaeological excavations at Bethsaida/Julias, Arav uncovered a Roman-style temple from the early first century. Identification has been established on the basis of floor plan and architectural remains as well as the discovery of a Roman incense shovel (Arav 1999, 18–24, 34–44; Arav, Freund, and Shroder 2000, 54–56). Arav suggests that this temple was dedicated to Livia and employed in the imperial cult, quite possibly at the time of the city dedication. Rather significant is the discovery of numerous fragments of clay figurines found in the vicinity of the temple—presumably for residents to purchase and take home. In one case, the fragment displays the folds of a draped cloth worn over the *chiton*. In another, a partial tiara is covered by a veil, possibly denoting a priestess figure (Arav 1999, 22, 32, figs. 16, 21). Yet, for most of these fragments, a more precise identification is impossible.

One figurine (fig. 2) does lend itself to identification since the upper portion of the woman's body is preserved (Arav 1995, 21, fig. 13). This four-centimeter-tall clay fragment (with tints of red remaining) shows a veiled female with the melonlike hairstyle typical for Livia during this period. Perhaps the closest parallel is found in a two-meter-tall white marble sculpture from Velletri where the distinct waves of hair frame the face (Strickert 2004, fig. 7).[15] Another is the statue of Livia from Velleia (figs. 1 and 3). It is reasonable to think that these figurines may have been miniature copies of a cult statue of Livia/Julia that stood at Bethsaida/Julias.[16] It is clear from his coins that the tetrarch Philip was bold enough to use human images, usually those of the imperial family. Some of those coin depictions bear characteristics that suggest copying from a statue familiar to Philip's own

Fig. 2. "Livia," clay figurine. Israel Antiquities Authority

Fig. 3. "Velleia Livia—head." Madrid Archaeological Museum

subjects. Such a statue of Livia/Julia in this rebuilt city of Bethsaida/ Julias could well have left a lasting impression on Josephus.

CONCLUSION

Scholars have long misunderstood Josephus' reference in *Antiquites* 18.28 to the renaming of Bethsaida/Julias in honor of Julia, the Caesar's daughter. It was often a case of mistaken identity, with the honor given to the dishonored daughter of Augustus and Scribonia. Recent archaeological discoveries, especially coin finds and artifacts related to a first-century temple, have demonstrated that the city was dedicated in 30 CE not to the younger, disgraced Julia, but to Livia/Julia the wife of Augustus. It is no longer necessary to conclude that Josephus' reporting was either careless or mistaken. His choice of epithet for Livia/Julia as "Caesar's daughter" was consistent with both literary and epigraphic examples for the decades following her death. Composing this paragraph with rich terminology, including both "wife of the emperor" and "daughter of Caesar," he described the impact of both Augustus and Livia/Julia on the founding of cities in first-century Palestine, among them Bethsaida/Julias.

CHAPTER NOTES

*Unless otherwise indicated, all translations are my own.

1. A shorter form of this article was published as "Josephus' Reference to Julia, Caesar's Daughter: *Jewish Antiquities* 18.27–28," *Journal of Jewish Studies* 53 (2002): 27–34.
2. Suetonius *Aug.*, 65; Dio *Hist.* 55.10.12–16. For a general summary of Roman evidence concerning Julia and Livia, see Greene 1999, 307–28, esp. 316–17.
3. Schürer 1973, 2:70. Louis Feldman footnotes Schürer's interpretation in the 1965 Loeb Classical Library edition of *Jewish Antiquities* (9:25).
4. Josephus *J.W.* 2.167. Here he mentions that Salome's will bequeathed land to Julia, wife of Augustus. In contrast, Josephus had only mentioned Julia, the daughter of Caesar, on one occasion (*J.W.* 2.25).
5. Greene 1999, 313. Greene credits this to a private correspondence between Louis Feldman and Richard Freund dated May 9, 1994.
6. The examples cited are of Straton's Tower (*Ant.* 13.313), Pacorus (*Ant.* 14.333), Antipater (*Ant.* 17.19), and two Egyptians (*Ag. Ap.* 1. 232–33).
7. Smith (1999, 337) does briefly call attention to this possibility though viewing it as without merit.
8. Rose 1997, 121–26, cat. 50; Bartman 1999, 123–26, epig. cat. 33. For a view that the group is dated to the Tiberian period, see Hausmann 1989, 233–45; Boschung 1989, 97.
9. Elizabeth Bartman (1999, 114–16) documents how a major shift occurs in the portrait depiction of Livia's hairstyle beginning with the *Salus Augusta* coin minted by Tiberius in 22 CE following her recovery from serious illness. One trend in development is the melonlike, wavy style as is typical of this piece and also a figurine discovered in the Roman temple in Bethsaida/ Julias. See Arav 1995, 21.
10. The 0.71 m. by 0.67 m. marble plaque is currently in Museo Archiologico, Parma, cat. 33. Bartman 1999, 211, epig. cat. no. 76.
11. The 0.74 meters by 0.61 meters by 0.36 meters marble base is from Aphrodisias. Rose 1997, 164, cat. 104; Bartman 1999, 210, epig. cat. 70. J. Reynolds (1980, 79–82) counters the view that it belongs to Livia.
12. Bartman (1999, 123) suggests that the two sculpture inscriptions dated during the reign of Caligula reflect his desire to subordinate his Claudian side to the Julian. Thus the expression "daughter of Augustus."
13. This is often lost in translation. In the Loeb edition, Feldman here translates both αὐτοκράτορ and Καίσαρος with "the emperor's."
14. Smith (1999, 338) notes that the term δύναμις occurs 538 times in Josephus, used throughout all four works. While he finds no real parallel for "fortifications" (Feldman's translation), 372 times it refers to bands of military troops and armies. More precisely, he speaks of garrisons in cities on nine occasions: *Ant.* 8.303, 393; 13.16; *J.W.* 1.46, 210; 2.332, 448; 5.510; and *Life* 411. See Smith 1999, 345 n. 302.

15. Other parallels noted by Bartman include a St. Petersburg gem of Livia holding a bust of Augustus (see Strickert 2004, fig. 12; Bartman 1999, fig. 81); the Paestum Livia with veil and wavy hair (Bartman 1999, figs. 88–89); the Lusitanian Aeminium Livia (Bartman 1999, fig. 150); and the Grumentum Livia (Bartman 1999, fig. 136).
16. For numerous parallels demonstrating Livia/Julia's role within the imperial cult, see Grether 1946, 222–52.

Fred Strickert

LITERATURE CITED

Arav, Rami. 1995. Bethsaida Excavations: Preliminary Report 1987–1993. In Arav and Freund 1995.

———. 1999. Bethsaida Excavations: Preliminary Report 1994–1996. In Arav and Freund 1999.

Arav, Rami, and Richard Freund, eds. 1995. *Bethsaida: A City by the North Shore of the Sea of Galilee.* Vol. 1. Kirksville, Mo.: Thomas Jefferson University Press.

———. 1999. *Bethsaida: A City by the North Shore of the Sea of Galilee.* Vol. 2. Kirksville, Mo.: Truman State University Press.

Arav, Rami, Richard A. Freund, and John F. Shroder, Jr. 2000. Bethsaida Rediscovered: Long-Lost City Found North of Galilee Shore. *Biblical Archaeology Review* 26 (Jan/Feb): 44–56.

Bartman, Elizabeth. 1999. *Portraits of Livia: Imaging the Imperial Woman in Augustan Rome.* Cambridge: Cambridge University Press.

Boschung, Dietrich. 1989. *Die Bildnisse des Caligula.* Das römische Herrscherbild 4. Berlin: Gebr. Mann.

Dio Cassius. 1914–17. *Roman History.* Translated by Earnest Cary. 9 vols. Loeb Classical Library. London: W. Heinemann.

Eusebius. 2003. *Onomasticon: Palestine in the Fourth Century.* Jerusalem: Carta.

Ferrill, Arthur. 1980. Augustus and His Daughter: A Modern Myth. *Studies in Latin Literature and Roman History* 11, Collection Latomus 168:332–46.

Greene, John T. 1999. The Honorific Naming of Bethsaida-Julias. In Arav and Freund 1999.

Grether, Gertrude. 1946. Livia and the Roman Imperial Cult. *American Journal of Philology* 67:222–52.

Hahn, Ulrike. 1994. *Die Frauen des Römischen Kaiserhauses und ihre Ehrungen im Griechischen Osten Anhand Epigraphischer und numismatischer Zeugnisse von Livia bis Sabina.* Saarbrücken: Druckerei und Verlag.

Hausmann, U. 1989. Zur Statuengruppe von Veleia. *Quaderni ticinesi di numismatica e antichita classiche* 18 (1989): 233–45.

Jones, A. H. M. 1937. *The Cities of the Eastern Roman Provinces.* Oxford: Clarendon Press.

Josephus. 1965. *Jewish Antiquities.* Translated by Louis Feldman. Vol. 9. Loeb Classical Library. Cambridge: Harvard University Press.

———. 1976. *Jewish War.* Translated by H. St. J. thackeray. Vol. 2. Loeb Classical Library. Cambridge: Harvard University Press.

Kindler, Arie. 1971. A Coin of Herod Philip—the Earliest Portrait of a Herodian Ruler, *Israel Exploration Journal* 21:162–63.

———. 1999. The Coins of the Tetrarch Philip and Bethsaida. In Arav and Freund 1999.

Kuhn, H. W., and Rami Arav. 1991. The Bethsaida Excavations: Historical and Archaeological Approaches. In *The Future of Early Christianity*, edited by Birger Pearson. Minneapolis: Fortress.

Meshorer, Ya'akov. 1982. *Ancient Jewish Coinage.* Vol. 2, *Herod the Great through Bar Cochba.* Dix Hills, N.Y.: Amphora Books.

———. 2001. *A Treasury of Jewish Coins: From the Persian Period to Bar Kochba.* Nyack, N.Y.: Amphora Books.

Perkounig, Claudia-Martina. 1995. *Livia Drusilla—Iulia Augusta: Das politische Porträt der ersten Kaiserin Roms.* Vienna: Böhlau Verlag.

Pliny, the Elder. 1938–63. *Natural History.* Translated by Harris Rackham. 10 vols. Loeb Classical Library. Cambridge: Harvard University Press.

Ptolemy. 1980. *Geographia.* Translated by F. E. Robbins. Loeb Classical Library. Cambridge: Harvard University Press.

Reynolds, J. 1980. The Origins and Beginnings of the Imperial Cult at Aphrodisias, *Proceedings of the Cambridge Philological Society* 206:79–82.

Ritter, Hans-Werner. 1972. Livias Erhebung zur Augusta. *Chrion* 2:313–38.

Rose, C. Brian. 1997. *Dynastic Commemoration and Imperial Portraiture in the Julio-Claudian Period.*Cambridge: Cambridge University Press.

Schürer, Emil. 1973. *The History of the Jewish People in the Age of Jesus Christ.* Vol. 2. Rev. ed. by Geza Vermes and F. Millar. Edinburgh: Clark.

Smith, Mark D. 1999. A Tale of Two Julias: Julia, Julias, and Josephus. In Arav and Freund 1999.

Strickert, Fred. 1995. The Founding of Bethsaida-Julias: Evidence from the Coins of Philip. *Shofar* 13:40–51.

———. 2002a. Josephus' Reference to Julia, Caesar's Daughter: *Jewish Antiquities* 18.27–28. *Journal of Jewish Studies* 53:27–34.

———. 2002b. The First Woman to Be Portrayed on a Jewish Coin: Julia Sebaste. *Journal for the Study of Judaism in the Persian, Hellenistic, and Roman Periods.* 33:65–91.

———. 2004. The Dying Grain Which Bears Much Fruit: John 12:24, The Livia Cult, and Bethsaida. In Rami Arav and Richard Freund, eds. *Bethsaida: A City by the North Shore of the Sea of Galilee.* Vol. 3. Kirksville, Mo.: Truman State University Press.

Suetonius. 1914. *Suetonius.* Translated by J. C. Rolfe. 2 vols. Loeb Classical Library. London: W. Heinemann.

Tacitus, Cornelius. 1977. *The Annals of Imperial Rome.* Translated by M. Grant. Penguin Classics. Harmondsworth: Penguin Books.

Velleius Paterculus. 1924. *History of Rome.* Translated by Frederick W. Shipley. Loeb Classical Library. London: W. Heinemann.

Heinz-Wolfgang Kuhn

Bethsaida in the Gospel of Mark

T HE EXTENT TO WHICH MARK, the oldest Gospel, contains information about the geographical activity of Jesus in Galilee and the
Gaulanitis can be demonstrated by its reference especially to Bethsaida.[1] The occurrences of Bethsaida in this Gospel (6:45, 8:22) can
help demonstrate what Mark knew about the places where Jesus had
worked. The basis for this hypothesis is that the Q saying in Luke
10:13–15, parallel to Matthew 11:20–24 (in modern research abbrevi-
ated as Q 10:13–15), actually reflects the historical activity of Jesus.
Arguments for the authenticity of the Q saying or at least for its
extreme proximity to the historical activity of Jesus were presented in
1991 in the Festschrift for Helmut Koester (Kuhn, in Kuhn and Arav
1991, 78) and more explicitly in 1993 in Münster, where the Bethsaida
Excavations Project was presented for the first time at the International
Meeting of the Society of Biblical Literature (Kuhn 1995a, 248–51; see
also the short summary in Kuhn 2000, 216). The arguments are reca-
pitulated here. In the older version of Luke, the saying reads:

> Woe to you, Chorazin! Woe to you, Bethsaida! For if the mighty
> deeds done in you had taken place in Tyre and Sidon, they
> would have repented long ago, sitting in sackcloth and ashes.
> But for Tyre and Sidon it will be more tolerable at the judgment
> than for you. And you, Capernaum, will you be exalted to
> heaven? You will be brought down to Hades. (10:13–15)

Two remarks first: this Q saying is without doubt tradition and
not merely a redactional wording by Q. Luke 11:31–32 parallel to Matthew 12:41–42, also from Q, is not as close to our saying as to constitute

115

an argument against its authenticity. There are three main arguments for the antiquity of the saying:[2]

1. *The criterion of convergence* (sometimes not distinguished from the closely related criterion of coherence): a saying attributed to Jesus fits into the critical picture of the historical Jesus on the whole and coheres not only with one or several presumably authentic sayings. What is the message of Jesus in our saying? Three smaller Jewish places are condemned in a clearly offensive way as being less penitent than the population of the notorious heathen cities Tyre and Sidon (see esp. Isa. 23 and Ezek. 26–28), whose willingness to be converted at the time is, according to the Hebrew Bible, by no means taken for granted. This would be consistent with Jesus' provocative manner of speaking, here regarding his own people (Lam. 4:6 is only a remote parallel), and with his acute consciousness of his mission (see, for example, the authentic saying Luke 11:20, parallel to Matt. 12:28; Kuhn 1966, 190–93).

2. *The criterion of dissimilarity to later Christian preaching:* a saying attributed to Jesus may be authentic when it is not in agreement with the preaching of the later church. The church, looking back on Jesus' entire work, would hardly have reduced here the ministry of Jesus simply to his miracles, but would also have mentioned his preaching (Hellenistic missionaries who primarily told miracle stories of Jesus are not recognizable as the source of this saying) (cf. Georgi 1964; Kuhn 1970, 302–8; 1971, 211–13; Koester 1990, 201–5).

3. *The criterion of dissimilarity to the situation of later Christian communities* (especially at Capernaum, which is emphasized by contrast in the saying of Jesus): a saying attributed to Jesus may be authentic when it does not fit into the later situation of Christian communities. According to Mark 1:21–34, a sizable Christian community probably existed at Capernaum already at the time of the composition of the Gospel around 70 CE (Kuhn 1995b, 72–82). The extremely negative view of this town expressed in this saying must therefore be older than the positive development at Capernaum; however, the saying does coincide with other older sources in placing Capernaum at the

center of Jesus' activity.[3] Chorazin does not occur at all in the subsequent canonical tradition.

Although the Q saying identifies the three places mentioned as locations of Jesus' activity with historical accuracy (indeed the locations form a triangle at the northern end of the Sea of Galilee), it appears that even the earliest evangelist no longer knew where Jesus really worked. Chorazin is not mentioned in the Gospel of Mark, and Bethsaida is only mentioned in passing. As far as Capernaum is concerned, it may be given special attention in the Gospel of Mark not because the evangelist was documenting historical facts, but because in his time, according to Mark 1, Capernaum had a Christian community of some importance that met in a private house attributed to Peter and located a short distance from the synagogue (Kuhn 1995b, 72–82). Conversely, the saying seems not to presuppose Christian communities in Tyre and Sidon that are known to have existed not later than the 50s CE (Acts 21:3–7).

There are three major problems related to the occurrence of Bethsaida in the Gospel of Mark. The first problem is the omission of the so-called Bethsaida section that is in the Gospel of Luke. One interpretation claims that Bethsaida does not appear at all in an older version of the Gospel of Mark, because the whole passage 6:45–8:26, in which Bethsaida is mentioned (6:45 and 8:22), was added later (Koester 1990, 284–86). The argument for this view is that the Gospel of Luke, which to a large extent follows the Gospel of Mark, does not include the Bethsaida section in Mark 6:45–8:26 (see how Luke's Gospel continues from 9:17 to 9:18).[4] But the fact that it is only in the Lukan version of the feeding of the five thousand (9:10b–17), just before the missing passage, that Bethsaida is mentioned (9:10b) seems to be evidence that Luke knew this passage even though he left it out.

Luke's omission begins with the first mention of Bethsaida in the Gospel of Mark and ends with its second and final occurrence. The hypothesis that Luke inserted the place-name Bethsaida, which frames the entire omission, as a kind of replacement just before the omission of the segment now missing in his Gospel, is a very probable explanation.

A somewhat less probable possibility is that in an older Gospel of Mark, which Luke would have had in front of him, the passage Mark 6:52 (not already from 6:45 on) to 8:26 was missing and that the itinerary of this hypothetical older Gospel of Mark led Jesus directly from the first reference to Bethsaida to the villages of Caesarea Philippi.[5] In this case Luke omitted only Mark 6:45–51, for whatever reasons, and instead localized the preceding feeding of the five thousand at Bethsaida. But this is difficult to explain.[6] Anyhow, in both cases the insertion of Bethsaida into the feeding of the five thousand would be a pure editorial construction of Luke without any basis in the tradition.

There is a better explanation for the absence of Mark 6:45–8:26 in Luke (see table 1). Luke may have seen the need to shorten the material from Mark due to the addition of material from Q. The reason for Luke's deletion of this particular passage can be explained by the fact that for the Gospel of Luke (despite the miracle stories 7:1–10 [parallel to Matt. 8:5–13] and 8:26–39 [parallel to Mark 5:1–20]), ministry to the heathen is the exclusive task of the church (see Hahn 1965, 111–19 [Engl. version, 128-36]) (cf. 24:46–47; explicitly in the Gospel of Matthew: 10:5–6; 15:24 [despite 8:5–13]), whereas Mark's "heathen passage" (which Luke apparently recognized as such) comes precisely in 7:1–8:21, in which Jesus' activity among the heathen (7:24–8:9) is framed by a contrast with Jewish authorities (7:1–23 and 8:10ff.) (see Kuhn 1971, 220; 1995b, 65, 86). This theme of Jesus' ministry to the heathen in 7:1–8:21 could therefore, apart from the need of shortening, be the reason for Luke's omission of the section Mark 6:45–8:26, that is, from Bethsaida to Bethsaida (Mark 6:45 and 8:22).

Table 1. Markan passage omitted by Luke (Mark 6:45–8:26)

	MIRACLES		
6:45–52 (v. 45: Bethsaida)	The last of six miracles (4:35ff.)		
6:53–56		Longer summary (corresponding to 3:7–12)	
7:1–23		Confrontation with Jewish authorities	
7:24–8:9	JESUS TURNS TO HEATHEN TERRITORY (Tyre, Sidon; Decapolis)		
8:10–21		Confrontation with Jewish authorities (and transition to the motif of the disciples' incomprehension in 8:27–10:45)	
8:22–26 (v. 22: Bethsaida)		Symbolic healing of a blind (corresponding to 10:46–52)	
	FROM CAESAREA PHILIPPI TO JERUSALEM		

A further pointer to the originality of the Bethsaida section in the Gospel of Mark is that the redactional work in the Bethsaida section 6:45–8:26 and in the rest of the Gospel arranges the material in such a similar and coherent way that two different redactors are very unlikely.[7] It is therefore much more probable (Kuhn, in Kuhn and Arav 1991, 78–79 n. 4; Kuhn 1995a, 247–48) that Luke simply omitted the entire Bethsaida section, starting with the strangely unsuccessful journey (Mark 6:45–52), for the reasons mentioned above.

Two more points are important in understanding the references to Bethsaida in relation to the Bethsaida section: Mark may have omitted the journey to Bethsaida in 6:53 (that is, changed the destination from Bethsaida to Ginosar)[8] because he wanted to withhold the journey to Caesarea Philippi with its (for Mark central) confession of Peter (8:27–30) and to make a connection between Jesus' sojourn in the Gaulanitis (8:22–9:29) and the final breaking off of his public work in Galilee (see Mark 9:30, where Jesus' last stay in Galilee seems to begin). The reference to Capernaum in the parallel story in John 6:17 instead of Bethsaida as in Mark 6:45 may originate from the so-called Semeia source, which the Gospel of John probably used. But the place-name Bethsaida, which is rarer in the tradition of Jesus, could be the older one.

The reference to Bethsaida in Luke 9:10 is understandable if Luke found the place-name Bethsaida in a section he did not reproduce: most likely Mark 6:45–8:26. Originally the story of the feeding, placed in a "remote place" (the feeding of five thousand: Mark 6:31, 32, 35; Matt. 14:13, 15; Luke 9:10 [variant reading], 12; cf. also the feeding of four thousand: Mark 8:4, Matt. 15:33), had nothing to do with Bethsaida. The story of the feeding of five thousand in John 6 (though there is no mention of a remote place) also does not suggest an older localization of the story at Bethsaida (Kuhn 1995a, 246–48). In the Gospel of Mark, the feeding of the five thousand occurs in a place *from where* Jesus sends his disciples away to Bethsaida (6:32–45), and in the Gospel of Matthew the name Bethsaida does not occur at all in this context because it was omitted from the passage where it occurs in Mark (6:45), that is, in Matthew 14:22.

The second major problem relating to Bethsaida in the Gospel of Mark is the localization of the healing of a blind man (Mark 8:22–26). The only occasion on which Jesus' activities in this place are mentioned in the Gospel of Mark is Jesus' journey to Caesarea Philippi.

According to Mark, Jesus left Galilee three times during his activity there (1:14–9:50): first during a series of four miracles in 4:35–5:43, when Jesus obviously goes to the Decapolis from the western bank of the Galilean Sea (5:1–20); then in the long "heathen passage" (7:24–8:9) in which Jesus first stays in the region of Tyre and in Sidon and then returns again to the Decapolis (7:31); and finally in his journey to the villages of Caesarea Philippi via Bethsaida,[9] where Jesus heals a blind man, and stays in the Gaulanitis apparently until 9:29. The redactor Mark does indeed possess sound geographical knowledge of Israel/Palestine: just as he has Jesus enter Jerusalem via Jericho (10:46), so in this passage he leads Jesus to Caesarea Philippi via Bethsaida (8:22). There must have been a road connecting the capital of the tetrarchy of Philip and the place in which he died, Julias (Josephus *Ant.* 18.4.6 §108), by the time of the upgrading of Bethsaida to the city of Julias about 30 CE.[10] At the time the Gospel of Mark was written (about 70 CE) the former territory of Philip, including Bethsaida and Caesarea Philippi,[11] had been under the rule of Agrippa II and at that time Jews lived there together with "Syrians" (Josephus *J.W.* 3.3.5 §56–57). The great-grandson of Herod the Great had received territories there in 53 CE and also held later parts of Galilee at the western shore of the Lake and Peraea.[12] Without doubt the road connection between Bethsaida and the capital Caesarea Philippi still existed.

There is no evidence that the village named as Bethsaida in Mark 8:22–23, 26 actually was named Bethsaida in the pre-Markan tradition that passed down the story. Even Mark himself, in a redactional phrase in 8:26b, refers to the locality at the end of the story as a village [κώμη], although Bethsaida had been a city [πόλις] since about 30 CE.[13] One can therefore draw the conclusion that neither the place-name Julias nor its expansion into a city had much impact on the population's perception. Since Philip died only three or four years later in 33/34 CE, there was not much time to expand the new city.[14] Both in the canonical Gospels and the rabbinic literature—as opposed to Josephus—the place is always referred to as Bethsaida; in pagan literature, on the other hand, it is referred to as Julias. The designation "city" can be found in the canonical Gospels in Luke 9:10 and John 1:44, whereas "village" only appears here in the Gospel of Mark (8:23, 26). As far as the Gospel of Luke is concerned, one can conclude from the alteration of the Markan text from κώμη to πόλις that Luke must have known about the "city" (Kuhn, in Kuhn and Arav 1991, 82).[15]

The question whether Mark first inserted Bethsaida into the traditional story of the blind man can be answered in three possible ways. The first possible solution is that the tradition localized the story at Bethsaida. This is not very likely, however, as the place-name only appears in the introductory sentence (Mark 8:22a), which must be attributed to Mark. This is especially clear in this case, since the introduction Καὶ ἔρχονται εἰς Βηθσαϊδάν does not fit well with the story following, which right at the beginning (8:23a) places Jesus "outside the village" (Bultmann 1931, 363–64 [Engl. version, 338, 340]). Furthermore, Mark symbolically frames the whole passage between Peter's confession and the entrance into Jerusalem with the healing of a blind at the beginning and end of the passage respectively (8:22–26 and 10:46–52). The meaning for the Gospel of Mark is that Jesus heals the eyes of the blind on the way to his passion, that the disciples also need to be healed of their spiritual blindness (see note 7). In the story of the healing of the blind outside Jericho, the place-name Jericho seems to be firmly anchored in the text on the basis of Mark 10:46b (see the "conflict of plural and singular" in 10:46, which points in 10:46b to ἐκπορευομένου αὐτοῦ ἀπὸ Ἰεριχώ as traditional) (Bultman 1931, 369 [Engl. version, 344]). It is unlikely, however, that both healing stories also happened to contain a locale Mark needed (Jericho before Jerusalem and Bethsaida on the way to Caesarea Philippi).

Another possibility would be that Mark had some vague knowledge of Jesus' general activity at Bethsaida and therefore mentions the place-name here; however, the Gospel gives no other indication of such knowledge, especially about Bethsaida.

The most likely explanation is that Mark inserted the name here on the basis of Mark 6:45, apparently being aware of the geographical location of Bethsaida (that the above discussed Q saying 10:13–15 speaks of miracles at Bethsaida can, of course, not be an argument for the originality of the place-name in this story). The following question must first be answered: what can be said about the geographical location of Bethsaida on the basis of Jesus' itinerary in Mark. From 8:10 onward, Jesus and his disciples were apparently on the western bank of the Sea of Galilee, after a sojourn in the Decapolis (unfortunately nothing definite can be said about the locality of Dalmanuta, which is mentioned here); from there they return "to the other shore again" by boat (πάλιν ... εἰς τὸ πέραν 8:13) and come to Bethsaida (8:22). As Bethsaida (et-Tell) lies beyond the River Jordan and the shore of the Sea of Galilee bends south at this point, it is possible that Mark had an accurate picture of the location when he had Jesus travel to Caesarea Philippi from Dalmanuta via Bethsaida. The geographical indications of Mark, however vague, also correspond to the assumed location of Bethsaida on et-Tell (or nearby). Similar observations can be made about the rabbinic literature, where Zaidan, or some such place-name, is associated with an abundance of very small fishes, which can be assumed especially for the shallow water at the mouth of the Jordan, at that time much nearer to et-Tell than today (Shroder et al. 1999).[16] The closest description of the location of Bethsaida/Julias (both are identified in Josephus *Ant.* 18.2.1 §28) is found in Josephus *Jewish War* 3.10.7 §515 in connection with his *Life* 72 §399, a description that perfectly matches et-Tell, today a little more than two kilometers from the shore.[17]

The third major problem relates to the first occurrence of Bethsaida in the Gospel of Mark. Two chapters before Jesus' journey via Bethsaida to Caesarea Philippi, Mark 6 recounts how, after the feeding of the five thousand, Jesus sends his disciples on ahead in a boat in the direction of Bethsaida. Again, as in Mark 8:13 (in connection with 8:22), the text says εἰς τὸ πέραν (6:45), when a boat trip to Bethsaida is meant, which speaks for Mark's possessing good geographical knowledge. Prior to this, Jesus apparently stayed on the western shore of the Sea of Galilee after his return from Nazareth (6:32). According to Mark, Jesus sees the disciples from the western shore drifting on the water; he walks across the water to their boat and arrives together with them not at Bethsaida (according to the story because of the wind), but at the fertile countryside with the name of Gennesaret on the northwestern shore of the Sea south of Tell el-Oreimeh (Tel Chinnereth).[18] Whereas the place-name of the original destination, Bethsaida, most probably is part of the story of Jesus walking on the water, the actual arrival in Gennesaret can be considered to be an editorial addition, as it is part of a Markan summary statement (6:53–56).[19] Reading the story, one can hardly conclude that Jesus' walk on the water happened near Bethsaida, an opinion expressed sometimes by scholars interested in this place. Mark changes the traditional destination Bethsaida to Gennesaret, because he wants to place 6:53–8:22 before Jesus' journey to Caesarea Philippi and, perhaps, does not want to put a discussion on purity with Pharisees and scribes from Jerusalem (7:1) into a more or less non-Jewish territory (it is characteristic of the tetrarchy of Philip that "Jewish" coins were minted—against Jewish law—for the first time with human images; for the time the Gospel of Mark was written, see the mixture of Jews and "Syrians" quoted above, p.120). Bethsaida is apparently situated with geographical accuracy in the region beyond the Galilean Sea and the Jordan River. Mark 6:45 is the only passage in the Gospel of Mark that can be based on an older tradition about Jesus' activity at Bethsaida, although the reference in the Gospel is limited now to Jesus sending his disciples "in the direction of Bethsaida" by boat.[20]

Several conclusions can be drawn from this discussion concerning Bethsaida in the Gospel of Mark. In a traditional story taken over by Mark (perhaps from a collection of six miracles, which can be found in Mark 4:35–6:52: see note 8), Jesus sends his disciples on ahead to Bethsaida on the other side of the Lake (6:45). But this place comes too early for the redactor Mark in his outline of Jesus' activity. Before letting him and his disciples go far away to Caesarea Philippi for Peter's confession of who Jesus is (in a heathen territory), he first wants to describe Jesus' ministry to the heathen in contrast to confrontations with Jewish authorities (7:1–8:10ff.). Thus Mark fetches Jesus back from the stormy lake to begin his last mission in his home country west of the Sea of Galilee (6:53), though Mark believes that the territory east of the Jordan River is not on the whole un-Jewish (see the scribes in 9:14 and Jesus' saying in 9:19). The Jewish character of Bethsaida at the time of Jesus' ministry (for the time of the evangelist see above) depends partly on the question whether Jesus worked here before, after, or during the elevation of the village to a city at about 30 CE, which was according to Josephus (*Ant.* 18.2.1 §28) enlarged "by many settlers"—if this is correct, certainly at least partly by non-Jewish colonists (Kuhn, in Kuhn and Arav 1991, 80).

Only after Jesus and his disciples have finished their work in Galilee (1:14–8:21) does Mark send them to the territory of Philip (8:22–9:29). On the way to the villages around Caesarea Philippi, they pass Bethsaida (8:22–26). From the region of Caesarea Philippi, Jesus and his disciples make their way to Jerusalem (see six times ὁδός [way, road], mostly ἐν τῇ ὁδῷ [on the way]: see Kuhn 1971, 224 n. 38), passing Galilee again (9:30–50), but without public activity there (see 9:30). Did Mark have any knowledge about Jesus' staying in the Gaulanitis and in the region of Paneas (cf. Josephus *J.W.* 2.9.2 §168) besides the two stories of Jesus' walking on water and Peter's confession? Mark knew nothing of an activity of Jesus in the Galilean Chorazin and little of an important ministry of Jesus at Bethsaida beyond the Jordan River (see Q 10:13–15); only this story of Jesus' walk on water (6:45–51), which Mark however changes (6:53), could be evidence in the Markan tradition for such activity at Bethsaida. The place-name Bethsaida in 8:22 probably belongs to the Markan redaction, taken over from 6:45.

Mark himself still knows of the location of Bethsaida and seems to localize it accurately beyond the Jordan River. This can be seen by the two occurrences of εἰς τὸ πέραν in 6:45 and 8:13 and the continuation of the journey to Caesarea Philippi in 8:27.

CHAPTER NOTES

All translations are my own. All biblical citations are taken from the *Novum Testamentum Graece*, Nestle-Aland, 27th ed.

1. The data of this article were checked by Lucas Grassal, Paul Benjamin Henke, and Peri Terbuyken. For checking the English of the article, I am very thankful to Prof. Dr. Alasdair Heron from Great Britain, who holds a chair at the University of Erlangen, Germany.
2. In using certain criteria for establishing the authenticity of a saying of Jesus, this article follows the traditional criteria (see Perrin 1967, 39–48) which have been partly misunderstood and partly misused. This is especially true for the criterion of dissimilarity, when one recognizes a dissimilarity compared to Jesus' Jewish environment. Of several new approaches, the most important seems that of Gerd Theissen and Dagmar Winter (1997); they speak in their book on the "Kriterienfrage" of the criterion of plausibility, but this term is very vague. Actually, the two main aspects of Theissen and Winter are related to the two main aspects of the criterion of dissimilarity regarding the Jewish environment and the later church. Since this article uses only the obvious criterion of convergence and the criterion of dissimilarity in its contrast to the later church, which is also part of Theissen's and Winter's "Plausibilitätskriterium," no further discussion of the criteria is needed.
3. Capernaum is not only the most frequently mentioned locality of all Galilee and the Gaulanitis in the canonical Gospels (sixteen times), but it also appears more than any other town or village in older gospel traditions: in Q the saying discussed above and Luke 7:1 with a parallel in Matthew 8:5 and even in John 4:46, and in Mark probably 2:1 (ἐν οἴκῳ εἶναι corresponds with the locality) and perhaps 1:21.
4. Other arguments (Koester 1990, 285), including doublets between the Bethsaida section and the rest of the Gospel (e.g., the feeding of the four thousand in 8:1–9 and the feeding of the five thousand in 6:32–44) and the vocabulary of the section (e.g., besides Mark 4:12, in an allusion to the Septuagint in Isaiah 6:9, συνίημι [to understand] occurs only 6:52, 7:14, 8:17, 21), are less convincing. The two feeding stories have different functions in Mark; three of the four occurrences of συνίημι refer to the same motif that the disciples do not understand the feeding.
5. Mark 6:52, the last verse of the feeding of five thousand, belongs to the same hand as 6:53–8:21 or 6:53–8:26 because of the motif of incomprehension of the feeding. Only in this respect is Walter Schmithals (1986, 337, 339; cf. 50) right to see in his older version of Mark 8:22ff. as following 6:51.
6. If Luke had deleted only this one story (Mark 6:45–51), there would have been no reason for inserting Bethsaida into the preceding story. A replacement makes sense only if the whole Bethsaida section was deleted, since

Luke did not localize Peter's confession in Caesarea Philippi (see Luke
9:18) and thus could not make use of Bethsaida for an intermediate stop.

7. Jesus' ministry among the heathen (Mark 7:24–8:9 resp. 7:1–8:21) and the
confrontation with Jewish authorities (Mark 2:1–3:6), frame Jesus' teaching and miracles (Mark 4:1–5:43, 6:32–52). Mark highlights the theological
significance of all these passages through further contrasting scenes (see
Kuhn 1995b, 61–68, 86). In the same way, Jesus' ministry among the heathen (taking up the theme of the antagonism of Jewish authorities in Mark
2:1–3:6) is framed again by similar confrontations with Jewish authorities
(Mark 7:1–23 and 8:10ff.). In addition, the longer summary 6:53–56, also
belonging to the Bethsaida section, corresponds in its framing function
with the longer summary in 3:7–12. Both summaries frame the whole passage of Mark 3:13–6:52 (Jesus' teaching and miracles including the contrasting scenes in 3:13–35 and 6:1–31). Finally, the healing of the blind in
Mark 8:22–26 corresponds to the healing of the blind in Mark 10:46–52.
Both stories frame the passage Mark 8:27–10:45, characterized by the
incomprehension of the disciples as they accompany Jesus to his Passion,
and thus the healing of the blind is given symbolic significance here (Jesus
takes away their blindness). For details, see Kuhn 1971, 216–22; 1995b,
61–68, 86. In addition, the withdrawal of Jesus into a house to instruct the
disciples also occurs several times: starting in the Bethsaida section in
Mark 7:17, later outside this section in Mark 9:28–29 and 10:10.

8. If Jesus' walking on the water (Mark 6:45–52) had only been an isolated
story, Mark would have been more likely to simply disregard it (because of
Bethsaida, which did not fit in his context as a working place of Jesus)
instead of changing Bethsaida to Ginosar in 6:53. I have suggested elsewhere, for other reasons (Kuhn 1971, 208–9), that Mark's two miracle stories in 6:32–52 were taken from an earlier collection of miracles (4:35–
5:43, 6:32–51).

9. For this route, see Kuhn 2000, 208–11; for all three routes, see Schmeller
1994.

10. On the topic of roads around the Sea of Galilee and in the Gaulanitis in the
first century CE, a thorough investigation is necessary. For the upgrading
of Bethsaida in the year 30 CE, see note 13 below.

11. Caesarea Philippi, again as capital, was briefly and unsuccessfully renamed
Neronias, apparently until the *damnatio memoriae* of Nero in 69 CE
(Schürer 1973, 471–79; 1979, 169–71). For the name Neronias, see Josephus *Ant.* 20.9.4 §211; see also the Agrippa II coin 4911 in Burnett, Amandry, and Ripollès 1992. For the *damnatio memoriae* of Nero, see Seyrig 1950,
286–89; Kienast 1996, 97.

12. Three coins of Agrippa II were found at Bethsaida (et-Tell) before 2003; for
the first coin, see Kindler 1999, no. 113 (no. 112 should not be regarded as
a coin of Agrippa II: see Burnett, Amandry, and Ripollès 1992, 671–72); the
second and third coins were found in 1997 and 2000 and analyzed for the
Bethsaida Excavations Project by Arie Kindler.

13. In contrast to Josephus *Antiquities* 18.2.1 §28, where the upgrading of Bethsaida is apparently dated about thirty years earlier, see his *Jewish War* 2.9.1 §168 for a later dating of the upgrading by Josephus (Kuhn, in Kuhn and Arav 1991, 87-90).

14. This is the reason one should not expect to find many traces of the upgrading in the excavations of Bethsaida (et-Tell); however, four coins of Philip (4 BCE–33/34 CE) and one coin of Antipas (4 BCE–39 CE) were found before 2003. The coins of Philip were found in 1988 (Kindler 1999, no. 110), 1990 (ibid., no. 109), 1994 (ibid., no. 26), and 2000; the coin of Antipas was found in 1995 (ibid., no. 25).

15. Further excavations and geological investigations have shown that Bethsaida (et-Tell) was not destroyed or deserted (at least not finally) during the First Jewish War, but probably existed until the earthquake of 363 CE (Kuhn 1999, 283–84; Arav, Freund, and Shroder 2000, 48). Concerning the destruction of Bethsaida in the Fifth Book of Ezra, a Christian pseudepigraphic (1:11, Spanish recension) see Wolter 2001, 798.

16. See esp. PT Sheqalim 6.50a.32–35. A Baraita tradition ascribed to Rabban Shimon ben Gamliel around the middle of the second century CE speaks of Tzaidan (a place in the area of the Sea of Galilee and Hulah Lake) which was rich in "more than three hundred kinds of [very small] fish" (Kuhn, in Kuhn and Arav 1991, 82; Freund 1995, 287–88).

17. According to Josephus (*J.W.* 3.10.7 §515), the Jordan River "cuts the Lake of Gennesar below (μετά) the town of Julias," that is, the town lies just north of the mouth of the Jordan River. According to *Life* 72 §399, there was a short distance of about two hundred meters between Julias and the camp of Josephus or the Jordan River to the west, respectively. This fits well with the distance that exists today between et-Tell and the eastern arm of the Jordan River. Though some question the identification of et-Tell with Bethsaida, I cannot discover any serious reasons against this assumption, well founded on the basis of Josephus, archaeology, and geology.

18. Regarding Gennesaret, it seems that Volkmar Fritz (1993; see also 1998; 2001) has given up his opinion of 1990 (182) that, after the destruction of Chinnereth about 700 BCE there had been in the Hellenistic era a refounding of the place (though it cannot be precisely located), with the new name Gennosar/Gennesaret, which existed at least until the Middle Ages. Perhaps only the countryside and the Sea of Galilee bore the name Gennesar/Gennesaret in the first century CE (cf. Fritz 2001, 79), but in the earlier rabbinic literature, especially Tosefta Eruvin 7.13, a town or village is presupposed. For the countryside, see Josephus *Jewish War* 3.10.8 §516–521; the spring Josephus called "Capharnaum" must be 'Ein et-Tineh at the southern foot of the hill in question (Fritz 1993, 299a).

19. Dieter Lührmann (1987, 123) tries to explain the occurrence of both localities in Mark 6:45 and 6:53 by interpreting the text in 6:53 as implying that the boat landed between διαπεράσαντες ... and ἦλθον at Bethsaida, which is linguistically insupportable. In the sentence Καὶ διαπεράσαντες ἐπὶ τὴν γῆν ... καὶ προσωρμίσθησαν [And when they crossed over for landing (after

the wind had ceased) they...made fast] the verb προσορμίζειν [make fast] takes up διαπεράσαντες.

20. Harald Hegermann (1964, 132–34, 137, 139) assumes that ὀψίας [in the evening] in two stories where the boat of Jesus and/or his disciples crosses the lake (Mark 6:45, 47; 4:35) and also the boat crossing to Bethsaida in Mark 8:13 and 22a suggest that in Mark's tradition Bethsaida was Jesus' regular overnight stay, but this is nothing more than an imaginative idea. According to 6:45–53, Bethsaida cannot be reached, 4:35–41 does not mention Bethsaida at all, and the events in 8:13 and 22a do not happen happen in the evening. The reason why two storm stories mention an evening (4:35, 6:47) has to do with a dangerous storm typical for the Sea of Galilee, the so-called eastern storm, "which usually starts in the early evening" (Nun 1989, 54). Hegermann (1964, 138) also speaks of Bethsaida as a place where Jesus can avoid Antipas; but this, too, is read into the Gospel of Mark.

LITERATURE CITED

Arav, Rami, and Richard A. Freund, eds. 1995. *Bethsaida: A City by the North Shore of the Sea of Galilee.* Vol. 1. Kirksville, Mo.: Thomas Jefferson University Press.

————. 1999. *Bethsaida: A City by the North Shore of the Sea of Galilee.* Vol. 2. Kirksville, Mo.: Truman State University Press.

Arav, Rami, Richard A. Freund, and John F. Shroder, Jr. 2000. Bethsaida Rediscovered: Long-Lost City Found North of Galilee Shore. *Biblical Archaeology Review* 26:44–56.

Bultmann, Rudolf. 1931. *Die Geschichte der synoptischen Tradition.* 2d ed. Forschungen zu Religion und Literatur des Alten und Neuen Testaments 29. Göttingen: Vandenhoeck & Ruprecht. Translated by John Marsh as *History of the Synoptic Tradition,* 2d ed. Oxford: Basil Blackwell, 1968.

Burnett, Andrew, Michel Amandry, and Pere Pau Ripollès. 1992. *Roman Provincial Coinage.* Vol. 1, *From the death of Caesar to the death of Vitellius (44 BC–AD 69).* Part 1: *Introduction and Catalogue;* Part 2: *Indexes and Plates.* London: British Museum Press; Paris: Bibliothèque Nationale.

Freund, Richard A. 1995. The Search for Bethsaida in Rabbinic Literature. In Arav and Freund 1995.

Fritz, Volkmar. 1990. *Kinneret: Ergebnisse der Ausgrabungen auf dem Tell el-'Orēme am See Gennesaret 1982–1985.* Abhandlungen des Deutschen Palästinavereins 15. Wiesbaden: Otto Harrassowitz.

————. 1993. Art. Chinnereth, Tel. In *The New Encyclopedia of Archaeological Excavations in the Holy Land* 1:299–301.

————. 1998. Ein Tell am See Gennesaret: Neue Ausgrabungen in Kinneret—Zur Frühgeschichte des Heiligen Landes. *Antike Welt: Zeitschrift für Archäologie und Kulturgeschichte* 29:431–38.

————. 2001. Kinneret—eine Stadt als Spiegel der Geschichte Israels. *Welt und Umwelt der Bibel* 20:77–79.

Georgi, Dieter. 1964. *Die Gegner des Paulus im 2. Korintherbrief: Studien zur religiösen Propaganda in der Spätantike.* Wissenschaftliche Monographien zum Alten und Neuen Testament 11. Neukirchen-Vluyn: Neukirchner Verlag. Translated as *The Opponents of Paul in Second Corinthians: A Study in Religious Propaganda in Late Antiquity.* Philadelphia: Fortress Press, 1986.

Hahn, Ferdinand. 1965. *Das Verständnis der Mission im Neuen Testament.* 2d corr. ed. Wissenschaftliche Monographien zum Alten und Neuen Testament 13. Neukirchen-Vluyn: Neukirchener Verlag. Translated by Frank Clarke as *Mission in the New Testament.* Studies in the Biblical Theology 47. London: SCM Press, 1965.

Hegermann, Harald. 1964. Bethsaida und Gennesar: Eine traditions- und redaktionsgeschichtliche Studie zu Mc 4–8. In *Judentum, Urchristentum, Kirche, Festschrift Joachim Jeremias,* edited by W. Eltester. Beihefte zur Zeitschrift für die neutestamentliche Wissenschaft 26. Berlin: Verlag Alfred Töpelmann.

Kienast, Dietmar. 1996. *Römische Kaisertabelle: Grundzüge einer römischen Kaiserchronologie.* 2d ed., rev. and enl. Darmstadt: Wissenschaftliche Buchgesellschaft.

Kindler, Arie. 1999. The Coin Finds at the Excavations of Bethsaida. In Arav and Freund 1999.

Koester, Helmut. 1990. *Ancient Christian Gospels: Their History and Development.* London: SCM Press; Philadelphia: Trinity Press International.

Kuhn, Heinz-Wolfgang. 1966. *Enderwartung und gegenwärtiges Heil: Untersuchungen zu den Gemeindeliedern von Qumran mit einem Anhang über Eschatologie und Gegenwart in der Verkündigung Jesu.* Studien zur Umwelt des Neuen Testaments 4. Göttingen: Vandenhoeck & Ruprecht.

———. 1970. Der irdische Jesus bei Paulus als traditionsgeschichtliches und theologisches Problem. *Zeitschrift für Theologie und Kirche* 67:295–320.

———. 1971. *Ältere Sammlungen im Markusevangelium.* Studien zur Umwelt des Neuen Testaments 8. Göttingen: Vandenhoeck & Ruprecht.

———. 1995a. Bethsaida in the Gospels: The Feeding Story in Luke 9 and the Q Saying in Luke 10. In Arav and Freund 1995.

———. 1995b. Neuere Wege in der Synoptiker-Exegese am Beispiel des Markusevangeliums. In *Bilanz und Perspektiven gegenwärtiger Auslegung des Neuen Testaments,* Symposium for Georg Strecker, edited by F. W. Horn. Beihefte zur Zeitschrift für die neutestamentliche Wissenschaft 75. Berlin: Walter de Gruyter.

———. 1999. An Introduction to the Excavations of Bethsaida (et-Tell) from a New Testament Perspective. In Arav and Freund 1999.

———. 2000. Jesu Hinwendung zu den Heiden im Markusevangelium im Verhältnis zu Jesu historischem Wirken in Betsaida mit einem Zwischenbericht zur Ausgrabung eines vermuteten heidnischen Tempels auf et-Tell (Betsaida). In *Die Weite des Mysteriums: Christliche Identität im Dialog, Festschrift Horst Bürkle,* edited by Klaus Krämer and Ansgar Paus. Freiburg: Herder.

Kuhn, Heinz-Wolfgang, and Rami Arav. 1991. The Bethsaida Excavations: Historical and Archaeological Approaches. In *The Future of Early Christianity,* Festschrift Helmut Koester, edited by Birger A. Pearson et al. (Kuhn, 77–91; Arav, 91–106) Minneapolis: Fortress Press.

Lührmann, Dieter. 1987. *Das Markusevangelium.* Handbuch zum Neuen Testament 3. Tübingen: J. C. B. Mohr (Paul Siebeck).

Nun, Mendel. 1989. *The Sea of Galilee and Its Fisherman in the New Testament.* Ein Gev: Tourist Department and Kinnereth Sailing Co.

Perrin, Norman. 1967. *Rediscovering the Teaching of Jesus.* London: SCM Press.

Schmeller, Thomas. 1994. Jesus im Umland Galiläas: Zu den markinischen Berichten vom Aufenthalt Jesu in den Gebieten von Tyros, Caesarea Philippi und der Dekapolis. *Biblische Zeitschrift,* n.s. 38:44–66.

Schmithals, Walter. 1986. *Das Evangelium nach Markus Kapitel 1–9,1.* 2d ed. Ökumenischer Taschenbuch-Kommentar zum Neuen Testament 2/1. Gütersloh: Gütersloher Verlagshaus Gerd Mohn; Würzburg: Echter Verlag.

Schürer, Emil. 1973. *The History of the Jewish People in the Age of Jesus Christ (175 BC–AD 135) I*, rev. ed. by Geza Vermes and Fergus Millar. Edinburgh: T & T Clark.

———. 1979. *The History of the Jewish People in the Age of Jesus Christ (175 BC–AD 135) II*, rev. ed. by Geza Vermes et al. Edinburgh: T & T Clark.

Seyrig, Henri. 1950. Irenopolis—Neronias—Sepphoris. *The Numismatic Chronicle* 6(10):284–89.

Shroder, John F., et al. 1999. Catastrophic Geomorphic Processes and Bethsaida Archaeology, Israel. In Arav and Freund 1999.

Theissen, Gerd, and Dagmar Winter. 1997. *Die Kriterienfrage in der Jesusforschung: Vom Differenzkriterium zum Plausibilitätskriterium.* Novum Testamentum et Orbis Antiquus 34. Freiburg (Schweiz): Universitätsverlag; Göttingen: Vandenhoeck & Ruprecht.

Wolter, Michael. 2001. *5. Esra-Buch. 6. Esra-Buch.* Jüdische Schriften aus hellenistisch-römischer Zeit III/7. Gütersloh: Gütersloher Verlagshaus.

Mark Appold

Peter in Profile:
From Bethsaida to Rome

S INCE ARCHAEOLOGICAL EXCAVATIONS began at the Bethsaida site, it has been customary in the pertinent literature, as well as in the project's advertisements, posters, book covers, and documentaries, to speak of Bethsaida as "the home of the apostles." Even though multiple attestations are lacking, one scriptural text in the Gospel of John (1:44) does indeed provide a Bethsaida connection for three of the apostles: Andrew, Peter, and Philip. The other "unnamed disciple," traditionally identified with John, the son of Zebedee, is also part of the context in this call scene, and consequently often emerges as yet another candidate for a connection with Bethsaida; of course, if that is true for John, why not also for his brother, James? The nature of this connection is never spelled out. Furthermore, the text never specifically says or suggests that the Zebedee sons are Bethsaida residents, nor does a close reading of the text demand that Bethsaida be seen as the birthplace for Andrew, Peter, and Philip. It will take another five centuries for this connection to be established in the tradition.

Writing in 530 CE, more than five centuries after the putative birth date of Peter, Theodosius, a Christian pilgrim, clearly identifies Bethsaida as the *birthplace* for Andrew, Peter, Philip, James, and John.[1] No longer are any questions asked and the assumption that Bethsaida is "the home of the apostles" is taken for granted.[2] Closer examination of the related texts and traditions, augmented by archaeological research, will today, however, lead to a more tenuous

133

position. Bethsaida as "the home of the apostles" will have to yield to a more nuanced understanding and perhaps to a revision of the phrase itself. As historical persons, stripped of later stories, legends, and elaborations, the apostles remain more in the shadows than in the light. If, for example, after more than a century of concentrated investigation and some of the most intensive research imaginable in the search for the historical Jesus, the results should still be controverted and inconclusive, will it be any different for these elusive apostles who have garnered, by comparison, significantly less attention?

Recognizing that historical reconstruction is extremely difficult, and in some cases, not possible, should not deter efforts to examine and to investigate the data. After all, there have been major advances in biblical studies and archaeological explorations in recent decades, particularly in terms of refinements and approaches. It is with this hope of forward movement that this short study[3] focuses on Peter, who is the most prominent of the disciples and who always appears first in the canonical lists of the followers of Jesus. The Johannine solitary reference to Peter's connection with Bethsaida (1:44) provides a unique window into the early years of Peter's life. Here is an access point for probing questions about the hidden years, a period in Peter's life about which virtually nothing is known. Here questions about background, upbringing, and occupation may legitimately be raised. The Fourth Gospel also contains another solitary textual reference that leads to the opposite end of the spectrum in Peter's life, his death. Although Peter's death is nowhere explicitly described in the New Testament, the text of John 21:18–19 presupposes that the reader knows what happened to Peter at the end of his life. The imagery of "stretching out your hands" and "being taken where you do not wish to go" may suggest a violent end, the memory of which was deeply embedded in Johannine communities at the turn of the first century. Since the reference in I Peter 5:13 asserts that the writer is in Babylon (meaning Rome), the presumption has grown that the end of Peter's life took place in Rome, even though there is no surviving evidence about how Peter ever came to be in Rome in the first place.

Therefore, when it comes to the early Peter and the late Peter, scholars are left with a conundrum—a paucity of early textual evidence and an abundance of later tradition. There are some who maintain that questions about historical Peter are really questions about the church and not about the historical conditions of a Galilean fisherman two millennia ago. It is true that massive traditions did, in fact, grow around the person of Peter, as is evidenced in the distance between the Simon engaged in a fishing cooperative on the north shore of the Kinneret and the Peter represented in the Vatican's bronze statue, regal in solemn pontifical vestments. Later traditions have often dictated the way in which Peter is perceived or the way in which these perceptions are anachronistically read back into earlier texts. Archaeological evidence, on the other hand, has begun to bring new dimensions into the discussion. Material finds can shed new light particularly on those areas where textual evidence is thin or contradictory.

The Bethsaida excavations, still in their infancy, despite more than a decade of work at the site, hold great promise for clarifying the milieu of Peter's early life. However, to date, the archaeological excavations at Bethsaida have not yielded any physical finds specifically related to Peter or to any of the disciples. Nor has any physical evidence come to light that would permit postulating an early Christian presence there. Just the opposite is true when it comes to the end of Peter's life. Extensive archaeological work in Rome has led to numerous claims for physical evidence directly related to Peter. But even archaeological efforts can end in an impasse where tradition still holds sway. When on a study tour through the extensive excavations under St. Peter's in Rome, this writer questioned the attendant guide about the validity of maintaining the discovery of Peter's bones there, the response was revealing. The guide, well trained in the intricacies of the issue, maintained that in the face of historical uncertainty, which admittedly was the case here, tradition takes precedence. This paper will weigh the relative merits of tradition and historical data in considering the perilous connection between faith and history, and the significance of material finds brought to light through archaeology.

To give any kind of assessment of either the early or the late Peter, one would have to depart from what may be called the essential middle of Peter's life, where the interpreter has the strongest and largest amount of primary textual data. Here archaeology has not played a significant role.[4] The task has been essentially an exegetical one. There are, however, strong parallels between textual analysis and archaeological investigation. Both struggle with the issue of stratigraphy, the science of identifying various strata. Just as archaeology lays bare layer after layer of human occupation and strives to describe the characteristics of each level, so exegetical studies strive to identify the successive layers of a text in order to determine what is late and what is early, what is dependent and what is independent (Crossan and Reed 2001, 15–20).

The biblical texts dealing with Peter are already laced with varying traditions and perspectives. By comparison, Paul leaves a legacy of firsthand autobiographical detail, travel plans, conflict issues, and personal theological material,[5] but nothing of the kind has come from the hand of Peter. The ancient tradition passed on by Eusebius that the Gospel of Mark contains the memoirs of Peter has long since been discredited on the basis of the Markan text itself. Also, the canonical epistles of Peter have been shown to be part of the pseudonymous literature that emerged in the generation after Peter.[6] The picture of Peter that the canonical texts yield for the middle years is not a uniform one. The all-important call experience, which marked a decisive change in the course of Peter's life and catapulted him into a life that would take him far beyond the confines of the Galilee, is described in different ways by each of the evangelists. These divergent traditions make it impossible to give a single account. The same can be said for pivotal episodes such as Peter's confession or Peter's denial of Jesus in the Passion account.

In the midst of this diversity there are some critical constants that do emerge. One is the dual portrayal of Peter as preeminent among the disciples, the spokesperson and authoritative interpreter, yet one who always needs correction and instruction. The evangelist Mark is particularly prone to underscore the weaknesses of Peter, whereas Matthew and Luke, while likewise recognizing Peter's foibles, tend to soften the image so that the community can still see Peter as the exemplary model for discipleship. Notably the Fourth Evangelist departs from this tradition. Not only is Peter not the first disciple to be called (Andrew, his brother is), but Peter is consistently pictured in the shadow of the unnamed Beloved Disciple. With the rhetorical tools of irony and misunderstanding, John paints a picture of the Beloved Disciple, not only as the source of the Johannine tradition, but above all as one who demonstrates both a loyalty to Jesus and an insight into his person that surpasses Peter's. All of this, however, is done without impugning the legitimacy of the Petrine traditions in other churches. There are striking differences at work here, but no final dichotomies.[7]

Evidence for the gradual yet profound transformation that Peter underwent, his struggle with Torah observance and gentile inclusion, as well as changes in leadership positions comes into view clearly against the background of his relationship with Paul. From the time of Paul's conversion when Peter appears as the principal leader of the Jerusalem community, and then Paul's first postconversion trip to Jerusalem when he visits with Peter but also with James the brother of Jesus, to the Jerusalem council when James is listed first along with Peter and John as "the pillars of the church," and then to the time when Paul writes his letter to the Galatians when Peter is no longer resident in Jerusalem, a significant shift in leadership is noticeable. Peter is no longer head of the church in Jerusalem. He yields to James, the brother of Jesus. This shift would have been precipitated by (Herod) Agrippa's political moves that ended in the execution of James, the son of Zebedee, the first disciple to be martyred. Peter's imprisonment was to follow (Acts 12:2–5). There is no reason to doubt the information in Acts that Peter's departure would have been triggered by these movements of persecution, suffering, and imprisonment. Through such events, Peter's views were changing. Nor was it just a matter of external pressure and political violence on the outside. There was pressure from the inside as well. Luke's account (Acts 11:2) that Peter had to defend himself before "the apostles and brothers in Judea" because of accusations lodged by "those of the circumcision party" will not be far off the mark. Peter's departure from Jerusalem marks a major shift in his activity in the early church.

One could credit Peter with the ability to straddle the heritage of both Jewish and gentile communities by living as a halakhic Jew among Jews and as a Gentile among Gentiles. Paul, however, didn't think so and when Peter made his trip to Antioch, in a test of church authority, Paul publicly reprimanded Peter for his duplicity in yielding to "the people from James" in the conflict over table fellowship with converted Gentiles.[8] Yet Paul never breaks with Peter, nor does Peter break with Paul. Scholars today have moved away from the old dualism of Paul's law-free approach and Peter's lingering legalism to a view of Peter as the centrist who, after all, had a huge stake in the Gentile mission. Unfortunately, no one knows how this all played itself out and into what areas Peter and his wife and other colleagues entered once they moved out of Samaria and beyond the coastland cities of Lydda, Joppa, and Caesarea, and then perhaps into Asia Minor, Greece, and Italy.[9] Direct evidence runs out at this point, and what remains are conflicting traditions and a growing welter of Peter stories and legends fueled by curiosity, church politics, and the drive to assert priority over other communities. These literary materials show how early Christians took the intimations and clues about Peter's character and ultimate fate contained in the New Testament account of the "middle years" and developed them into full-fledged stories not only about Peter's last years but about the preceding ones as well.

Throughout all of the "middle years" following the death of Jesus, there is for Peter no Bethsaida connection, with perhaps one exception right at the very beginning. In the Markan and Matthean resurrection accounts, the disciples are instructed to return to Galilee, for "there you will see him" (Mark 16:7; Matt. 28:10). Would they have gone back to old haunts and familiar places that played such pivotal roles in Jesus' Galilean ministry? Could Bethsaida be in the picture at this point? The question is made more pressing because of the now well-known identification that the Fourth Gospel makes between Bethsaida and the brothers Peter and Andrew and also Philip. What is striking, however, is that in all the extant body of Petrine literature and references, canonical and apocryphal (of all the texts that claim the name of Peter—gospel, *kerygmata*, epistles, apocalypses, acts, and Gnostic writings), only in the Fourth Gospel is Bethsaida identified as the "city of Peter." Why was this detail important for John but for no one else?

First it should be noted that the claim for Bethsaida as the "home of the apostles" does not enjoy multiple attestation, but is rather the result of a single extant tradition. A closer look at the exact wording of that tradition reveals the complexity of translating it. Both of the Greek prepositions used, ἐκ and ἀπό, as well as the simple genitive case for Andrew and Peter, can be used interchangeably to indicate source, origin, or a point from which a particular relationship ensues. The nature of this relationship is not specified. It is easy to see how initially the use of the genitive could suggest the place of birth.[10] Yet to speak of a person as being of this place or that town may have nothing to do with one's birthplace. People speak of Jesus of Nazareth, not Jesus of Bethlehem, even though the prevailing birthplace tradition for Jesus is Bethlehem. The constructions used in John 1:44 could just as well suggest the place of work or the location of one's residence, temporary or permanent. It might also indicate an area where one is so familiar that the person is identified with the place. There is nothing in the text itself or in the surrounding context that would necessitate one or the other translations.

Of greater significance is simply the mention of the name Bethsaida itself. Only in John's Gospel is Bethsaida associated with specific individuals. In the synoptic references, the feeding of the crowds, and the woe statements against Chorazim, Capernaum, and Bethsaida, the connection is with whole groups of people. In the synoptic Gospels, Bethsaida is the location for an event. In the Johannine text, Bethsaida is associated with a person or persons. Why is this association of such importance for the Johannine community, when otherwise this connection appears in no other textual tradition? It has been noted in Johannine scholarship that place designations in the Fourth Gospel play a special role. Such designations are distinctive in John's tradition and are characteristic of his text. In the case of Bethsaida, one possible explanation is etiological in nature. The interest in a specific location may emerge out of later worship centers where small groups gathered in house church settings and where those gatherings, much like Paul's reference in Corinth to the Peter group or the Apollos group, would be shaped by the remembrance of the name of one of the disciples whose lives were intimately allied with the area around the north shore of the Sea of Galilee (Kundsin 1925, 54–58). Such an interest could have been a factor affecting the successive redactions of the Johannine text.

A more probable explanation for the interest in Bethsaida has to do with the distinctive character of John's text as the carrier of some of the oldest strands of information embedded in Palestinian Judaism. This gospel is the preserve of many geographic locations that do not occur anywhere else in New Testament tradition—Bethany on the other side of the Jordan, Cana of Galilee, Aenon by Salim, Jacob's well by Sychar, Ephraim near the wilderness, or Tiberias, founded by Herod Antipas. Unique also is the use of Jewish-Aramaic terms like "messiah" or "cephas" when they are transliterated into Greek. Information about Jerusalem, Samaria, and the Galilee proves to be astonishingly accurate as do the details about Jewish festivals and customs. A correct rendering of the precise name of Peter as "Simon, son of John," and of "Judas, son of Simon" reflects an amazingly close acquaintance with the culture and practices of the motherland.[11] While the Bethsaida reference in John 1:44 appears to be lodged in an early segment of the tradition,[12] it is not possible textually to extricate it, define its contours, and stratigraphically demarcate it in the successive levels of redaction in the Fourth Gospel. Attempts over the years have been made to identify a signs source and an underlying Passion narrative.

But today it is commonly recognized that all these attempts have reached an impasse, since the unity of language and style in the Fourth Gospel is so thoroughgoing. The text has been "johannicized" at every level. Unlike the synoptic Gospels where multiple traditions allow comparison and, for example, the establishment of dependency and independency in isolating textual traditions, nothing of the kind is possible for John's Gospel, which remains an independent and singular tradition.[13]

Nonetheless, if John's independent Bethsaida reference represents an early piece of tradition that shows no interest in confirming the birthplace of Peter, the question still remains, what is the nature of Peter's connection with Bethsaida? Does the reference prove that Bethsaida was Peter's home, the place where he was raised, the location where he would reside? While this is always a possibility, it would have to be said that neighboring Capernaum carries the greater weight of evidence. Even though the final assessment is not without its problems and the claims of the Franciscan excavators may be overstated, the Capernaum "Peter house" is one of the very few credible localizations of New Testament textual statements. The synoptic Gospels (Mark 1:29–31 and parallels) uniformly speak of "Simon's house" located there. Archaeological excavations, begun there almost a century ago, made breakthrough discoveries between 1968 and 1985 when three distinct strata were laid bare, exposing a fifth-century octagonal church built to commemorate "Peter, the prince of the apostles," then a fourth-century house church and shrine, and finally a courtyard house, larger, yet somewhat similar to the courtyard houses discovered at Bethsaida.[14]

Could Peter have had homes both at Bethsaida and Capernaum? Of course. One could also easily imagine that Peter lived in Bethsaida and subsequently moved to Capernaum or vice versa. Admittedly, the Capernaum home has the difficulty of belonging not to Peter, but to his mother-in-law. But living with the extended family would not be out of the question in first-century Galilee. The fact that the evangelist Mark (1:29) refers to "the house of Peter and Andrew" is a reminder of the same. The Capernaum model has distinct advantages over the Bethsaida model. It has textual attestation on its side when it speaks of Peter and Andrew not just in the genitive case, but explicitly mentions the word "house." Capernaum also has an early and sustained pilgrim history with an abundance of written graffiti. The same cannot be maintained for Bethsaida.

If the case can be maintained that the primary focus for Peter's Bethsaida connection is not on the location as a birthplace, then the next reasonable assumption is to see Bethsaida as Peter's workplace. It was here that he stored his fishing nets and equipment and shared a boat with his brother. He would have resided in Bethsaida, at least for some time, because his occupation demanded it. Without exception, the New Testament texts always identify Peter as a fisherman. His close relationship to the Zebedees, a family of fishermen, well off enough to have hired hands, could easily indicate the existence of a larger business cooperative in which they all participated. Pickling and smoking fish at Magdala, also a lakeside village just north of Tiberias, helped to make fishing a thriving industry whose products, Strabo indicates (16.2.45), would reach as far as Rome. Fishing rights on the Kinneret were not free and would have to be purchased from Herod's administration. Total taxes could have been anywhere from 25 percent to 40 percent of one's income (Culpepper 2000, 14–15; Crossan and Reed 2001, 210). Peter and his colleagues must have had the resources to pay such fees and to carry on a business. Consequently, they would not have shared the desperate lot of day laborers or indentured peasants. On the other hand, they would not have been among the ranks of the economically secure. Luke's assessment of them as "uneducated and ordinary" (Acts 4:13) would have paralleled their depressed economic status as well. The first-century Galilee boat now housed in the Yigal Allon Museum at Ginosar may provide further insight into the economic conditions that prevailed for fishermen of the Galilee. The hull's construction and the materials used reveal the work of a skilled boatbuilder who had to make do with sparse resources and inferior materials.[15] It is reasonable to assume that Peter's fishing occupation suffered from similar limitations.

How would Peter's fishing occupation fit with what to date is known about first-century Herodian Bethsaida? The one certain and undisputed fact is that it was a fishing village. Archaeological efforts have recovered an abundance of fishing implements, hooks, weights, anchors, and what is presumed to be a fisher's seal to substantiate the claim. Its first-century proximity to the lake, once deemed a problem, is now assured, providing access through a harbor and waterways to the lake. On-site building structures of this time period are all fairly modest, a reminder that the fishing industry was no bonanza. House-hold wares, cooking vessels, wine jugs, and eating bowls, of which there are many, are, with few exceptions, common ware, hardly indic-ative of an opulent lifestyle. This was not an economic boom area. Herod Philip's tetrarch generated only half of the income of his half brother Antipas in neighboring Galilee, and despite what Josephus calls Philip's building expansion in Panias and then in Bethsaida, the tetrarchy remained on the lower end of the economic scale. When Philip traveled through his territories, so Josephus recounts, it was only with a small, select entourage so as not to burden his people. Bethsaida was no Tiberias or Sepphoris, let alone a Caesarea Maritima or a Herodium. No frescoes, mosaics, or marble columns have been found there. No public inscriptions, texts, or tablets. No civic struc-tures providing entertainment, such as a theater or hippodrome, bath-house or administrative basilica. Peter would have left Bethsaida not very long after Philip elevated it to the rank of a city in 30 CE and per-haps never returned,[16] but even after its significant change in rank, Bethsaida remained modest in size and appearance.[17]

If Peter knew Bethsaida and worked there when it was still a vil-lage (still called so by Mark in 8:26), what kind of culture would he have experienced? In his later standoff with Paul, Peter gave every indi-cation of being an observant Jew, careful to heed the ritual require-ments of the Torah, concerned about kosher food and circumcision. Clearly, he was raised in a Jewish home. To date, however, there is no clear archaeological evidence that would substantiate a strong Jewish presence in Bethsaida. Whereas limestone fragments, which typify Judaism in the archaeological record, have been found in houses in Capernaum with first-century layers and hundreds of such fragments in first-century contexts have been found at Jodefat and Gamla, only a few such fragments have been found at Bethsaida, hardly enough to document a Jewish presence. Unless one considers some of the houses as candidates for a synagogue, there is also no evidence in Bethsaida of a synagogue or of a *miqweh* (a ritual bath). Similarly, there is no evi-dence of physical remains that would suggest an early Jewish/Christian presence.[18] Bethsaida also has no pre-Constantinian pilgrimage record and no graffiti to support such a record. Clearly the data are meager and offer in most cases only circumstantial evidence. The absence of ritual baths, *miqwaoth*, the surprising abundance of pig bones (5 per-cent of the total collected), Philip's very un-Jewish coinage with images, and the possible remains of a small Roman temple[19] all dovetail with what is already known about Philip's thirty-year popular and tolerant rule in general and Bethsaida in particular.

Located at the crossroads of major thoroughfares that led north to Caesarea Philippi, south to Tiberias, and west to Cana, Sepphoris, and Nazareth, Bethsaida was more exposed to an influx of people from the north and the east, from Batanaea, Trachonitis, Auranitis, and Gaulonitis, all areas under Philip's control. As such it was characterized by a mixed population and strong Greek influence. Peter's name, Simon,[20] and the names of Andrew and Philip are distinctly Greek. Even though it was not uncommon for Jewish parents to give their children Greek names, when they did, it was a reflection of the larger culture in which they lived. In its longer overall history, Bethsaida was usually more pagan than Jewish. Later rabbis would regard this area as the Diaspora. The years Peter spent in Bethsaida would have exposed him to a unique diversity of peoples and practices, influenced by the neighboring Decapolis. It is not impossible to imagine that this gentile influence could cause a devout Jew like Peter to retain his workplace in Bethsaida while establishing his family home in Capernaum, which was under the rule of Antipas (Herod), known for his considerable respect for Jewish traditions. On the other hand, having to live in a mixed population of "Jews and Syrians," as Josephus puts it (*J.W.* 3.57), may have prepared him for his later outreach to the uncircumcised and for his centrist position in earliest Christianity.

From the early years of Peter, the Galilean fisherman, where so much detail of family and background remains in the shadows, where textual witness is weak, and where archaeology will continue to face the challenges of clarifying the contexts, the focus now shifts to a closing assessment of the end of Peter's life where the textual witness is again weak and where archaeology is faced with another set of challenges to clarifying the traditions. The literary sources for considering the late years of Peter raise more questions than they give answers. The fragmentary character of these sources leads one to hypotheses and inferences. Where one would expect direct information, there is none. Late tradition confidently speaks of Peter's move to Rome. But Acts breaks off its account of the missionary activity of Peter and doesn't give the slightest allusion to any stay in Rome. When Paul writes his letter to the Romans in 57/58 CE, there is no mention of Peter, which is unthinkable if he in fact had been there. In the long debate over this issue, there are some who doggedly argue that Peter never even stepped foot into Rome. And yet the clues already alluded to in John 21 and I Peter clearly suggest Peter's martyrdom there. While no early sources prior to the second half of the second century actually report this event, the added inferences from I Clement 5 and the Letters of Ignatius have led to the cautious affirmation of Peter's martyrdom in Rome. Prior to the second century, there is no evidence for interest in the relics and burial places of the great martyrs, but from that time period on, one witnesses a steady expansion of the tradition.

Later tradition will also attach the memory of Peter to different places in Rome, most notably the Vatican hill and the catacombs under the Basilica of St. Sebastian. Here the work of the archaeologist enters again into the picture. If such work holds promise for Bethsaida, it holds even greater promise for Rome, although the final results may be less clear, as is the case with the purported discovery of the bones of Peter. The problem of the bones of Peter is of relatively recent origin and was never really a concern of archaeology. The bones were traditonally assumed to be under St. Peter's in Rome. There were, however, discrepancies that prompted over the years a number of theories and hypotheses to account for the varying traditions. Then in wartime 1939, extensive, secretive, and prolonged excavations began at St. Peter's. In his 1950 Christmas message, Pius XII announced that "the grave of the Prince of the Apostles has been found" (see Cullman 1953, 138), conceding at the same time that remains of human bones could not be identified. Engelbert Kirschbaum S.J. persisted with the work, discovering a number of bones underneath the famous red wall. In his 1959 publication, he announced that "bones were removed from a grave now recognized to have been that of St. Peter, and that they are in fact the bones of an elderly man" (Kirschbaum 1959, 195). When the bones were submitted to technical tests, however, they were reported to be those of a woman. Kirschbaum dropped his claim and the bone problem was put to rest. It came as a shock when in June of 1968, Paul VI disclosed that the bones of Peter had been convincingly identified. What caused the change? An Agatha Christie-like story unfolds when one reads the publications of Margherita Guarducci, professor of Greek epigraphy at the University of Rome, who was responsible for the new assessment. Her thesis of cryptolanguage was almost universally rejected by epigraphical authorities and her story of a box containing the all-important bones (which, incredibly, had been removed in 1943 from the excavation site by Msgr. Kaas, director of the work, and then reappeared years later without any further comment) was not believed. The story weakens any confidence one might have in the new position.[21] But it is a position now, not likely to change. In fact, it has never been addressed again. At this point tradition preempts history and becomes purported history.

Textual studies and the work of the archaeologist are all perilous trades and, in the case of Peter, underscore how elusive his historical record continues to be.

CHAPTER NOTES

Unless otherwise indicated, all translations are my own. All biblical citations are taken from the New Revised Standard Version.

1. Baldi 1982, 266. Writing in the fourth century CE, the church historian Eusebius speaks of Bethsaida as "the city of the apostles Andrew, Peter, and Philip."
2. Tradition has a tendency to grow and to be shaped by piety and sometimes by confusion and misunderstanding. By the eighth century, Willibald, bishop of Eichstätt in Bavaria, in his pilgrimage to the Holy Land, mentions the church in Bethsaida where the house of Peter and Andrew earlier had stood. The place was almost certainly confused with el-Araj, a few hundred meters from the mouth of the Jordan, or el-Mesadiyeh, on the shore to the southeast. Biblical Bethsaida would no longer be in the picture. By the time of pilgrimages, spurred by the crusades of the twelfth century, reports circulated, identifying Bethsaida as the home not only of five apostles, but of James the son of Alphaeus as well. The expansion is clearly due to confusion over the two Jameses.
3. The scope of this study is determined by the circumstances surrounding its initial presentation. An adapted version was presented at the SBL International Conference in Rome on July 8, 2001.
4. The one notable exception is the archaeological work done in Capernaum on the purported "house of Peter" (or perhaps more accurately, the house of Peter's mother-in-law).
5. Of course, Paul's texts too have been subject to redaction, as is clearly evidenced particularly by the Corinthian and Philippian correspondence.
6. A contrary point of view is maintained by Margherita Guarducci, whose discovery of the bones of Peter, hailed by the Vatican as authentic, is yet to be considered in this study. As for the First Epistle of Peter, Guarducci maintains that "it is certainly authentic—of Peter himself" and "it follows that Peter dictated his first Epistle at Rome..." (1960, 26, 28).
7. Carrying on the tradition of Oscar Cullmann's work on Peter, Pheme Perkins' recent monograph (2000) on Peter underscores the balance maintained in the preservation of independent traditions about Peter. Though the Johannine communities do not derive their legitimacy from the Petrine tradition, they recognize the validity of the witness to Jesus in other communities.
8. Both Paul and Peter never leave Judaism, and although at Antioch they are at loggerheads with one another over the issue of kosher foods and the boundaries between Jew and Gentile, they do not break fellowship. Their dispute, however, would become the source of unending controversy in succeeding centuries. Cf. Smith 1985, 209–14.
9. Virtually nothing is known about the entire second half of Peter's missionary activity except the fact that it occurred. See Cullmann 1958, 52. Actually, something similar can be maintained for Paul, for whom the first half

of his missionary activity in the Transjordan and then in Syria/Cilicia remains almost totally in the shadows. Even though nothing is known of Peter's mission activity after he leaves the homeland, his name is clearly connected with three major population centers: Antioch, Corinth, and Rome.

10. Thus, Bargil Pixner, "the Father of Bethsaida," in his 1982 pioneering essay, "Putting Bethsaida-Julias on the Map," a study that would lead to serious excavations at the site, could begin his article by referring in his opening sentence to "Bethsaida, birthplace of the Apostles Peter and Andrew, and home of the Apostle Philip" (1982, 165).

11. For an extensive discussion of these aspects, see Hengel 1989, 110–35; Davies 1996, 43–64.

12. John 12:21, which places Bethsaida in Galilee, is the product of a later redaction.

13. A very helpful overview of the complicated history of Johannine research on this issue is given in Culpepper 2000, 297–321.

14. Fred Strickert (1998, 22–28) argues that "the house of Peter" did not come about until the fourth century after the gospel reports had established a connection between Peter and the town of Capernaum; however, the abundance of graffiti-like inscriptions on the walls of the central room go back to the second century and underscore a long tradition of reverence for the place as a location connected to Peter.

15. For further discussion see Crossan and Reed 2001, 85, 86.

16. Except possibly during the brief interlude following the crucifixion of Jesus and the time when Peter returned to Jerusalem.

17. Pausanias derides Panopeus for claiming status as a *polis* when it had no government buildings, gymnasium, theater, or fountains. Similarly, Strabo didn't think Thebes even merited recognition as a respectable village. One could only guess what they may have said about Bethsaida.

18. The excitement over the "Bethsaida cross" has now subsided, since stratigraphical studies have placed it outside of the Christian era.

19. Heinz-Wolfgang Kuhn (2000, 222–29) argues that instead of supporting a small Roman temple committed to the cult of Caesar, the evidence, at best, might indicate the presence of a small pre-Christian pagan temple or shrine dedicated to a local deity.

20. Andrew and Philip are purely Greek names without any semitic counterparts. Peter, who is commonly referred to as "Simon Peter" in John, on two accounts (1:42 and 21:15) is addressed by his family name, Simon. Only twice is the similarly sounding semitic form of Simeon used. Otherwise, it is "Simon," which is native Greek. The added name of Kepha, Aramaic for Peter or rock, and its hellenized form of *Kephas*, is not a given name at all, but rather a descriptive title. Just as Simon says to Jesus, "You are the Christ," so Jesus says to Simon, "You are Peter."

21. For a study of the sequence of events see Walsh 1982. For a concise, current overview, see Thümmel 2003, 1166.

Literature Cited

Baldi, Donatus. 1982. *Enchiridion, Locorum Sanctorum.* Jerusalem: Franciscan Press.

Crossan, John, and Jonathan Reed. 2001. *Excavating Jesus.* San Francisco: Harper.

Cullmann, Oscar. 1958. *Peter.* Philadelphia: Westminister Press.

Culpepper, Alan. 2000. *John, the Son of Zebedee.* Minneapolis: Fortress.

Davies, W. D. 1996. Reflections on Aspects of the Jewish Background of the Gospel of John. In *Exploring the Gospel of John*, edited by R. A. Culpepper and C. C. Black. Louisville: Westminster John Knox Press.

Guarducci, Margherita. 1960. *The Tomb of St. Peter.* New York: Hawthorne Books, Inc.

Hengel, Martin. 1989. *The Johannine Question.* Philadelphia: Trinity Press International.

Kirschbaum, Engelbert. 1959. *The Tombs of St. Peter and St. Paul.* New York: St. Martin's Press.

Kuhn, Heinz-Wolfgang. 2000. Jesu Hinwendung zu den Heiden im Markuse-vangelium. In *Die Weite des Mysteriums*, edited by K. Krämer and A. Paus. Freiburg: Herder.

Kundsin, Karl. 1925. *Topologische Überlieferungsstoffe im Johannes-Evangelium.* Göttingen: Vandenhoeck & Ruprecht.

Perkins, Pheme. 2000. *Peter.* Minneapolis: Fortress Press.

Pixner, Bargil. 1982. Putting Bethsaida-Julias on the Map. Christian News from Israel 27 (4).

Smith, T. V. 1985. *Petrine Controversies in Early Christianity.* Tübingen: J.C.B. Mohr.

Strickert, Fred. 1998. *Bethsaida, Home of the Apostles.* Collegeville: Liturgical Press.

Thümmel, Hans Georg. 2003. Petrus. In *Religion in Geschichte und Gegenwart*, edited by H. D. Betz, D. S. Browning, B. Janowski, and E. Jüngel. Vol. 6. Tübingen: Mohr Siebeck.

Walsh, John Evangelist. 1982. *The Bones of St. Peter.* Garden City, N.Y.: Doubleday & Co., Inc.

Fred Strickert

The Dying Grain Which Bears Much Fruit: John 12:24, the Livia Cult, and Bethsaida

R ECENT ARCHAEOLOGICAL RESEARCH at Bethsaida on the northeast
side of the Sea of Galilee provides a new perspective for the context of the ministry of Jesus and for the development of the early
church. In particular, findings from archaeology provide new eyes for
understanding the saying of Jesus in John 12:24:

> Very truly, I tell you, unless a grain of wheat falls into the earth
> and dies, it remains just a single grain; but if it dies, it bears
> much fruit.

The context for this saying is not Bethsaida, but Jerusalem
during the last week of Jesus' life; however, it is uttered when Philip
and Andrew, two Bethsaida disciples, report that there are "Greeks"
wishing to see Jesus. A saying about grain sown and bearing fruit is by
no means unusual in the teaching—evidenced by the parables of the
sower, the mustard seed, and the seed sown secretly. However, what is
unique is the connection to the death and resurrection of Jesus. This
can be understood against the background of the role of Livia, wife of
Augustus, in the imperial cult and in particular its importance in the
city of Bethsaida.

149

AN EARLY SAYING OF JESUS

The grain saying of John 12:24 has many characteristics that point to its earliness in the sayings tradition. In fact, according to *The Five Gospels* (Funk et al. 1993, 441–42), which records the work of the Jesus Seminar, it is one of only four sayings in the Gospel of John that are considered possibly authentic.[1] This saying is printed in gray, which means that it reflects the ideas of Jesus although not his exact words. This is somewhat surprising because there is no synoptic or Thomas parallel; however, a parallel in 1 Corinthians 15:36–37 does demonstrate that the imagery "has deep roots in the Christian tradition" (Funk et al. 1993, 411). The Pauline parallel reads:

> What you sow does not come to life unless it dies. And as for what you sow, you do not sow the body that is to be, but a bare seed, perhaps of wheat or of some other grain.

Since 1 Corinthians is usually dated to the early 50s CE, this would point to wide use of the saying in the first two decades after the death of Jesus on 7 April 30 CE.[2]

The dying grain is combined with two other short sayings of Jesus in John 12:24–26 which seemed to be linked already in a pre-Johannine source:

> Very truly, I tell you, unless a grain of wheat falls into the earth and dies, it remains just a single grain; but if it dies, it bears much fruit. Those who love their life lose it, and those who hate their life in this world will keep it for eternal life. Whoever serves me must follow me, and where I am, there will my servant be also. Whoever serves me, the Father will honor.

Rudolf Schnackenburg has identified these three sayings as "a unit, firmly rooted in tradition and catechesis of the primitive church."[3] What stands out the most about these latter two sayings is that parallels occur in Mark 8:34–35, but in reverse order. These sayings occur in the context of the confession of Simon Peter which is linked geographically to the area of Caesarea-Philippi, just north of Bethsaida. That episode is preceded in Mark 8 by the second feeding miracle and the healing of the blind man at Bethsaida (Brodie 1993, 48–66; Strickert 1998, 125–30). Even though it is a major revision from Mark, Luke 9 places the confession of Peter and the sayings about losing one's life and being a servant directly after the Bethsaida feeding of the five thousand episode. The tendency of form critics (Bultman 1931), of course, has been to completely separate the sayings of Jesus from their context in the Gospels and to discount this contextual data as devoid of interpretive information. John 12:20–23, however, seems to bring this principle into question. The fact that John 12:21 refers to Bethsaida disciples in introducing these three sayings should not go unnoticed.

Years ago, C. H. Dodd analyzed this short dying grain parable (John 12:24) and asked whether it also "should not be accepted as representing an element in the tradition as primitive and authentic as anything" contained in the synoptic Gospels (1963, 366–69). He noted that in form it is very similar to a number of synoptic parables (salt, kingdom divided, eye, lost sheep),[4] which he refers to as the form of an "observed invariable sequence" or "law of nature" that "if A occurs, then B occurs" (Dodd 1963, 366–69). Parables based on observation of agricultural practice are common to Jesus, especially seed parables— the parables of the sower, the mustard seed, the seed sown secretly. Even with individual words and phrases, there is a high degree of similarity: ὁ κόκκος τοῦ σίτου [a grain of wheat] is not unlike the κόκκος σινάπεως [a grain of mustard seed] of the mustard seed parable (Mark 4:31), and πεσὼν εἰς τὴν γῆν" [falling into the earth] is almost identical to ἔπεσεν εἰς τὴν γῆν [it falls into the earth] of the parable of the sower (Mark 4:8). Only the introductory "very truly I say to you" and "it remains alone" (John 6:15) have a distinctively Johannine ring (Sanders 1968, 292; Brown 1966, 471). More important than individual expressions, however, is the similarity in motif with the mustard seed parable that the one becomes many (Funk et al. 1993, 441). According to Dodd, "It appears, therefore, that we have here a pericope which in form, in the character of its imagery, and in the whole manner in which it is presented...associates itself closely with the tradition of parabolic teaching as we know it from the Synoptics."[5]

The final words in the John 12:24 text, καρπόν φέρει [it bears fruit], are significant. The concept of bearing fruit is quite common in the New Testament. The actual epithet καρπόφορος [fruit bearing] occurs only a single time in Acts 14:17. This is a sermon by Paul in the town of Lystra in Asia Minor against the backdrop of a temple of Zeus in which Paul points to the one creator God worshipped in Judaism as καρπόφορος. Likewise in letters written in a Greco-Roman context (Rom. 7:4, 5; Col. 1:6, 10), the metaphor is used for Christian behavior—with the verbal form καρποφορέω.

The predominant expression used in the synoptic Gospels is καρπόν ποιεῖν [to produce fruit], used a total of fourteen times in Q (Matt. 3:8 = Luke 3:8; Matt. 3:10 = Luke 3:9; Matt. 7:16–20 [five times] = Luke 6:43–44 [twice]), Matthew's unique material (Matt. 13:36, 21:43), and Luke's unique material (Luke 13:9). The Markan parable of the sower uses καρπον δουναῖ [to give fruit] (Mark 4:7, 8). This is followed by Matthew 13:8 while Luke makes an alteration to καρπόν ποιεῖν [to produce fruit] (Luke 8:8). Only in the final verse of the explanation to the parable of the sower do all three writers use καρπο-φορέω (Mark 4:20; Matt. 13:23; Luke 8:15). This same expression is repeated by Mark in the parable of the seed sown secretly (Mark 4:28). Thus out of twenty-two occurrences of the various forms of the expression "to produce fruit," the synoptic Gospels only have four from the καρπόφορος [fruit bearing] root.

In contrast, John uses exclusively καρπός φερεῖν [to bear fruit]. The first occasion is the Passover week dying grain saying (John 12:24). Three chapters later, also in the context of Passover week, Jesus gives the "I am the vine; you are the branches" discourse, which employs καρπός φερεῖν seven times (John 15:1–16). This is clearly a favorite Johannine expression. With John's often subtle sacramental theology, one can see a clear link between the two sayings, one focusing on the fruit of sown grain and the other on the fruit of the vine. The dying grain saying thus provides an introduction to the grain and vine motifs common to both Passover and Eucharist. The point is that through the single grain and the single vine comes much fruit.

Unlike the synoptic Gospels, there is no reference to a Thursday evening Passover meal nor to the Eucharistic words in John 12–15. Rather one is directed back to the previous Passover when Jesus stayed behind at Bethsaida (John 6), where the same disciples, Philip and Andrew, played leadership roles, and when Jesus fed the five thousand by taking the grain of the field and producing much fruit (Strickert 1998, 115–24).

THE DEMETER MYTH

While, in many respects, the saying of John 12:24 is very similar to other sayings of Jesus, there is one critical difference. The grain does not represent the word or the kingdom as in the synoptic parables. Rather it represents a person whose death is inevitable and necessary.

The parable not only speaks of the seed "falling into the earth," but twice it is also mentioned that the seed "dies."[6] The use of the article ὁ κόκκος τοῦ σίτου [the grain of wheat] makes it clear that the parable is not about seeds in general, but about one particular seed,[7] whose death will lead to bearing much fruit.

There is no question that the closest parallels for this symbolism are found in a Hellenistic religious background and especially mystery religions where the annual cycle of death and rebirth was dramatized with an ear of grain (Holtzmann 1908; Brown 1966, 472; Barrett 1960, 352; Sanders 1968, 293). Most popular were the mysteries of Eleusis where Demeter (also known as Brimo, Ceres [Roman], Deo, and Doso, and sometimes identified with her daughter, Kore, Kore Persephone, and Isis [Egypt]) traveled to the underworld to bring back her daughter Kore (Persephone, Persephassa, Proserpina [Roman], also known as Brimo, Core, Despoina [Arcadian]) so that the earth could bring forth corn. In time, hopes of individual immortality were thus linked to this agricultural festival (Rose 1970, 324).

The grain myth goes all the way back to the eighth or seventh century BCE Homeric *Hymn of Demeter*, which details the abduction of Demeter's daughter Kore to the underworld, her rescue, and finally the explanation of the life cycle of grains with the four-month period in which the fields are barren corresponding to the return of Kore to the underworld each year. The planting thus is understood as a mystery in which the seed is sown apparently to death below the surface of the ground, yet sprouts new life and an abundant crop for another year (Rice and Stambaugh 1979, 171–83; Meyer 1987, 20–30).

With the Demeter myth as the heart of the Eleusinian mysteries, the sanctuary soon became prominent in the religious life of Athens. A late fifth-century BCE document describes how the Athenians made regular grain payments to support the sanctuary:

> Resolved by the council and the people…, on the proposal of the drafting committee: that the Athenians give first-fruits of the grain to the Two Goddesses according to the ancestral custom and the oracle of Delphi.

After explaining the details of this transaction, the document concludes: "May there be many good things and an abundance of grain of good quality to those who do this…."[8]

At about the same time, Herodotus documents the festive nature of the annual processions from Athens to Eleusis (*Hist.* 8.65). This same procession is alluded to a generation later (405 BCE) by the playwright Aristophanes in *The Frogs*. Here Dionysius, on a journey to the underworld, encounters initiates into the Eleusinian mysteries who celebrate in death as they did in life. The chorus sings a processional hymn to Proserpina:

> March, chanting loud your lays,
> Your hearts and voices raising,
> The Saviour goddess praising
>   Who vows she'll still
> Our city save to endless days,
> Whate'er Thorycion's will. (lines 378–83)

The leader then responds to introduce another hymn, this time to Demeter:

> Break off the measure, and change the time, and now with
>   chanting and hymns adorn
> Demeter, goddess mighty and high, the harvest-queen,the
>   giver of corn. (lines 384–85)

Here in the final line, the epithet καρπόφορος is used of Demeter. She is "the harvest queen, the giver of corn" [τὴν καρποφόρον βασίλεαν].

The same basic expression had been used of Demeter by Herodotus in describing fertile Mesopotamia which abundantly brings forth the grain of Demeter (Δήμητρος καρπὸν ἐκφέρειν), an expression repeated verbatim several lines later (*Hist.* 1. 193). From inscriptions from Pessinus (*CIG* 4082) and Paros (*IG* 12 (5).226), it would appear that the epithet Καρπόφορος was in fact well known for Demeter. Although he is later (second century CE), Pausanius mentions in Tegea a temple (presumably built in earlier times) of Demeter and Kore which was called Καρπόφορος (*Descr.* 8.53.7).

A similar situation occurs in Rome with Demeter's equivalent Ceres—literary references point to the spread of this cult in Rome by at least the fifth century BCE (Spaeth 1996, 1). In fact, it was understood that the name Ceres itself derived (with the similarity of "c" and "g" sounds) from the idea of bearing fruit. The Augustan scholar Varro quotes the earlier poet Ennius as saying "She, because she bears fruits, (is called) Ceres" [*Quae Quod gerit fruges, Ceres*].[9] It is not surprising then that the Latin *frugifera* [bearing fruit]—equivalent of Καρπόφορος—is used as an epithet of Ceres.[10] As Barbette Stanley Spaeth notes, "The Greeks gave Demeter the epithet *Karpophoros* (Bearer of Fruit), while the Romans called Ceres *Frugifera* (Bearer of Fruit)" (1996, 130). The impact of the dying grain myth is widespread.

There are two major problems with the Demeter cult as background for the particular grain saying in John 12:24. First, its Hellenistic character does not seem to fit the other evidence of an early, possibly authentic saying of Jesus. Second, the emphasis in John is on an action that really risks losing one's life and requires a death that is real. As Raymond Brown has pointed out, this is weakened by "the automatic and immutable character of this cycle" (1966, 472). It does seem far-fetched to make a connection between this saying of Jesus and Hellenistic mystery religions.

THE GREEK CONNECTION

An adequate explanation for the connection between the grain imagery of one becoming many and death becoming life has long eluded scholars. John offers a clue by setting this saying in the context of the Jerusalem Passover when Greeks[11] wish to see Jesus. The mention of Greeks is highly significant. On the one hand, it is totally unexpected from a historical perspective because Greeks would not be permitted to eat the Passover meal (Exod. 12:48; Josephus *J.W.* 6.422–27; Schackenburg 1980, 381), and it is unusual from a literary perspective because the Greeks are not mentioned again after this introduction. Their place in the episode is more symbolic than historical. The author seems to be giving the reader a clue perhaps to the upcoming gentile mission, but perhaps also to the significance of this saying. This is underscored further by including as intermediaries Philip and Andrew, the only disciples with truly Greek names. Likewise the author reminds the reader that these disciples are from Bethsaida—a piece of information that had already been mentioned once in John 1:44—an area noted for its "mixed population" (Josephus *J.W.* 3.58). In order to understand the saying of Jesus in John 12:24, the reader should look to the Greek cultural and religious setting of Bethsaida.[12]

LIVIA CULT

The mention of Bethsaida in John 12 is significant because it was a center for the imperial cult and especially the cult honoring Livia,

who was known also as Julia. Livia, the second wife of Augustus and
the mother of Tiberius, was perhaps the most popular woman of the
Roman Empire and played an important role in the imperial cult.
Upon the death of Augustus in 14 CE, while she was denied deification, she was adopted into the Julian clan, receiving the name Julia
Augusta [Ἰουλια Σεβαστη] (Tacitus *Ann.* 1.8.14; Dio *Hist.* 56.32.1,
56.46.1, 57.12.2; Suetonius *Aug.* 101.2; Giacosa 1983, 22–24). While
this made the succession of Tiberius possible, it also elevated Livia's
role as Empress Mother and increased her popularity in the provinces.

In Palestine, two cities were thus renamed Julias in her honor:
Betharamptha in Perea[13] and Bethsaida (Josephus *J.W.* 2.168; *Ant.*
18.28; Strickert 1995b, 40–51) on the northeast shore of the Sea of
Galilee. Herod the Great, under the patronage of Augustus, of course,
had already established the imperial cult in the region by building
temples to Augustus at Caesarea Maritima, Sebaste, and Paneas (which
was later renamed Caesarea Philippi by Herod's son Philip). It is not
surprising, then, that Herod's two sons Antipas and Philip, who had
been raised in Rome, chose to continue this patronage by honoring
Livia with the dedication of cities in their tetrarchies.[14] There is no
question concerning the importance of Livia in the imperial cult and
there is no question of her significance in Palestine. How then is she
related to this saying of Jesus about dying grain coming to life?

The link between Jesus' saying about the dying grain and the
Demeter myth is in the person of Livia, and the key to understanding
this linkage is a coin minted by Herod Philip in 30 CE (Strickert 2002b;
Meshorer 2001, plate 51, no. 107) at the rededication and renaming of
Bethsaida to the city of Julias. This particular coin (fig. 1) bears the
image of Livia on the obverse surrounded by the inscription ΙΟΥΛΙΑ
ΣΕΒΑΣΤΗ [Julia Sebaste] and on the reverse the depiction of an out-
stretched hand holding three ears of grain with the inscription ΚΑΡ-
ΠΟΦΟΡΟΣ [Karpophoros/fruit bearing] and the date ΛΔ.

The date ΛΔ points to the thirty-fourth year of the rule of Philip
corresponding to the year 30/31 CE—a year in which Philip minted at
least two other coins (Kindler 1999, 245–49). Philip portrayed his own
image on another rare, smaller coin minted that same year (fig. 2)
(Meshorer 1982, plate 8, no. 12). As in previous mints, his primary
coin was one depicting the emperor (Tiberius)[15] on the obverse and
the temple of Augustus at Caesarea Philippi on the reverse (fig. 3). The
only unique feature about this particular issue (Meshorer 1982, plate

Fig. 1. "Julia Sebaste," Coin of Herod Philip. Caesarea Philippi, 30 CE. The Israel Museum, Jerusalem

Fig. 2. "Philip," Coin of Herod Philip. Caesarea Philippi, 30 CE. The Israel Museum, Jerusalem

Fig. 3. "Tiberius," Coin of Herod Philip. Caesarea Philippi, 30 CE. The Israel Museum, Jerusalem

Fig. 4. "Augustus and Livia," Coin of Herod Philip. Caesarea Philippi, undated. The Israel Museum, Jerusalem

8, no. 10a) is the inclusion at the end of the typical inscription ΕΠΙ ΦΙΛΙΠΠΟΥ ΤΕΤΡΑΡΧΟΥ [in the tetrarchy of Philip] of the abbreviation ΚΤΙΣ referring to Philip's role as a founder [κτίστης] of cities.[16] In particular this points to the founding of the city of Julias where Philip had made improvements and added population to the fishing village Bethsaida (Josephus *Ant.* 18.28; *J.W.* 2.168). It has been argued elsewhere (Strickert 1995a, 179) that the undated coin depicting the double image of Augustus and Livia under the legend ΣΕΒΑΣΤΩΝ (fig. 4) makes up the fourth coin in this commemorative mint (Meshorer 1982, plate 7, no. 6; Maltiel-Gerstenfeld 1982, 148–49).

    The ΚΑΡΠΟΦΟΡΟΣ legend and the grain symbolism on the ΙΟΥΛΙΑ ΣΕΒΑΣΤΗ coin point to her role as a Demeter/Ceres figure. As Gertrude Grether has noted:

> The tendency of the art of the period seems to have been to stress her office as priestess of Augustus and her association with the deities of plenty and fertility. The general idea expressed is that, since Augustus is no longer on earth but has taken his place among the divinities, his blessings must come to the Roman people through the mediation of his priestess, Julia Augusta. (1946, 245)

The extent of the assimilation of Livia with the goddess Demeter/Ceres is confirmed by inscriptions from throughout the empire:

* From the island Gaulos near Malta:
  CERERI IULIAE AUGUSTAE DIVI AUGUSTI MATRI TI CAESARIS AUGUSTI

Translation: [dedicated to] Ceres Julia Augusta, wife of the
deified Augustus, mother of Tiberius Caesar Augustus
(Spaeth 1996, cat. 1.1; Bartman 1999, epig. cat. 50)

- From Lampsacus:
  'Ιουλίαν Σεβαστὴν 'Εστίαν νέαν Δήμητρα
  Translation: [dedicated to] Julia Augusta Hestia, the new
  Demeter
  (Spaeth 1996, cat.1.2; Bartman 1999, epig. cat. 55)

- From Amphrodisias:
  Θεᾶς 'Ιουλίας νέας Δήμητρος
  Translation: [dedicated by the priests] of the goddess, Julia,
  the new Demeter
  (Spaeth 1996, cat. 1.3)

- From Nepet:
  Cereri August
  Matri Agr
  Translation: [offerings dedicated] to Ceres Augusta,
  mother of the fields
  (Spaeth 1996, cat. 1.6; Bartman 1999, epig cat. 63)

- From Cyzicus:
  "Αυτοκράτορα Καίσαρα θεόν θεοῦ υἱόν
  "Σεβαστὸν καὶ Λιουίαν θεὰν Δήμητηρά...
  Translation: The god Imperator Caesar Augustus, son of a
  god, and the goddess Livia, Demeter...
  (Bartman 1999, epig cat. 7)

The impression is quite clear that the fruits of Demeter/Ceres are now
bestowed through the benefactress Livia/Julia.

The cult of Ceres had arrived in Rome as early as the fifth century BCE and was worshipped at the Aventine where Temples of Ceres,
Liber, and Libera paralleled the Eleusinian triad. The prominence of
Ceres is also documented by the fact that nine different coin types of
Ceres were used already for the years 48 through 42 BCE (Spaeth 1996,
98); however, it was Augustus himself who appears to have initiated
the link between Livia and Demeter/Ceres (Grether 1946, 226). The
influence for this may have been derived from the fact that Octavian
himself had been initiated into the Eleusian mysteries in 31 BCE just
after the battle of Actium (Dio *Hist.* 54.7). On that occasion, the
people of Eleusis erected statues to both Octavian and Livia. An
inscription on the base for the latter read:

'Ο δ [ἤμ] ος
Λιβίαν Δρουσίλλαν
[Αὐ]τοκράτορος Καίσαρος
γυναῖκα

Translation: The people [dedicated the] statue of Livia
Drusilla, wife of Imperator Caesar
(Bartman 1999, epig cat. 1)

Her statue, however, does not survive. Susan Wood argues that Livia
herself may have been initiated into the Eleusinian rituals when she
accompanied Augustus on a second trip to Eleusis in 19 CE (2000, 92–
93; Dio *Hist.* 54.9.10).

Shortly thereafter, the link between Livia and Demeter/Ceres
began to appear in Rome. Following the return of Augustus from campaigns in Spain and Gaul, the Senate decreed in 13 BCE the erection of
the Ara Pacis Augustae to celebrate the return of peace—the *Pax
Romana*. This is the first time that identifiable mortal men and women
were to appear on an official state relief in Rome. No less than ninety
figures make up a stately procession on the north and south friezes
with Augustus and Livia being dominant, projecting the image of a
ruling couple with shared powers—they alone wear both veil and
laurel wreath—and emphasizing the relation between lasting peace
and the continuation of this dynasty (Bartman 1999, 86–93).

The larger than human status of Livia is emphasized by the similarities in her depiction with a mother figure on the eastern panel
often named Italia[17] who, crowned with a wreath of wheat and pop-
pies, holds two children in her lap. Flanked by nymphs, with a grazing
sheep and a reclining lamb at her feet, and surrounded by various
plants and fruits such as pomegranates, grapes, and nuts, the Italia
figure clearly portrays the ideal nurturing figure which Spaeth identifies as the goddess Ceres (1994, 65–100). The Augustan visual message
is one that is paralleled in writing by Ovid:

Peace nourishes Ceres
and Ceres is the nursling of peace.[18]

Likewise Horace, writing in 13 BCE, the year of Augustus' campaigns in
Spain and Gaul, declares:

The fatherland yearns for Caesar. (For when he is here),
the cow in safety roams through the fields, Ceres and

nourishing Prosperity nurture the fields, the ships fly
over the pacified sea. (*Saec.* 4.5.16–19)

Upon Augustus' return, Horace declares the promise fulfilled: "Your
era, Caesar, has brought back abundant fruits to the fields" (*Saec.*
4.15.4–5).

One might wonder how effective was such a subtle connection
between the figure of Livia and Italia and the symbolism of Ceres on
the Ara Pacis Augustae; however, Augustus seems to have assisted
that merging of figures in his choice for the dedication of the altar—
on 30 January, the birthday of Livia, in the year 9 BCE. It seems to be
no accident that in 7 CE, following the adoption of Tiberius by Augustus, the emperor dedicated two other altars in Rome, the Arae Cereris
Matris and Opis Augustae, serving to link Livia and the goddess Ceres
(Grether 1946, 226). Likewise Augustus restored the ancient Temples
of Ceres, Liber, and Libera which were then rededicated by Tiberius in
17 CE (Tacitus *Ann.* 2.49).

The identification of Livia with Ceres was very useful in that the
goddess seemed to represent a variety of symbols. Not only was the
connection with fertility [καρπόφορος], peace, and prosperity, but the
ancient myth of Ceres and Proserpina (Demeter and Kore) represented
the virtues of chastity and motherhood. Ceres was the ideal symbol
for the Augustan program and Livia as the grand mother played the
role perfectly (Spaeth 1996, 113). With the death of Drusus, the heir
apparent, on a military campaign in 9 BCE, Livia along with her son
had moved into the spotlight.

Beginning in 2 BCE and continuing to his death in 14 CE, coins
of Augustus depicted on the reverse a seated female who holds a scep-
ter in her right hand and wheat stalks in the left (Spaeth 1996, fig. 40;
RIC 1:56.219; *BMCRE*, Augustus 544). This same imagery was adopted
on official state coins of Tiberius (see fig. 5)—the tribute coin (*BMCRE*
1, 124–27, nos. 30–60, plates 22.20–23.9; RIC 1:95.25–29)—and of
Claudius in 42 CE after the deification of Livia (*BMCRE* 1, 195, no. 224,
plate 37.7). Only in the case of the latter does the inscription make
clear that the figure on the coin is Livia: *Diva Augusta* (see fig. 6). However, it has been commonly held by scholars that this was the intent
also of Augustus and Tiberius and the portrait features of the seated
figure, although less than distinct, are similar to the depiction of Livia
on statues.[19] Just as important as the intent of the minter, however,

Fig. 5. "Tribute Penny," Denarius of Tiberius. Lyons. © Copyright The British Museum

Fig. 6. *"Diva Augusta,"* Dupondius of Claudius. Rome, 42 CE. © Copyright The British Museum

may be the understanding of those who held these coins. In the provinces during the rule of Tiberius, a number of imitations of this figure do include the name Livia in the inscription (*RPC* 341–Caesaraugusta, 711–Hippo Regius, 3919–Cyprus; Bartman 1999, 118 n. 25). There are numerous examples of other Livia coins from the provinces with a variety of other images as well. For example, a coin from Alexandria in 10/11 CE depicts Livia on the obverse with Euthenia/Abundantia on the reverse (*RPC* 5053).

Wood notes that "during the period of her widowhood, Livia first began to be explicitly identified as 'Ceres Augusta'" (2000, 112). According to Elizabeth Bartman, "Ceres was Livia's most politically innocuous (and consequently, most widespread) divine evocation" (1999, 93). In addition to coin images, Bartman has catalogued a large corpus of sculpted portraits of Livia that includes a significant

Fig. 7. "Livia on sardonyx." Museo Archeologico, Florence

representation of Ceres/Demeter figures. Perhaps the most common mark of identification of Ceres in art is the *corona spicea*—a crown of wheat. Here Ovid's rendition of the myth of Ceres and Proserpina seems to have been influential. He describes the daughter's return as affecting the land:

> Only then did Ceres recover her expression and her spirit and she put the wheat sheaf garland on her hair; and a great harvest was produced in the fallow fields and the threshing floor scarcely received the heaped up wealth. (*Fast.* 4.615–18)

This is depicted well by a sardonyx cameo from the Tiberian era which presents Livia facing left, veiled, and wearing a very distinct floral wreath (fig. 7).[20] This is common in numerous statues as well.

In Tibullus, where *Pax* is given the attributes of Ceres, the stalk of wheat is held forth in the hand—as in the case of the seated women on the imperial coins mentioned above. Tibullus describes the role of *Pax* including a descriptive reference to the wheat imagery:

> Meanwhile let Peace tend our fields. Bright Peace first led under the curved yoke the cows about to plow the fields; Peace nourished the vine plants and stores the grape juice so that pure wine might flow for the son from the father's jar. In peace shine the hoe and plowshare, but decay masters the sad arms of the harsh soldier in the darkness.... Then come to us, nourishing Peace, and hold the wheat stalk in your hand, and let fruits pour out of your shining breast (*Corp. Tib.* bk. 2:1.10.45–50, 67–68).

The *corona spicea*, handheld wheat stalks, cornucopia, and other floral arrangements thus, when employed in sculptural representations of Livia, serve to identify her with Ceres/ Demeter.

The Ceres Borghese (fig. 8) with a likely provenance of the vicinity of Rome brings together several of these characteristic symbols.[21] Wearing the floral wreath, Livia stands erect while clutching a cornucopia of fruit to her left side and extending her right hand with stalks of wheat. Bartman suggests that this "reflects an important portrait of Livia" in Rome since a similar figure has been discovered near Spanish Corduba (1999, 106).

In contrast to the highly decorated Ceres Borghese, the Velletri statue (fig. 9) is highlighted alone by the stalks of wheat held erect in the left hand.[22] The figure of Livia herself is dominant, dressed in chiton and himation, veiled, and with waves of hair framing her face. Yet there is no question. It is Livia in the guise of Ceres.

Perhaps the closest parallel to the depiction on the Philip coin commemorating the city of Bethsaida/Julias is a cameo figure from Vienna (fig. 10).[23] The figure of Livia, enthroned and diademed, faces to the left gazing at a bust of Augustus that she holds in her right hand—thus providing a dating for this piece shortly after Augustus' death in 14 CE. It is the depiction of the stalks of grain, however, that is important here. Unlike other parallels where the ears of grain are bunched together, here the artist has depicted three distinct ears. Like the depiction on the coin of Philip, they are held in the left hand—in this case oversized perhaps for emphasis. One should also not overlook the similarity in context. Just as the gem depicts Livia in mourning

Fig. 8. Ceres Borghese, "Portrait de l'Impératrice Livie figurée en Cérès, épouse d'Octave-Auguste en 38 av. JC." Paris, Musée du Louvre

Fig. 9. "Velletri Livia." Wells (Norfolk), Holkham Hall

Fig. 10. "Cameo of Livia." Vienna Kunsthistorisches Museum

following the death of Augustus, so also the coin of Philip, dated to the year 30 CE, is clearly a response to Livia's death.

The Ceres/Demeter imagery serves to convey ideas of fertility, prosperity, and peace as well as virtues of motherhood and chastity—all of which were important in the Augustan program. At the same time, one should not overlook the role of the Ceres/Demeter myth focusing on life and rebirth. So while the gem depicts Augustus in his deified state, that message of continuity of life is affirmed in the symbol of the wheat stalks. There is mourning, yet there is also a message of hope. The program of Augustus will be continued in the role of Livia as benefactress. According to the will of Augustus, Livia had been adopted into the Julian gens and granted the title *Sebaste* ensuring the succession of Tiberius, yet in fact setting up a co-regency where she ruled alongside as empress mother.

Καρπόφορος Epithet

As seen above, Καρπόφορος [fruit bearing] was the dominant slogan associated with the goddess Demeter. The coin of Philip dedicated to Julia/Livia is apparently the only known example of Καρπόφορος on a coin. It is important to note that the epithet does not merely call attention to the goddess Demeter, but it explicitly describes Livia herself as Καρπόφορος identifying the imperial mother with the goddess.

A parallel for this comes from an inscription on a large stele from Ephesus dating from 19 to 23 CE. While dedicated to Livia, the decree describes the special favors granted to the *Demetriastai* [priests of Demeter] among whom several are named including

ἱερεῖς ... τῆς Σεβαστῆς Δήμητρος Καρποφόρου
[Priests...of Augusta Demeter Karpophoros]
(*SEG* 4.515; Bartman 1999, epig. cat. 45; Spaeth 1996, cat. 1.4)

This is the beginning of a trend in which the epithet Καρπόφορος is appropriated by women of the imperial family so that later inscriptions will designate in a similar way the following imperial women.

- Agrippina the Elder, wife of Germanicus and mother of Caligula:
  Αἰολίς Καρποφόρος (from Mytilene on Lesbos)

- Agrippina the Younger, sister of Caligula, daughter of Agrippina the elder, wife of Claudius, mother of Nero:

Αἰολίς Καρποφόρος (from Thermae)
Αἰολίς Καρποφόρος (from Mytilene)

- Sabina, wife of Hadrian:
Δημητήρ Καρπόφορος (from Tchelidjik)
Καρπόφορος (from Athens)
(Spaeth 1996, cat. 4.1, 6.1, 6.2, 12.3, 12.4)

While the use of such later examples must be treated carefully, it would seem to indicate that the use of the epithet for Livia herself may have been more extensive than the evidence of two examples might attest. Since the coins of Philip were intended only for circulation within his meager territory northeast of the Sea of Galilee, one would expect this to be the case for Philip's subjects to understand the inscription.

LIVIA COINS IN A JEWISH PROVENANCE

In a well-known episode, Jesus, confronted by Jerusalem authorities concerning taxes, calls for a coin and says, "Render to Caesar the things that are Caesar's, and to God the things that are God's" (Mark 12:17). The saying revolves around the image of Caesar Tiberius depicted on the coin. A lesser-known detail is that the reverse depicts an image of Livia, seated and in the guise of *Pax* (fig. 5) (*BMCRE*, no. 35). For over thirty years, this particular coin type had circulated throughout the Roman Empire—minted regularly at the official Roman mint at Lugdunum by Augustus beginning in 2 BCE, continued by Tiberius, and then copied frequently in the provinces including the "tribute penny" presented to Jesus in Jerusalem. The significance of this is quite clear—Livia was a well-recognized figure even among those living far on the eastern edges of the Roman Empire on Palestinian soil. As benefactress also for the Jewish people, her role would be familiar.

The Roman procurators of Judaea residing in Caesarea Maritima also issued their own coins, among which were a number dedicated to Livia. In deference to Jewish custom, no images of Livia were depicted (Meshorer 1982, 42). Yet during the years 15 through 26 CE, Valerius Gratus issued no less than six different coins with a ΙΟΥΛΙΑ [Julia] inscription (fig. 11).[24] The symbols employed were inoffensive cornucopia, amphorae, vine leaves, and olive leaf wreathes. Still, those symbols did point to the concept of fertility and abundance associated with the empress mother.

Fig. 11. "Julia," Coin of Procurator Gratus, 17 CE. The Israel Museum, Jerusalem

Fig. 12. "Julia Kaisaros," Coin of Procurator Pontius Pilate, 29 CE. The Israel Museum, Jerusalem

In the year 29 CE, and again in 30 CE, following Livia's death, the new procurator Pontius Pilate continued the practice of issuing Livia coins now with a ΙΟΥΛΙΑ ΚΑΙΣΑΡΟΣ [Julia of Caesar] inscription (fig. 12).[25] Only Pilate, known for his willingness to test the boundaries of Jewish law (Josephus *Ant.* 18.55–62; *J.W.* 2.167–77; Philo, *Embassy* 38.299–305), did not refrain from images that were associated with the imperial cult such as the *simpulum* and the *lituus*. In addition, imagery of three ears of grain, which are significant for Livia, appear on Pilate's coins. The frequency of these Livia coins in modern coin markets attests to their wide circulation. The holders of such coins were surely aware of the importance of this individual named Julia.

When one considers the high distribution of the tribute coins of Tiberius, the Julia coins of Procurators Gratus and Pilate, and the Julia Sebaste coins of Herod Philip, it is clear that the impact of this powerful woman was understood throughout first-century Palestine.

THE DEATH OF LIVIA

The Demeter myth of the dying grain was spread throughout the Roman Empire through its appropriation by Livia the wife of Augustus; and the impact of Livia on Palestinian soil was communicated through the naming of cities and the minting of coins. It is, however, at the point of her death in 29 CE that the connection of Livia and the dying grain myth is made explicit. The evidence for this is the use of grain imagery on Livia coins both by Pilate and by Philip in 29 and 30 CE.

It is well known that Livia sought apotheosis for herself, as had been the case with Julius Caesar and her husband Augustus. In the eastern provinces, she was already treated as a goddess while living. Yet in Rome, these attributes of Ceres and other goddesses were still seen as more symbolic. Perhaps it was the degree to which such honors were bestowed upon her, especially in the provinces; perhaps it was her growing popularity and power in Rome itself. However, there was a definite falling out between Tiberius and Livia during her latter years, so that he exiled himself in 26 CE to Capreae, from which he ruled. Even news of her death was not enough to bring him back to Rome. Fear that her followers might stage a grandiose funeral and pressure for her apotheosis, he stayed away, only sending orders that her funeral be kept simple and he asked the Senate to declare a year of mourning (Dio *Hist.* 58.2; Suetonius *Tib.* 51; Tacitus *Ann.* 5.1–2)— a significant move in contrast to the declaration forbidding mourning following Augustus' death since he was to be seen as a god (Dio *Hist.* 56.41). It was the continued popularity of Livia and a grassroots movement that led to her deification by Claudius in 41 CE (Dio *Hist.* 60; Suetonius *Claud.* 11).

The Pontius Pilate coin of 29 CE is clearly influenced by Tiberius' instructions for a year of mourning to commemorate Livia's death. Thus the inscription ΙΟΥΛΙΑ ΚΑΙΣΑΡΟΣ [Julia of Caesar] gives honor to her special role as wife of Augustus and mother of the emperor and the *simpulum* on the obverse points to her role as priestess in the imperial cult. Yet it is the use of grain imagery on the reverse that calls attention to Livia as the new Demeter.

Fig. 13. "Livia with Augustus and the bust of a young man on a sardonyx." St. Petersburg, Hermitage

The motif of drooping ears of grain on this particular coin resembles the Vienna gem where Livia, holding the bust of Augustus, was clearly in mourning. In contrast, Ceres Borghese (fig. 8) and Velletri (fig. 9) statues portrayed Livia with erect stalks of wheat. What is especially interesting about the Pilate coin is that three distinct ears of grain are depicted rather than the common, less-distinct bunches of ears found on many statues.

A gem from St. Petersburg (fig. 13) may perhaps offer insight into interpretation since it also portrays a trinity of figures.[26] The positioning of Livia and Augustus—this time an actual figure rather than

a bust—closely parallels the Vienna gem. Here Livia, bedecked with
the Ceres *corona spicea*, is portrayed as priestess with the veil and her
uplifted right hand. New to this depiction is the central character of
a young boy. His identity, while debated for years, must remain
uncertain. The obvious connection with Tiberius cannot be proven
because of lack of facial resemblance and the incongruency of age
(Bartman 1999, 103). Nevertheless, the youthful figure surely represents the future and the promise of the Augustan dynasty. With both
Augustus and Livia depicted with divine attributes, the empire's
future would be in the hands of youthful mortals—including Tiberius. The coin of Pilate would seem to follow this idea. The single
erect ear of grain in the center would likely represent the living
Emperor Tiberius while the two drooping ears would represent the
now fallen Augustus and Livia. Such a depiction is not unlike the
Vienna gem where, in Livia's handheld bundle, the lower ear of grain
seems to recede giving way to two stronger, healthier looking stalks.
Here this lower receding stalk would represent the deceased, though
deified Augustus. The Pilate coin has taken that one step further in
response to the death of Livia in 29 CE and the Roman Senate's declaration of a year of mourning. The representation of the drooping ears
of grain on the coin of Pilate was thus consistent with that decree.
With Augustus and Livia now dead, Pilate's future was clearly dependent upon his favor with Tiberius.

Like the Pilate coin, Agrippa 1 also employed the imagery of
three grain stalks in a coin minted in 42 CE (fig. 14). Only this time all
the stalks of grain are presented as erect (Meshorer 1982, plate 10, no.
11). There is no connotation of mourning. The timing of this coin is
significant. In 41 CE, Livia finally achieved her goal of apotheosis
when her grandson Claudius became emperor and declared her deification. On that occasion, Claudius reissued the common Tiberian and
Augustus state coin which depicted the seated Livia in the guise of
Ceres holding an ear of grain (fig. 6) (*BMCRE* 1975, 224). The inscription *DIVA AUGUSTA* [goddess Augusta] makes the explicit connection
with her role as the new Demeter and her deification. It was thus fitting that Agrippa 1—as the grandson of Livia's dear friend Salome who
had been educated in Rome alongside Claudius, as well as Caligula
and Drusus, son of Tiberius—would commemorate Livia's deification
far away on Palestinian soil.

Fig. 14. Coin of Agrippa 1, 42 CE. The Israel Museum, Jerusalem

On the other hand, it is somewhat surprising that Philip was to employ the symbolism of three erect ears of grain on his Julia Sebaste coin of 30 CE (fig. 1)—eleven years prior to Livia's apotheosis. In fact, that same year Pilate was to reissue the Julia coin with the drooping ears of grain. It would appear that Philip was part of a grassroots movement in support of Livia's deification—a movement at odds with the official position of the emperor and the Roman Senate. Yet there is no ambiguity concerning the coin of Philip. The ears of grain are presented more in the traditional pose of Ceres/Demeter, erect and held in an outstretched hand—a sign of vitality and health. The two legends ᾽Ιουλια Σεβαστη [Julia Sebaste] and ΚΑΡΠΟΦΟΡΟΣ [fruit bearing] underscore the continued benevolence of the Livia figure.

It would seem that this might be a risky move for Philip since it went against the position of Tiberius; however, Philip continued to mint an image of Tiberius on his larger denomination in 30 CE while the Julia Sebaste coin was smaller. At the same time, one must note that the Tiberius coin in that particular year included a significant variation, the mention in the inscription of Philip's role as founder of cities [ΚΤΙΣ].[27] This information, combined with the notations in Josephus (*Ant.* 18.28; *J.W.* 2.168), provides the convincing evidence that this especially large mint in the year 30 CE was part of a greater program in which Philip honored Livia with the foundation of a city—the village Bethsaida, now expanded and rededicated as Julias (Strickert 1995b, 40–51).

While the minting of a coin may be a decision that can be made in short order, the founding of a city requires years of planning and preparation, especially when improvements and expansion are included. In the case of the city of Bethsaida/Julias, it is likely that construction began as early as 25 CE with his original target date for dedication as 30 January 33 CE—Livia's ninetieth birthday. The decision was perhaps a response to Livia's recovery from serious illness in 22 CE[28] and an act of appreciation for a lifetime of beneficiary service. After all, Philip had been educated in Rome along with other potential client rulers under the watchful eye of Livia, and his appointment as tetrarch of the Golan in 4 BCE and retention in office after the deposing of Archelaus in 6 CE were likely due in part to her influence (Strickert 1998, 79, 94–95). At the same time, there may also have been political factors since Agrippa 1, a member of a younger generation of Roman-trained client rulers, had returned to Palestine in 23 CE at about the age of thirty-three. The brothers Antipas in Galilee and Philip in the Golan having provided long and successful rule since 4 BCE, Agrippa 1 found himself as a trained client king without a kingdom.

What better way to demonstrate stability and prosperity—and to ensure Philip's continuation as ruler—than to found a city and to dedicate it to the empress mother. By incorporating the motifs of Ceres/Demeter on the Julia Sebaste coin, Philip was also recalling the great virtues of the Augustan program—the recognition of motherhood, peace, and prosperity; the natural progression of the life cycle. In short, Ceres/Demeter was a natural image for a political figure seeking a continuation of the status quo. There was also a natural connection with the establishment of a new city. Before grain was discovered, people wandered without boundaries. The settled farming society was thus the beginning of law, the beginning of civilization. Thus in commenting on Vergil's *Aenead* 4.58, Servius writes:

> Ceres…is in charge of the founding of cities,
> as Calvus teaches: "She taught the sacred laws."
> (Spaeth 1996, 98)

Thus is found the well-known custom of encircling the boundaries of a city with the furrow of a plow. The Ceres/Demeter motif on the Julia Sebaste coin would have served Philip well.

Yet one must also be careful not to overestimate the propaganda value of such a coin since the coins of Philip were circulated only within his own Golan region—especially for such a small denomination. For Philip himself, having been educated in Rome during that period when Augustus began utilizing the Ceres motif and quite possibly present at the dedication of the Ara Pacis Augustae where the connection with Livia began, the symbolism would have been meaningful. So also it is to some degree with the other Herodians, Agrippa and Antipas, as well as with Pilate and other Roman officials. Yet what about the local populace? Even with the proliferation of Livia/Demeter statues and coins throughout the eastern Mediterranean and with an appreciation of some degree of cosmopolitanism in the Palestinian setting, would the impact of these coins be lost on Philip's subjects?

Perhaps the answer to this comes from the recent archaeological excavations at Bethsaida/Julias under the direction of Rami Arav. Among the ruins, Arav has identified a Roman-style temple from the early first century—identification has been established on the basis of floor plan and architectural remains, as well as the discovery of a Roman incense shovel (Arav 1999, 18–24, 34–44)—which he suggests was dedicated to Livia and employed in the imperial cult, quite possibly at the time of the city dedication. Rather significant is the discovery of numerous fragments of clay figurines found in the vicinity of the temple—presumably for residents to purchase and take home. In one case, the fragment displays the folds of a draped cloth worn over the chiton. In another, a partial tiara is covered by a veil denoting possibly a priestess figure (Arav 1999, 22, 32, figs. 16, 21). Yet, for most of these, a more precise identification is impossible.

One figurine (fig. 15), however, does lend itself to identification since the upper portion of the woman's body is preserved (Arav 1995, 21, fig. 13). This four-centimeter-tall clay fragment (with tints of red remaining) shows a veiled female with a hairstyle typical for Livia during this period. Perhaps the closest parallel is found in the two-meter-tall white marble Velletri sculpture (fig. 9) where the distinct waves of hair frame the face.[29] Beginning with Tiberius' *Salus* coin (fig. 16) minted in 22 CE, there was a clear development in Livia's hairstyle which has been characterized by Bartman as the tendency "to exaggerate those waves into melonlike segments that cover the head uniformly with distinguishing between side waves and crown."[30] Although facial features in this miniature clay figurine are clearly generic, it seems only logical to identify the figurine as Livia.

Fig. 15. "Livia," clay figurine. Israel Antiquities Authority

Fig. 16. "Livia as *Salus*," Dupondius of Tiberius.
Rome, 22 CE. © Copyright The British Museum

There are no similarities between the figurine fragment itself
and the Julia Sebaste coin of Philip. A connection can only be made
indirectly in that the Velletri parallel does depict Livia holding ears of
grain in her left hand. However, the depiction on Philip's coin is most
unusual, with the disembodied arm reaching out with the grain.
While the depiction of ears of grain on coins is quite common, as is
the complete figure of the seated Livia, no parallel for the handheld

grain has been found earlier than the Philip coin.[31] Several years ago at a conference in Germany, Robert Wenning suggested that such a representation must be dependent upon a well-known statue. One possibility, of course, is that the artist employed by Philip at his mint was aware of such Livia statues from travels throughout the empire. No less improbable is the conjecture that the coin imagery was based on such a statue that stood prominently in Bethsaida/Julias—Philip, after all, was not hesitant to employ human images on his coins. The handheld grain imagery on the Julia Sebaste coin would thus serve as a constant reminder of the significance of the Livia cult in Bethsaida/ Julias in the same way that the tetrastyle temple on his Augustus and Tiberius coins called to mind the temple of Augustus at Caesarea Philippi. The coin epigraph ΚΑΡΠΟΦΟΡΟΣ likewise must be understood in this context—familiar to all of Philip's subjects because of the Livia cult and perhaps even utilized, as at Ephesus, as a dedicatory inscription.

LIVIA AND THE DYING GRAIN SAYING OF JOHN

There is no question that the role of Livia as priestess in the imperial cult helped to spread the Demeter myth throughout the empire, including first-century Palestine. There is now strong evidence that the depiction of stalks of grain on sculptures and on coins and the common epithet ΚΑΡΠΟΦΟΡΟΣ were commonplace. Because of the coincidence of the respected Livia's death in 29 CE less than a year before the death of Jesus of Nazareth (April 7, 30 CE), one must take seriously this phenomenon as background for the dying grain saying in John 12:24. The mention of "Greeks" wishing to see Jesus and the intermediary role of two Bethsaida disciples seem to be clues that should not be discounted too quickly.

With the death of Livia, a new dimension was added to the dying grain myth. No longer was rebirth considered automatic and immutable. The seed of grain had fallen into the earth and died. Just as the followers of Jesus looked in hope for his resurrection, so the adherents of the cult of Livia looked forward to her deification—a process that was not complete until the rule of Claudius in 41 CE. Although she had frequently been identified with Ceres while alive, Livia's death by no means led to an automatic rebirth. Yet it was a grassroots movement in the provinces that led to her exaltation. Her death led to the bearing of much fruit.

CHAPTER NOTES

Unless otherwise indicated, all translations are my own. All biblical citations are taken from the New Revised Standard Version.

1. Only John 4:44 received a pink or "probably" designation, while John 12:25 and 13:20 are both colored gray, which means that the ideas are close to those of Jesus.
2. Hans Conzlemann (1975, 281) notes that the analogy of human life and the cycle of nature is common in the ancient world, yet what is new in the Christian saying is the necessity of death as a condition of life.
3. Schnackenburg 1980, 384. See also Brown 1966, 471, 473–74; Haenchen 1984, 97; Barrett 1960, 353; Dodd 1963, 368. Like John 12:24, verse 25 is also printed in gray in *The Five Gospels* (Funk et al. 1993).
4. Matt. 5:13; Mark 3:24; Matt. 6:22–23; Matt. 18:12–13. See also Schnackenburg 1980, 383.
5. Dodd 1963, 369. Similar opinions are expressed in Brown 1966, 471–73; Schnackenburg 1980, 383.
6. Raymond Brown (1966, 472) states, "the peculiar feature of this parable is the insistence that only through death is the fruit borne."
7. Cf. Brown (1966, 467) who refers to "a parabolic use of the article" as in Luke 8:5, 11. See also Barrett 1960, 352.
8. *IG* I.76.1–46. Translation in Rice and Stambaugh 1979, 185–87.
9. Varro *Ling.* 5.64. See also Cicero *Nat. d.* 2.26.67, 3.30.52, 24.62.
10. Seneca, *Phoen.* 219; Claudianus, *Rapt. Pros.* 2. 138; Germanicus, *Arat* 38; similary Ovid (*Metam.* 5.490) makes use of the epithet *frugum genetrix*.
11. The term here is Ἕλληνές which refers to Gentiles, not Ἑλληνίσται which would refer to Greek-speaking Jews. John does not use ἔθνος to refer to the Gentiles, but to the Jewish people. Ernst Haenchen suggests that John 12:20 refers to the "Greek world in general, and thus also the pagan world" (1984, 96). See also Brown 1966, 466; Schnackenburg 1980, 381; Barrett 1960, 351; Sanders 1968, 290; Hoskyns 1947, 423.
12. The reference to Bethsaida of Galilee perhaps focuses on "Galilee of the Gentiles" as a territory of mixed culture and should be contrasted with Jerusalem rather than making a distinction between Galilee and Golan (Strickert 1998, 21). See also Brown 1966, 466; Barrett 1960, 351.
13. This city was first renamed as "Livia" and then changed to "Julia." Josephus *J.W.* 2.168.
14. Salome also bequeathed territories on the southern coast to Julia. Josephus *J.W.* 2.167.
15. Kindler 1971, 162–63. Coins with Augustus' image were minted in 1, 8, and 12 CE and with Tiberius' image in 15, 26, 29, 30, and 33 CE.
16. Ya'akov Meshorer originally interpreted this as a reference to the thirtieth anniversary of the founding of Caesarea Philippi (1982, 42, 49). Citing my earlier study (Strickert 1995a), he has changed his view to see this as a reference to the founding of Bethsaida/Julias (Meshorer 2001, 88).

17. Both figures are veiled and crowned in a similar fashion. Bonnano 1976, 28.
18. *Pax Cererem nutrit, Pacis alumna Ceres.* Ovid *Fast.* I.704.
19. *BMCRE* 1:91; Spaeth 1996, 171; Bartman 1999, 103; Wood 2000, 88–89; Grether 1946, 227. For a contrary view, see Pollini 1990, 334–57, esp. 350.
20. Bartman 1999, 190, fig. 185=Spaeth 1996, fig. 10—from Museo Archeologico 14549, Florence. Height 4.5 cm.
21. Bartman 1999, 45, fig. 45, cat. 3—Musee du Louvre (Paris) Ma 1242. Height 2.53 meters, probably from near Rome.
22. Bartman 1999, 152, fig. 132, cat. 15—Wells (Norfolk), Holkham Hall. From the Villa Ginnetti in Velletri, white marble, height 2.08 meters.
23. Bartman 1999, 104, fig. 79, cat. 110—Sardonyx from Vienna, Kunsthistorisches Museum IX A 95. Height 10 cm.
24. Meshorer 1982, 173; Gratus coin for year 17 CE, Meshorer 1982, plate 31, no. 16.
25. Meshorer 1982, 180, 283; Pilate coin of 29 CE, Meshorer 1982, plate 31, no. 21.
26. Bartman 1999, 105, fig. 81, cat. 105—sardonyx gem, St. Petersburg, Hermitage Z 149. Diameter 8.3 cm.
27. For analysis of epigraphs, see Strickert 1995a, 182.
28. Tacitus *Ann.* 3.68. Upon Livia's recovery, Tiberius responded in 22 CE. by issuing a series of coins in her honor including the Salus dupondius which expressed appreciation at Livia's health as well as the well-being of the entire empire. *BMCRE* 1.131, nos. 81–84; Giacosa 1983.
29. Other parallels noted by Bartman include the St. Petersburg gem illustrated above, Bartman 1999, fig. 81, cat. 105; the Paestum Livia with veil and wavy hair, figs. 88–89, cat. 24; the Velleia Livia, figs. 96–97, cat. 33; the Lusitanian Aeminium Livia, fig. 150, cat. 44; and the Grumentum Livia, fig. 136, cat. 21.
30. Bartman 1999, 117. Brigette Freyer-Schauenberg describes this development as the "Kiel type"(1982, 209–24). See also Wood 2000, 118; Strickert 2002b.
31. Arie Kindler (1999, 246–47) notes two parallels, one minted by Agrippa for his wife Kypros (Meshorer 1982, 250) and another minted by Agrippa 2 (Meshorer 1982, 246), which are likely dependent on the Philip coin.

180   *Fred Strickert*

LITERATURE CITED

Arav, Rami. 1999. Bethsaida Excavations: Preliminary Report, 1994–1996. In Arav and Freund 1999.

Arav, Rami, and Richard Freund, eds. 1995. *Bethsaida: A City by the North Shore of the Sea of Galilee.* Vol. 1. Kirksville, Mo.: Thomas Jefferson University Press.

———. 1999. *Bethsaida: A City by the North Shore of the Sea of Galilee.* Vol. 2. Kirksville, Mo.: Truman State University Press.

Aristophanes. 1955. *The Frogs.* In *The Five Comedies of Aristophanes.* Translated by Benjamin Bickley Rogers. Garden City, N.Y.: Doubleday.

Barrett, C. K. 1960. *The Gospel According to St. John.* London: S.P.C.K.

Bartman, Elizabeth. 1999. *Portraits of Livia: Imaging the Imperial Woman in Augustan Rome.* Cambridge: Cambridge University Press.

Bonnano, A. 1976. *Roman Relief Portraiture to Septimius Severus.* British Archaeological Reports, Supplement 6. Oxford: Oxford University Press.

Brodie, Thomas L. 1993. *The Quest for the Origin of John's Gospel: A Source-Oriented Approach.* New York: Oxford University Press.

Broeckh, August, et al. 1828. *Corpus Inscriptionum Graecarum.* 13 vols. Berlin: Berolini.

Brown, Raymond E. 1966. *The Gospel According to John, I–XII.* The Anchor Bible, vol. 29. Garden City, N.Y.: Doubleday.

Bultmann, Rudolf. 1931. *The History of the Synoptic Tradition.* London: Blackwell.

Cicero, Marcus Tullius. 1965. *Selected Works.* Translated by Michael Grant. Baltimore: Penguin Books.

Conzelmann, Hans. 1975. *1 Corinthians.* Translated by James W. Leitch. Hermeneia Series. Philadelphia: Fortress.

Crawford, M. H. 1974. *Roman Republican Coinage.* 2 vols. New York: Cambridge University Press.

Dio, Cassius. 1914–17. *Roman History.* Translated by Earnest Cary. 9 vols. Loeb Classical Library. London: W. Heinemann.

Dodd, C. H. 1963. *Historical Tradition in the Fourth Gospel.* Cambridge: University Press.

Freyer-Schauenberg, Brigette. 1982. Die Kieler Livia. *Bonner Jahrbuch* 182:209–24.

Funk, Robert W., Roy W. Hoover, and the Jesus Seminar. 1993. *The Five Gospels: The Search for the Authentic Words of Jesus.* New Translation. New York: Polebridge Press.

Giacosa, Giorgio. 1983. *Women of the Caesars: Their Lives and Portraits on Coins.* Translated by R. Ross Holloway. New York: Arte e Moneta Publishers.

Grether, Gertrude. 1946. Livia and the Roman Imperial Cult. *American Journal of Philology* 67:222–52.

Haenchen, Ernst. 1984. *John.* Translated by Robert W. Funk. Hermeneia Series. Philadelphia: Fortress.

Herodotus. 1998. *The Histories/ Herodotus*. Translated by Robin Waterfield. New York: Oxford University Press.

Holtzmann, H. J. 1908. *Evangelium, Briefe und Offenbarung des Johannes*. Tübingen: Mohr.

Horace. 1964. *Horace*. Edited by Jacques Perret and translated by Bertha Humez. New York: New York University Press.

Hoskyns, E. D. 1947. *The Fourth Gospel*. London: Faber & Faber Ltd.

Inscriptiones Graecae. 1873. Berlin: W. de Gruyter.

Josephus. 1958–65. *Works*. Translated by H. St. J. Thackeray. 9 vols. Loeb Classical Library. Cambridge: Harvard University Press.

Kindler, Arie. 1971. A Coin of Herod Philip: The Earliest Portrait of a Herodian Ruler. *Israel Exploration Journal* 21:162–63.

———. 1999. The Coins of the Tetrarch Philip and Bethsaida. In Arav and Freund 1999.

Maltiel-Gerstenfeld, Jacob. 1982. *260 Years of Ancient Jewish Coins*. Tel Aviv: Kol Printing Service Ltd.

Mattingly, Harold. 1975. *Coins of the Roman Empire in the British Museum*. London: British Museum.

Mattingly, Harold, et al. 1923. *Roman Imperial Coinage*. 9 vols. London: Spink.

Meshorer, Ya'akov. 1982. *Ancient Jewish Coinage*. Vol. 2, *Herod the Great through Bar Cochba*. Dix Hills, N.Y.: Amphora Books.

———. 2001. *A Treasury of Jewish Coins*. Nyack, N.Y.: Amphora Books.

Meyer, Marvin W., ed. 1987. *The Ancient Mysteries: A Sourcebook*. San Francisco: Harper & Row.

Ovid. 1916. *Metamorphoses*. Translated by F. J. Miller. Loeb Classical Library. London: W. Heinemann.

———. 1931. *Fasti*. Translated by J. G. Frazer. Loeb Classical Library. London: W. Heinemann.

Pausanias. 1971. *Guide to Greece*. Translated by Peter Levi. Harmondsworth: Penguin Books.

Philo of Alexandria. 1962. *The Embassy to Gaius. Philo*. Vol. 10. Translated by F. H. Colson. Loeb Classical Library. Cambridge: Harvard University Press; London: W. Heinemann.

Pollini, John. 1990. Man or God? Divine Assimilation and Imitation in the Late Republic and Early Principate. In *Between Republic and Empire: Interpretations of Augustus and His Principate*. Berkeley: University of California Press.

Rice, David G., and John E. Stambaugh. 1979. *Sources for the Study of Greek Religion*. Society of Biblical Literature Sources for Biblical Study 14. Chico, Calif.: Scholars Press.

Rose, Herbert Jennings. 1970. Demeter. In *The Oxford Classical Dictionary*. 2d ed. Edited by N. G. L. Hammond and H. H. Scullard. Oxford: Clarendon Press.

Sanders, J. N. 1968. *A Commentary on the Gospel according to St. John*. Edited by B. A. Mastin. New York: Harper & Row.

Schnackenburg, Rudolf. 1980. *The Gospel according to St. John, II.* New York: The Seabury Press.

Spaeth, Barbette Stanley. 1994. The Goddess Ceres in the Ara Pacis Augustae and the Carthage Relief. *American Journal of Archaeology* 98:65–100.

———. 1996. *The Roman Goddess Ceres.* Austin: University of Texas Press.

Strickert, Fred. 1995a. The Coins of Philip. In Arav and Freund 1995.

———. 1995b. The Founding of Bethsaida-Julias: Evidence from the Coins of Philip. *Shofar* 13:40–51.

———. 1998. *Bethsaida: Home of the Apostles.* Collegeville, Minn.: The Liturgical Press.

———. 2002a. Josephus' Reference to Julia, Caesar's Daughter: *Jewish Antiquities* 18.27–28. *Journal of Jewish Studies* 53:27–34.

———. 2002b. The First Woman to Be Portrayed on a Jewish Coin: Julia Sebaste. *Journal for the Study of Judaism in the Persian, Hellenistic, and Roman Periods* 31:65–91.

Suetonius. 1914. *Suetonius.* Translated by J. C. Rolfe. 2 vols. Loeb Classical Library. London: W. Heinemann.

Supplementum Epigraphicum Graecum. 1923. Leiden.

Tacitus, Cornelius. 1977. *The Annals of Imperial Rome.* Translated by M. Grant. Penguin Classics. Harmondsworth: Penguin Books.

Tibullus. 1931. *Catullus, Tibullus, and Pervigilium Veneris.* Translated by J. P. Postgate. Loeb Classical Library. London: W. Heinemann.

Varro, Marchus Terentius. 1938. *De Lingua Latina.* Translated by Roland G. Kent. Loeb Classical Library. London: W. Heinemann.

Wood, Susan E. 2000. *Imperial Women: A Study in Public Images, 40 BC–AD 68.* Leiden: E. J. Brill.

Richard A. Freund

Ereimos: Was Bethsaida a "Lonely Place" in the First Century CE?

BETHSAIDA AND "THE LONELY PLACE"

BETHSAIDA (LITERALLY, THE HOUSE OF THE FISHERMAN) was an important location on the Sea of Galilee mentioned by name in the Apocrypha, the writings of Josephus, Greco-Roman and rabbinic literature, and the New Testament. Its importance in early Christianity is amplified by the fact that, according to the Gospel of Luke, the only major miracle mentioned in all four Gospel accounts, the so-called "feeding of the multitudes" (at or near the site of Bethsaida), occurred. The exact location where the miracle occurred is known simply in Greek as *ereimos* and is generally translated as "solitary," "desolate," "deserted," "desert," "lonely place," or "wilderness."

Some have speculated that the location of the *ereimos* was completely distinct from Bethsaida and located the site on the northwest side of the Sea of Galilee in what is today called Tabgha.[1] Unfortunately, the northwest side of the Sea of Galilee is anything but a desert or wilderness and so the question of where to locate both the feeding and "lonely place" remains. In the only account that gives a clear link to a named location, the Gospel of Luke, places the feeding in a "lonely place" near Bethsaida (Luke 9:10–17). For the Gospel of John, the miracle of the feeding occurs on the eastern side of the Sea, while the Gospel of Matthew simply places it near the Sea of Galilee on a hill. It is reasonable, therefore, to assume that perhaps the "lonely place" might be located on a hill on the eastern side of the Sea of Galilee near the site of Bethsaida.

The location of Bethsaida has been in dispute until the recent excavations of the Bethsaida Excavations Project. Up until 1987, the site presently being excavated was called et-Tell. It is located on a large (twenty-acre) artificial mound situated at the northeast corner of the Sea of Gailiee. The site is presently set back from the Sea, located at some distance from any other ancient settlements and, according to the ongoing geological study of the area, was located in front of an active floodplain with direct access to the Sea of Galilee in antiquity (Shroder and Inbar 1995; Shroder et al. 1999). It was quite isolated in antiquity and therefore fulfills many of the characteristics of a lonely, solitary location. It presents itself as a natural candidate for the *ereimos* mentioned in the Gospels.

One part of the Bethsaida Excavations Project involves the comparison of the geology, geography, and archaeological finds associated with the site with ongoing literary investigations of citations connected with it. This chapter will present some of this information gathered during the excavations together with literary investigations related to possible meanings of *ereimos* in antiquity to determine if (and if so, why) this site, et-Tell/Bethsaida, may have been adjacent to a site that could be designated as a "lonely place" in the first century CE.

Searching for Bethsaida in Medieval Maps

The earliest extant map (Nebenzahl 1986, 19) of the area around the Sea of Galilee is a twelfth-century copy of a fourth-century map associated with writings of Jerome (fig. 1) that provides evidence about the lost fourth-century map of Eusebius of Caesarea. In this map, Bethsaida is located on the east side of a river shown as the Dan, but is also on the west side of a river shown as the Jor. A myth had been circulating about the division of what is today called the Jordan River into a Jor and a Dan River and seems to have affected the mapping of the area in this period (Nebenzahl 1986, 19). The area described in the twelfth-century map does in fact contain scientifically validated information about a series of seasonal rivers, the Meshoshim and Yehudiye Rivers, that meet in the Beteiha Plain; but the map of Jerome and Eusebius apparently called them the Jor and Dan Rivers and thus began the first in a number of different maps that confused the location of the city of

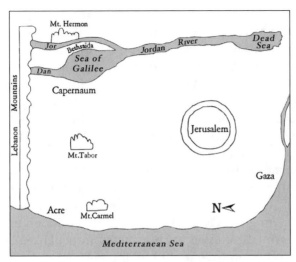

Fig. 1. Map of Bethsaida after the fourth century CE version associated with the writings of Jerome and Eusebius of Caesarea

Bethsaida (in relation to the rivers) and the events associated with it in the literature of antiquity (specifically, Josephus, the New Testament, and rabbinic literature).

The medieval maps also seem to regularly confuse Bethsaida and another city, Chorazin, in maps dating from the thirteenth century. In the thirteenth-century Matthew Paris map in the St. Albans Bible at Oxford, "Corozain" (Chorazin) and Bethsaida are both on the west side of the Sea of Galilee.[2] In a thirteenth-century map preserved in the Library of Florence, "Corozain" is located on the east side of the Jordan River, Capernaum is directly adjacent on the western side of the Jordan (on the Sea of Galilee) followed by Bethsaida Civitas. In between Capernaum and Bethsaida is found an indication of a *tabula* (table) where the feeding of the multitudes took place on what appears to be a river spur of the Sea of Galilee leading northward (Vilnay 1965, 251).

From this time onward, Bethsaida seems to migrate farther to the west of the Jordan River and closer to most of the other traditional, Byzantine pilgrimage sites along the northwest shore of the Sea of Galilee (especially close to the traditional location of Capernaum). A permanent change in the placement of Bethsaida and Chorazin on medieval maps occurred in the thirteenth century. Burchard of Mount Sion, a thirteenth-century Dominican monk, wrote a pilgrimage account based on his ten-year stay in the area, including a map with distinctive designations. Apparently it was he who first instituted the exchange of Bethsaida and Chorazin's locations on medieval maps. The exchange of the two sites might be based on theological consider-ations rather than geographic information. Bethsaida was a significant location in the New Testament and early pilgrim traditions, while Chorazin had few or no substantive literary traditions associated with it. If the Roman-period site of Bethsaida was "lost" (destroyed, aban-doned, or forgotten by the time the pilgrimage sites became popular) as the present excavations suggest, it must have been particularly dif-ficult for pilgrim guides to explain. Chorazin, although set back from the other pilgrimage sites on the northwest shore of the Sea of Galilee, had a large and impressive set of buildings at the site with active set-tlement throughout the Byzantine and early medieval periods. Per-haps because of the large remains present at the site of Chorazin (and the absence of a site near other pilgrimage locations), the two sites were exchanged. Burchard's map apparently influenced many other maps for centuries to come. Although the original of Burchard's map is lost, Lucas Brandis of the fifteenth century preserved a map designed after Burchard's account. In it, Chorazin is on the east side and Bethsaida has moved from the east to the west side of the Jordan River, or from between the Jor and Dan Rivers to the other side of the renamed and unified Jordan River (Nebenzahl 1986, 61–62). In the fourteenth-century Marino Sanuto and Peturs Vesconte map pre-served in their *Secrets for the True Crusaders to Help Them Recover the Holy Land*, Chorazin is located on the east side of the Jordan, Caper-naum is on the west side, and Bethsaida has migrated just south of Capernaum (fig. 2). Again, as in earlier maps, a mesa is found in between Capernaum and Bethsaida on a small mount north of Beth-saida (Nebenzahl 1986, 45). In one fifteenth-century map "Corozaim" is located on the east, with "Capharnau" and "Betsaida" on the west but the mesa is found on the east side north of "Corozaim" and another unnamed mesa on the west side, just north of the city of "Bet-saida" (Nebenzahl 1986, 53, plate 18). Continuing in the fifteenth, sixteenth, and seventeenth centuries, most maps placed Chorazin on the east side, Capernaum on the west, and Bethsaida directly to the south of Capernaum and to the north of Magdala, when indicated.[3]

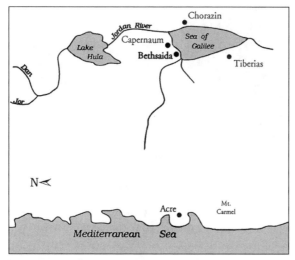

Fig. 2. Map of Bethsaida on western shore of the Sea of Galilee in Marino Sanuto and Peturs Vesconte's map preserved in their "Secrets for the True Crusaders to Help Them Recover the Holy Land"

This is generally the pattern through the eighteenth century. A variation is found in the fifteenth-century map of Bernhard von Breitenbach, which placed Chorazin on the east side of the Jordan, Capernaum and Magdala on the west side, and Bethsaida farther west and inland from Magdala (Nebenzahl 1986, 64). A rare exception is Natale Bonifacio's sixteenth-century map, which placed Chorazin, Capharnau, and Bethsaida on the west side of an oddly shaped Jordan River (Nebenzahl 1986, 98).

Another exception involves the introduction of a different location for Julias (as opposed to Bethsaida-Julias being the same as Bethsaida and Julias) on the east side of the Jordan farther to the east from Chorazin. The city of [Bethsaida-]Julias mentioned in the writings of Josephus, Pliny, and Ptolemy became distinct from Bethsaida. In the fifteenth-century map in Sanuto and Vesconte's *Tabula Nova Terrae Sanctae* (a version of Claudius Ptolemy's *Geography*), Julias sits on the west side of the Jordan. In the writings of Josephus and Pliny, Julias is said to be on the east side of the Jordan with Hippos, but in some medieval maps accompanying the writings of Ptolemy, Julias is on the west side. In the coordinates given in most of the manuscripts of

Fig. 3. Map of Julias (Bethsaida) after first century
Ptolemy's *Geography* (5.15.1–7)

Ptolemy's *Geography* (5.15.1–7), Julias is due north of Tiberias on the
west side of the Jordan and not on the coast of the Sea of Galilee at all
(fig. 3). This placement was apparently based upon a scribal error and
should be corrected to a reading that places it directly on the northeastern shore of the Sea of Galilee on the eastern side of the Jordan
River.[4] Despite traditions to the contrary, the idea of Bethsaida[-Julias]
being on the west side of the Sea of Galilee seems to have prevailed
into the modern period.

      Because of, or perhaps in spite of, this scribal error, maps starting
in the sixteenth century (Gerardus Mercator's 1537 map, for example)
placed Bethsaida and Capernaum on the west side and Chorazin and
Julias on the east side, apparently the first reference to Julias as separate
from Bethsaida (McCown 1930, 35). It appears that in the Renaissance,
as a larger selection of texts were examined in the preparation of maps,
the issue of Bethsaida-Julias (of Philip Herod and Josephus) on the eastern side of the Jordan began to conflict with the biblically oriented
map tradition present since the thirteenth century. To resolve this conflict, Mercator and others from the sixteenth century onward simply
placed Julias on the east side of the Jordan (near Chorazin) across the

sea from Bethsaida (Nebenzahl 1986, 97 [Christian von Adrichom 1533–85], 85 [Abraham Ortelius 1527–98], 119 [Jan Jansson 1588–1664], 129 [Thomas Fuller 1608–61], 115 [Franciscus Haraeus 1620]). The introduction of a distinctive location, Julias, may have also resolved the differences between any other extant map traditions of the period which still placed Bethsaida on the east side of the Jordan. The sixteenth-century *Theatrum Terrae Sanctae* of Christian von Adrichom, in particular, praised the thirteenth-century Burchard and, following him, placed Chorazin on the east and Bethsaida on the west, adding Julias next to Chorazin (Nebenezahl 1986, 94). Some, such as the sixteenth-century map of Peter Laicksteen and Christian Sgrooten, placed Bethsaida and Julias together on the west side south of Capernaum, but placed another "Iuliada" next to Chorazin on the northeast shore of the Sea of Galilee (Nebenzahl 1986, 83, 87). Another variation of this is the sixteenth-century Plancius map of the Holy Land, which includes a designation "Chorazim et Iuliada" on the northeastern shore of the Sea (Nebenzahl 1986, 102).

THE DESERTUM BETHSAIDA, BETHSAIDA, AND BETHSAIDA-JULIAS

The influence of the sixteenth-century map of *Theatrum Terrae Sanctae* of Christian von Adrichom on the study of modern and early modern preconceptions about possible biblical roads and sites cannot be minimized (Nebenzahl 1986, 96–97). Certain innovations that he introduced in his maps influenced the first seventeenth-century Hebrew maps of Yaaqov ben Abraham Zaddiq (who produced the first modern Hebrew map of Israel) and others, including Philippe Briet, Nicholas Visscher the Elder, and the eighteenth-century maps of Georg Matthaeus Seutter (Nebenzahl 1986, 110–11, 123, 133, 144). On their maps, Bethsaida appears on the west side of the Jordan on the main road of antiquity, the Via Maris [way to the sea], which leads directly to Ptolemais/Acre. Two other cities linked with Bethsaida figure prominently in Zaddiq's detailed maps. Julias and Chorazin are placed on the east side of the Jordan River, and another location, simply designated "Desertum Bethsaida," appears on the east side just south of Julias. "Desertum Bethsaida" is apparently the translation of the Greek word *ereimos*, which was associated in the New Testament with the feeding of the multitudes near Bethsaida. Unfortunately, in some later maps even this is confused as on the seventeenth-century map of

Nicholas Sanson d'Abbeville, which places the Desertum north of Julias (Nebenzahl 1986, 134).

During the Enlightenment, the use of classical texts such as those of Pliny, Josephus, and Ptolemy (as opposed to the Bible) in establishing geographic locations apparently precipitated another change in the location of Bethsaida in some maps. In the eighteenth-century map of Adrian Reland, for example, Julias Gaulanitica was located on the east side of the Jordan as described by Josephus, and Bethsaida and Chorazin are not mentioned, probably because Josephus and Pliny do not mention cities by these names (Nebenzahl 1986, 143). A hybrid version of this appears in Jean Baptiste Bourguignon's eighteenth-century map in which Bethsaida is on the west side of the Sea of Galilee and the Jordan River, but on the northeast coast is found the designation "Julias" in large print, and in smaller print "vel Chorozain," to indicate that Julias was thought to be another name for Chorazin.[5]

This short analysis of the medieval and premodern map tradition demonstrates that Bethsaida grew from one to three locations over the course of time in the following manner.

- The most ancient map traditions of Eusebius and Jerome apparently located Bethsaida on the northeast shore of the Sea of Galilee between two rivers, the Jor and the Dan. The traditions about these rivers became unified into one Jordan River. Bethsaida, while continuing to be placed between two rivers, was moved on some maps farther to the northwestern shore of the Sea of Galilee. Despite literary traditions indicating that Julias was located on the northeast shore of the Sea of Galilee and on the east side of the Jordan River, some manuscripts of Ptolemy's *Geography* contained incorrect coordinates for the city of Julias, placing it on the western side of the Sea of Galilee. A selective understanding of the Fourth Gospel traditions about "Bethsaida of Galilee," combined with this Ptolemy reference, may have contributed to the western migration of Bethsaida on maps originating from the thirteenth century onward.

- The knowledge of [Bethsaida-]Julias on the east side of the Jordan River (Josephus and Pliny) as well as pre-Ptolemy traditions may have created the need to reconcile the conflicting location. By the fourteenth century, maps showed a city called Julias on the northeastern shore of the Sea of Galilee while a Bethsaida on the west (although not all traditions held this) was indicated at approximately the location of modern day Tabgha.

- By the sixteenth and seventeenth century, the premodern systematic rereading of the Gospels and classical Greco-Roman literature seems to have created a third location that reconciled many of the previous questions. The "feeding of the multitudes" apparently occurred at a "lonely place" (Desertum Bethsaida) on the eastern side of the Sea of Galilee in an underpopulated area near the [Bethsaida-] Julias of Pliny and Josephus, but across the Sea from the then firmly established location of Bethsaida on the northwestern shore of the Sea of Galilee.

THE MODERN EXCAVATIONS AT ET-TELL

The confusing medieval map traditions were further complicated in the modern period by the rise of early-nineteenth-century adventurers and archaeologists who added their own observations to the mix. Since the nineteenth century, some (including Edward Robinson) have suspected that et-Tell, a mound some two kilometers north of the Sea of Galilee and a few hundred meters from the Jordan River, was Bethsaida. Since 1987, et-Tell has been under excavation. Following a series of probes in 1987 and 1988 initiated by Rami Arav on behalf of the Golan Research Institute and Haifa University, which eliminated other reasonable proposals for the identification of Bethsaida, et-Tell is now identified on Israeli maps as Bethsaida and the plain in front of the tell is designated as the Beteiha (sometimes even Bethsaida) Plain. The present identification was initially based upon cumulative evidence that included among other elements:

- the absence of any other historically validated site (with or without a medieval church/synagogue/building);

- et-Tell's status as the largest artificial mound in the area, and near a likely location of the city;

- the absence of a large settlement in the Late Hellenistic–Early Roman level in the probe excavations of other sites proposed as Bethsaida (at el-Araj and el-Mesadiyeh); and

- the presence of a systematic and extensive Late Hellenistic–Early Roman level at et-Tell and the lack of such a level
  at the other proposed sites.[6]

The archaeological and geological investigations at the site
during the past seven years have given insights into the question of
whether this site, et-Tell/Bethsaida (especially in the Hellenistic-
Roman periods) may have been located next to an area that could be
described as *ereimos* and therefore reconcile the literary descriptions.
The rest of this article will concern itself with the nature of the archaeological and geological data in relation to the literary information.

FROM TZER TO BETHSAIDA—FROM AN IRON AGE FORTIFIED PORT TO A ROMAN FISHING CENTER

Bethsaida is known to have been a significant site in the Iron Age
through the Roman Period for a number of reasons. As excavations at
the site uncovered a massive Iron Age gate complex and walls, it
became clear that the site must have been known in antiquity, but perhaps by another name. According to the ancient literary sources that
mention it by the name Bethsaida, the ancient city was originally situated at the northern edge of the Sea of Galilee with a port that had
direct access to the important fishing opportunities there. Bethsaida is
mentioned in the New Testament, Josephus, Pliny, and in classical rabbinic literature, including the Mishnah, Tosefta, both Talmudim, and
the Midrashim. Bethsaida was also apparently known in an earlier
period by a similar name (either Tzed [fishing] or Tzer [fortress]
through the interchanging of the similar Hebrew letters "resh" and
"dalet") in the period of the Hebrew Bible (Iron Age).[7] The Iron Age
name of Tzed may have persisted into the Hellenistic and Roman
period with the addition of Beth (Tzer) indicating that perhaps it had
been transformed from a port city to a fishing center in this time
period. A remnant of the earlier name may have been preserved in association with the lakefront property located directly adjacent to it on the
northern Sea of Galilee. This general area was known in antiquity as
Gennosar and was known as one of the most fruitful agricultural
regions in the country.[8] Although it is commonly thought that Gennosar encompassed only the northwest area of the Sea of Galilee, it may
have included both sides of the Jordan River, with the river running
between the two sides of the area. Given the present understanding of

the original name of the city as Tzer, located on the northeast shore of the Sea of Galilee, the name Gennosar may have originally been derived from the Hebrew word *Gannei*[9] which would mean the "Gardens of Tzer." If so, the disappearance of the ancient Hebrew Bible's city of Tzer may be explained by its renaming in the Persian or Greco-Roman periods. Some city names that became centers of industry or populations centers for an area became prefixed in the Second Temple period with Beth- [House of]. For example, the ancient biblical city of Gilgal, mentioned in early traditions in the Hebrew Bible (Deut. 11:30; Josh. 4:19, 5:9–10), became Beth-Gilgal in the Persian period (Neh. 12:29). Succoth in the Hebrew Bible (Gen. 33:17, Josh. 13:27, and other references) became Beth Socoth (Hieronymus *Qu. Hebr. Gen.* 53:8). Since it was in the Second Temple period that the designation Beth-[House of] was added to some city names that previously did not have this designation, this appears to be what happened to Bethsaida. The fortified city on the northeast shore of the Sea of Galilee became known as Bethsaida and lost its more ancient name of Tzer (perhaps with the development of commercial fishing at the site), but the Hebrew designation was retained in a small way by the name of the lush surrounding plain: the Gardens of Tzer-Gennosar.

In the New Testament, Bethsaida is mentioned by name twice in the Gospel of Mark, once in Matthew, twice in Luke, and twice in John. It appears, however, to have been known by another designation in the Gospel accounts as well. The only miracle account found in all four Gospels is the so-called "feeding of the multitudes" narrative. Because it is linked with Bethsaida in some of the literary accounts, an understanding of these accounts may provide insights into the physical location of Bethsaida. In Luke 9:10–17, when the five thousand are fed, the Lukan narrative states that it took place at Bethsaida (9:10), but in 9:12 the text states that the people should go in search of lodging and provisions elsewhere since it was "a lonely place" [*ereimos*]. In Matthew's parallel version of the feeding of the multitudes (14:13–21), no specific name is given to the place of the feeding, but it begins with Jesus arriving (14:13) at "a lonely place" [*ereimos*] that can be reached by boat. Later in the narrative (14:15) the disciples state that "this is a lonely place" [*ereimos*] with no provisions for the crowds. Similarly in the Markan parallel (6:30–44), although it occurs in an unnamed location, the narrative states three times (6:31, 6:32, 6.35) that the place is "a lonely place" [*ereimos*], again that can be reached by boat. *Ereimos* appears to be used here as specific terminology rather than as a random choice of vocabulary to describe an unknown location. Again, the reference is to the lack of provisions at the location and the need to go elsewhere to feed the hungry. In John 6:1–15, which is a parallel to the synoptic descriptions of the feeding of the five thousand, no specific location is designated (although Jesus withdraws to an unknown mound in the area in connection with the narrative). At the end of John's account, the disciples get into their boat and sail to Capernaum (6:16–24) and Jesus makes reference to the Hebrew Bible's feeding of the multitudes account that occurs in the book of Exodus in the *ereimos* (6:31, 6:49).

In Mark's second version of the feeding of the multitudes (four thousand are fed in 8:1–10), the location is again described as *ereimos* (8:4) and following the narrative the action moves to the healing of the blind man at Bethsaida (Mark 8:22–26), suggesting, at least by the proximity of the two narratives, that they are located in the same place. In the Matthean parallel to the second version of the feeding of multitudes (four thousand are fed in 15:32–39), the entire narrative takes place at "a lonely place" [*ereimos*] and at the end of the narrative Jesus gets in a boat and proceeds to the region of Magdan (or Magdala?) on the west side of the Sea of Galilee, suggesting that the original "lonely place" was on the east side of the Sea. In short, Bethsaida seems to have been known by the Gospel writers by its Hebrew name, "the house of the fisherman" and the region of Bethsaida (and perhaps by virtue of its elevation above the lake on the mound) by a more metaphoric Greek name, *ereimos*, a wilderness or simply "a lonely place."

THE GEOLOGY AND GEOGRAPHY OF BETHSAIDA

The geological history of Bethsaida goes back millions of years to the creation of the Dead Sea Rift and the volcanic flows that gave Bethsaida its basalt rock formations. Bethsaida sits astride the major Jordan River–Dead Sea Rift, which extends northward to Syria and south to Africa. Along this fault line (and the Jordan River), a natural route of transit developed (Beitzel 1991, 65–75), despite the fact that the area is prone to earthquakes and other geological phenomena. As cities began to emerge in the Near East some five thousand years ago, the area of Bethsaida may have played a role in the trade between the major civilizations of Mesopotamia and Egypt. Archaeological evidence suggests that a village with fishing and weaving industries existed at et-Tell during much of this period. The importance of this fishing village seems to have been altered as the access to the Sea of Galilee changed. According to the present status of Bethsaida geological information, Bethsaida had full boat and fishing access to the Sea of Galilee at that time. As recently as two thousand years ago, only indirect boat and fishing access was available to the site, and presently Bethsaida has no access to the Sea of Galilee. Evidence now suggests that, up until and including the Roman period, the Sea of Galilee may have been much larger than its present size or may have included a series of estuaries leading off of a large lagoonlike section just north of the present-day coast (Shroder and Inbar 1995; Inbar 1982a, 1982b, 1987; Inbar and Even-Nir 1989). This change may be attributed to a number of different factors that include the fluctuations of the water table on the Sea of Galilee, periodic flooding and sediment buildup, and abrupt fault displacement leading to the active seismicity well known in the region. The fact that the entire area of the Beteiha Plain (Bankier 1995) is located on the Dead Sea–Jordan Rift fault system, has made the area prone to fault creep, subsidence, upwarping, and earthquakes. Other forms of land changes, tsunami (lake tidal waves), and sediment buildup along the Jordan River (immediately adjacent to the tell) are well known and historically documented over the past two thousand years. What is not known is how important this information could be for the understanding of archaeological sites located in the northern Upper Galilee and Golan region. The combination of fault slippage, tectonic uplift, and sediment discharges from the Jordan River may have quickened the pace of the natural processes present in this unique geological area. In a single documented flood in the upper Jordan River near the site of et-Tell in 1969, for example, twenty times the annual sediment discharge occurred (Inbar and Even-Nir 1989). In addition, deforestation and overgrazing, which have continued throughout the modern period, and the draining of Lake Hula in the twentieth century have radically changed the locale. These geological phenomena have contributed to the disappearance of other ancient ports such as Ephesus. These geological factors may help to explain the mysterious disappearance of Bethsaida in antiquity. In addition, it is not surprising that when Byzantine Christian pilgrims were searching for a fishing village on the northern shore of the Sea of Galilee and did not find it, they may have established small relic sites directly on the shore to commemorate their search for Bethsaida at places such as el-Araj and el-Mesadiyah, despite the lack of ancient foundations. In general, the medieval pilgrim accounts collected by Dr. Elizabeth McNamer (McNamer 1999) show that most pilgrims did not search beyond the confines of the well-known pilgrimage sites and routes that were located on the Sea of Galilee of the medieval period. More important, sites that could not be found but were important to the pilgrim experience were placed near other well-known sites.

One of the major questions raised by the present state of geological information on Bethsaida is whether ancient writers ever recorded the topographical environment of lagoons and estuaries in the area. Simply put, do any writers in antiquity corroborate modern geological findings in any way? The answer is affirmative. Geological information that has helped solve one of the major mysteries about the disappearance of Bethsaida is also, in part, found in the ancient literature.

The plain in front of Bethsaida is referred to by local tradition in Arabic as "Beteiha." This name may preserve some ancient insight into the history of the site. In Aramaic, for example, the word *betah* means a hollow, columnlike receptacle for collecting rainwater kept near the house.[10] The name may also reflect a topography of swamps and marshes and may preserve the traditional knowledge of the legendary sediment discharges of the Jordan River at this location, or swamps and marshes. Even the traditional name for the larger surrounding area, the Land of (and the Lake of) Gennesaret, found in Strabo, Josephus, the Gospel of Luke, and I Maccabees[11] may indicate more than just a variant on the Hebrew *kinneret*. Strabo states that the Jordan waters "…a country that is fertile and all productive. It also contains a lake that produces the aromatic rush and reed; and likewise marshes. The lake is sometimes called Gennesaritis [*limnei Genneisaritis*]" (Stern 1976, 288). One of the Greek terms used by Josephus in *Antiquities* 18.28 to describe the area in front of Bethsaida is *pros limnei tei Genneisaritidi*. While the word *limnei* in Greek is one way of referring to a small pond or lake, it is also a well-known Hellenistic phrase referring to marshy lands or standing water (Liddel-Scott 1977, s.v. "limnei").

In Josephus' *Life* (71–73) he refers to the fact that there was a marshy area in front of Bethsaida (where he was injured in a battle that must have taken place in 66 or 67 CE) and that it was possible to sail directly from Taricheae (Magdala) to Bethsaida. The rabbis also describe the area of Bethsaida as containing marshes and swamps (PT

Sheqalim 6:2, 50a). Most of the Gospels use the term *thalassa*,[12] a general word for sea, when describing the Sea of Galilee, but Luke uses the word *limnei* to describe it. It is Luke who also provides the most detailed information on the traditions of Bethsaida in the Gospels; he may have possessed special materials concerning Bethsaida and its environs. The geological information gained from the investigations at Bethsaida may also contribute to the understanding of another topographical reference in Josephus. In his description of the Lake of Gennesaret, Josephus in *Jewish Wars* 3.10 states:

> Now Jordan's visible stream arises from this cavern, and divides the marshes and fens of the Lake Semechonitis: when it has run another one hundred and twenty furlongs, it first passes by the city Julias, and *then passes through the middle of the Lake of Gennesaret.*[13]

If Josephus is referring to the Gennesaret region investigated above, the Jordan River is running through the middle of this northwest/northeast area and into the Sea of Galilee. Lacking an understanding of this built-up region, medieval and premodern cartographers of the Holy Land have mistakenly created ludicrous scenarios that have a snaking Jordan River passing through the entire length of the Sea of Galilee.[14] A similar report also appears in the Babylonian Talmud.[15]

The present state of the geological information on Bethsaida also helps unravel the problem of the dimensions of the Sea of Galilee in antiquity compared to the present period. It is clear from the ancient dimensions of the Sea of Galilee (Pliny states that it was 16 by 6 miles [140 by 40 stadia]) versus the present dimensions (12.5 by 7 miles: Stern 1976, 1:471, 478) that the Sea has significantly changed over the past two thousand years. Based on evidence gathered by a geology and geography team headed by John F. Shroder and Michael Bishop of the University of Nebraska at Omaha and Moshe Inbar of Haifa University, it seems that there was a marshy, lagoonlike area (and/or estuaries)[16] in front of Bethsaida some two thousand years ago. This lagoon might have allowed a recognizable Jordan River to pass through it if the Lagoon of Gennesaret was, as it was understood by some writers in antiquity, both a part of the larger Sea of Galilee and a name for the lagoon to the north of the Sea. This situation is therefore partially corroborated in ancient and premodern observations and demands further study.

EARTHQUAKES THAT SHAPED RELIGIOUS HISTORY

The question asked at the outset was whether the Bethsaida uncovered and researched for the past seventeen years could be described as a "lonely place" in the first century CE or not. The answer is yes and no. The geological and literary information suggests a place slightly isolated from other locales around the Sea of Galilee by the first century CE. A secondary question that developed in these investigations was when the site was abandoned. It is clear from the archaeological and literary information that the site was not abandoned in the first century CE as was Gamla. The archaeological information, including some second- and third-century coins, some distinctive second- and third-century pottery,[17] and perhaps a structure or two, suggests that a settlement persisted at the site through the second and third century. The literary information, including rabbinic and apocryphal, suggests a known settlement through the third century CE. The tectonic information of the Galilee region provides additional information for identifying a more exact date. Earthquakes are well documented along the Dead Sea–Jordan Rift system upon which Bethsaida sits. In the past three thousand years, major earthquakes can be documented with a one- to two-hundred-year periodic frequency. Some of these quakes also are related to the above-mentioned tsunami on the Sea that would have swept the Beteiha Plain as well.

Earthquake terminology was well known to the biblical writers and is found in the earliest writings dating from the ninth century BCE (2 Sam. 22:8–9; 1 Kings 19:11), as well as in literary prophets from the eighth-sixth century BCE (Amos 1:1; Isa. 5:25, 13:13, 29:6; Ezek. 38:19; Zech. 14:5). Minor and major recorded earthquakes that affected the region occurred in 1927, 1896, 1837, 1759, 1546, 1457, 1303, 1202, 1157, 1114/5, 1033/34, 859, 756, 749, 551, 363, 306, 115, first century CE, and the first century BCE (Amiran, Arieh, and Turcotte 1994; Amiran 1950; Netzer 1981, 28, 134 n. 22; Boling 1984, 6:169–70). Because no systematic finds have been found at et-Tell after the third century CE and because no Byzantine presence has been discovered at the site, the "disappearance" of the site must be linked to some events in the third to the fourth centuries. The prevailing theory is that the earthquakes of the second through the fourth centuries may have initiated a slow process of deterioration of gainful employment possibilities at et-Tell and ultimately led to its abandonment before the arrival of significant Byzantine pilgrims in the area. The demise of Bethsaida during this period, however, may have also coincided with the establishment of new settlements located in different nearby areas around the Sea of Galilee. The earthquakes of 115, 306, and especially 363 CE may have caused a step-by-step destruction of the fishing industry in particular as the sedimentation from the Jordan River built up the coastline of the Sea of Galilee to a point where commercial fishing from Bethsaida was impossible. It was presumably during this period that the Byzantine presence in the area led to the establishment of a small site at el-Araj which, because it was located in a floodplain (and periodically flooded), ultimately led to the permanent establishment of Tabgha (Heptapegon) as the official site of the feeding of the multitudes for Byzantine pilgrims because of its proximity to other pilgrimage sites. The establishment of the Tabgha site in the fourth century is corroborated by the visit of the pilgrim Lady Egeria there in 380 CE. Also in the fourth century, St. Paula had as her guide St. Jerome, who called the place where Tabgha is located by the other designation for Bethsaida—*ereimos*.

The Tuba II catastrophic flood event mentioned by Shroder, Bishop, Kevin J. Cornwell, and Inbar in the second volume of this series (1999) can be dated to approximately 1,600 to 1,800 years ago and would have effectively ended commercial fishing from Bethsaida after this time. The rise of other sites in the lower Golan and nearby Galilee may indicate how the Tuba II flood created the impetus for establishing newly located cities. The site identified as Chorazin, for example, which is directly across the Jordan from Bethsaida, is a Byzantine village/city and may represent the post-363 CE settlement pattern in the area. A Syriac manuscript, *Harvard Syriac 99*, mentions twenty-one urban centers that suffered damage as a result of the earthquake that destroyed the temple restoration project initiated under Emperor Julian in 361 CE, including some of the sites in the area around Bethsaida. On the basis of the calculations available from the date mentioned in the manuscript, it is possible to date the time and day of the earthquake to 19 May 363 CE ("...at the third hour, and partly at the ninth hour of the night...") (Brock 1977, 274, 276, 279–80). Because of this information, several archaeological sites have been reassessed regarding damage and dating (Russell 1980, 47–62; Hammond 1980, 65–67; Nathanson 1986, 26–36; Groh 1988, 80–94). Apparently the damage in Palestine extended to cities such as Tiberias and Sepphoris where many of the rabbinic teachers and academies could be found in the mid-fourth century CE (Brock 1977, 276; Russell 1980).

Bethsaida is located directly along a major fault line and would have been devastated by the earthquake if the epicenter were along the fault line. In the period preceding such an earthquake, pre-shocks, lifting, or flooding may have changed the water resources located at the original port and its channels leading from the Sea of Galilee. In any case, the earthquake of 363 CE may have put a permanent end to the settlement history of the fishing village of Bethsaida and other smaller settlements in the Golan and Galilee. Earlier large sediment discharges along the Jordan River may have preceded the 363 CE earthquake and may have made Bethsaida progressively less attractive to continued settlement by the fourth century CE. I. Karcz and U. Kafri (1978, 237–53) have demonstrated two main earthquake indicators in the study of supposed archaeoseismic damage in Israel that appear at et-Tell. The first indicator is the total destruction (or perhaps abandonment) of a site without extensive evidence of strife or warfare as is the situation at et-Tell. The second indicator is evidence of extensive structural damage such as fissures, displaced walls, etc. This is consistent with the structural damage found at et-Tell, making the site similar to (using these criteria) other archaeoseismic damage sites in Israel. Although it is not altogether clear when the archaeoseismic damage occurred at et-Tell, there is no evidence that a systematic settlement survived there into the Byzantine period.

Despite the carbon 14 dates associated with the catastrophic floods, it is impossible to be any more precise than 1,800 to 1,600 years ago in dating the period when the site would have been abandoned following the Tuba II catastrophic flood and subsequent sedimentation of the low-lying estuaries used for fishing access to the Sea. Although the number of literary accounts and damage assessments is greatest in the wake of the 363 CE earthquake, it is possible that this was just the final part of a slow process that had begun after the earthquakes of 115 and 306 CE.

This seismic activity may also indicate that the changes were not permanent. Two premodern reports demonstrate that a fishing site in this locale thought to be Bethsaida continued in a much later period. The French traveler Pierre Belon, in 1547 CE, and a Portuguese Christian pilgrim in 1560 CE, state that fishing was possible at Bethsaida and the latter reports that he was fed quantities of fish there. In the recent 1994 excavations at Bethsaida, a sixteenth-century European coin was found. The number of pilgrim reports[18] that specifically mention Bethsaida after the well-documented earthquake of 1546 (and the stoppage/division of the Jordan) may indicate that the site did enjoy changing conditions because of the geological phenomena associated with the area (Braslavsky 1938, 323–36).

THE SEARCH FOR "THE LONELY PLACE"

GEOLOGY AND LITERARY CRITICISM

As mentioned above, the first-century CE sources, the New Testament and Josephus, suggest that Bethsaida was accessible by boat (and by roads) but isolated. Geological studies indicate that the site et-Tell/Bethsaida may have been accessible by boat through the first century CE and may have been slightly isolated. It is possible, however, that in addition to the geological factors that may have contributed to Bethsaida being designated "in the wilderness," the designation of Bethsaida as *ereimos* may also be a literary reference. It is important to consider this possibility since one of the major problems with most attempts at comparing archaeology to a literary text is that serious literary analysis of the text as a text is not also considered. The New Testament is a serious literary composition with internal considerations that invite analysis and, since the concept of *ereimos* is one of the few elements that link most of the Gospel accounts together in the feeding of the multitudes account, the following sections will analyze possible literary meanings of the *ereimos* references. While the concept of "a lonely place" may indicate something about the archaeology, geology, and geography of the location, it may also be a literary metaphor that connects the different Gospel accounts together in a literary way. The question explored in the rest of the chapter is the meaning of *ereimos* in light of modern literary, archaeological, and geological analyses.

WAS BETHSAIDA JESUS' SINAI?

One of the points about the location of Bethsaida as "a lonely place" or "wilderness" centers upon whether the Gospel writers saw some connection between the word Bethsaida and the words "lonely place" or "wilderness." This may have been a metaphor for Jesus and may correspond to a fulfillment of the same set of activities that were a literary matrix from the Hebrew Bible. This is a well-known phenomenon in the

New Testament as Jesus is seen as fulfilling all sorts of different prophecies and events that first appear in the Hebrew Bible. The suggestion here is that the events regarding the feeding of the multitudes recorded in the New Testament were somehow preordained in the biblical book of Exodus account of the "walking of the Israelites on dry land in the midst of the Sea" recorded in Exodus 14–15, and the account of the feeding of the Israelite multitudes (with the miraculous quails and manna) in the midst of the desert in Exodus 16. The word *ereimos* is used over fifty times in the New Testament to denote "desolation," "desert," and "wilderness," and generally these passages refer to the historical "desert" and "wilderness" found in the Hebrew Bible. The word appears hundreds of times in the Septuagint translation of the Hebrew Bible and Apocrypha in Greek with a wide variance of meanings, but generally "wilderness," "desert," "destroyed," or "empty place" are the meanings of the different Hebrew and Aramaic terms alluded to. Among the most ancient Greek writers, Herodotus uses the word *ereimos* to describe a thinly populated place or even an abandoned city that has been reinhabited (*Hist.* 3.102, 4.17 ff, 6.23, 8.65).

The sequence of events seems to be key in the overall structure of the New Testament accounts of the feeding of the multitudes. The Bethsaida accounts in Matthew, Mark, and John all state that first the multitudes were fed at a lonely place/wilderness, and then Jesus had an experience "in the midst of the sea" in almost a counternarrative parallelism of the Exodus account. In the Exodus account, Moses has a walking through the sea experience that is then followed by the feeding of the multitudes account. This is a common form of literary parallelism when the author attempts to borrow from a well-known symbolic account, but then updates and enhances it with a totally new twist. In this case, Jesus (the new Moses) feeds the people first and then leads them back through the Sea. The connection to the Exodus feeding account in the Gospel according to John is the clearest of all the Gospels. In John 6:1–15, the feeding of the multitudes takes place when "Jesus withdrew to the mountain by himself" and then in 6:49 it is clearly alluded to: "Your fathers ate manna in the wilderness [*ereimos*] and they died." In this case, the feeding of the multitudes is a direct New Testament counterparallel to the events unfolding in the biblical book of Exodus. In John 6:15–21, Jesus walks on the sea (as opposed to the Israelites who walked on dry land in the midst of the sea in Exodus). In Matthew 14:13–21, Jesus feeds the multitudes at *ereimos* and then walks on the sea in Matthew 14:22–27. In Mark 6:32–44, Jesus feeds the multitudes at *ereimos* in 6:31, 6:32, and 6:35, and later this narrative is linked with Bethsaida in 6:45 where he begins his walking in the midst of the waters. In Luke 9:10–17, Jesus feeds the multitudes at Bethsaida which is referred to in 9:12 as "a wilderness." In Luke the only hint of a "sea passage" equivalent is found in 8:22–25 where no walking in the midst of the sea is recorded, only the calming of the seas, an account that is paralleled in Mark and Matthew. In all of these cases, however, there appears to be an echo of the Exodus feeding account in the wilderness. While Jesus' "walking on the sea" is clearly not equal to the Israelites' "walking in the midst of the sea," it is easy to see how they might be connected in the mind of the Gospel writers. The point of the Gospel writers, however, is also not the same as the biblical book of Exodus account. It is Jesus alone who has enough faith to walk "on the waters," even though he has clearly demonstrated God's power before the people by feeding the multitudes. If so, the entire sequence of events and the calling of Bethsaida an *ereimos* is a literary metaphor with little bearing upon the actual geological placement of the city.

UP OR DOWN THE JORDAN RIVER?

The geology of the area may have affected the literary metaphor of the Gospel writers. Today, the Sea is over two kilometers from et-Tell, but geological research suggests that two thousand years ago or more, an estuary led from the bottom of Bethsaida into an enlarged deltaic lagoon next to the Jordan River and led into the Sea. This has been confirmed by follow-up trench-digging during the 1994 season, and it also provides insights into the "walking on the water" sequences of John and Matthew. It may explain the *ereimos* references as well. *Ereimos* may indicate a location upriver, far removed from the active fishing villages located on the banks of the Sea of Galilee, requiring time to sail up the shallow estuary to the ancient site of Bethsaida.

BY THE DESTROYED OR ANCIENT RUIN?

Besides the metaphoric reasons for describing Bethsaida as a biblical wilderness or isolated upriver port, the possibility also exists that *ereimos* means something altogether different. The Gospel accounts may have derived *Tzaida* from both the Hebrew and Aramaic derivations of the root. Consistently in Aramaic translations of the period, the root *tzdy* is used to translate the Hebrew words for "destroyed place," "destruction," and "desolation" such as in Targum Onqelos of Genesis

1:2 (*Tohu*) and Exodus 23:29.[19] The derived word "*ereimia*" does appear in the Septuagint Greek translation as a translation for the Hebrew word *harav* or *harevah* in Isaiah 61:4 and Ezekiel 35:4 and the word *shemamah* in Ezekiel 35:9. *Ereimos*, therefore, may mean a destroyed portion of a city. In this case the *ereimos* of Bethsaida may mean some ancient ruined part of the city that was located in the newer Roman-period city. The Syriac translation of *ereimos* in the New Testament is invariably *atra hurba* (the destroyed place). In the Syriac translation of Luke 9:10, "the *ereimos* of Bethsaida" is referred to as *Atra Hurba d'Bethsaida* (the destroyed place of Bethsaida) and may indicate a tradition of a destroyed location at the site of Bethsaida, or perhaps a destroyed site near a more ancient Iron Age city. Although parts of et-Tell were destroyed in the modern period (and it is difficult to discern how and when certain parts were destroyed), the most impressive parts of the mound are a large Iron Age gate, palace, and temple complex on one side of the mound, to the east of the main Roman-period discoveries. This Iron Age section of the mound presently contains a roadway that leads through what must have been a destroyed gate complex into the upper Hellenistic and Roman superstratum. The Iron Age gate complex was not fully restored in the Roman period, but was massive and provided easy access into the upper city. This is quite normal in ancient cities, since many sites were rebuilt only in certain areas and quarried stone from destroyed areas provided easy building materials. If so, *ereimos* might refer to a destroyed area of the mound that provided an entrance to the city, but that, in the time of the apostles, provided a clear metaphor of past (and perhaps future) events.

The possibility exists that Bethsaida did contain a destroyed area because of earlier earthquake damage. Josephus writes emotionally in *Antiquities* 15.5.2–5 about the earthquake of 31 BCE that undoubtedly severely impacted sites in the northern region of Israel. The destruction on the fault line affected the entire line of villages along the Jordan River down to the Dead Sea. The use of the designation *atra hurba* or "destroyed place" may be an indication of the status of the city when the Gospel writers came in contact with it in a period before or after 70 CE. In addition, the Gospel writers may be referring only to a part of the area of Bethsaida that was not being used and may explain how they were so glibly able to predict the end of the city in Matthew 11:21 and Luke 10:13.

The Depopulated *Ereimos*

The designation of an *ereimos* may also simply be a demographic fact. Josephus states that the area around the Sea of Galilee was densely populated in the first century CE and any area that was not densely populated was in fact "a lonely place" (Byatt 1973, 51–60). The areas to the east of et-Tell/Bethsaida are in a floodplain with the modern small, seasonal *Meshoshim* and *Yehudiye* Rivers that make it impossible to have permanent settlement on the northeast shore of the Sea of Galilee. This area may have been one of the few areas around the Sea of Galilee in the first century CE that was relatively desolate and unpopulated because it was near a floodplain and hence a wilderness.

In an Exile, Diaspora, or Spiritual Desert

Ereimos is a word that hints at a number of different literary elements. One element may also be the idea of the "diaspora" or "a place of escape or exile." One finds, for example in Josephus (*J.W.* 7.438), that the weaver Jonathan led his followers in Cyrene into the *ereimos*. Josephus relates that, at the end of the destruction of Jerusalem in 70 CE, the Jews made a final request to let their women and children go "into the *ereimos*" (*J.W.* 6.351). The use of the word among Greek-speaking Jews may have been indicative of many different shades of meaning for a wilderness. One such meaning would be "exile." The word *ereimos* appears in the Septuagint translation (including the Apocrypha) hundreds of times in a variety of meanings. The most striking examples can be found in exilic and postexilic writings (Jeremiah, Ezekiel, Lamentations, II Isaiah, parts of Psalms, Zechariah, Haggai, and Malachi),[20] perhaps indicating the spiritual desolation faced by the Jews during the exile and the idea of diaspora. In these contexts, *ereimos* may be used to indicate exile. The terminology is used in the New Testament to relate Jesus' experience to Moses' experience of bringing the people out of the spiritual desolation of Egypt to the Promised Land. This *ereimos* may also be a place of ascetic or spiritual meditation, again linking Moses' experience on top of Mount Sinai with Jesus' experience at the *ereimos*. It is not a coincidence that the word for the ascetic location for monks spiritually communing became associated with the term. The *ereimos* became the hermitage.

The metaphor of the wilderness was also a pristine reminder of the place in between their Egypt and Promised Land, an apt metaphor to describe Bethsaida, on the border between Babylonia and the rest of southern Israel. In this sense, the use of *ereimos* to describe Bethsaida in the Gospels can mean a frontier town just beyond the borders of the historical land of Israel. This is the view that the rabbis have of Bethsaida (BT Kiddushin 75b, 66a; Baba Kama 79b; Baba Batra 54b; Hullin 134b; Menahot 109a). It was a border town that was both in and out of the historical land of Israel—both in the Diaspora and in Israel.

Different proposals present themselves when attempting to understand the unique language of the New Testament. Some possibilities are presented by the geology, geography, and archaeology of the Bethsaida excavations, while others are literary issues that are not easily resolved by a simple reading of the text. It is therefore important to try to consider both simultaneously. The proposals in this chapter present *ereimos* as:

- a lonely place (isolated or upriver from the main activity of fishing along the Sea of Galilee)

- a destroyed place (either from earthquakes, uplift, and/or flooding)

- a destroyed place from an earlier period of occupation

- a wilderness (a reenactment of Moses' feeding of the multitudes in the desert of Sinai)

- an exile or diaspora (a time when the Jews were living outside of the land)

- an ascetic or spiritual "desert" in general (a place of meditation—Mount Sinai)

All in all, Bethsaida was perhaps both a literary and geographic wilderness.

CHAPTER NOTES

Unless otherwise indicated, all translations are my own. All biblical citations are taken from the Revised Standard Version.

1. See Pixner 1985, 196ff. Father Bargil Pixner has suggested two separate "feeding" accounts, the first on the west side of the Sea and the second on the east side. He emphasizes the tradition of Mark and Matthew, which have two stories of the feedings of the multitude(s) and holds that Luke and John telescope the first feeding into the geographic setting of the second.

2. Perhaps this explains the John 12:21 reference, "Bethsaida of Galilee." The idea that Bethsaida was in Galilee may be explained in a number of different ways. Although the city was technically in Golan in the period of Philip-Herod (until 34 CE), in 54 CE King Agrippa was given Tiberias, Magdala, and Julias (Josephus *J.W.* 2.13.2) and therefore at the time of the formulation of John's Gospel, Bethsaida should have been included as part of Galilee. The Gospels themselves are also not always reliable when it comes to geographic designations because they are not intended as geography textbooks and they were formulated by authors (or transmitted by scribes) who lived outside Palestine and after the events, and were not always familiar with the geography they were writing about. In addition, the connection to "Galilee" as an entire literary unit for the life of Jesus (especially in the Gospel of John) may have outweighed the need to accurately designate it in the Golan. Even the writings of Josephus contain errors of this sort with regard to certain geographic locations with which one might assume he was familiar. See Safrai 1989, 295ff.

3. Nebenzahl 1986, 50 (William Wey's Sanuto), 59 (Vesconte's *Tabula Nova Terrae Sanctae*), 77 (Tilleman Stella), 79 (Giacomo Gastaldi), 105 (English Bible of 1599), 107 (John Speed), 117 (Willem Janszoon Blaeu), 125 (Claes Janszonius Visscher).

4. Claudius Ptolemaeus (Ptolemy), a second century CE astronomer from Alexandria, lists the following cities of Galilee (*Geog.* 5.15.3):
   Sapphuri: 66° 40' longitude 32° 25' latitude
   Caparcotni: 66° 50' longitude 32° 35' latitude
   Julias: 67° 5' longitude 32° 15' latitude
   Tiberias: 67° 15' longitude 32° 5' latitude
   Chester McCown (1930, 35) suggests that the Julias reference should be corrected by slightly emending the Greek letters used for designating the longitude on the map to read 67° 25' (instead of 67° 5'), placing it directly over the east of the Jordan River to the north of the Sea of Galilee. Otherwise, Julias is not even on the Sea of Galilee, but to the west of the Sea of Galilee and inland.

5. Nebenzahl 1986, 151. For example, the same map has "Scythopolis" listed as "vel Bethsan."

6. Nothing found before the probes of Rami Arav suggests any systematic and extensive Hellenistic-Roman settlement at any other site on the

northeast shore of the Sea of Galilee. In fact, the random Hellenistic and
Roman shards, high lake levels, and periodic flooding in the area (all mentioned in the earlier surveys) all suggest what the geologists in the Bethsaida Excavations Project have written: that other sites closer to the Sea of
Galilee were created as a result of the catastrophic flooding and sedimentation, and the random Hellenistic-Roman shards found there are the
result of "float" from sites upstream. See Arav 1988, 1989, 1991, 1992;
Kuhn and Arav 1991.

7. In the lists of fortified cities located around the Sea of Galilee in Joshua 19,
an enigmatic reference has been resolved by the discovery of the Iron Age
stratum of Bethsaida. This chapter lists the allocations to the tribe of
Naphtali in Galilee, perhaps including territory on the eastern side of the
Jordan. The Hebrew text of Joshua 19:35 reads "the fortified cities of
"HaTziddim, Tzer, and Hamat, Raqat, and Kinneret." The designation of
HaTziddim may refer to an ancient group of this name or it may refer to
the designation of "the hunters/fishermen." In the Hebrew Bible, the root
tzud/tzid appears over forty times; and the root is generally linked to hunt-
ing, trapping, or catching food. Substituting *Tzed* for *Tzer* would render
this passage "The fishing villages [HaTziddim] which were Tzed, Hamat,
Raqat and Kinneret." See Arav 1993, 42–43.

8. Josephus *Ant.* 3.515–18 and in most rabbinic citations as well (see Genesis
Rabbah 98). The Onqelos translation and interpretation of Deuteronomy
33:23 that cites Gennosar as part of the Naphtali tribe possession (not in
the Hebrew text) is an unusual example, since an early printing (the
Sabioneta edition of 1557) of Onqelos preserves the reading of Gennosar
as *Genezer* (the "Valley of the Nazarene"), connecting it with the root of
Nazareth and early Christianity as opposed to Gannei-sar, the way that it
is normally written.

9. The Greek spelling of the site, Genneisar, might suggest a double meaning
to a bilingual Greek and Hebrew/Aramaic speaker of the period. The *Gen-
nei-* is a stem that may indicate "birth" in Greek and the area was well
known for its fruitful nature and products. This type of bilingual Greek
and Hebrew/Aramaic wordplay is a common form of popular derivation
for bilingual linguistics, and is found in many rabbinic passages about the
location such as BT Eruvin 30a (see Eilberg-Schwartz 1987, 765ff.). The
rabbis often would take a Greek word and read or interpret it as if it were a
Hebrew word (or vice versa) or even change lettering in an attempt to
"squeeze" a new interpretive perspective from a biblical text. Many Greek
names given to Hebrew locations reflect this bilingual interplay.

10. See Jastrow 1903, s.v. "betah." Used in rabbinic sources as well, for example, Mishnah Ohilot 12.3.

11. The first reference to the name is I Maccabees 11:63–74, which refers to an
area on the northwest shore, "the water of Gennesar," using a word meaning a spring or well, rather than a fixed body of water. Luke refers to the
area as the Lake of Gennesaret (Luke 5:1–2, 8:22–23, 33). The passages in

Luke 5 are preceded by an indication that the place where Jesus was located was a "lonely place" (Luke 4:42).

12. Luke does not use *thalassa* to refer to the Sea of Galilee although he does use it in other contexts (17:2, 17:6, 21:25). The other Gospels do use the word for the Sea of Galilee: Matthew uses it eleven times, Mark seven times, and John seven times.

13. Elsewhere (*J.W.* 3.57, 4.456) Josephus calls it the "Sea of Tiberias." Pliny calls it the Lake of Gennesaret and (Lake of) Tarichaeae (*Nat.* 5.71).

14. For example, Thomas Fuller's 1650 map (Vilnay 1965, 251).

15. BT Baba Batra 74b; BT Bekorot 55a. The rabbis identified Gennesaret as a place where small dwellings were built seasonally for tending to the crops, but not a place of permanent residence (perhaps because of the rising water table). See Mishnah Maaserot 3.7

16. Shroder and Inbar 1999. Dr. Shroder's study includes radiocarbon dating of bones and pottery samples dug from trenches at the bottom of et-Tell. The soil samples, radiocarbon dating, and pottery samples found in these trenches conclusively demonstrate that there was a riverbed open in the area directly adjacent to the tell some two thousand years ago.

17. The Roman-period pottery designated as "Kefar Hananya" and dating from the second and third century CE is much more prominent than was first thought. See Adan-Bayewitz 1993.

18. McNamer 1999, 399–400. Father Bonifacus de Stephanis (1551) and Johannes Cotovicus (1600) include unique information about Bethsaida compared to earlier reports.

19. Other references are Lev. 26:22, 31, 32, 33, 34, 35, 42; Num. 21.30; Deut. 28:37. See Jastrow 1903, 1262.

20. Jer. 2:6, 15, 24, 31; 4:11, 26–27; 7:34; 9:2, 10, 12, 26; 12:10, 12; 13:24; 17:6; 22:6; 23:10; 31:2; 33:10; 34:22; 44:2; 48:6; 49:13; 50:12; Lam. 4:19, 3l; 5:9; Ezek. 5:14; 6:14; 13:4; 14:8; 19:13; 20:10, 13, 15, 17, 18, 21, 23, 35, 36; 23:42; 25:13; 26:20; 29:9–10, 12; 30:12; 33:28–29; 34:25; Isa. 50:2; 51:3; 52:9; 54:1; 58:12; 61:4; 62:4; 63:13; 64:10; Ps. 136:16; Zech. 2:13; Hag. 1:9; Mal. 1:3–4.

LITERATURE CITED

Adan-Bayewitz, D. 1993. *Common Pottery in Roman Galilee: A Study in Local Trade.* Jerusalem: Bar-Ilan University Press.

Amiran, D. H. K. 1950. A Revised Earthquake Catalogue of Palestine. *Israel Exploration Journal* 1:223–46.

Amiran, D. H. K., E. Arieh, and T. Turcotte. 1994. Earthquakes in Israel and Adjacent Areas: Macroseismic Observations since 100 B.C.E. *Israel Exploration Journal* 44 (3–4): 260–305.

Arav, Rami. 1988. Et-Tell and el-Araj. *Israel Exploration Journal* 38 (3): 187–88.

———. 1989. Et-Tell, 1988. *Israel Exploration Journal* 39 (1–2): 99–100.

———. 1991. Bethsaida, 1989. *Israel Exploration Journal* 41 (1–3): 184–85.

———. 1992. Bethsaida, 1992. *Israel Exploration Journal* 42 (3–4): 252–54.

———. 1993. Bethsaida, Tzer and the Fortified Cities of Napthali. In *The Nineteenth Archaeological Conference in Israel Abstracts.* Jerusalem.

Arav, Rami, and Richard Freund, eds. 1995. *Bethsaida: A City by the North Shore of the Sea of Galilee.* Vol. I. Kirksville, Mo.: Thomas Jefferson University Press.

———. 1999. *Bethsaida: A City by the North Shore of the Sea of Galilee.* Vol. 2. Kirksville, Mo.: Truman State University Press.

Bankier, L. 1995. Control of geomorphic process mechanics, timing of events and environmental reconstruction of the western Beteiha Plain, Master's thesis, University of Nebraska at Omaha.

Beitzel, B. J. 1991. The Via Maris in Literary and Cartographic Sources. *Biblical Archaeologist* 54:65–75.

Boling, R. G. 1984. *Joshua: A New Translation with Notes and Commentary.* The Anchor Bible, vol. 6. New York: Doubleday.

Braslavsky, J. 1938. The Earthquake and Division of the Jordan in 1546. *Zion* 6:323–36.

Brock, S. P. 1977. A Letter Attributed to Cyril of Jerusalem on the Building of the Temple. *Bulletin of the School of Oriental and African Studies* 40:274.

Byatt, A. 1973. Josephus and Population Numbers in First Century Palestine. *Palestine Exploration Quarterly* 105:51–60.

Eilberg-Schwartz, H. 1987. Who's Kidding Whom? A Serious Reading of Rabbinic Word Plays. *Journal of the American Academy of Religion* 55 (4): 765–75.

Groh, D. E. 1988. Jews and Christians in Late Roman Palestine: Towards a New Chronology; *Biblical Archaeologist* 51:80–89.

Hammond, P. C. 1980. New Evidence for 4th-Century A.D. Destruction of Petra. *Bulletin of the American Schools of Oriental Research* 238:65–67.

Inbar, Moshe. 1982a. Measurement of Fluvial Sediment Transport Compared with Lacustrine Sedimentation Rates: The Flow of the River Jordan into Lake Kinneret. *Hydrological Sciences Journal* 4:439–49.

———. 1982b. Spatial and Temporal Aspects of Man-induced Changes in the Hydrological and Sedimentological Regime of the Upper Jordan River. *Israel Journal of Earth Sciences* 31:53–66.

————. 1987. Effects of a High Magnitude Flood in a Mediterranean Climate: A Case Study in the Jordan River Basin. In *Catastrophic Flooding*, edited by L. Mayer and D. Nash. Boston: Allen and Unwin.

Inbar, Moshe, and M. Even-Nir. 1989. Landslides in the Upper Jordan Gorge. *Pirineos, Journal on Mountain Ecology* 134:23–40.

Jastrow, M. 1903. *A Dictionary of the Targumim, the Talmud Babli and Yerushalmi, and the Midrashic Literature*. Philadelphia: Traditional Press.

Josephus. 1958–65. *Works*. Translated by H. St. J. Thackeray et al. 9 vols. Loeb Classical Library. Cambridge: Harvard University Press.

Karcz, I., and U. Kafri. 1978. Evaluation of Supposed Archaeoseismic damage in Israel. *Journal of Archaeological Science* 5:237-53.

Kuhn, Heinz-Wolfgang, and Rami Arav. 1991. The Bethsaida Excavations, Historical and Archaeological Approaches. In *The Future of Early Christianity, Essays in Honor of Helmut Koester*, edited by B. A. Pearson. Minneapolis: Fortress Press.

Liddel, Henry George, and Robert Scott, eds. 1977. *A Greek-English Lexicon*. Oxford: Clarendon Press.

McCown, Chester. 1930. The Problem of the Site of Bethsaida. *Journal of the Palestine Oriental Society* 10:32–42.

McNamer, Elizabeth. 1999. Medieval Pilgrim Accounts of Bethsaida and the Bethsaida Controversy. In Arav and Freund 1999.

Nathanson, B. G. 1986. Jews, Christians and the Gallus Revolt in Fourth-Century Palestine. *Biblical Archaeologist* 49:26–36.

Nebenzahl, K. 1986. *Maps of the Holy Land*. New York: Abbeville Press.

Netzer, E. 1981. Greater Herodium. *Qedem* 13. Jerusalem: Israel Exploration Society.

Pixner, Bargil. 1985. The Miracle Church at Tabgha on the Sea of Galilee. *Biblical Archaeologist* 48:196–216.

Pliny the Elder.1938. *Natural History*. Loeb Classical Library. Cambridge: Harvard University Press.

Ptolemy. 1975. *Geography*. Loeb Classical Library. Cambridge: Harvard University Press.

Russell, K. W. 1980. The Earthquake of May 19 A.D. 363. *Bulletin of the American Schools of Oriental Research* 238:47–62.

Safrai, Z. 1989. The Description of the Land of Israel in Josephus' Works. In *Josephus, the Bible and History*, edited by L. H. Feldman and G. Hata. Detroit: Wayne State University Press.

Shroder, John F., and Moshe Inbar. 1995. Geologic and Geographic Background to the Bethsaida Excavations. In Arav and Freund 1995.

Shroder, John F., Michael P. Bishop, Kevin J. Cornwell, and Moshe Inbar, 1999. Catastrophic Geomorphic Processes and Bethsaida Archaeology, Israel. In Arav and Freund 1999.

Stern, M. 1976. *Greek and Latin Authors on Jews and Judaism,* Vol. 1. Jerusalem: Monson Press.

Vilnay, Z. 1965. *The Holy Land in Old Prints and Maps*. Jerusalem: Rubin Mass.

Hector Avalos

Bethsaida in Light of the Study of Ancient Health Care

I N VOLUME 1 OF THE BETHSAIDA EXCAVATIONS PROJECT publication series, John Rousseau attempted to place the healing of the blind man in Mark 8:22–26 within the sociohistorical context of Jesus and Bethsaida (1995). Indeed, Bethsaida and health care have been linked textually since at least the writing of Mark. Given the subsequent discovery of Greco-Roman miniature vessels and other items with possible medical uses, it is now an opportune moment to reassess the role of Bethsaida in the health care systems of ancient Palestine during the Greco-Roman period.

Such an examination is particularly important in light of a movement toward the medical anthropological study of ancient health care now emerging within Near Eastern and biblical studies.[1] The aim of this chapter is to explain the medical anthropological approach to ancient health care, and to place Bethsaida within the context of Greco-Roman health care systems, especially since Rousseau's study of healing at Bethsaida.

MEDICAL ANTHROPOLOGICAL APPROACHES

Prior to about the 1980s, most studies of health care in the Bible focused on ancient "medicine." One common concern of such studies is the identification of specific diseases mentioned in the Bible. An example of his approach is the article by Max Sussman in the *Anchor Bible Dictionary* (1992, 6:6–15), where he discusses specific modern diagnoses for a catalogue of conditions described in the Bible.

A second impulse in the study of biblical medicine seeks to explain how biblical healing practices were somehow superior to non-biblical medicine. This apologetic emphasis is exemplified by John Wilkinson, *The Bible and Healing: A Medical and Theological Commentary* (1998), which sought to show that Jesus' healings were not any sort of magic, but rather were based on authentic miracles.[2]

Given the dearth of information about specific diseases, some writers have lessened the emphasis on finding modern diagnoses for ancient conditions. Such writers argue that new questions need to be posed to ancient data. Many new questions came from the field of medical anthropology. The field itself is relatively new within anthropology.[3] Arthur Kleinman, perhaps the foremost medical anthropologist today, did not begin to write his best-known works until the 1980s.

At the heart of the medical anthropological approach is the concept of health care as a system. A health care system may be defined as a set of interacting resources, institutions, and strategies that are intended to maintain or restore health in a particular community. There have been other rubrics applied to the study of systems that involve healing, medicine, etc. The rubric "health care system" is preferred over "healing system" because the latter restricts its focus to healing rather than the maintenance of health and prevention of illness. The rubrics "medical system" and "medicine" bear too many misleading associations with modern scientific medicine.

In any case, a health care system usually includes, but is not limited to, the presuppositions regarding the causes and diagnosis of illness, the options available to the patient, and the modes of therapy administered. Other dimensions include any social or geographic differences in accessibility to what is perceived to be the best care available in the society as well as the attitudes toward the patient in the society and toward the health care expert. Most health care systems, modern or not, offer a plurality of options for patients. Furthermore, health care issues shape and are shaped by religion. The new question is: How does a socioreligious conceptual framework affect and interact with the type of health care that a society devises for its members?

HEALTH CARE AND EARLY CHRISTIANITY

Early Christianity can be seen as a movement within Judaism that sought to address some of the health care problems perceived to exist in other Jewish traditions as well as in Greco-Roman traditions (Avalos 1999).[4] The solutions proposed by early Christians attracted converts and contributed to the success of the Jewish sect(s) that became known as Christianity.

According to some counts, there are about forty-one healings ascribed to Jesus in the Gospels (Kelsey 1995, 44–45). Health care, then, should not be seen as just a literary topos or an excuse to show-case Jesus' power in the New Testament. Healing may not just be a sign of the arrival of the kingdom of God. Health care, far from being a peripheral service, can be the core of a new religious movement. As such, healing can be the principal factor in attracting converts who desperately want to relieve themselves of one of the most universal of human problems—illness.

The excavations at Bethsaida provide a piece of the picture concerning health care in ancient Galilee. According to the New Testament, some of the first disciples were born at Bethsaida (for example, John 1:44). To understand the role of Bethsaida in the rise of Christianity, it is helpful to think in terms of the problems encountered by patients with the various health care systems that competed for clients in the Greco-Roman world. Looking at the health care systems available in the ancient Near East, it can be shown that: (1) there were problems voiced about the health care system in Greco-Roman and Jewish sources; (2) Christianity was aware of those problems and attempted to address them; and (3) the proposed solutions may have attracted converts. This chapter will examine these problems, discuss how Christianity responded to them, and then assess how the excavations at Bethsaida may illuminate the relationship between health care and the rise of Christianity.

THE PROBLEMS OF POLYTHEISM AND MONOLATRY

In contrast to modern Western medicine, religion and health care were intricately intertwined in most of the ancient world. Thus, the religious framework of a culture was of utmost importance in determining the type of health care that a culture developed. Such influence, however, was not unidirectional. Health care issues also helped to shape religious frameworks. At the most basic level, the number of gods in a religious system affected a health care system in a fundamental manner. The two basic systems are polytheism and monolatry.

Polytheism, as a religious system that acknowledges the existence and/or legitimacy of many gods, provided patients with a number of divine options. If one deity does not provide an answer, the patient may go to another deity. On the other hand, a polytheistic system can also complicate the options available to a patient. Healing rituals, for example, may become long and elaborate due to the sheer number of supernatural beings that must be entreated or repelled. One example may be seen in a ritual against what is termed as "malaria" by Simo Parpola, an Assyriologist.[5] In order to perform this ritual, one needs:

> a figurine of the daughter of Anu (the primary sky-god)
> a figurine of Namtar (a minor god of the underworld)
> a figurine of Latarak (a little-known figure)
> a figurine of Death
> a substitute figurine made of clay
> a substitute figurine made of wax
> 15 drinking tubes of silver for Gula (goddess of healing) and
>   Belet-seri (Mistress of the desert)
> 7 twigs of tamarisk
> 7 twigs of date palm
> [7 bot]tles of wine
> 7 bottles of beer
> [7 bottles] of milk
> 7 bottles of honey

The figurines of the deities, which were probably assembled in the presence of the patient or in some sacred area, represent the supernatural beings that need to be appeased. The foods were probably intended as offerings to gain the favor of those deities. Prayers to those deities were probably combined with medical treatments applied to the patient, and the entire ritual might last hours or even days.

The catalogue of items needed for the ritual against malaria illustrates that labor-intensive rituals were related, in large part, to the number of supernatural beings that were to be contacted, appeased, or repelled. In fact, sometimes the consultant had to spend much of the time in the performance of complicated rituals and in the procurement of paraphernalia for different gods, even if a single illness was the object of the ritual.

The fact that such labor-intensive rituals affected the immediate availability of some health care consultants is also evident in a letter where the king, probably Esarhaddon (681–669 BCE), orders Marduk-shakin-shumi, an *ashipu* (the term for one of the main healing consultants of Mesopotamia) to perform an antiwitchcraft ritual before the twenty-fourth day of the month. The *ashipu* replies, in part: "We cannot make it; the tablets are too numerous; (god only knows) when they will be written. Even the preparation of the figurines which the king saw (yesterday) took us five to six days" (Parpola 1993, 255.8–13). The text again reflects how the complexity of Mesopotamian polytheism resulted in a labor-intensive system of rituals that affected the availability of the healers, as well as the schedule of rituals. Even with assistants, one type of consultant could not always accomplish the numerous tasks needed in exorcism in the time requested by the king.

The principal effect of monolatry is, perhaps, the automatic bifurcation of a health care system into legitimate and illegitimate options. Since only one god can be approached for healing, all other gods, whether they are believed to exist or not, are automatically rendered illegitimate. In some ways, then, monolatry offers fewer options.

At the same time, a monolatrous system theoretically simplifies the search for the healing deity and thus the therapeutic ritual. Since only one sender/healer of disease is possible, the liturgy is reduced to appeasing or contacting only one deity. For example, in the biblical story of Elisha and Naaman (2 Kings 5:11), the expected ritual for curing "leprosy" is as follows: "He would surely come out [of his house] and he shall stand and call upon the name of Yahweh, his god; and he shall wave his hand over the [afflicted] area; and he shall remove the 'leprosy.'"[6] No long liturgy is expected, and the only deity that has to be consulted is Yahweh.

The effects of monolatry, however, cannot be oversimplified. Even in apparently monolatrous systems, such as Catholicism, one finds that patients can resort to a variety of saints and lengthy prayers (repetition of rosary prayers) that can render therapeutic rituals complex. This is because the large number of saints can become the equivalent of the numerous gods to which one could appeal in frankly polytheistic systems. Likewise, some forms of Judaism in the first century CE approached polytheism insofar as therapeutic strategies are concerned.[7]

As it concerns the Jesus movement, the New Testament texts portray Jesus as simplifying therapeutic strategies as found in Second Temple Judaism and Greco-Roman health care systems. Although Yahweh is ultimately responsible for illness and healing within Judaism, it is clear that a variety of demons and supernatural beings were active in human affairs. Thus, Douglas L. Penney and Michael Wise note Rabbi Huna's comments on Psalm 91:7: "Everyone among us has a thousand demons on his left hand and ten thousand on his right" (1994, 627). In the Testament of Solomon 18, which may have been originally a Jewish work composed as early as the first century, one finds some thirty-six specific demons corresponding to illnesses of specific areas of the body. Some examples are:

Demon	Area of Body
Ruax	head
Artosael	eyes
Oropel	throat
Sphandor	shoulder

Some of the Dead Sea Scrolls also indicate that a variety of demons could be responsible for disease. For instance, 4Q560 is apparently intended to repel, among other entities, "The male Wasting-Demon, the female Wasting-Demon," and diseases that may have been synonymous with the names of the demon (for example, "Fever, and Chills, and Chest Pain") (Penney and Wise 1994, 632). As such, late Second Temple Judaism sometimes did not differ much from frank polytheistic religions in their attribution of disease to supernatural beings.

The numerous stories of demon possession in the New Testament clearly attest that early Christianity also assumed that demons could cause disease. Demons are responsible for conditions ranging from what may be epilepsy to paralysis. Thus, in Mark 5:9 the main locutor for the demons says, "My name is Legion; for we are many." Concerning the origin of the enemies of Christianity, Paul says (Eph. 6:12), "For our struggle is not against enemies of blood and flesh, but against the rulers, against the authorities, against the cosmic powers of this present darkness, against the spiritual forces of evil in the heavenly places." So, Christian etiologies for disease did not differ much from that of other Jewish traditions insofar as the role of demons is concerned. As shall be argued below, what is distinctive in early Christianity is the relative simplification of its therapeutic strategy despite the belief in a variety of demons as causes of disease.

PROBLEMS POSED BY TEMPLES

A small temple from the Roman era has been identified at Bethsaida (Arav 1999, 18–25; Arav, Freund, and Shroder 2000, 55–56). Temples are usually part of almost any health care system in antiquity. All temples/shrines may have one or more of at least three possible functions in a health care system:

1. petitionary function, if a shrine/temple is used as a place to petition a deity for health either by the patient or through a proxy;

2. therapeutic function, if, aside from simple petitions, a shrine/temple is used for the direct application of *materia medica* or for healing rituals;

3. thanksgiving function, if a shrine/temple is used as a place to thank deities for healing; such a practice may be voluntary or enjoined by the cult.

Temples in the ancient world can be compared on the basis of the combinations of functions that they might have. Thus, the Asclepius temples in Greece have all three functions. The Levitical view of the temple, inferred from attitudes toward impurity expressed in Leviticus 13–21, did not allow a therapeutic function, but it did allow a thanksgiving function. In other Hebrew traditions, a shrine or temple could have a petitionary function (for example, Hannah at Shiloh in 1 Sam. 1) or a therapeutic function, as was probably the case with the temple of Jerusalem prior to Hezekiah's expulsion of Nehushtan/metal serpent, a well-known therapeutic device (2 Kings 18:5; Num. 21:5–10). The particular configuration of functions in any temple then serves as a lens to study the cultural reasons for that configuration.

However, there were also problems with temples. One problem was that the more famous a temple became for its healing, the more crowded it could become. Strabo notes that the temple of Asclepius at Epidauros was "always full of the sick."[8] An increased number of visitors meant a decrease in access for some. Likewise, travel to a healing temple could be cumbersome and expensive.[9] Finally, the rituals involved in an Asclepius temple could be time-consuming and painful, especially if anesthesia was insufficient for some of the surgical procedures known to be administered at Asclepius temples.

OTHER PROBLEMS OF HEALTH CARE SYSTEMS

Among the most constant problems with Greco-Roman health care was its cost. Speaking of the consequences of the establishment of the traditions of Asclepius and Hippocrates, Pliny the Elder (23?–79 CE) laments, "Afterwards there was no limit to the profit from medical practice, for one of the pupils of Hippocrates, Prodicus, born in Selymbria, founded *iatraliptice* (ointment cure) and so discovered revenue for the anointers even and drudges of the doctors."[10]

New Testament writers were aware of the cost of physicians, and make at least two allusions to this problem. In this context, the most important one is found in Mark 5:25–26, which describes the healing of a hemorrhagic woman as follows, "Now there was a woman who had been suffering from hemorrhages for twelve years. She had endured much under many physicians, and had spent all that she had; and she was no better, but rather grew worse." This is a clear criticism of physicians, who are seen as ineffective and an economic drain on the patient.

The cost of health care was sometimes related to the expensive ingredients that were needed in therapy. Philostratus, in his *Life of Apollonius of Tyana*, ridicules those who are ensnared by the promise of cures from exotic pharmaceuticals, "They are given all the spices which the gardens of India yield; and the cheats exact vast sums of money from them for all this, and yet do nothing to help them at all."[11] Tatian, the second-century Christian writer, went so far as to reject the use of all pharmaceuticals in his *Oratio ad Graecos* (18).

Temporal restrictions also could pose a problem. Second Temple Judaism could impose restrictions on the Sabbath, at least as portrayed by Christian sources (Matt. 12:10ff.). Greco-Roman physicians also were not available all of the time. Seasonal fluctuations in disease as well as self-imposed time limitations by physicians meant that some patients were left waiting for treatment. Galen, the famous Roman physician, mentions a "customary three-day period of delay according to many physicians who follow Thessalus and others. They insist on keeping up this custom as if it is a revelation from God" (*On Physicians* 89).

The notion of purity also seemed problematic to early Christian writers. The effect of purity laws on those suffering with chronic skin diseases, sometimes mistranslated as "leprosy," means that Jewish families were sometimes fractured (see Lev. 13:44–46). That is to say, since those afflicted with diseases were removed from the community, then family members were separated from the sick individual.

Finally, there was the problem of access to therapeutic loci. This problem is highlighted in John 5:2–9.

> Now in Jerusalem by the Sheep Gate there is a pool, called in Hebrew Beth-zatha, which has five porticoes. In these lay many invalids—blind, lame, and paralyzed. One man was there who had been ill for thirty-eight years. When Jesus saw him lying there and knew that he had been there a long time, he said to him, "Do you want to be made well?" The sick man answered him, "Sir, I have no one to put me into the pool when the water is stirred up; and while I am making my way, someone else steps down ahead of me." Jesus said to him, "Stand up, take your mat and walk." At once the man was made well, and he took up his mat and began to walk. Now that day was a Sabbath.

The biblical author is clearly aware that one of the problems with this pool was its difficult access to those with physical challenges. The story also notes that this place was crowded, and consequently a patient might not benefit even if he or she could travel there. The biblical author emphasizes that the patient had been there a long time. All of these problems with therapeutic loci, though they may have literary motives in the Bible, were echoed in Greco-Roman literature.

EARLY CHRISTIAN RESPONSES

As argued above, early Christians, as portrayed in the New Testament, were aware of the problems of health care in the Greco-Roman world and in its parent Jewish traditions. Furthermore, early Christians sought to address those problems, consequently attracting converts. The New Testament portrays Jesus and his disciples as addressing these problems in two major ways.

The foremost solution was renewed emphasis on simple faith as a therapeutic strategy. This could solve two problems. First, faith logically could transcend the problems of distance, accessibility, and cost.

Since only faith was required, then theoretically it was no longer necessary to go anywhere for health care (for example, the story of the centurion in Matt. 8:5–10). It was not necessary to fight one's way into crowded therapeutic loci (John 5:1–18). Faith made temporal restrictions unnecessary, since healing was now theoretically available at any time. Faith, therefore, simplified therapeutic strategies significantly.

Another simplification came with the emphasis on using the name of Jesus to achieve cures. Repeatedly, Christian sources claim that only the name of Jesus is required to effect healing. Already, in Mark 9:38 (which most scholars see as the earliest gospel) is found the notion of the sufficiency of Jesus' name: "John said to him, 'Teacher, we saw someone casting out demons in your name, and we tried to stop him, because he was not following us.'"

The value and sufficiency of Jesus' name continues in Luke 10:17: "The seventy returned with joy, saying, 'Lord, in your name even the demons submit to us!'" The emphasis on appealing to a single name in Christianity may, in fact, be a critique and response to the multiplicity of names being used in the therapeutic techniques reflected in Jewish incantations, amulets, and the Testament of Solomon.

The author of Luke and Acts may have constructed this critique by centering the whole issue of Jesus' name in the healing of the paralytic (Acts 3–4). The episode begins at the gate of the temple, the center of traditional Judaism, where a paralytic is begging for alms. Instead of alms, the disciples bid him to stand up and walk "in the name of Jesus Christ of Nazareth" (Acts 3:6).

The use of the single name of Jesus is raised again in the speech of Peter and John before Annas, Caiaphas, and other traditional Jewish authorities in Acts 4:10–12:

> Let it be known to all of you, and to all the people of Israel, that this man is standing before you in good health *by the name* of Jesus Christ of Nazareth, whom you crucified, whom God raised from the dead. This Jesus is the stone that was rejected by you, the builders; it has become the cornerstone. There is salvation in no one else, for there is *no other name* under heaven given among mortals by which we must be saved. (Emphasis added)

Indeed, the whole episode mentions the use of "the name" of Jesus some ten times, a clear sign that the author wishes to emphasize the point.

The simplicity of Christian therapeutic ritual was sufficiently generalized to enable Origen (c. 185–c. 254 CE) to use it as an argument against Celsus: "But even if it be impossible to show by what power Jesus wrought these miracles, it is clear that Christians employ no spells or incantations, but the simple name of Jesus, and certain other words in which they repose faith, according to the Holy Scriptures" (*Cels.* 1:6, in Roberts and Donaldson 1965, 4:399).

Indeed, it was no longer necessary to entreat a number of angels, as could sometimes happen in Second Temple Judaism (Testament of Solomon). No longer was it necessary to consult a large number of Greco-Roman deities. The return to a sort of therapeutic monolatry simplified therapeutic strategies immediately.

Faith alone eliminated the need for fees. But early Christian authors also emphasized that fees should not be charged to patients. Thus, Matthew 10:8 states, "Cure the sick, raise the dead, cleanse the lepers, cast out demons. You received without payment; give without payment." This animosity toward fees, seen as an advantage of early Christianity relative to other health care systems, is advertised by Irenaeus in his *Against Heresies*, when speaking of the miracles done by the church: "She [the Church] exerts day by day for the benefit of the Gentiles, neither practicing deception upon any, nor taking any reward from them" (22:4, in Roberts and Donaldson 1965, 1:409). Tertullian also notes that, in general, there are no fees for entrance into the Christian temple: "Even if there is a chest of a sort, it is not made up of money paid in entrance fees, as if religion were a matter of contract."[12]

It cannot be claimed that Christianity healed anyone any more than any other health care system; however, if all health care systems were relatively equal in their ability or inability to heal, then the advantages of Christianity, at least for some patients, reside in the other benefits discussed.

Thus, even if Christianity could not heal blindness any more than the Asclepius physicians could, at least Christians could argue that they did not charge for their practice or expect remuneration. Even if going to the Asclepius temple was no more effective than praying to Jesus, at least one did not incur all of the problems that travel to a crowded shrine might pose for a patient. Even if Jesus did not heal a patient, at least the patient would not have to endure surgical procedures that were painful and no more effective.

Finally, in some ways early Christianity came to resemble the Asclepius tradition, which generally did not see the sick as too impure to enter the Asclepius temple. Purity of thought rather than of body became more important. This resulted theoretically in the reintegration of the chronically ill, in particular, into the family and community. At the very least, this Christian attitude of not seeing the ill as impure seems an attempt to reverse the fracture of the family that might have resulted from Levitical laws concerning the chronically ill.

It is true that not all patients would be attracted by the benefits that early Christianity was marketing. Yet, there might be sufficient numbers who were attracted. The most important testimony for this attraction comes from the Gospels themselves. The authors portrayed people coming for healing precisely because of the factors discussed above (cost and inefficacy of physicians). If such factors were not thought to be important, then the writers would not have been prompted to use them at all.

HEALTH CARE REFORM AT BETHSAIDA

Bethsaida has a special place in the portrayal of Christianity as a health care reform movement. Mark 8:22–26 tells the story of Jesus' healing of a blind man at Bethsaida. The passage bears repeating:

> They came to Bethsaida. Some people brought a blind man to him and begged him to touch him. He took the blind man by the hand and led him out of the village; and when he had put saliva on his eyes and laid his hands on him, he asked him, "Can you see anything?" And the man looked up and said, "I can see people, but they look like trees, walking." Then Jesus laid his hands on his eyes again; and he looked intently and his sight was restored, and he saw everything clearly. Then he sent him away to his home, saying, "Do not even go into the village."

According to one tradition, Jesus tells the blind man not to reenter Bethsaida. According to another tradition, Jesus prohibits the formerly blind man from telling anyone at Bethsaida about the healing.[13]

While it is plausible that the moral of the story is that Jesus does not yet want people to fully recognize him as the Messiah, it is also curious that Jesus' actions parallel some of the modes of healing found in the Asclepius tradition. Three parallels with Asclepius, in particular, may be noted.

1. Asclepius also healed a man, Alcetas of Halieis, who "first saw the trees in the sanctuary after the god placed his fingers in the patient's eyes."[14] Note that both the Gospel of Mark and this Asclepius Testimony use the same Greek word (ὄμματα) for "eyes."

2. Asclepius used spittle to heal, though not in the case of Alcetas.

3. Asclepius often preferred places outside the city. Major settings, such as Asclepieia, were located outside the city, as at Epidauros, Pergamon, and Athens.[15]

But the story of the healing at Bethsaida also illustrates some of the advantages, at least as portrayed by early Christian writers, of Jesus' healing practices. First, note that, unlike the Asclepius cult, the patient was not required to go to a temple. Second, the ritual was very simple. While it is true that Asclepius sometimes healed with spittle, therapy at Asclepieia could involve elaborate preliminary rituals. As Matthew Dillon notes, "the full cycle of Asklepiad rituals was abstinence, ritual bathing, payment of a fee, sacrifice, incubation, faith, healing and thanksgiving" (1994, 255).

Note also that there was no charge for Jesus' service. Asclepieia usually expected some sort of remuneration from patients. Finally, the use of spittle may itself be a commentary on the cost of health care. As noted by Pliny (*Nat.* 28.7:36–39), some prescriptions included spittle, but the message in the Gospel of Mark could be that Jesus needed no expensive substances, but rather the inexpensive and readily available spittle. This use of inexpensive therapeutic substances would continue a commentary on the cost of health care that began in Mark 5:25–34.

The question of this authenticity of Jesus' healing is not relevant in this context. As long as people believed that Jesus healed, it would have been sufficient to attract those in need of healing. Jesus' relatively simple and inexpensive treatment may be seen in light of Galileans increasing awareness of other health care systems with which to compare Christianity.

As mentioned, there is archaeological evidence that Bethsaida probably was home to the principal health care systems and practices found in the ancient Mediterranean basin. In her letter of March 13, 2001, Sandra Fortner of the University of Munich notes that the following, and still unpublished, items from the Greco-Roman period at Bethsaida may bear possible medical uses:

1.   At least five miniature ointment vessels similar to others known to be associated with pharmacists and pharmaceuticals.[16] The small size may mean that the substances in them could not be produced in vast quantities, and substances not produced in vast quantities were probably a bit more costly than more readily available substances.

2.   At least five bronze spatulas. These could be used for applying cosmetic or medicinal substances, or for manipulating parts of the body being treated.[17]

3.   A pair of bronze tweezers that could be used to extract objects or work with affected areas of the body.

These instruments, if they have medical purposes, confirm what is known from other sources, that Bethsaida was, during the Greco-Roman period, in an area where multiple health care systems were in effect. Bethsaida probably had a number of physicians at any one time. Indeed, the nearby village of Capernaum could boast of a number of physicians, if one judges by Josephus. In his *Life* (403–404), Josephus relates how he was taken to Capernaum [Κεφαρνωκόν] after falling off a horse in battle. He says that physicians [ἰατρούς], presumably local ones, were summoned for his treatment.

Note that the Gospels place a number of healings at Capernaum (Matt. 8:5; Mark 1:21–28, 2:1–12; Luke 7:1–10; John 4:46–54).Perhaps the reason for this many healings at Capernaum is that the town was known for its physicians, and Jesus' healing there would form a polemic juxtaposition with non-Christian health care.

Likewise, it can be hypothesized that the reason some traditions placed the healing of the blind man at Bethsaida was precisely to highlight the contrasts between Jesus' practices and those of others in a place that may have been famous for its wide variety of healers. The healing of the blind man at Bethsaida would have made the point even stronger, especially if Asclepian traditions about curing the blind were well known in the area.[18] Of course, how much Mark knew of such healing traditions at Bethsaida is difficult to discern. But Mark may have preserved some genuine tradition about a healing by Jesus at Bethsaida.

CONCLUSION

Bethsaida was a place where multiple health care systems could be observed. There is evidence of Jewish and Greco-Roman cultural traditions at Bethsaida, including a structure that may have been a Roman temple, which may have functioned as a place to petition for health, a place for therapy, and/or a place to give thanks for a healing. Thus, Bethsaida may represent one locus where the problems and advantages of health care voiced in the Greco-Roman world could be compared directly side by side.

Any nascent Jewish sect in the Galilee would certainly be familiar with the problems posed by various health care systems. The miniature vessels found at Bethsaida support the hypothesis that expensive medicines were part of at least some of the health care practices there. The bronze spatulas and pair of tweezers found there may attest to secular or religious Greco-Roman healing practices. Someone had to pay for the manufacture of these items, and these costs were probably transferred to patients.

Christianity advocated a radical simplification of therapy and the concomitant elimination of cost. Such health care practices may have attracted converts who were not satisfied with the health care of Greco-Roman or previous Jewish traditions. Christian practices may have also posed a challenge to non-Christian physicians at Bethsaida and elsewhere, something indicated clearly in Mark 5:25–26. Indeed, Mark 8:22–26 may be seen as continuing a critique of non-Christian health care begun at least at Mark 5:25–26. As such, Mark or his sources may have sought to make a case for the advantages of Christian health care practices by placing healing stories precisely in the Galilean towns (Capernaum and Bethsaida) known for their physicians. Further excavations may show the extent to which health care practitioners were active in Bethsaida and other parts of Galilee.

CHAPTER NOTES

*Unless otherwise noted, all biblical citations are from the New Revised Standard Version.

1. For examples of these approaches, see Avalos 1995, 1999; Pilch 1985, 1986, 1991, 2000.
2. For a critique of scholarship (for example, Kee 1986) that attempts to make distinctions between magic, miracle, and medicine, see Avalos 1999, 85–87.
3. For a historical and methodological survey of medical anthropology, see Johnson and Sargent 1990.
4. For other studies of healing in Jesus' ministry, see Davies 1995; Kee 1986; Smith 1978; Twelftree 1993.
5. Parpola 1993, 296, reverse, lines 3–14. Parpola does not document his diagnosis of the Akkadian phrase, *GIG di'u*, as malaria. My explanations of the deities are in parenthesis, and the words in brackets are based on reconstructions by Parpola.
6. Author's translation. "Leprosy" may describe a variety of skin diseases here.
7. On whether "monotheism" is an appropriate description of the main theological framework of Second Temple Judaism, see Hayman 1991.
8. Strabo, *Geogr.*, 8.6.15, cited in Edelstein and Edelstein 1945, 1:380: τὸ ἱερὸν πλῆρες ἔχοντος ἀεὶ τῶν τε καμνόντων.
9. For more details on cost of going to Asclepieia and other types of Greco-Roman temples, see Avalos 1999; Dillon 1994, 251–54.
10. *Nat.* 29.2 (Jones, LCL): Nec fuit postea quaestus modus, quoniam Prodicus Selymbriae natus, e discipulis eius, instituit quam vocant iatrilipticen et unctoribus quoque medicorum ac mediastinis vectigal invenit.
11. Philostratus, *Life of Apollonius* 7.39 (Conybeare, LCL): ἀρώματά τε ὁπόσα ἡ Ἰνδικὴ κηπεύει, καὶ χρήματα μὲν αὐτοὺς λαμπρὰ ὑπὲρ τούτων πράττονται, ξυνδρῶσι δὲ οὐδέν.
12. *Apol.* 39: 5 (Glover and Rendall, LCL): Etiam si quod arcae genus est, non de honoraria summa quasi redemptae religionis congregatur.
13. On the form critical and redactional issues with the passage, see Mann 1986, 335–37; Appold 1995; Rousseau 1995; Ruis-Camps 2000.
14. Testimonia of Asclepius 423 (Edelstein and Edelstein 1945, 1:224–25): ἐδόκει οἱ ὁ θεὸς ποτελθὼν τοῖς δακτύλοις διάγειν τὰ ὄμματα καὶ ἰδεῖν τὰ δένδρη πρᾶτον τὰ ἐν τῶι ἱαρῶι.
15. For the Asclepius temple at Athens, see Aleshire 1989; for Epidauros, see Tomlinson 1983; for Pergamon, see Radt 1988.
16. For other examples of miniature vessels from Israel, see Hershkovitz 1986. It may also be speculated that such miniature vessels might provide dosage standards for certain medicines.
17. For possible parallels from the Greco-Roman period, see Michaelides 1984, esp. plate 74; Borobia Melendo 1993.
18. In an electronic mail communication sent on 5 December 2002, Rami Arav informed me that the Arabic name for Bethsaida was Tel e-Shafi,

which means "mound of healing." The name may preserve an ancient tradition about Bethsaida's fame in healing.

Literature Cited

Aleshire, Sara B. 1989. *The Athenian Asklepieion: The People, Their Dedications, and the Inventories.* Amsterdam: J. C. Gieben.

Appold, Mark. 1995. The Mighty Works of Bethsaida: Witness of the New Testament and Related Traditions. In Arav and Freund 1995.

Arav, Rami. 1999. Bethsaida Excavations: Preliminary Report, 1994–1996. In Arav and Freund 1999.

———. 2002. Electronic communication to the author, 5 December 2002.

Arav, Rami, and Richard A. Freund, eds. 1995. *Bethsaida: A City by the North Shore of the Sea of Galilee.* Vol. 1. Kirksville, Mo.: Truman State University Press.

———.1999. *Bethsaida: A City by the North Shore of the Sea of Galilee.* Vol. 2. Kirksville, Mo.: Truman State University Press.

Arav, Rami, Richard Freund, and John F. Shroder Jr. 2000. Bethsaida Rediscovered: Long-Lost City Found North of Galilee Shore. *Biblical Archaeology Review* 26 (1): 45–56.

Avalos, Hector. 1995. *Illness and Health Care in the Ancient Near East: The Role of the Temple in Greece, Mesopotamia, and Israel.* Harvard Semitic Monographs 54. Atlanta: Scholars Press.

———.1999. *Health Care and the Rise of Christianity.* Peabody, Mass.: Hendrickson Press.

Borobia Melendo, Enrique Luis. 1993. Instrumentos médicos hispanoromanos: La especilla en la práctica médica romana. *Revista de arqueología* 13 (142): 46–49.

Davies, Stevan L. 1995. *Jesus the Healer: Possession Trance and the Origins of Christianity.* New York: Continuum.

Dillon, Matthew P. J. 1994. The Didactic Nature of Epidaurian Iamata. *Zeitschrift für Papyrologie und Epigraphik* 101:239–60.

Edelstein, Ludwig, and Emma Edelstein. 1945. *Asclepius: A Collection and Interpretation of the Testimonies.* 2 vols. Baltimore: Johns Hopkins University Press.

Fortner, Sandra. 2001. Letter to the author, 13 March 2001.

Galen. 1988. On Physicians. In *Galeni De optimo medico cognoscendo libelli versionem arabicum primum edidit, in linguam anglicum vertitt, commentatus est Albert Z. Iskander.* Corpus medicorum graecorum suplementum orientale 4. Berlin: Akademie-Verlag.

Hayman, Peter. 1991. Monotheism—A Misused Word in Jewish Studies? *Journal of Jewish Studies* 42 (1): 1–15.

Hershkovitz, Malka. 1986. Miniature Ointment Vessels from the Second Temple Period. *Israel Exploration Journal* 36:45–51.

Johnson, Thomas M., and Carolyn F. Sargent. 1990. *Medical Anthropology: Contemporary Theory and Method.* New York: Praeger.

Josephus. 1926–1965. *Works.* Translated by H. St. Thackeray et al. 10 vols. Loeb Classical Library. Cambridge: Harvard University Press.

Kee, Howard Clark. 1986. *Medicine, Miracle and Magic in New Testament Times.* Cambridge: Cambridge University Press.

Kelsey, Morton. 1995. *Healing and Christianity*. Minneapolis: Ausburg.

Kleinman, Arthur. 1980. *Patients and Healers in the Context of Culture: Explorations of the Borderland between Anthropology, Medicine and Psychiatry*. Berkeley: University of California.

Mann, Christopher S. 1986. *Mark: A New Translation with Introduction and Commentary*. Anchor Bible 27. New York: Doubleday.

Michaelides, Dimitrios A. 1984. A Roman Surgeon's Tomb from Nea Paphos (Part 1). *Report of the Department of Antiquities of Cyprus*, 315–32.

Parpola, Simo, ed. 1993. *Letters from Assyrian and Babylonian Scholars*. State Archives of Assyria X. Helsinki: Helsinki University Press.

Penney, Douglas L., and Michael O. Wise. 1994. By the the Power of Beelzebub: An Aramaic Incantation Formula from Qumran (4Q560). *Journal of Biblical Literature* 113 (4): 627–50.

Philostratus. 1912. *Life of Apollonius of Tyrana*. Translated by F. C. Conybeare. 2 vols. Loeb Classical Library. Cambridge: Harvard University Press.

Pilch, J. J. 1985. Healing in Mark: A Social Science Analysis. *Biblical Theology Bulletin* 15 (4): 142–50.

———. 1986. The Health Care System in Matthew: A Social Science Analysis. *Biblical Theology Bulletin* 16 (3): 281–83.

———. 1991. Sickness and Healing in Luke-Acts. In *The Social World of Luke-Acts*, edited by Jerome Neyrey. Peabody, Mass.: Hendrickson.

———. 2000. *Healing in the New Testament: Insights from Medical and Mediterranean Anthropology*. Minneapolis: Ausburg Fortress.

Pliny. 1938–63. *Natural History*. Translated by D. E. Eichholz, W. H. S. Jones, and H. Rackham. 10 vols. Loeb Classical Library. Cambridge: Harvard University Press.

Radt, Wolfgang. 1988. *Pergamon: Geschichte und Bauten, funde und Erforschung einer antiken Metropole*. Cologne: Du Mont.

Roberts, Alexander, and James Donaldson, eds. 1965. The Ante-Nicene Fathers. Reprint, Grand Rapids: Eerdmans.

Rousseau, John. 1995. Healing of a Blind Man. In Arav and Freund 1995.

Ruis-Camps, Josep. 2000. El ciego de Betsaida/Betania (Mc. 8, 22–26). *Estudios Bíblicos* 58:289–308.

Smith, Morton. 1978. *Jesus the Magician*. San Francisco: Harper & Collins.

Sussman, Max. 1992. Sickness and Disease. *Anchor Bible Dictionary*, edited by D. N. Friedman et al. New York: Doubleday.

Tatian. 1982. *Oratio ad Graecos and Fragments*. Edited by Molly Whittaker. Clarendon: Oxford.

Tertullian. 1931. *Apology/De Spectaculis*. Translated by T. R. Glover and G. H. Rendall. Loeb Classical Library. Cambridge: Harvard University Press.

Tomlinson, Richard A. 1983. *Epidauros*. Austin: University of Texas Press.

Twelftree, Graham H. 1993. *Jesus the Exorcist: A Contribution to the Study of the Historical Jesus*. Peabody, Mass.: Hendrickson.

Wilkinson, John. 1998. *The Bible and Healing: A Medical and Theological Commentary*. Grand Rapids: Eerdmans.

Richard A. Freund

The Tannery of Bethsaida?

THE INDUSTRY OF TANNING IN THE HELLENISTIC
AND ROMAN PERIOD

A TANNERY WAS A LARGE-SCALE INDUSTRY in antiquity and was located in key places where accessibility to resources, environmental conditions (water, population base for workers, wind to remove odors, etc.), and a trade route to justify preparation of both primary materials and sometimes finished products were found. A tannery required ready access to large numbers of animal skins that could be brought along a major trading route, tanning materials such as oak bark, large amounts of water, and a physical plant that included as many as five or six large installations or vats. These items were not always in ready supply in the ancient Near East and evidence in Israel of tanneries is sparse. A tannery usually involved a number of different operations in an open-air series of round vats, which were usually sealed by clay or other natural material.

The industry of tanning was an extremely lucrative business in the Hellenistic and Roman periods, and was apparently tightly controlled in the Roman eastern provinces by taxes and by guilds of leather workers as well as the various types of workers who used leather to create a variety of other products including sandals, writing implements, religious objects, saddles, handbags, purses, weapons, and armor. Guilds of these workers existed throughout the Hellenistic and Roman provinces in places such as Arsinoe, Thebes, Fayum, Aphroditopolis, and Panopolis. From the first half of the second century BCE, a

233

petition from a tanner in Hellenistic Egypt includes key details of the
infrastructure necessary to support a tannery there and how he was
apparently licensed by the state to work in the profession (Forbes 1966,
5:35):

> To the *epimelethus* Porotheus from Petosiris, tanner living at
> Crocodilopolis. I work in the State shops. I have living quarters
> like the others and there I dwell. The tax farmer Philippus has
> conceded us the right to work the raw hides, we detach the
> hair, we deliver the wool to the weavers of coarse stuffs [*kaso-
> poioi*] and we deliver to the tax farmer for the Royal Treasure
> the receipts of the sale of the hides.

The rabbis and later Islamic literature (Al-Hassan and Hill 1986, 197–
201) wrote extensively on the ordinances regarding a tannery and the
standards of work. The rabbis created a whole series of additional
questions, because tanning involved a dead animal that immediately
placed the profession within the categories of the ritual purities system. Ritual purity was a metaphysical ideal that, although biblically
founded, was implemented in very specific ways in the Hellenistic
and Roman periods (Neusner 1973a, 12). Certain materials were seen
as inherently able to contract or pass on impurities. Since dead animals were one of the major sources of ritual impurity, the use of the
skin of a dead animal for a holy purpose (scrolls for the writing of holy
scripture, but also phylacteries and other religious items) presented an
enormously complex philosophical question that the rabbis
embraced. With a large proportion of the entire rabbinic tractate
Kelim [utensils] in the Mishnah and Tosefta (hundreds of pages)
devoted to the utensils of leather (chapters 16, 23–26 are also devoted
to utensils made of wood, bone, pottery, glass, and metal), the question of how, why, and where a tanner was able to work continued to
be a well-known issue to the Galilean rabbis. A legal paradox was created that apparently the rabbis needed to resolve. The rabbis make it
abundantly clear that coming into contact with a dead animal is a vio-
lation of purity laws, especially when the Temple was standing, but
even after the destruction of the Temple it remained a problem. The
rabbis created philosophical categories for allowing the use of finished
products that involved seemingly problematic materials according to
the laws of purity as long as the production of the finished materials
was properly supervised by them. This meant that they also partially

controlled the industries associated with leather, wood, bone, pottery, glass, and metal, and so places where tanneries were located were also bastions for a rabbinic presence. This does not mean that these places were the location of a rabbinic academy, court, or even a synagogue; rather, the opposite was true. The very fact that the location may have had a questionable industry may have obviated the presence of a rabbinic academy, court, or synagogue, but it also meant that rabbinic presence was necessary. The fully defined leather product is tanned, and according to rabbinic interpretation the final product is purified through the final production process (and thereby becomes susceptible to ritual impurity again). Ritual and nonritual objects were made from leather and therefore were very important for the daily life of Jews. Gloves, mezuzot (placed on every doorpost), shoes, ritual phylacteries (put on for daily prayers), and the most important of all of these items, the Torah and other biblical scrolls as well as rabbinic manuscripts were all made of leather. The skins were first impure and then when completed as leather, were subject to the same laws of purities as other objects that might come into contact with another, new source of impurity. A mysterious line was crossed in the process of tanning and rabbinic supervision and control was crucial to the process. First, the animals that were chosen for use were among the kosher animals described in the Bible and rabbinic literature. Second, the animals had to be ritually slaughtered under rabbinic supervision, and then the different parts of the preparation of the skins were carefully monitored. When the leather was completed, it no longer possessed the same impurities as when it was only partially finished. This created a unique opportunity for Jews and non-Jews to participate in the process of creating ritual (and nonritual) objects. This type of activity, which involved the setting of legal boundaries, was also the basis of much of rabbinic literature in general and the rabbinic interest in Bethsaida in particular.

ON THE BORDERS OF THE LAND

BETHSAIDA AND ITS TANNERY

The rabbinic classifications of the "Land of Israel" are extremely relevant when investigating a border town such as Bethsaida. Richard Sarason has noted "that virtually every Mishnaic case involving the

Land of Israel deals with issues of boundaries and confusion of boundaries, both spatial and social" (1986, 112). These borders were not necessarily intended to be politically defensible or representative of historical boundaries of any one kingdom or period, but rather, represented a series of issues that linked rabbinic communities of similar background and traditions together. The Diaspora was considered by some rabbinic sources to be ritually impure, so being on the border between the land of Israel and the Diaspora made Bethsaida an especially interesting place for the rabbis. Since the Jordan River was for some rabbinic issues the line of demarcation between the land of Israel and the Diaspora, many questions relating to borders were decided based on individual precedents. The Mishnah of tractate Ohilot 18.7 relates:

> If a man bought a field in Syria that lies close to the Land of Israel and he can enter it in ritual purity (there is a corridor of land which is just over the border and touches his land), it is ritually pure (and considered as if it were a part of the Land of Israel even though it is not), and it is subject to the laws of Tithes and Seventh Year produce; but if he cannot enter it in ritual purity it is deemed impure.

In general, the role of the Tosefta is to provide a follow-up or additional information to the mishnaic presentation of a topic common to both the Mishnah and Tosefta. While the language of the Mishnah and Tosefta will be similar, the Tosefta will usually employ its own style and choice of vocabulary for a topic. Tosefta Ohilot 18.2 contains supplementary and complementary data about the traditions mentioned in Mishnah Ohilot 18.7. The Tosefta relates its information in similar language but contains some exemplification:

- 18.2: The land of the Gentiles—if one can enter it in ritual purity, it is ritually pure. And how near must it be so that one may be able to enter it in ritual purity? Rabban Shimon ben Gamliel says: "Even a single furrow intervenes."

- Rabbi Shimon said: "I can make it possible for priests to be fed with ritually pure food (even) in the tannery of Bethsaida [*BeTz[a]idan*][1] and in the villages of Lebanon because they are near the sea or the river."

- They said to him: "The fish pools [*pesanim*][2] intervene."

- 18.3: The assumption concerning roads taken by immigrants from Babylonia, even though they are surrounded by the land of the Gentiles, is that they are ritually pure.

- 18.4: Cities surrounded by the Land of Israel, for example, Susita and the villages around it, Ashkelon and the villages around it, even though they are free of tithe and of the rule of the sabbatical year, are not subject to the law governing the land of the Gentiles.

The "tannery of Bethsaida" mentioned in 18.2 must have been an important element in the historical memory of the city, since it appears in other places in rabbinic literature. While some have argued that the reading here should be "the tannery of Sidon," it appears both from critical studies of manuscript traditions and the geographic location of Sidon itself (which is far from the traditional borders of the land of Israel) that the reading of Bethsaida is to be preferred here (Freund 1995, 267–311). The rabbinic tradition that was used by the Tosefta Ohilot 18.2 is an example of a place near the border of Syria (mentioned in the Mishnah) where one could enter the Diaspora in a ritually pure state. This location appears to be near the Jordan River and close to where fish pools were found. Since there is a significant need for a good source of fresh water for tanning purposes, it makes good sense that the tannery was located in Bethsaida, at the intersection of the Jordan and Sea of Galilee, and not at Sidon on the Mediterranean Sea.

The other traditions found in Palestinian Talmud 18.3 and 18.4 cited above confirm that the eastern land routes bordering Galilee and the Jordan are meant and not the northern border with Tyre and far northern Sidon. The land route to Babylonia passed north and east of Bethsaida, and Susita is one of the Decapolis cities around the Sea of Galilee. The logistical, contextual, and text-critical arguments found in these traditions demonstrate that the famous tannery of the rabbis was located in Bethsaida and not in Sidon, and that Rabbi Shimon was acquainted with the city of Bethsaida. It is possible that in a large city such as Sidon a single tannery stood out for the rabbis, but it is more likely that this tannery was located in a much more strategic place, such as Bethsaida on the border between the Galilee and the Diaspora leading to Babylon. It also appears that, because of a remarkable coincidence of logistical, contextual, and text-critical arguments found in rabbinic literature, the role of the tannery of Bethsaida became highlighted.

In the Palestinian Talmud, tractate Avodah Zarah 1.10, 40b, and in Mishnah Ketubot 7.10, traditions relating to the tannery (and tanners) of Bethsaida are highlighted. In discussing problems that might arise from Jews' renting Jewish properties to non-Jews, the rabbis use the legal precedent of nearby Syria. In a Diaspora community the issue appears to be very clear: Jews find themselves as a minority living among non-Jews, and feel compelled to rent and sell land and rooms to non-Jews to maintain good relations. The question appears to be less clear in the land of Israel where Jews are supposed to be in the majority. The city of Bethsaida, on the border, provides them with a way of discussing the nuances of the issue. The Palestinian Talmud continues:

> In a place in which it is customary to sell [houses to a non-Jew], one sells him even a residence or rents him even a residence.[3] Rabbi Aha, Rabbi Tanhum bar Hiyya in the name of Rabbi Eleazar ben Rabbi Yose said: "and even a small stall, for example, like the *(BeTz[a]idan) Bethsaida* Tannery." It is therefore not the end of the matter that one may rent out the entire house, but even a single room [in a house]. (Emphasis added)

The implication from this story is that one can have non-Jews and Jews living in the same residences, a situation that would probably not be advisable for the furtherance of Jewish observance but perhaps a necessity in border towns.

In the most ancient manuscript tradition of the Mishnah (Codex Kaufmann A50), Ketubot 7.10 mentions the tannery in Bethsaida, apparently a well-known place name:[4]

> And these are compelled to divorce their wives: he that is afflicted with boils...a coppersmith or a tanner, whether these defects were known before the marriage or not. Of all of these, Rabbi Meir says: Although the husband made it a condition with her [to marry him despite his defects], she may say, "I thought I could endure it, but now I cannot endure it." *It once happened in Bethsaida* that a tanner died and had a brother who was a tanner. The Sages said: She may say, "your brother I could endure; but you I cannot endure." (Emphasis added)

Of the over fifty Bethsaida references in classical rabbinic literature (until the early medieval period), almost fifteen are of a highly personal nature and relate to halachic (legal) observations made at the town/city apparently because of some event that occurred there (Freund 1995) using a specific formula known as *maaseh* literature. The highly personal rabbinic texts related to Bethsaida are important since it is extremely difficult to glean historical information from rabbinic texts in general and even more difficult to compare historical events in rabbinic texts with archaeological information. Some of the Bethsaida references use a formulaic statement that has been seen by scholars as being more authentic than general statements (without this formula) in rabbinic texts. It is important to note that even though almost one-third of the Bethsaida rabbinic texts are framed with the formulaic statement *"maaseh"* [it once happened], this does not guarantee their historical authenticity. These *maaseh* narratives appear to be one-time, original statements of a historical "fact," but it still does not mean that they can be totally relied upon for accurate historical information, although they do provide a measure of comparison that is unprecedented especially combined with the rather specific nature of the tannery's location at Bethsaida. As Jacob Neusner has stated regarding these types of formulas:

> It was the convention of rabbinic historiography to invent dramatic "incidents" out of the evidence of conflict, and so to represent as a clash of personalities what was originally a difference of some seriousness to be sure, in matters of law. (Neusner 1984, 91)

Of the fifteen different Bethsaida citations that use the *maaseh* formula, half of the issues that use this formula are questions about Bethsaida's location and most of these traditions contain elements relating to a unique relationship between Jews and non-Jews. The traditions under consideration in this chapter begin with a descriptive setting linked to a historical example or precedent using the Hebrew word *maaseh*. Neusner has described this word as indicative of a form of narrative: "What separates legal narratives from conventional, testimonial, and debate sayings is their historical focus, the reference in the past tense to a one-time action, ruling, setting, or event" (Neusner 1973b, 3:23–24). Gary G. Porton writes about this literary form:

Narratives are introduced by "it once happened [*maaseh*]."
Often the narratives contain debates. The narrative seems to
have been frequently used for transmitting sayings of the
Patriarch Gamliel and his family and many of our narratives
do discuss the Patriarchs. (Porton 1988, 130)

The legal precedent created concerning the Bethsaida tanner and his
wife is both personal and unusual. The scene assumes that the woman
and the Bethsaida tanner have no children and according to the biblical law of levirate marriage, she ought to be compelled to marry the
brother, who is also a Bethsaida tanner. She is exempted by the majority of the sages. The rabbis have gone out of their way to limit the legal
precedent by mentioning that it was enacted for a Bethsaida tanner's
wife. It opens the door for another challenge for a more mainstream,
normative community to also ask for an exemption, but it does not
assume it. This is the power of the Bethsaida tannery example. It is
apparently well known enough for the public to understand that it is
a precedent of the sages of the land of Israel but specific enough in its
location and qualifications to allow later sages to either use the precedent to extend the exemption for some other location or limit it to the
Bethsaida location.

One more rabbinic tradition from Bethsaida indicates that in
addition to the actual tannery, there were scribes there who worked
with finished products in a type of scrollery. The Babylonian Talmud
Shabbat 115b states:

Our Rabbis taught: Benedictions and amulets, though they
contain letters of the (divine) name and many passages of the
Torah, must not be rescued from a fire (on the Sabbath) but
must be burnt where they lie, they together with their (divine)
names. Hence it was said: they who write down benedictions
are as though they burnt the Torah. *Maaseh beachad shehayah
kotev BeTz[a]idan [It once happened at Bethsaida]* that someone
was once writing [semiprofessionally for amulets and such—
the divine name]. Rabbi Yishmael was informed thereof, and
he went to question him (about it). As he was ascending the
ladder, he (the writer) became aware of him (so) he took a
sheaf of benedictions and plunged them into a bowl of water.
In these words did Rabbi Yishmael speak to him. The punish-
ment for the latter (diluting in water the benedictions) is

greater than the former (writing down the benedictions in general). (Emphasis added)

The reference here explores the complex world of the sanctioned rabbinic scribe and those who would write the divine name for ritually sanctioned items (that was closely monitored by rabbinic academies, courts, and synagogues) and the more popular (nonsanctioned) use of Jewish amulets and benedictions. The split between the more formal, sanctioned religious literature and the less formal, popular (and non-sanctioned) religious amulets, magic bowls, incantations, and benedictions is a very common element in ancient religion (Naveh and Shaked 1985, 1993; Neusner, Frerichs, and McCracken-Flesher 1989). The use of the divine name in sanctioned religious literature was carefully regulated by the rabbis especially after the destruction of the Temple in Jerusalem to ensure that the name would not be misused by a variety of different sects. The fact that the scribe above is described only as "someone" and not a rabbinically sanctioned figure is apparent. It is not clear whether the person is a Jew or a non-Jew. The unknown scribe is writing the divine name on small scrolls of benedictions that would be inserted in amulets and, although they are not considered to be holy by rabbinic standards, they are nonetheless in need of rabbinic supervision. The fact that it just says *beechad* [someone] is an important distinction when compared with the next text. The rabbis often hid the identities of individuals who did not share the normative religious view behind designations such as *echad* [someone] or *acher* [another one]. This was the name given to the scholar Elisha ben Abuya, who is referred to in rabbinic texts simply as *acher* (Mishnah Hagigah 2:1; Tosefta Hagigah 2:3; BT Hagigah 15a–b; PT Hagigah 2:2, 77b–c).

The scribe destroys his handiwork (by dipping it in water) rather than have the rabbi see what he has done. The incident at Bethsaida points up the fact that the writer is not being directly monitored by rabbinic authority and thus Rabbi Yishmael, one of the leading rabbinic figures of the second century CE, scolds the nonsanctioned scribe for his decision to destroy the work rather than allow supervision. It also points out that the scribe does in fact respect the authority of the rabbi but was not willing to have his work subjected to his scrutiny. In what appears to be a parallel version of this tale (with a twist), the identity of the unknown scribe may in fact illustrate the enormously distinctive nature of Bethsaida. In the Tosefta of Avodah Zarah 3.7, a specifically mentioned non-Jewish scribe is writing Jewish texts and in the only legal precedent of its kind in this period, this is permitted by the dages:

> *Maaseh b'goy echad BeTzaidan* [It happened that there was a non-Jew in Bethsaida] who used to write scrolls of the Law [Sefarim] and the *Maaseh* [incident] came before the Sages and they said it was permitted to take it from him. (Emphasis added)

The unique nature of these two incidents at Bethsaida cannot be minimized. Perhaps because of its unique location, the religious identity of the individuals who live in this location, or the difficulty in distinguishing rabbinically certified Jews from nonrabbinically certified Jews in this area, the text refers to the individual as a non-Jew. All of these references point to a unique religious environment at Bethsaida in the second century CE.

What makes both of these references to Bethsaida more relevant is their connection to the literary traditions of the New Testament associated with the site and the archaeological information that has been gleaned from seventeen years of excavations at Bethsaida. The existence of material culture related to the tanning industry has emerged from excavations at Bethsaida. At the same time, the existence of an imperial cult temple at Bethsaida (Arav 1999, 18–24) near what may be the remains of a tannery raises the possibility that in the first and second century CE a tanning industry did exist at Bethsaida. The question of whether the tannery was an industry related to the first century CE imperial cult temple or whether it emerged later will be considered. The fact that the New Testament also has literary references that refer to the tanning industry/tanners among the population of Bethsaida also is relevant. Peter, who according to the Gospel of John 1.44 was from Bethsaida, demonstrates a close knowledge and friendship with tanners, one of the more despised professions of the period (because of persistent odors and related problems). In the book of Acts 9:43, 10:6, and 10:32, Peter is shown as staying in the home of and knowing tanners in other locations, raising the assumption that as he is used to living with tanners, he must be from a location with tanners, that is, Bethsaida.

THE PROBLEM OF THE TANNERY

Tanneries are well known in antiquity but little is known about the installations necessary to maintain them from archaeological contexts. Leather-making was important in antiquity, especially for the Jews. Tanning, although never mentioned in the Hebrew Bible, was used for shoes, sandals, and straps and harnesses for donkeys, camels, and horses, and was also used for storing and transporting liquids. All writing materials were made from leather, including scrolls, *tefillin* (phylacteries with biblical verses fixed inside of a leather mount), and *mezuzot* (biblical verses written on scrolls and placed in doorposts). The terms that became the standard rabbinic terms for the profession, however, were Greek words *bursi* (tanner), *bursekai* (tannery), and *bursiyyon* (the hide when it was being processed). The tannery, according to Mishnah Baba Batra 2.9, was to be located in the east part of the city, and at least fifty cubits from the outskirts of the city. This tractate states that the tannery should be fifty cubits (seventy-five feet) away from the settlement, apparently to have prevailing winds remove the powerful odors produced by the chemicals associated with the tanning process. The tradition is much more complicated than it seems at first glance:

> Carrion, graves, and tanneries must be kept fifty cubits from a town. A tannery must only be placed on the east side of the town. Rabbi Akiva, however, says that it may be placed on any side except the west, providing it is kept fifty cubits away. (Mishnah Baba Batra 2.9)

According to rabbinic literature, a tannery, unlike any other place of business, did not require a *mezuzah* and was unfavorably compared in this regard to both a bathhouse and a bathroom in BT Yoma 11a. Apparently because of the semipermanent state of discoloration associated with the skin of the tanner and smells associated with the tannery, BT Hagigah 4a even exempted tanners from having to make the biblically ordained pilgrimage to Jerusalem. While the rabbis lauded all types of work and crafts as worthy of divine attention, only tanning was singled out in popular sayings as being a demeaning craft.

> "It was taught: Rabbi said: No craft can disappear from the world—happy is he who sees his parents in a superior craft, and woe to him who sees his parents in a mean craft. The world cannot exist without a perfume-maker and without a

tanner—happy is he whose craft is that of a perfume-maker, and woe to him who is a tanner by trade. (BT Pesachim 65a; BT Baba Batra 16b; BT Ketubot 82b)

What does all of this have to do with the tannery at Bethsaida? First, the fact that the tanning profession is singled out at Bethsaida in rabbinic literature is an indication of its importance at the site. It is not an insignificant profession in rabbinic literature, but rather was quite a well-known industry based upon the number of references to it in rabbinic literature. This would mean that rabbinic attention to the tannery of Bethsaida was probably pointed and deliberate. Second, according to rabbinic information about tanning, the location of the tannery must have been unique at the site, with regard to wind patterns (on top of the hill overlooking the entire Sea of Galilee) that may have allowed the fumes to dissipate without affecting the larger cities of the area located to the southwest and perhaps the inhabitants of the site. Third, while Bethsaida was not a noted rabbinic center in the way that Yavne, Usha, Sepphoris, and Bet Shearim were known (with academies, courts, and synagogues) in rabbinic literature, it may have had a sufficient rabbinic presence for parts of the tanning industry that required minimal rabbinic supervision. Based upon the rabbinic traditions attached to the site, this seems to be the case. Finally, Bethsaida, both in literary texts and in archaeological excavations, was located on trade routes to allow the shipping of the skins (and the final products) from north and south, east and west. Locations of rabbinically supervised industries were tied to the trade routes. While most rabbinic centers were not necessarily known as being centers for industry, places such as Kefer Hananya (pottery) and Tiberias (glass) that did have specific associated industries were located on major trade routes similar to Bethsaida.

Since Bethsaida became an imperial cult site in the early first century CE, it is important to look at another Roman imperial cult site, such as Pergamon where, in 1990, an early Roman industrial installation with basins and cisterns identified as a tannery was discovered to the northwest of the site (Mellink 1992, 145). The best example is at Pompeii. At this site, one room was used "for the mechanical treatment of the hides...it was separated by a low wall from a back room, which had 15 round pits (1.25–1.60 m in diameter and about 1.50 deep), lined with stucco, in the walls of which there were two steps to allow the workmen to descend into these pits and clean them out.... In the

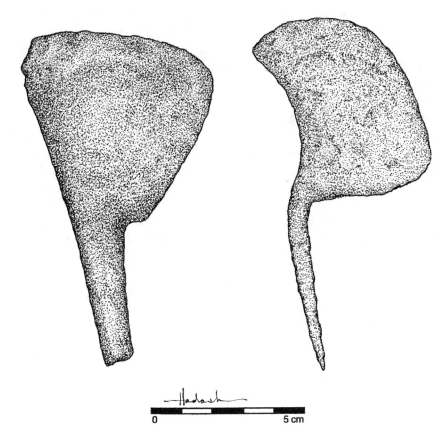

Fig. 1. Half-moon scrapers used in tanning from Roman period, left (drawn after R. J. Forbes, *Studies in Ancient Technology*, 5:62, photo 14 [Leiden: Brill, 1966]), and Bethsaida, right (Area A, 1993, Locus 730, basket 2216)

first room were found many instruments, which differed little from those now in use. There were the blunt-edged concave scrapers, the currier's knife, the half-moon knife, awls (or other steel edging tools?) and other tools" (Forbes 1966, 56).

The half-moon knife is an extremely distinctive artifact (Forbes 1966, 62, photo 14). The half-moon knife is so unusual, that when a half-moon knife was discovered at Bethsaida with other bronze and stone scrapers in a round stone structure in Area A in 1993 (Locus 730, basket 2216, see fig. 1), no one could immediately identify the item. It was only later that comparative studies revealed the use of this distinctive item as a scraper used in tanning as noted above at Pompeii. The round stone structure excavated in this area has very pronounced walls (Arav 1995, 7ff.). The discoveries in this area indicate a Greco-Roman context for the round structure. Eastern Terra Sigillata pottery, and Hellenistic and Roman period cooking pots and plates were all found in loci 550 through 730. The western slope of the mound nearest this round stone structure has not been fully excavated to date and therefore it is difficult to conjecture whether these finds are part of the original structures on the mound from a later second or third century CE context or whether the tannery would have been located in another area of the mound and the finds were dumped in the round structure, but there are no other Hellenistic-Roman period structures to the west of the rounded structure except massive basalt boulder Iron Age buildings.

At Hurvat Sumaq, some forty miles to the west of the Bethsaida excavations (on the way to Haifa), a workshop building from the second to fourth centuries was uncovered, which appears to be a tannery located to the east of the synagogue (Wolff 1993, 158). Abundant water resources were necessary for the tanning industry and, since the odor was so profound from the tanning chemicals, it was necessary to have these facilities in a nonresidential quarter. Location to the east of dwellings because of the prevailing west-east wind patterns is also important. The presence of certain vegetation used in tannage, such as alum, oak galls, gall nuts, bark, and wood of oak, is important as well. Dung and urine were also extremely effective and easily available agents for tanning. The specific tanning agents are mentioned in the context of a sacrifice of an ox in a Babylonian text (800 BCE), indicating that the center for cult sacrifice, a temple, was sometimes located directly adjacent to the tanning works (Forbes 1966, 45).

At Bethsaida, a number of these elements have been discovered in Area A near the round stone structure directly adjacent to the Roman-style temple there,[5] which corroborates the tannery theory as well. Rami Arav holds that this round stone structure is most likely a Hellenistic and early Roman granary. Tithes received at a cult center would certainly need a storage area directly adjacent. A pollen analysis conducted in 1996 in the area of the imperial cult temple showed high percentages of three taxa in the temple plaster: quercus (oak) 35 percent, olea (olive) 3 percent, and linim (flax) 14 percent.[6]

The high percentage of oak implies that more than just tree residue is present there. Other tree taxa are present in minute amounts, but the high percentage of oak may imply that oak by-products (tannin) were being used in the area in high concentrations. Two possibilities present themselves: that the tannin may have been in liquid form and tithed in high concentration at the Roman temple or that the structure was no longer in use as a temple at a later period (the rabbinic tannery would have been in use from the second to third century CE, over one hundred years after the Roman temple had been in use), and was used for storage or as a small tannery. The coin finds in the area directly adjacent to the Roman temple indicate a second- and perhaps third-century settlement at Bethsaida.[7] If this was indeed a Roman temple and an anathema to the rabbis, it is understandable that the rabbis would have been happy to turn it into a tannery in a later period to diminish its importance, and why they would have written about it as a distinct location. In general, tanneries were located east of the city and not on top of the mound. Usually only monumental buildings would achieve such an elevated status. A tannery located in a central place like the most elevated part of a city familiar to the rabbis would have been distinctive enough to be mentioned so prominently in rabbinic literature. It may have represented for the rabbis an opportunity to take a hellenized (Jewish) city and have the city now be a site for a despised profession—an ignoble victory over Hellenism of sorts. In this same rabbinic period, there was a synagogue, Kh. ed-Dikke, which was built some 1.5 kilometers to the north of the Bethsaida site, probably to avoid the noxious odors created by the tannery and later by the residue of the tanning process (Urman and Flesher 1995, 503–9). It is also possible that the tannery was located to the east of the settlement as prescribed in rabbinic texts[8] and that the existence of these finds on top of the mound is not directly related to a tannery building, but rather to a storage building for the tannery.

Dating the existence of a tannery at Bethsaida is difficult. An imperial city might have had a cult center at one part of a site, and the existence of animal sacrifices for cult purposes might have allowed for abundant stock at the site; however, throughout the second century, literary accounts still record abundant wildlife in the area (the pheasants of Hadrian are mentioned in the Talmud in this area in Ecclesiastes

Rabbah 2.8). Directly adjacent to the Roman-style temple, another architectural layer was found dating from a period after the temple, which was dated with coin finds to the second and early third century. In fact, the materials may indicate that the use of the top of the mound of the city as a tannery may have begun a few generations after the Roman-style temple was no longer in use. This may indicate that the tannery may have begun its work in a second-, third-, or fourth-century context and begun its use only after it was no longer functioning as a cult center. The named rabbinic traditions would place it in the later period rather than the early Roman period.[9]

Bethsaida could have had a tannery in the first century as well. So far, no clear dwellings from this later period at Bethsaida have been found, although some structures and small finds indicate the existence of some settlement on the mound. The existence of nonresidential buildings to block the prevailing winds east-west and a small population located on the eastern side of the mound might have allowed the tanning professionals to continue their work without major obstacles. More important, since imperial cities had precincts specifically set aside for the cult, locating a tannery in this very prominent area would mean that very few people would be affected by the odors since the cult site was not living space. In fact, Bethsaida may have been an excellent industry center for Philip Herod's small kingdom in the first century. By the city of Bethsaida passed roads for overland transport north and south in the Roman Empire, west to the port of Ptolemais on the Mediterranean Sea, and by water to the port of Tiberias—in the world of Philip Herod's small kingdom, this was an important center indeed.

CHAPTER NOTES

1. This is the reading of the Erfurt manuscript according to the Zuckerman-del 1970 edition of the *Tosephta*, which does not list any other variants for this reading.

2. The Tosefta reads "*pesanim*," a word with no apparent parallel that appears to be in need of some reconstruction. It should perhaps read "*pesaqin*," which could be the naturally occurring pools mentioned by commentators of Alfasi on BT Moed Qatan 4b. See Jastrow 1903, s.v. "*pesaqot*," which points to the Latin *piscine*, meaning reservoir, swimming bath, or fish-tank.

3. According to this section, Jews did not rent to non-Jews for fear of impurities regarding the dead. The Temple Scroll, for example, lists as a seemingly Levitical prohibition: "You shall not defile your land. Do not do as the Gentiles do as they bury their dead all over the place, they even bury them in the middle of houses..." (Martinez 1996, 169).

4. The so-called "Lowe" manuscript at Cambridge University (Lowe [1883] 1996) for Gittin 7.5 reads fully with two yud's: "BeTzaidan" while Ketubot 7.10, Gittin 4.7, and Avodah Zarah 3.12 read without two *yud*'s: "BeTz[a]idan." The PT Leiden manuscript of the Mishnah reads with two yud's: "BeTzaidan" for Mishnah Avodah Zarah 3.12 and Gittin 7.5, but Gittin 4.7 and Ketubot 7.10 read without two *yud*'s: "BeTz[a]idan."

5. "West of the main building, the Iron Age remains descend abruptly resulting perhaps from an Iron Age retaining wall that supported the upper structures. At this point an oval structure built with massive boulders was discovered (W70). It measures 6.8 by 5.5 m. This structure had a partition wall of 0.90 m. wide, in this center. The oval house served perhaps as a granary and dates from the Hellenistic period. West of the granary few structures were discovered" (Arav 1995, 16).

6. Information provided by P. Geyer and Professor J. Shoenwetter after analyses carried out at Arizona State University, May 1997. A full report was presented in Shoenwetter and Geyer 2000, 63–73.

7. Approximately 10 percent of the coins in areas A and B can be dated to the period of the second and third century, with city coins of different mints and Tyre and Tiberias predominating. There is an occupation gap after Constantine I. See Arav 1995, 53–60; Kindler 1999.

8. Usually cited from Mishnah Baba Batra 2.9. The Mishnah states that the tannery should be fifty cubits (seventy-five feet) away from the settlement. This rabbinic tradition has been over-interpreted by archaeologists to place any theoretical tannery (as well as cemeteries and garbage dumps) fifty cubits away from a city because of the odors (and purity laws) while in reality, one often finds cemeteries and dumps in direct proximity to villages and towns. This is one of the problems that result from the use of rabbinic texts as archaeological or city planning guidebooks.

9. The Tosefta Ohilot text on the "Tannery of Bethsaida" is quoted in the name of Rabbi Shimon (usually Rabbi Shimon without any other designation is held to be Rabbi Shimon Ben Yohai), a post-Hadrianic Rebellion,

second-century CE source. The PT Avodah Zarah text on the "Tannery of Bethsaida" is quoted in the name of "Rabbi Aha, Rabbi Tanhum bar Hiyya in the name of Rabbi Eleazar ben Rabbi Yose." Rabbi Tanhum bar Hiyya, who lived at Tiberias in the third century CE, is relating this in the name of the earlier rabbinic source, Rabbi Eleazar ben Rabbi Yose, a Galilean (usually thought to be the son of Rabbi Yosi HaGelili), also a post-Hadrianic Rebellion, second-century CE source. This means that in the second and third centuries CE, the tannery was known to rabbinic, Galilean sources.

LITERATURE CITED

Al-Hassan, A. Y., and D. R. Hill. 1986. Islamic Technology, *Ma'alim al Qurba* (On the Duties of the Mutasib). Cambridge: Cambridge University Press.

Arav, Rami. 1995. Bethsaida Excavations: Preliminary Report, 1987–1993. In Arav and Freund 1995.

———. 1999. Bethsaida Excavations: Preliminary Report, 1994–1996. In Arav and Freund 1999.

Arav, Rami, and Richard Freund, eds. 1995. *Bethsaida: A City by the North Shore of the Sea of Galilee*. Vol. 1. Kirksville, Mo.: Thomas Jefferson University Press.

———. 1999. *Bethsaida: A City by the North Shore of the Sea of Galilee*. Vol. 2. Kirksville, Mo.: Truman State University Press.

Beer, G., ed. 1968. Mishna Codex Kaufmann A50, Limited Edition of the Budapest Manuscript, Vols. 1 and 2. Jerusalem: Qedem.

Forbes, Robert J. 1966. *Studies in Ancient Technology*. Vol. 5. Leiden: Brill.

Freund, Richard. 1995. The Search for Bethsaida in Rabbinic Literature. In Arav and Freund 1995.

Jastrow, Marcus. 1903. *A Dictionary of the Targumim, the Talmud Babli and Yerushalmi, and the Midrashic Literature*. Philadelphia: Traditional Press.

Kindler, Arie. 1999. The Coin Finds at the Excavations of Bethsaida. In Arav and Freund 1999.

Lowe, W. H., ed. [1883]. 1967. *The Mishnah on Which the Palestinian Talmud Rests*. Cambridge: Cambridge University Press; reprint, Jerusalem: Makor Publishing.

Martinez, Florentino Garcia. 1996. *The Dead Sea Scrolls Translated*. Leiden: Brill.

Mellink, M. J. 1992. Archaeology in Anatolia. *American Journal of Archaeology* 96:151-53.

Mishna. 1976. *Mishna Codex Parma* (De Rossi 138), Limited Edition of Bibliotheca Palatina, Parma, Italy, Vols. 1 and 2. Jerusalem: Makor Publishing.

Naveh, Joseph, and Shaul Shaked. 1985. *Amulets and Magic Bowls-Aramaic Incantations of Late Antiquity*. Jerusalem: Magnes Press, Hebrew University.

———. 1993. *Magic Spells and Formulae-Aramaic Incantations of Late Antiquity*. Jerusalem: Magnes Press, Hebrew University.

Neusner, Jacob. 1973a. *The Idea of Purity in Ancient Judaism*. Leiden: Brill.

———. 1973b. The Rabbinic Traditions about the Pharisees before 70. Leiden: Brill.

———. 1984. *In Search of Talmudic Biography*. Chico: Scholars Press.

Neusner, Jacob, Ernst S. Frerichs, and Paul Virgil McCracken-Flesher, eds. 1989. *Religion, Science and Magic: In Concert and in Conflict*. New York: Oxford University Press.

Palestinian Talmud. 1971. Palestinian Talmud, Manuscript Codex Scaligerianus 3, Limited Edition of the Leiden Manuscript, Vols. 1–4. Jerusalem: Qedem.

Porton, Gary G. 1988. *Goyim: Gentiles and Israelites in Mishnah-Tosefta.* Atlanta: Scholars Press.

Sarason, R. 1986. The Significance of the Land of Israel in the Mishnah. In *The Land of Israel: Jewish Perspectives,* edited by L. Hoffman. Notre Dame: Notre Dame Press.

Shoenwetter, J., and P. Geyer. 2000. Implications of Archaeological Palynology at Bethsaida, Israel. *Journal of Field Archaeology* 27 (1): 63–73.

Urman, Dan, and Paul V. M. Flesher. 1995. *Ancient Synagogues.* Vol. 2. Leiden: Brill.

Wolff, S. R. 1993. Archaeology in Israel. *American Journal of Archaeology* 97:158–59.

Zuckermandel, Moses Samuel, ed. 1970. *Tosephta.* Jerusalem: Wahrmann.

Mark D. Smith

Eusebius of Caesarea and the Fate of Bethsaida

O NE UNUSUAL ASPECT of the Bethsaida excavations is that there has been little occupation of the tell since the first couple of centuries CE; in many places, it is possible to dig down just a few centimeters and encounter shards of ancient pottery. The first century CE is well attested throughout the site, during which time it appears that Bethsaida/Julias was a thriving town, even boasting a Roman temple that may have been dedicated to Julia (= Livia, the wife of Augustus). The second century, however, is not nearly so well attested in the excavated areas. Thus far, excavators have discovered one modest dwelling in Area B, a few random walls not connected to any decipherable structure, and a small portion of paved floor in Area A as well as a couple of coins dating to the reign of Trajan. In addition, excavators regularly encounter Galilean bowls, manufactured for a local constituency in Kefar Hananya, some of which may date to the late first to early second centuries. After the mid-second century, very little has been found: a couple of coins not associated with any structures and some random shards testify to little more than the occupation of transient squatters.

The literary testimonia raise a similar enigma. There is a significant amount of evidence about the Bethsaida of the New Testament. Josephus wrote about Philip the Tetrarch's rebuilding of the city and giving it a new name, Julias; he also wrote of a significant battle fought near Bethsaida in late 66 or early 67 CE.[1] Pliny the Elder also attests to the "lovely" first-century town of Julias.[2] There is even some evidence of a rabbinical community there, perhaps into the second century.[3] Thereafter, the only written sources to mention Bethsaida/Julias offer no information about its history or inhabitants; rather, they tend to be preoccupied with quoting or commenting on the New Testament.[4] Both archaeological and literary evidence seem to indicate that something has changed from the first century. What became of Bethsaida/Julias? When was it abandoned and why? The one author who can offer some hint is Eusebius, bishop of the Metropolitan See of Caesarea around 300 CE.

Eusebius was a polymath. Renowned as the most learned scholar of his day, he was a remarkably prolific author, producing treatises on theology and philosophy as well as apologetic works, biblical commentaries, and other resources for studying the Bible, a chronicle, panegyrics, and accounts of martyrs. He is best known, however, as the "Father of Church History" and the biographer of the emperor Constantine. In the midst of his prodigious literary activity, Eusebius produced four works in which he makes mention of Bethsaida: the *Demonstratio Evangelica*, the *Commentary on Isaiah*, the *Chronicon*, and a modest work on *Place-Names in Holy Scripture*, better known as the *Onomasticon*.

In his *Demonstratio Evangelica*, Eusebius comments on Isaiah 9:1–6 and Matthew 4:12–25 concerning the importance of Galilee: "Shortly after, in the same Gospel [Matthew] you will find that Matthew was called from Galilee, and again, in another [Gospel], Levi. And Philip, according to John, came 'from Bethsaida,' 'from the *polis* of Peter and Andrew.' This was also in Galilee."[5] This first reference is a bit disappointing. Since there is no evidence that Eusebius was concerned with distinguishing between Galilee and Gaulanitis, little can be gleaned from these comments that one cannot learn from the text of the Gospels.

Eusebius' second reference to Bethsaida, found in the *Chronicon*, is problematic on several counts. Since only a few fragments of the original Greek text are extant,[6] scholars must rely upon translations: Jerome's Latin version (to which he made liberal additions) and an Armenian version, based on the Greek, perhaps dating from the sixth century.[7] Given these significant textual problems, one should interpret the *Chronicon* with caution. In his section of chronological canons, the first edition of which he probably composed in the early 290s (Barnes 1981, 113), Eusebius makes reference to Philip's rebuilding of

Bethsaida, which he here calls by its Herodian name, Julias, an event he places in the third year of the 200th olympiad, the 2,039th year of Abraham, and the tenth year of Tiberius' reign (c. 24/25 CE, though numismatic evidence suggests that he is probably off by a few years). In this rare case, a Greek fragment survives, preserved by Syncellus, in addition to the Latin and Armenian versions. Unfortunately, the Greek text stops short of the reference to Julias.[8] The Latin version reads: "Philip the Tetrarch called Paneas Caesarea Philippi, in which he had constructed many buildings, and he called another city, Julias."[9] This entry is remarkably similar to Josephus' references to the cities renamed by Philip.[10] Since Eusebius often used Josephus as a source, there is good reason to suspect that he did so in this case (Barnes 1981, 114). What is curious, however, is that Eusebius nowhere else refers to Bethsaida as Julias. It is possible that Eusebius' original version read "Bethsaida," which was subsequently changed to Julias in the Latin, but that is doubtful, since the Armenian version, which also calls the city Julias, seems to have been based on the original Greek and not on Jerome's Latin version. In addition, if Eusebius relied upon Josephus as his source for this entry, he probably used the name Julias because it is by far the most common name the latter uses for the town.[11] Eusebius, then, in this work, probably strayed little from Josephus' lead. Thus far, little of moment for understanding the fate of Bethsaida has been revealed.

Eusebius' reference to Bethsaida in his *Commentary on Isaiah* is both more interesting and more troubling than the previous references. Once again, commenting on Isaiah 9:1, Eusebius notes that the prophet refers to "Galilee by the sea and across the Jordan." He then explains:

> "By the sea" speaks of all the region on both sides of Lake Genesaret, which the Gospel remembers as "the sea," and therefore says, "Jesus, going beside the 'sea' of 'Galilee,' saw two brothers." There the disciples of our Savior were lying at anchor. Indeed Capernaum and Bethsaida and Chorazin and the rest of the villages, which the evangelical writing refers to as around the Lake of Tiberias, are still now pointed out.[12]

Two issues are worthy of note in this passage. First, Eusebius lumps together Capernaum, Bethsaida, and Chorazin, the so-called "evangelical triangle," as villages around the Sea of Galilee. There are two reasons

Eusebius may have used these three names as a group: their geographical proximity, and the fact that Q (Matt. 11:21; Luke 10:13) treats them together as the cities over which Jesus pronounced woes. Since it is well known that Eusebius seldom wrote a sentence that does not contain some sort of biblical allusion, this grouping should occasion no surprise. Perhaps for a combination of these reasons, Eusebius seems to treat these three towns as a sort of group label for all of the villages around the northern part the lake.

The second significant issue Eusebius raises in this passage is his enigmatic note that these villages "are still now pointed out." What does he mean? The subject of the verb must be αἱ λοιπαὶ κῶμαι, probably including the three towns specifically named. Since the verb is passive, it is not clear who does the pointing. Further, what does he mean by "pointed out"? Does he mean that there are, in Eusebius' own time, local guides who are able to take the curious to each of these specific sites? Or does he mean something more general, a sort of folk memory, by which, perhaps, learned locals are able, from a place like Tiberias, to point to the general location of towns Jesus is said to have visited in the Gospels? The former interpretation might lead one to conclude that the site of Bethsaida (as well as Chorazin and Capernaum) was still known at the turn of the fourth century. Both interpretations are plausible, but the latter better accounts for the ambiguities in Eusebius' language. The final reference to Bethsaida in Eusebius' works may help in understanding what Eusebius knew of Bethsaida in his own time.

The fourth work in which Eusebius mentions Bethsaida is the *Onomasticon*. Both the date and the purpose of this book are disputed. Although some argue that the *Onomasticon* should be dated somewhere around the time of Helena's pilgrimage in 326 (Wallace-Hadrill 1960, 56; Thomsen 1903, 131; cf. Schwartz 1909, 1434), recent studies have suggested that this was more probably an early work, produced in the 290s (Barnes 1981, 110–11; Pohlsander 1996). Whether Eusebius wrote this work simply to facilitate the study of the Bible, or whether he had in mind a guide for prospective pilgrims has been another bone of contention.[13] The extent of pilgrim visits to "Holy Places" before Helena's famous pilgrimage is not at all certain.[14] Further, one might expect a handbook for pilgrims to be structured geographically, as many later examples would suggest.[15] The structure of the *Onomasticon*, however, would lend itself more readily to use as an aid to biblical exegesis, since it is arranged alphabetically and, within each alphabetical section, entries appear in order of the books of the Bible (Barnes 1981, 106ff.).

Although the *Onomasticon* does not contain any references to Julias, as one might expect from Eusebius' entry in the *Chronicon*,[16] it does make one mention of the city of Bethsaida, appropriately listed under the letter *beta* in the section on the Gospels: "Bethsaida, the *polis* of Andrew and Peter and Philip. It lies in the Galilee [region] near Lake Gennesaret."[17] This is a disappointing entry, since it includes virtually nothing that cannot have been derived from the New Testament, and even on that basis, it is incomplete. There is no reference to Bethsaida as the place where Jesus walked on water (Mark 6:45) or healed a blind man (Mark 8:22), no reference to the curse of Chorazin, Bethsaida, and Capernaum (Matt. 11:21; Luke 10:13), no mention of Luke's narrative which implies that Bethsaida (or its environs?) was the "lonely place" where Jesus fed the five thousand (Luke 9:10). Indeed, almost all of this entry comes from John 1:44 and 12:21, with the exception of using "Genesaret" as the name of the lake, which occurs only in the synoptic Gospels (Matt. 14:34; Mark 6:53; Luke 5:1). It is here that this inquiry must begin, for in this entry, one learns something of significance about the character of the *Onomasticon*. Eusebius is not attempting to be thorough or systematic. His treatment of various sites is a combination of impressionistic references to the Bible and geographical notes based either upon Eusebius' own travels or his sources (Barnes 1981, 109). It is well known that, in addition to the Bible, Eusebius relied upon Josephus and Origen in many places (Thomsen 1903, 140; Klostermann 1902; Fischer 1939, 169ff.; Barnes 1981, 108; Wallace-Hadrill 1960, 204), but there is no recognizable influence of either of these sources in the entry on Bethsaida, despite his apparent dependence on Josephus in his *Chronicon*, which, according to Jerome, Eusebius had composed earlier (Klostermann 1902, 1–3; cf. Barnes 1981, 111).

Scholars of the *Onomasticon* have noted the irregular nature of Eusebius' entries. Some are very brief and refer only to biblical material, while others are considerably more detailed, containing much that probably came from Eusebius' personal experience of a region. Since Eusebius spent most of his life in Caesarea Maritima, it is not unreasonable that he may have traveled over much of the biblical landscape. D. S. Wallace-Hadrill argues that there is a consistent pattern in the amount of personal detail in the entries. Those sites in the middle region, between Galilee and Jerusalem, seem to receive the most up-to-date discussion, presumably a reflection of Eusebius' greater personal experience of that area (1960, 205). Since the entry on Bethsaida refers to a place on the north of the Sea of Galilee, and it receives such a short, exclusively biblical treatment, it is possible that Eusebius had never visited the area, in which case his entry is of no value for understanding the status of Bethsaida around the turn of the fourth century. Is this conclusion, and the assumption upon which it is based, warranted? The only way to be sure is to analyze the other references to towns around the Sea of Galilee in the *Onomasticon*. If they, like Bethsaida, receive only brief entries, based primarily on biblical data, Eusebius is probably revealing his personal ignorance of the region. If, however, Eusebius has more to say, alternative explanations must be sought.

In addition to Bethsaida, Eusebius includes entries on four other towns in the region: Capernaum, Chorazin, Gadara, and Gergesa. Beyond these, there is one entry on Galilee and a couple of references to Tiberias (though there is no separate entry on Tiberias). The following are translations of the relevant entries:

> Capernaum (Matt. 4:13). Beside Lake Gennesaret. Until today it is a village of Gentiles in Galilee. 'On the border of Zebulun and Naphtali.'[18]

> Chorazin (Matt. 11:21). A village in Galilee which Christ cursed, according to the Gospel. It is now deserted, separated from Capernaum by two mile stones. (1966, 174, line 23)

> Gadara (Matt. 8:28). A city on the other side of the Jordan from Scythopolis and Tiberias, toward the east, in the mountains, near the foothills where there are baths of warm water. (1966, 74, line 10)

> Gergesa (Mark 5:1). There the Lord cured the demoniacs. Now there appears in the hills a village by the Lake of Tiberias into which the swine cast themselves. It [the village] lies farther up [the hillside?]. (1966, 74, line 13)

> Galilee (I Kings 9:11). There are two Galilees, of which one is called Galilee of the Gentiles, lying along the border of Tyre. There Solomon gave to Chiram 20 cities, of the land of Naphtali. The other [Galilee] is on both sides of Tiberias, near the

lake of the same name, a region allotted to Zebulun. (1966, 72, line 1)

Eusebius does not appear, based upon these entries, to be ignorant of the geography around the Sea of Galilee. He is knowledgeable enough to use Tiberias as a reference point for situating other cities, and he has something to say about the layout and current situation of all four of the other towns in the region: Capernaum is now a city of the Gentiles; Gadara is near some hot springs; Gergesa is a contemporary village lying in the hills above the lake;[19] Chorazin is deserted.[20]

In light of the particular information Eusebius provides concerning other sites around the Sea of Galilee, it is unlikely that his lack of specificity concerning Bethsaida can be attributed to his lack of geographical knowledge of the region. Indeed, his relative silence about Bethsaida is distressingly loud. The most probable explanation is that Eusebius said so little about Bethsaida because he simply knew nothing more. He was surely in the right neighborhood when describing Chorazin and Capernaum, but Bethsaida did not even merit a note like Chorazin, that it was deserted. It is, of course, possible that this is an anomaly, that Eusebius simply chose not to include anything more about Bethsaida, even though he knew more, as one might infer from his reference in his *Commentary on Isaiah*. Or he may never have visited the area, relying instead on an unnamed written or oral source that simply left him nothing about Bethsaida. Scholars know of many travels undertaken by Eusebius, both within Palestine and northward to Antioch, Nicea, and Constantinople. Moreover, it is evident, both in the *Onomasticon*, and throughout many of his other works, that Eusebius is interested in the topography of Palestine, and proud of his superior knowledge of it.[21] There is, therefore, a significant probability that Eusebius did indeed visit the region around the north shore of the Sea of Galilee.

While there is no reason to posit Eusebius' personal ignorance of the Galilee region, or his dependence upon an unknown source, there is good reason why Eusebius, despite the probability that he visited the region, may have known nothing about Bethsaida: he could not find it. It is possible that the floods that caused major alluvial deposits at the mouth of the Jordan had already begun their work of pushing the coast away from the city of fishermen. Anyone trying to locate the site would most likely look along the shore of the lake, not two kilometers inland, where the tell resides at present. In addition, Bethsaida may have been so thoroughly ravaged by some combination of destruction, neglect, and earthquake that there was little evidence of past habitation already by Eusebius' time (there is in fact literary and geological evidence of two significant earthquakes dating to 115 and 130 CE).[22] Whatever the reasons, knowledge of the location of Bethsaida, city of apostles, may well have been lost by the turn of the fourth century. And, if Bethsaida's location was already unknown, there arose an interesting task for those who desired to undertake a pilgrimage to New Testament sites, as well as for the guides who sought to lead them. The result was the marvelous inconsistency and confusion between sites that is apparent in so many medieval pilgrimage accounts.[23]

Appendix of Greek and Latin Sources on Bethsaida

Claudius Ptolemy, *Geography* (second century CE)
   [Cities] of Galilee:
   Sapphorei (or Sepphoris)
   Kaparkotnei (or Capernaum)
   Julias
   Tiberias [lake].[24]

Gospel of the Nazareans [Hebrews] (second century CE)
   In these cities (namely Chorazin and Bethsaida) many wonders have been wrought; as their number the Gospel according to the Hebrews gives 53.[25]

Aelius Herodianus, *Partitiones* (second century CE)
   Every pronunciation of written words beginning with the syllable "β" combined with "η" are such as: Bethlehem, Bethesda, Bethsaida, Bethphage, which are names of places in Jerusalem [*sic*]. (1963, 5, line 14)

Origen of Alexandria [and Caesarea Maritima] (third century CE)

   Commentary on John. And Jesus says to this Philip who had been found by Andrew, "follow me." To follow Jesus is to obey the Word, Wisdom, Righteousness, thinking and acting properly. Bethsaida means, in the Greek language, house of the hunters [fishermen?] to whom Jesus said, "follow me and I will make you fish for people." (1903, frag. 23)

   Fragments of Commentary on Exodus. "Woe to you Chorazin; woe to you Bethsaida, for if the signs that happened in you had taken place in Tyre and Sidon, they would long ago have clothed themselves in sackcloth and ashes and repented. But I say to you, it will be better for Tyre and Sidon than for you," etc. For the Savior, having foreknowledge of the faithlessness of those in Chorazin and those in Bethsaida, and those in Capernaum, and that it is better for the land of Sodom on the day of judgment than for those cities, what marvelous [monstrous?] things took place in Chorazin and in Bethsaida, seeing that, because of these things, it is better on the day of judgment for the Tyrians and Sidonians than for the citizens of these cities? (*MPG* 12:280, line 28; cf. *Philocalia* 27.11)

   Commentary on Matthew. "Mark, having made a change, wrote a slightly differing version [of the story of Jesus walking on the water]." There follows a quotation of Mark 6:45.[26]

Epiphanius, *Panarion* (fourth century CE)
   [Jesus, while staying in Capernaum, did other signs]. There he healed the man with the withered hand, as well as healing the mother-in-law of

Peter who, though he was from Bethsaida, had married a woman from Capernaum—for there was not a great distance between these places.[27]

Pseudo Epiphanius, *Index apostolorum*
This Philip was the Apostle from Bethsaida; he was from the village of Peter and Andrew. He was the one who proclaimed the Gospel in the region above Phrygia, and died in Hierapolis. (Schermann 1907, 110)

Pseudo Athanasius, *Synopsis scripturae sacrae* (fourth century CE?)
He heals the blind man in Bethsaida. (*MPG* 28:392)

Basil of Caesarea (fourth century CE)

Regulae Morales [28]

Against Eunomius. For immediately from this voice, we perceive the [son] of Jonah, from Bethsaida, the brother of Andrew, the one who was called from the company of fishermen to the service of Apostleship. (*MPG* 29:577, lines 46ff.)

John Chrysostom (fourth century CE)

Exposition of Psalms. [Christ, like the Prophets, did much crying and lamenting, as when he says] "Woe to you, Chorazin. Woe to you, Bethsaida." And again, whenever he speaks thus, "Jerusalem, Jerusalem, city that kills the prophets." (*MPG* 55:260, lines 60ff.)

Homily on Matthew. Jesus came to reproach the cities in which most of his miracles were performed, because of their lack of repentance, saying, "Woe to you, Chorazin. Woe to you, Bethsaida." Then, in order that you might learn that it was not from their nature that these cities were so cursed, he sets forth the name of the [latter] city, from which came five apostles. For Philip and those two pairs of leaders were from there.[29]

Homily on John.[30] [Christ called this apostle] who was roaming around this lake [of Galilee] with his father and his brother James, stitching up torn nets.... This, therefore, is the fisherman, the one roaming around lakes toting nets and fish, the one from Bethsaida of Galilee, the son of a poor fisherman father, and poorest of the poor.... This unlettered man, this loner, this man from Bethsaida, the son of Zebedee.[31]

Homily on Acts. Where now is the conceit of the Greeks? Where, the name of the Athenians? Where, the nonsense of philosophers? The man from Galilee, the man from Bethsaida, the rustic yokel, he prevails over all of these. (*MPG* 60:47)

Homily on Ephesians. And Christ came to reproach the cities, saying, "Woe to you Chorazin; Woe to you Bethsaida," in order that he might set them free from reproach. (*MPG* 62:74, lines 38ff.)

On Babylon, Against Julian....One will find the citizen of an obscure polis, or rather, not a polis at all, but the tiniest of villages, for [that citizen] was from Bethsaida "of Galilee" (as the region is called) from which that blessed one came. (Schatkin 1967, sec. 18, line 8)

On Isaiah. [Prophets, like Jeremiah, often lament]. So also is the case with Christ, who says, "woe to you Chorazin; woe to you, Bethsaida." This is also a form of teaching. For what the rational word did not restore, the lament often made right. (Dumortier 1955, 1.3)

Quod regulares feminae viris cohabitare non debeant. [Jesus wept over the forthcoming destruction of Jerusalem.] So also over Bethsaida, he did not treat its future with counsels or with signs, but with sorrow alone, repeatedly pronouncing the woe over the cities just as we ourselves do over those who are on death's door. (Dumortier 1955, 2.68)

Homily on Genesis[32]

Pseudo Chrysostom, *On Peter and Paul*
The blessed Peter is the Apostle of Christ from Bethsaida of Galilee, in which our Lord Jesus Christ performed most of his marvelous works, and from which city Philip got his start. (*MPG* 59:495, lines 4ff.)

Didymus Caecus (fourth century CE)

On Zechariah. [Quotation of the woes from Matt. 11:21.] For even though prodigious mighty works had been performed by Jesus, the citizens of Chorazin and Bethsaida, being Jews, did not repent, whereas if they had been among the Tyrians and Sidonians who had repented, the citizens of Chorazin and Bethsaida would likewise have become repentant. (1962, 3.83.13)

Fragments on Psalms. I will bless the hunt of those who hunt for blessings. The hunt is blessed by the blessing of the Lord for which the fishers and hunters sent by the Lord hunt, upon all the high mountains and in the holes of rocks—which is a symbol they bear who dwell in the village of hunters—namely Andrew, Peter and Philip. For these all dwell in Bethsaida, which is interpreted as "the house of hunters." (Mühlenberg 1975, frag. 1186)

On Genesis[33]

Jerome (fourth to fifth century CE)

On Illustrious Men. Simon Peter the son of John, from the village of Bethsaida in the province of Galilee, brother of Andrew the apostle, and prince of the apostles.... (1879, ch. 1)

Commentary on Matthew. "Woe to you, Chorazin, woe to you, Bethsaida...." Chorazin and Bethsaida, cities in Galilee, were lamented over by the Savior because, after so many signs and virtuous works, they would not do penance. Tyre and Sidon, cities given to idolatry and other vices, were preferred. They were preferred because Tyre and Sidon had only trampled upon natural law, whereas in the case of Chorazin and Bethsaida, after they transgressed against both natural and written law, they paid little heed to the signs done among them. We may ask where it is written that the Lord did signs in Chorazin and Bethsaida. We read above: "And he traveled among all the cities and villages, curing all the sick" and the rest. Among the other cities and villages, therefore, the Lord had done signs in Chorazin and Bethsaida.... Whereas Chorazin and Bethsaida are condemned because they would not believe in the Lord when he was present, Tyre and Sidon are justified because they believed his apostles. (1977, 2.11.22–24)

Nonnus, *Metric Paraphrase of John* (fifth century CE?)
You, Philip, follow. And while the hearing was still warm in his ears, he was accepting the story, and he applied the voice to his footsteps. And Philip had his own hometown, Bethsaida, the same place where Andrew lived, and where the bold Simon made his home. And Philip, by means of his own story, soothed Nathaniel, who was resting easily beneath a tree. (Scheindler 1881, lines 168ff.)

John of Damascus, *Epistle on the "Holy, Holy, Holy"* (seventh to eighth century CE)
[Peter] the 12 stringed lyre of the Apostles, the son of Jonah from Bethsaida, the one martyred in Rome under Nero, would reveal himself as a liar if...[he claimed, as have some others, that] the Thrice Holy was the one crucified for us. (1969, 4.14.27)

CHAPTER NOTES

All translations are my own.

1. For further discussion, see Greene 1995.
2. See chapter 4 of this volume.
3. For further discussion, see Freund 1995.
4. See Claudius Ptolemy, *Gospel of the Nazareans*, Aelius Herodianus, and Origen in the appendix.
5. διὸ μετὰ βραχέα τοῦ εὐαγγελίου εὑρήσεις ἀπὸ τῆς Γαλιλαίας τὸν Ματθαῖον κεκλημένον, καὶ ἐν ἑτέρῳ δὲ πάλιν τὸν Λευίν. καὶ ὁ Φίλιππος δὲ κατὰ τὸν Ἰωάννην "ἀπὸ Βηθσαϊδὰ" ὡρμᾶτο "ἐκ τῆς πόλεως Ἀνδρέου καὶ Πέτρου." καὶ αὕτη δὲ τῆς Γαλιλαίας ἦν (1913, 9.8.7).
6. The few remaining fragments of the Greek text have been collected by A. Schöne (Eusebius 1967). Cf. Dindorf 1829; Cramer 1967; Bauer 1909.
7. The Latin was edited by R. Helm (1956); the Armenian was edited and translated into German by J. Karst (1911). There was also a Syriac translation, but it is of little assistance for determining the text of the original. For further discussion, see Mosshammer 1979; cf. Barnes 1981, 111ff.
8. Φίλιππος τετράρχης Πανιάδα ἀνακτίσας Καισάρειαν Φιλίππου προσωνόμασεν (1911, 212).
9. "Filippus Tetrarcha Paneadem in qua plurimas aedes construxerat Caesaream Filippi uocauit, et Juliadem aliam ciuitatem." Karst's rendition of the Armenian version substantially agrees with that of Jerome: "Philippos der Vierfürst erbaut Pennada und Kesaria, welches er das philippische nannte, und eine andere Stadt, Juliada" (1911, 212).
10. "Philip built a city near the sources of the Jordan, in Paneas, [which he named] Caesarea [Philippi], and in lower Gaulanitis, he built Julias" (*J.W.* 2.168). "Philip too made improvements at Paneas, the city near the sources of the Jordan, and called it Caesarea. He also raised the village of Bethsaida on Lake Gennesaret to the status of a polis [by adding] many residents and other power. He called the city by the same name as Julia, the Emperor's daughter" (*Ant.* 18.27–28).
11. For further discussion of the relevant Josephan texts, see Smith 1999.
12. "παράλιον" δέ λέγει πᾶσαν τὴν ἀμφὶ τὴν Γενησαρὲτ λίμνην χώραν, ἧς μέμνηται τὸ Εὐαγγέλιον ὡς "θαλάσσης," λέγει δ' οὖν, "παράγων δὲ ὁ Ἰησους παρὰ τὴν 'θάλασσαν' τῆς 'Γαλιλαίας' εἶδεν δύο ἀδελφούς." ἐντεῦθέν τε καὶ οἱ μαθηταὶ τοῦ σωτῆρος ἡμῶν ὡρμῶντο. ἥ τε Καφερναοὺμ καὶ ἡ Βηθσαϊδὰ καὶ ἡ Χωραζὶ καὶ αἱ λοιπαὶ κῶμαι, ὧν μέμνηται ἡ εὐαγγλικὴ γραφὴ περὶ τὴν λίμνην τῆς Τιβεριάδος εἰσέτι καὶ νῦν δείκνυνται (1975, 1.54).
13. Wallace-Hadrill argues the latter (1960, 202–5).
14. For further discussion, see Hunt 1982; cf. Rousseau and Arav 1995, 117.
15. See McNamer, forthcoming.
16. Eusebius does, however, refer to Λιβιάς as an alternative to Julias, seven times (1966, 12, 16, 44, 48(3x), 168). But he never does so with reference to Bethsaida; in all seven places, Eusebius uses Λιβιάς to refer to Betharam-

phtha in Peraea which, according to Josephus, Antipas rebuilt and renamed Ἰουλίας (*J.W.* 2.168; *Ant.* 18.27–28).

17. Klostermann's Greek edition (1966, 58, line 11) reads: Βηθσαϊδά (Matt. 11:21). πόλις Ἀνδρέου καὶ Πέτρου καὶ Φιλίππου. κεῖται δὲ ἐν τῇ Γαλιλαίᾳ πρός τῇ Γεννησαρίτιδι λίμνη. Jerome's Latin translation, included in the same edition, reads: "Bethsaida ciuitas in Galilaea, Andreae et Petri et Filippi apostolorum, prope stagnum Genesareth" (59, line 13). There are four textual variants in the Latin version. Two concern the spelling of Bethsaida (Bethsaidan) and Genesareth (Genesar [A] or Genessareth [H]), and the other two do not include *in* and the first *et*. None of the textual variants for the Greek or the Latin pose any problems for the interpretation of the entry. Jerome's only substantive addition is his identification of Andrew, Peter, and Philip as apostles.

18. 1966, 120, ln. 2. If Eusebius is correct that Capernaum was a village of Gentiles around the turn of the fourth century, serious questions arise about the genesis of the marvelous and massive synagogue built there within a short time after Eusebius wrote. Both Richard Freund and Rami Arav, in personal conversations, have raised questions about the authenticity of this building. Eusebius seems to lend credence to their suspicions. Why would a small village of Gentiles lavish a great quantity of funds on the construction of a synagogue far more grand than any Jews in town would be able to utilize? Perhaps this building had purposes other than that of a gathering place for Jews to study and worship? One should not, however, be overly hasty in assuming that Eusebius considered Capernaum to be the site so identified today. For further discussion, see Rousseau and Arav 1995, 39–47.

19. The fact that Eusebius distinguishes between Gadara and Gergesa appears to be his attempt to resolve the sticky textual problems encountered in Matthew 8:28, Mark 5:1, and Luke 8:26,37. Unfortunately, if he was correct about the existence of such a village on the hillside east of the lake, he has solved a textual problem only to create an archaeological problem, for no such village has yet been discovered. The traditional candidate, Kursi, with its Byzantine church and monastery, has revealed no remains dating from the first century. There is, however, some evidence of earlier remains south of Kursi. For further discussion, see Rousseau and Arav 1995, 97–99.

20. Eusebius' reference to Chorazin is problematic on archaeological grounds. On the one hand, his reference to the "two milestones" that separate Chorazin from Capernaum presupposes travel on the Roman road that is still visible (a branch of the *Via Maris*) and the distance is approximately correct. On the other hand, some archaeologists have dated the construction of the town and synagogue at the present site of Chorazin to the second or third century (e.g., Levin 1982, 42; cf. Finegan 1992, 96). If the synagogue and town of Chorazin were already built by his time, Eusebius could hardly refer to the site as deserted unless, of course, he was referring to another site or fabricating this portion of the entry. However, his accurate reference to location and the lack of such fabrication in his other

entries renders both of these alternative explanations less than probable. Further, Yeivin, the latest excavator of Chorazin, dates the foundation of the synagogue and the surrounding town to the late third- or early fourth century (Yeivin 1987, 35; cf. Finegan 1992, 96). If he is correct, there was a brief chronological window during which Eusebius' reference to Chorazin would make sense. If he composed his *Onomasticon* in the later 290s, he must have done his research, including travel, some time before that. He therefore may have visited the Galilee region anywhere between about the 280s and the time of writing. It is possible, then, that during this limited time-span Eusebius did visit Chorazin, only to find a deserted site. He wrote about what he had experienced, perhaps never aware that sometime very near the date of the publication of his *Onomasticon,* this entry was in the process of being rendered obsolete by the construction of the new town. (Yeivin mistakenly suggests that Eusebius composed his *Onomasticon* in the late fourth century [well after he was dead], and thus referred to the fourth-century town, which subsequently suffered severe earthquake damage c. 360 [35].) The first-century town of Chorazin has not been discovered, but much of the area remains to be excavated. In addition, some shards from that time have been found on the opposite side of the modern road, indicating a hopeful site for future excavations. Cf. Yeivin 1987, 322–36; Rousseau and Arav 1995, 53.

21. Wallace-Hadrill 1960, 205; cf. Barnes, who suggests that this interest in the concrete and historical is one of the primary differences between Eusebius and Origen (1981, 110).

22. The most recent geological evidence suggests that the flood(s) that deposited the heavy layers of sediment that, at least in part, moved the coastline of the lake away from Bethsaida, were caused by earthquakes that resulted in landslides upstream, which temporarily blocked the flow of the Jordan, subsequently breaking with predictable effects. John Shroder et al. (1999) suggest that the evidence of historic landslides upstream from Bethsaida may date from second to fourth centuries CE. In addition, David Amiran et al. report that there is historical evidence of only two significant earthquakes in the region between the time of Pliny and that of Eusebius, in 115 and 130 (or 128, according to some sources). There was also a destructive earthquake in the area of Tyre and Sidon in 306, which would only be relevant if Eusebius visited this region after that date (1994, 265).

23. For further discussion, see McNamer, forthcoming.

24. 1966, 5.16.4. Ptolemy simply lists these towns along with his own peculiar notations of their physical location, which I have omitted.

25. Translated in Hennecke and Schneemelcher 1963, 1:151.

26. With two slight textual variants (Origen 1970, 11.5.53).

27. 1922, 2:268. In two separate citations, he quotes John 1:41–45 (1922, 2:266, 267).

28. Quotation of Matt. 11:21, with no significant textual variation (*MPG* 31:700, line 21).

29. *MPG* 57:424, lines 45 ff. These two pairs of leaders were presumably Peter and Andrew, and James and John (see his *Homily on John*).
30. This work includes two references to Bethsaida; the first is a quotation of John 1:43–44 (*MPG* 59:123).
31. *MPG* 59:30–31. It appears that Chrysostom anticipated by more than a century Theodosius' suggestion that James and John came from Bethsaida (see Geyer 1898, 138; cf. Baldi 1982, 266).
32. Quotation of Matt. 11:21 (*MPG* 53:220, lines 39 ff.).
33. Quotation of Matt. 11:20–21, with two minor textual variants (1976, cod. 232, lines 18 ff.).

LITERATURE CITED

Amiran, David, E. Arieh, and T. Turcotte. 1994. Earthquakes in Israel and Adjacent Areas: Macroseismic Observations since 100 B.C.E. *Israel Exploration Journal* 44:260–305.

Arav, Rami, and Richard Freund. 1995. *Bethsaida: A City on the North Shore of the Sea of Galilee*. Vol. 1. Kirksville, Mo.: Thomas Jefferson University Press.

———. 1999. *Bethsaida: A City on the North Shore of the Sea of Galilee*. Vol. 2. Kirksville, Mo.: Truman State University Press.

Baldi, Donato. 1982. *Enchiridion Locorum Sanctorum*. 1935. Reprint, Jerusalem: Franciscan Printing Press.

Barnes, Timothy D. 1981. *Constantine and Eusebius*. Cambridge: Harvard University Press.

Bauer, Adolphus. 1909. *Anonymi Chronographia Syntomos e Codice Matritensi No. 121 (nunc 4701)*. Leipzig: Teubner.

Cramer, John. 1967. *Anecdota Graeca e Codd. Manuscriptis Bibliothecae Regiae Parisiensis 2*. 1839. Reprint, Hildesheim: G. Olms.

Didyme l'Aveugle [Didymus Caecus]. 1962. *Sur Zacharie*. Edited and translated by Louis Doutreleau. 3 vols. Sources chrétiennes 83, 84, 85. Paris: Cerf.

———. 1976. *Sur la Genèse*. Edited by Pierre Nautin and Louis Doutreleau. Sources chrétiennes 233. Paris: Cerf.

Dindorf, Wilhelm, ed. 1829. *Syncellus. Corpus Scriptorum Historiae Byzantinae*. Bonn: E. Weber.

Dumortier, Jean. 1955. *Saint Jean Chrysostome. Les cohabitations suspectes*. Paris: Les Belles Lettres.

Epiphanius. 1922. *Ancoratus und Panarion*. Edited by K. Holl. Vol. 2 of *Epiphanius Werke*. GCS 31. Leipzig: Hinrichs.

Eusebius. 1911. *Die Chronik aus dem Armenischen übersetzt mit textkritischem Kommentar*. Edited by J. Karst. Vol. 5 of *Eusebius Werke*. GCS 20. Leipzig: Hinrichs.

———. 1913. *Die Demonstratio evangelica*. Edited by I. A. Heikel. Vol. 6 of *Eusebius Werke*. GCS 23. Leipzig: Hinrichs.

———. 1956. *Die Chronik des Hieronymus*. Edited by R. Helm. Vol. 7 of *Eusebius Werke*. GCS 47. Berlin: Akademie-Verlag.

———. 1966. *Das Onomasticon der biblischen Ortsnamen*. Edited by E. Klostermann. Vol. 3.1 of *Eusebius Werke*. GCS 11.1. 1904. Reprint, Leipzig and Hildesheim: Georg Olms.

———. 1967. *Eusebi chronicorum cononum quae supersunt*. Edited by A. Schöne. 1866. Reprint, Berlin: Weidmann.

———. 1975. *Der Jesajakommentar [Commentary on Isaiah]*. Edited by J. Zeigler. Vol. 9 of *Eusebius Werke*. GCS. Berlin: Akademie-Verlag.

Finegan, Jack. 1992. *The Archeology of the New Testament*. Rev. ed. Princeton: Princeton University Press.

Fischer, H. 1939. Geschichte der Kartographie von Palästina. *Zeitschrift des deutschen Palästina-Vereins* 62:169–89.

Freund, Richard. 1995. The Search for Bethsaida in Rabbinic Literature. In Arav and Freund 1995.

Geyer, Paulus. 1898. *Itinera Hierosolymitana saeculi III–VIII* [CSEL XXXIX]. Vindobonae.

Greene, John. 1995. Bethsaida-Julias in Roman and Jewish Military Strategies, 66–73 CE. In Arav and Freund 1995.

Hennecke, E., and W. Schneemelcher. 1963. *New Testament Apocrypha*. 2 vols. Philadelphia: Westminster.

Herodianus, Aelius. 1963. *Herodiani partitiones*. Edited by Jean Francois Boissonade. 1819. Reprint, Amsterdam: Hakkert.

Hunt, E. D. 1982. *Holy Land Pilgrimage in the Later Roman Empire A.D. 312–460*. Oxford: Clarendon.

Jerome. 1879. *Hieronymi de Viris Inlustribus*. Edited by W. Herding. Leipzig: Teubner.

———. 1977. Commentaire sur s. Matthieu. Translated and edited by Emile Bonnard. Vol. 1. Sources chrétiennes 242. Paris: Cerf.

John, of Damascus, Saint. 1969. *Die Schriften des Johannes von Damaskos*. Edited by Bonifatius Kotter. Patristische Texte und Studien 7. Berlin: De Gruyter.

Klostermann, Erich. 1902. *Eusebius' Schrift*. Texte und Untersuchungen 23.2b. Leipzig: J. C. Hinrichs.

Levin, Lee. 1982. *Ancient Synagogues Revealed*. Detroit: Wayne State University Press.

McNamer, Elizabeth. Forthcoming. Medieval Traveler and Pilgrim Accounts of Bethsaida.

Migne, Jacques-Paul. 1857–87. *Patrologiae cursus completes*. Bibliotheca universalis, series graeca. Paris: P. Geuthner. (*MPG*)

Mosshammer, Alden. 1979. *The "Chronicle" of Eusebius and the Greek Chronographic Tradition*. Lewisburg, Penn.: Bucknell University Press.

Mühlenberg, Ekkehard. 1975. *Psalmenkommentare aus der Katenenüberlieferung*. Patristische Texte und Studien 15. Berlin: De Gruyter.

Origen. 1903. *Der Johanneskommentar [Commentary on John]*. Edited by Erwin Preuschen. Vol. 4 of *Origenes Werke*. GCS 10. Leipzig: Hinrichs.

———. 1970. *Commentaire sur l'évangile selon Matthieu [Commentary on Matthew]*. Edited and translated by Robert Girod. Vol. 1. Sources chrétiennes 162. Paris: Cerf.

Pohlsander, Hans. 1996. *Helena: Empress and Saint*. Chicago: Ares.

Ptolemy, Claudius. 1966. *Geographia*. Edited by C. Nobbe. 1843–45. Reprint, Hildesheim: Georg Olms.

Rousseau, John, and Rami Arav. 1995. *Jesus and His World*. Minneapolis: Fortress.

Schatkin, Margaret. 1967. *Critical edition of, and introduction to, St. John Chrysostom's "De sancto Babyla, contra Iulianum et gentiles."* Ph.D. diss., Fordham University.

Scheindler, August. 1881. *Paraphrasis s. evangelii Ioannei*. Leipzig: Teubner.

Schermann, Theodor. 1907. *Prophetarum vitae fabulosae*. Leipzig: Teubner.

Schwartz, Edouard. 1909. Eusebios von Caesarea. In *Realencyclopädie der classischen Altertumswissenschaft* 6, edited by F. Pauly and G. Wissowa. Stuttgart.

Shroder, John, M. Bishop, K. Cornwell, and M. Inbar. 1999. Catastrophic Geomorphic Processes and Bethsaida Archaeology, Israel. In Arav and Freund 1999.

Smith, Mark. 1999. A Tale of Two Julias. In Arav and Freund 1999.

Thomsen, P. 1903. Palästina nach dem *Onomasticon* des Eusebius. *Zeitschrift des deutschen Palästina-Vereins* 26: 97–141, 145–88.

Wallace-Hadrill, D. S. 1960. *Eusebius of Caesarea.* London: A.R. Mowbray.

Yeivin, Z. 1987. Ancient Chorazin Comes Back to Life. *Biblical Archaeology Review* 13 (5): 322–36.

Nicolae Roddy

The Antichrist at Bethsaida

T HE TRAVELS OF SIR JOHN MANDEVILLE,[1] a fourteenth-century pilgrimage account that has been called "one of the most popular books of its age" (Braude 1996, 133–58), carries within its pages an intriguing editorial aside:

> In Chorazin will Antichrist be born, as some men say; and others say he shall be born in Babylon; for the prophet saith, "Out of Babylon shall come a serpent that shall devour all the world." This Antichrist shall be nourished at Bethsaida, and he shall reign in Capernaum; and therefore saith Holy Writ, "Woe unto thee, Chorazin! Woe unto thee, Bethsaida! And thou, Capernaum." And all these towns are in the land of Galilee. (Wright 1969, 183)

The obvious literary connection between this legend and Jesus' condemnation of the unrepentant Galilean cities in Q (Matt. 11:20–24; Luke 10:13–16) offers an all too easy solution to the question of origin for this tidbit of Antichrist biography; likewise, the paraphrastic reference to Jeremiah 8:16–17 cited in support of the claim that the Antichrist will be born in Babylon. A more satisfying etiological assumption, with roots deep in rabbinical and early Christian exegesis, is that the Antichrist's biography was not simply invented on the basis of the condemnations in Q, but that scripture was readily martialed in response to some social phenomenon.[2] Unfortunately, it is rarely the case that these literary responses can be tied to the natural or human events that sparked them. Often the best that can be done is to follow the written evidence back to its earliest time and place and then, on

273

the basis of current historical knowledge, attempt to determine its most likely social origin. The present chapter will trace the history of the Antichrist of Galilee legend back to its earliest surviving attestation; it will then suggest that this unique aspect of the Antichrist legend is no mere literary fiction based on Q, but a tradition that likely arose within the social situation of late-fourth-century Galilee itself.[3]

THE GALILEAN ANTICHRIST IN MEDIEVAL PILGRIMAGE ACCOUNTS

By the fourteenth century, the Antichrist legend had become a kaleidoscope of composite and often conflicting traditions, of which Mandeville's biographical details offer only a very small part.[4] On the one hand, that the Antichrist represents the great Final Enemy of the church whose appearance signals the imminent consummation of history is clearly the dominant and unifying theme. On the other hand, portraits of the Antichrist that had taken shape over the previous twelve centuries came to be quite varied, depending largely upon the social circumstances of the group for whom the Antichrist or his minions posed a threat. The influence of the book of Daniel on the synoptic Apocalypse (Mark 13:1–37; Matt. 24:1–25, 46; Luke 21:5–38), certain Pauline and Johannine writings, and especially the Apocalypse of John, interpreted in light of the challenges faced by the primitive church, provided the raw materials for these varied and ambiguous portraits of the Final Enemy.[5] Literature and interpretations influenced by these texts show that the Antichrist may be one or many, Jew or Gentile; he may confront the church as the eschatological, demonized other exercising tyrannical power over the church, or he may arise as an insidious deceiver or false prophet from within the congregation itself; for indeed, one of the more intriguing aspects of the Antichrist is found in the alternative meaning of the term, namely "in place of Christ." Finally, it is a commonplace that the Antichrist has been associated with many and varied figures throughout history, from Nero, emperor of Rome, to Justinian, emperor of New Rome; from Mohammed the prophet, to Pope John XXII; from Adolph Hitler to former Secretary of State Henry Kissinger.[6]

The Galilean Antichrist legend circulated widely among medieval pilgrimage accounts. The most recent surviving account, somewhat later than Mandeville's, is found in a mid-fourteenth-century work called *Account of the Holy Land*, based on a work attributed to Philippus Brusserius Savonensis. It carries the following observation:

> Near [the Sea of Galilee] is the city of Peter and Andrew, Bethsaida by name, upon which the Lord shed his lustre by his presence…. Four miles from Bethsaida is Chorazin, in which Antichrist, the world's seducer, is to be nurtured. It was of these two cities that Jesus said, "Woe to thee, Bethsaida! Woe to thee, Chorazin!" (1971, 35–36)

Although the Antichrist is not directly associated with Bethsaida here, the reference is clearly part of the same tradition, with probably no direct literary connection with Mandeville's account.

Paul Hamelius traces Mandeville's reference to the Antichrist directly to Friar Odoric de Pordenone's *Travels in the Far East* (1987, 19–21, 74), but there are a number of other possible candidates for the source of this legend among medieval accounts. The overall lack of originality among the sources betrays the fact that many of these "observations" are not eyewitness reports at all, but popular "travel guides" circulating in pamphlet form among people who enjoyed reading or writing about the Holy Land, but were not likely to actually go there themselves. One must not be naive in assuming that the authors of many of these so-called pilgrimage accounts had actually traveled to Palestine, since following the series of failed crusades that took place during the twelfth and thirteenth centuries, few Europeans were likely to risk reentering lands from which even the intransigent Franks had been expelled.[7]

An anonymous twelfth-century western pilgrimage account known as Pseudo-Beda comes somewhat closer to the source of the Galilean Antichrist legend. Its striking similarity to the Savonensis text, including the omission of Capernaum from the cities, suggests a more direct connection here than with Mandeville's *Travels*:

> From Bethsaida came Peter and Andrew, James and John, and James the son of Alpheus. Four miles from Bethsaida is Chorazin, wherein shall be brought up Antichrist, the deceiver of the world. Of Chorazin and Bethsaida the Lord said: "Woe to thee, Chorazin, woe to thee Bethsaida." (1971, 6:53)

In addition to Pseudo-Beda, there are a number of other surviving twelfth-century manuscripts that attest to the legend, Bishop Theodorich (1971, 5:66) and John of Würzburg (1971, 5:67) among them. John's account provides a direct source for Theodorich; in fact they were likely acquainted, and at least one of their accounts seems to have been known to Pseudo-Beda as well. Theodorich and John agree:

> From Bethsaida came Peter and John, Andrew, and James the son of Alpheus. Six miles from Bethsaida is Chorazain, wherein Antichrist, the misleader of the world, will be nursed. Of Chorazain and Bethsaida Jesus said: "Woe to thee, Chorazain. Woe to thee, Bethsaida."

Theodorich and John appear almost certainly to have traveled to Palestine, but they are not the source of the Galilean Antichrist legend. Although the Franks held Jerusalem during this time and had established strategic outposts throughout Palestine and parts of Syria around Antioch, travel away from crusader outposts was still fraught with peril. The danger of Saracen marauders often prevented pilgrims from venturing too far away from the safety of crusader garrisons, so many pilgrim writers simply relied on earlier materials they had on hand. Lacking originality and any indication of firsthand observation in their accounts of Galilee, it seems likely that neither John nor Theodorich actually visited that region. In any case, at the time of their travels, the sites of Bethsaida and Chorazin were lost to history and only Capernaum, a site that had remained occupied until around the turn of the millennium, had a chance of being identified with any degree of certainty. In addition, apart from being an eyewitness to holy sites within Jerusalem, John of Würzburg freely admits to borrowing from earlier accounts. He writes, "about those [sites], however, which are situated far off in the neighboring province, we have not proposed ourselves to speak, knowing that they have been already sufficiently described by others" (1971, 5:2).

One final western pilgrim witness to the legend, this one ascribed to a certain Fetellus within decades of Pope Urban II's invasion and assault upon Antioch and Jerusalem during the First Crusade (1095), undertakes to describe the condition of the holy sites and knows a sparse form of the Antichrist legend:

> From Bethsaida were Peter and Andrew, John and James, James the son of Alpheus. Four miles from Bethsaida is Corozain, in which Antichrist will be nourished. (1971, 5:28)

All of the aforementioned medieval pilgrimage accounts draw inspiration and supplementary information from the Scottish bishop Admanan's *De Locis Sancti*, a work based on the detailed eyewitness testimony of the French bishop Arculf, who traveled through Palestine in the late seventh century. Admanan, however, is not aware of the Galilean Antichrist legend, and neither are the turn-of-the-millennium readers who followed in Arculf's footsteps—pilgrims like Willibald, Bernard the Wise, or Saewulf—even though Bethsaida, Chorazin, and Capernaum are often mentioned in their accounts.

At this point it may appear that the Galilean Antichrist legend was simply a western literary fiction devised sometime during the early twelfth century; but although we have come to a historical dead end in the West, a detour opens toward the East. A Russian pilgrim traveling at the turn of the twelfth century knows a somewhat different version of the tradition. Although his account is often vague and geographically unreliable, the Russian abbot Daniel insists that he described nothing that he did not actually see (Wilson 1971, 4:viii–ix). Of Capernaum he writes:

> [Capharnaum] was formerly a very important and populous town, but at present it is deserted, and situated not far from the Great Sea. Of this Capharnaum the prophet said, "Woe unto thee, Capharnaum: Thou shalt be exalted to heaven, and thou shalt be brought down to the depths of hell." In this city Antichrist is to appear, and for this reason the Franks have abandoned it. (Wilson 1971, 4:54)

The Galilean Antichrist legend also appears in a twelfth-century Armenian work that circulated as part of the Life of St. Nersus. Paired with the Antichrist from the tribe of Dan legend, it asserts that the Antichrist "will be born in Chorazin, a village of the people of Israel" (Boussett 1896, 254–55). This twelfth-century text was compiled from sources dating to as early as the fifth century; however, since it was compiled after the Franks conquered Jerusalem, without further examination one cannot tell whether the Antichrist reference was supplied from western sources or whether it had been transmitted in the East all along. In any event, it is clear that some form of the Galilean Antichrist legend was known in the East; but in which direction was the transmission?

EARLIEST LITERARY ATTESTATION FOR THE GALILEAN ANTICHRIST LEGEND

The source of the Galilean Antichrist tradition in the aforementioned medieval pilgrimage accounts can be traced to certain western apocalyptic theological tractates. The legend is found in the early-twelfth-century writings of Lambert of St. Omer, whose massive theological reference work *Liber Floridus* states:

> Antichrist, Son of Perdition, will be born of the tribe of Dan who was the son of Jacob by Pala [that is, Bilhah], the hand-maiden of Rachel. Antichrist will be born in Corozaim, nurtured in Bethsaida, and reign in Capernaum. He will make his way to Jerusalem and sit in the temple of God as if he were God.[8]

Although not a direct source for Lambert's description of the Galilean Antichrist, the widely known tenth-century letter composed by Adso, later abbot of Montier-en-Der, witnesses to the presence of an earlier, common tradition. In his *De Ortu et Tempore Antichristi* (On the origin and time of the Antichrist) addressed to Gerberga, sister of the Frankish king Otto I, sometime around 954, Adso asserts that the Antichrist will be born in Babylon of the tribe of Dan, and that he will be

> brought up and protected in the cities of Bethsaida and Corozain, the cities the Lord reproaches in the Gospel when he says, "Woe to you, Bethsaida; woe to you, Corozain." (McGinn 1994, 89–96)

Adso's treatise on the Antichrist, which appears in the genre of the *vita sancti* (Emmerson 1979, 179–90), is the earliest surviving western reference to the Galilean Antichrist tradition. Adso's account provides the West with its "summary of the traditional teaching about the Final Enemy" in which he reflects the "standard western view…that Antichrist will be born in Babylon" (McGinn 1994, 101). Adso also introduces an aspect of the Antichrist legend that can be traced as far back as Irenaeus of Lyons, namely, that the Antichrist will come from the tribe of Dan.

Although Adso formalizes the picture of the Antichrist in the West, he acquires a great many of his apocalyptic ideas from non-western sources. In addition to the Galilean Antichrist legend, there is also in Adso the tradition concerning the rise of a Last World Emperor who will defeat every end-time adversary of God but the Antichrist himself. For these legends, scholars must look eastward to one of the most important of western apocalyptic sources, the *Revelations* of Pseudo-Methodius, a seventh-century Syrian text that had been introduced into the West through its Greek translation sometime during the Carolingian period.

THE *REVELATIONS* OF PSEUDO-METHODIUS

The *Revelations* of Pseudo-Methodius has been called the "crown of Eastern Christian apocalyptic literature."[9] Attributed to Methodius of Patera, a fourth-century martyred bishop, this text was produced in response to the meteoric rise of Islam in the eastern regions of Byzantium. It provides the earliest surviving witness to the Galilean Antichrist tradition, as well as the legend concerning the Last World Emperor, a powerful Byzantine king who will overthrow Muslim rule before surrendering his own crown to God (Alexander 1971, 47–82). Pseudo-Methodius is clearly a compilation of earlier traditions, for seams in the text emerge that are readily apparent even in translation. Toward the end of the text, the Galilean Antichrist and Last Emperor legends are brought together.

According to Pseudo-Methodius, when the divinely chosen "king of the Greeks" has thoroughly defeated the Muslims, as well as the newly escaped barbarian tribes that his predecessor Alexander the Great had locked away in the North, he will come to Jerusalem and dwell there ten years. When the Christian empire's foes have all been vanquished, the Final King will hang his crown upon the wood of the Holy Cross on Golgotha and expire, at which time "the Son of Perdition, the false Christ will be revealed." At this point the text interjects that the Final Enemy, the Son of Perdition over whom the Final King will not be able to triumph, will be

> conceived in Chorazin, born in Bethsaida, and will reign in Capernaum. Chorazin will boast of him, for he will have been born there; Bethsaida, for he will have been brought up there. Because of this our Lord lamented over the three of them in his Gospel saying, Woe to you, Chorazin! Woe to you, Bethsaida! As for you, Capernaum, who were exalted to the skies, you shall go down to Sheol. (Martinez 1985, 1971, XIV)

Scholars are at a loss to find any earlier written mention of the Galilean Antichrist legend than this; however, it is certain that this passage has been interpolated into the text. The line, "As soon as the Son of Perdition has been revealed..." repeats and carries forth the line preceding the passage, "And then the Son of Perdition, the false Christ, will be revealed." The Son of Perdition is said to be revealed *before* the King of the Greeks offers his abdication and his life on Golgotha; then, after the King has died, the text again affirms that "the Son of Perdition will be revealed." (Martinez 1985) The passage concerning the Antichrist's boyhood haunts seems out of place, intruding upon the continuity of the narrative like some hastily inserted afterthought. In addition, the Antichrist's Danite connection, an earlier tradition that may have come to be circulated as part of the Galilean Antichrist legend, seems also to have been rather carelessly inserted into the structure of the narrative.

In the absence of any earlier literary attestation, it is impossible to know the actual source of the Galilean Antichrist legend with any certainty. It may even be that this is its earliest writing and that the compiler has introduced some local oral tradition into his work. The original text was almost certainly composed in Syriac (Martinez 1985, 25), which places it in the general proximity of the Galilean cities. In fact, Michael Kmosko, one of the leading scholars on Pseudo-Methodius, argues that this apocalyptic work was compiled by a Melkite Syrian who left Syria for Palestine in the wake of Heraclius' conquests over the Avars (Pseudo-Methodius' "tribes of the north") and the Persians;[10] for in addition to the mention of the Galilean cities, the finalized version of the text reflects concerns for Palestinian geography:

> [The sons of Ishmael] then fled from the desert of Yathrib, and entered into the cultivated land. They made war with the kings of the nations and devastated them. They destroyed and captured and subdued all the kingdoms of the nations, and the whole Promised Land came to be under their dominion. The Land was filled with them and with their camps. They were like locusts; they used to walk naked; they ate flesh from vessels of flesh, and drank the blood of animals. (Martinez 1985, V)

> Egypt, Syria and the places of the East will be subjugated to the yoke of tribute and tax. One out of seven will be in the distress of captives. And the Promised Land will be filled with men

from the four winds of heaven, like the locusts which are gathered by a whirlwind. (Martinez 1985, XI)

The sons of the king of the Greeks will seize the regions of the desert and will finish by the sword any survivor left among them in the Promised Land. (Martinez 1985, XIII)

Kmosko's position, it should be noted, has since been sufficiently challenged to leave the exact provenance of this seventh-century Syriac apocalypse in question. In any event, it is clear that the Galilean Antichrist legend enjoys a very long and expansive history, which can be traced from fourteenth-century western Europe all the way back to seventh-century Syria and, perhaps, Palestine.

"WOE TO YOU, CHORAZIN; WOE TO YOU, BETHSAIDA!"

Every occurrence of the Galilean Antichrist legend is supported by Jesus' pronouncement against the Galilean cities in Matthew 11:21 and Luke 10:13. These woes are the product of Q, the hypothesized sayings source utilized by the authors of these Gospels.[11] Whether or not Q witnesses to the actual words of Jesus is not the concern; in any event, the pronouncement reflects a high degree of frustration on the part of early Jewish-Christian missionaries, clearly a minority, that these cities have not been receptive to their messianic assertions about Jesus.[12]

There is considerable agreement among New Testament scholars that Q underwent at least one redaction before being picked up by Matthew and Luke (Koester 1990, 133–35). Dale Allison attributes the woes against the cities to Q^3, the third and most recent of Q redactions (1997, 33, 53). One of the characteristics of Q^3 is that it reflects a concern for geography—it mentions the most places, and most of these are in Galilee.[13] Q^3's emphasis on the Galilean cities prompts Allison to observe:

One might guess, from the mention of Chorazin, Bethsaida, and Capernaum...that Q was the product of a group in the south, or, alternatively, of a group which had moved from the north to the south. One might also, given that Chorazin, Bethsaida, and Capernaum are very near each other at the north end of the Sea of Galilee, and because those three cities are not otherwise significant in the biblical tradition, guess that Q was put together in that area.[14]

It is almost certainly the case that Q's mention of these cities is no mere literary fiction, one that could have been produced anywhere, but a witness to actual frustrations arising among Jewish followers of Jesus in the vicinity of these Galilean cities. Furthermore, Q must have been of special interest for the author of Matthew, for despite the central importance of Jerusalem in the passion of Jesus, the missionary concerns of the gospel writer clearly focus upon Galilee (Matt. 28:10, 16). Although scholars cannot pinpoint Matthew's provenance with any certainty, it is commonly thought that this Gospel took shape amid polemical tensions between Jewish followers and nonfollowers of Jesus. While any sizable community in Syria or Palestine could have served as this arena, Galilee presents itself as a particularly attractive candidate as the "starting point of the reorganization of Judaism" (Koester 1982, 177).

Once the names of the condemned cities passed into the Gospel accounts, they became fair game for speculation wherever the Gospels circulated. An author interested in portraying the Antichrist in an *imitatio christi* might conceivably seize upon the Galilean cities in the interest of having the Final Enemy follow in the footsteps of Jesus. But Jesus himself, according to the Gospel tradition, was neither born nor nurtured in these cities, and the mere fact that he is reported to have uttered a curse against them is not sufficient to account for the origin of the Galilean Antichrist legend. Given the specific features of the legend, it seems reasonable to suppose that certain Christians availed themselves of these condemnations in justifying some anti-Jewish polemic; for before the rise of Islam, from the perspective of eastern Christians perceiving some large-scale, external threat, an Antichrist who is not explicitly Roman is nearly always explicitly or implicitly Jewish.[15]

Something of the Jesus movement's ongoing frustration with other Jews may be found in the Antichrist's Danite connection. Irenaeus of Lyons, writing around 180, seems to be the earliest witness to this legend, which clearly affirms the notion of a Jewish Antichrist. Irenaeus supports the assertion that the Antichrist will come from the tribe of Dan by citing Jeremiah 8:16, as well as the fact that the name of the tribe is missing from the list of tribes sealed in Apocalypse 7:5–7:

> "We shall hear the voice of his swift horses from Dan; the whole earth shall be moved by the voice of the neighing of his

galloping horses: he shall also come and devour the earth, and the fullness thereof, the city also, and they that dwell therein." This, too, is the reason that this tribe is not reckoned in the Apocalypse along with those which are saved. (*Adv. Haer.* V.xxx.2)

Hippolytus, too, knows the Danite Antichrist legend and cites Genesis 49:16–18 for support (*Antichr.* XV). However, it is hardly possible that the Danite legend sprang full-blown from any of these obscure biblical passages, especially since some of its more important scriptural proof texts, like Genesis 49:16–18, are contextually positive and hardly descriptive of any sort of enemy:

Dan shall judge his people as one of the tribes of Israel. Dan shall be a snake by the roadside, a viper along the path, that bites the horse's heels so that its rider falls backward. I wait for your salvation, O Lord.

Wilhelm Bousset's *religionsgeschichte* approach attempted to identify the roots of the Danite Antichrist legend in haggadic materials and in the Testament of the Twelve Patriarchs (1896, 171–72), but these sources are also either too vague or ambiguous to account for the tradition (Hill 1995, 99–117). Again, it is far more likely that scripture was interpreted in ways that support the appearance of some social phenomenon. One must ask under what conditions this clearly anti-Jewish notion would come about and what possible reason anyone outside the traditional vicinity of Dan, in northern Galilee, would have for spinning such a legend? Despite the lack of a clearly identifiable referent, a sociological etiology for the Antichrist is more satisfying than a merely literary one. C. E. Hill suggests that "Christian representation of the Antichrist as false messiah, even a Danite, must be seen in the context of the ongoing debate between Jews and Christians over the Messiah and over the correct interpretation of the Old Testament prophetic scriptures" (Hill, 1995, 105).

THE GALILEAN ANTICHRIST

Having said this, one must realize that reliable evidence for a Jewish-Christian presence in lower Galilee[16] during the second and third centuries CE is all but lacking. Of course, the most obvious reason for this is the lack of material remains that might allow the objective archaeologist to be able to distinguish between things Jewish and

Jewish-"Christian." Anything short of a representational symbol or epigraph scratched on a potsherd would not be sufficient to distinguish one from the other. Sometimes the reverse telescoping of Christian history by less objective interests has resulted in the misinterpretation of archaeological data, as in the case of the so-called *domus ecclesia*, a late-fourth-century octagonal-shaped structure built over the supposed site of Peter's house in Capernaum.[17] But in any event, it seems reasonable to assume that some communities associated with the Jesus movement were present in the region; however, it is impossible to ascertain their numbers or to know for certain how they may have interacted with other social groups.[18]

On the Jewish side of the equation, the record is equally silent concerning a pre-fourth-century Christian presence in the vicinity of the condemned cities of lower Galilee. Qoheleth Rabbah recounts a colorful story about a visit to Capernaum made by Rabbi Joshua's nephew, Hanina, in which tensions with the *minim*, generally but perhaps naively thought to be Jewish followers of Jesus, are reflected:

> Hanina, the son of R. Joshua's brother, came to Capernaum, and the *minim* worked a spell on him and set him riding upon an ass on the Sabbath. He went to his uncle, Joshua, who anointed him with oil and he recovered from the spell. R. Joshua said to him, "Since the ass of that wicked person...has roused itself against you, you are not able to reside in the land of Israel." So he went down from there to Babylon where he died in peace. (Cohen 1939, I.8, 4)

Elsewhere in Qoheleth Rabbah, the inhabitants of Capernaum, specifically the *minim*, are identified as sinners (VII.26, 3). The problem here is that in neither of these cases is it clear that the *minim* are Jewish followers of Jesus.[19] The inability to distinguish between Jewish followers and nonfollowers of Jesus (if the former were present) even may have affected the fifth-century Christian historian Epiphanius who observed that, until the fourth century, the population of Capernaum was entirely Jewish (*Pan.* 30). On the basis of the archaeological record, there is nothing with which to refute him.

It is not until the legalization of Christianity in the fourth century, which immediately capitalized on the growing interest among Christians for making pilgrimages to biblical places, that Christians begin demonstrating a historically discernible presence in the region.

As Richard Horsley writes, "The 'Christianity' that suddenly appears in Galilee in the mid-fourth century was not indigenous to Galilee, but was something developed outside and then imposed on the land-scape" (1996, 108). It therefore may be suggested that if the Galilean Antichrist legend, like its earlier Danite counterpart, arose amid tensions between Christians and Jews in or around Galilee, the most fertile period for the growth of such anti-Jewish slander would be during the mid- to late-fourth century. Certainly by that time, the focus of any conflict would not have been at Bethsaida or even Chorazin; however, neither Capernaum nor especially nearby Tiberias should be discounted.

Excavations at Bethsaida indicate that a massive earthquake in 115 CE may have destroyed the city, sealing its fate against any further significant habitation (Strickert 1999, 347–72). There is little in the material remains to suggest that any concerted effort at rebuilding the city took place after the early second century. Chorazin, roughly six miles northwest of Bethsaida, appears to have rebounded from the earthquake in somewhat better shape.[20] Tosefta Makot (3.8), compiled sometime around the third century, describes Chorazin as a "medium-sized town."[21] Excavations there have uncovered a synagogue dating to the third century; however, this synagogue, and presumably the rest of the town, was destroyed by yet another massive earthquake, in 363, an event which Eusebius attributes to the fulfillment of Jesus' condemnation of Chorazin. Finally, a gap in coinage finds between 340 and 390 (Nathanson 1986, 26–36) indicates an earlier abandonment, attesting to the fact that Chorazin enjoyed only an intermittent history as a viable town.

Capernaum, by contrast, seems to have continued as a thriving port city despite natural setbacks and social upheavals. A second- or third-century Roman bathhouse located outside the zone of the Franciscan excavations suggests a Roman presence, perhaps witnessing to the increased military presence in Galilee following the death of Agrippa II and again following the Bar Kokhba revolt (Horsley 1996, 115). Finally, archaeologists have identified a period of controlled building and steady growth for the Late Roman and Early Byzantine periods (Laughlin 1993, 58–59).

With the advent of imperial Christianity early in the fourth century, interest in the Holy Land intensified, resulting in the establishment of Christian shrines and a steady stream of pilgrims to places

associated with Jesus mentioned in the Gospels. An infamous pro-
moter of the imperial Christian presence in Palestine was Joseph of
Tiberias, ostensibly a former adviser to the court of the patriarch at
Tiberias, who upon conversion to Christianity received the title of
comes (companion of the emperor). With imperial protection and support, Joseph soon set about building churches and shrines throughout
Galilee, including Capernaum (Avi-Yonah 1984, 167–68). The sudden
appearance of lavish Christian structures throughout Galilee must
surely have been met with disdain by conservative Jewish religious
leadership; however, there is no evidence to suggest that Joseph's
building program was anything more than an annoyance to the
Jewish population as a whole. It is most likely that Christian shrines
were despised less for their religious function than they were as symbols of Byzantium's increased meddling in local affairs. Any tensions
present as a result of the introduction of the Christian religious
dimension to a long and continuous Roman presence in Palestine
were only exacerbated by the increased enforcement of existing
Roman law under Constantine. With the accession of Constantius II,
new pro-Christian, anti-Jewish legislation was enacted which struck at
the heart of Jewish economy, the textile industry in particular.[22] Contemporary rabbinic frustrations may be reflected in Song of Songs Rabbah: "This is the wicked government that incites all the people and
leads them astray with its lies."[23] Whether the hardships endured
were in fact economically painful or just politically symbolic, pockets
of resentment began growing in Galilean urban industrial centers like
Sepphoris and Tiberias. In 351, with imperial interests focused on
problems toward the West, armed rebellion broke out in Galilee.

The Gallus Revolt, the third major Jewish insurrection against
the Roman Empire, began in Sepphoris (Diocaesarea) (Nathanson 1986,
34). According to Jerome, the rebels overtook the soldiers garrisoned at
Sepphoris. Now armed with military weapons, the rebels carried their
insurrection to Tiberias, another Jewish industrial city that had been
affected by recent imperial, anti-Jewish legislation. Aurelius Victor, a
fourth-century historian, reports that the uprising was led by one Patricius, who was raised to "a sort of kingship" *(sub regni speciem)*. From
Galilee the revolt spread southward to Lydda, where rebels succeeded in
blocking the Roman route between Antioch and Alexandria (Avi-
Yonah 1984, 178–79). The initial success of the rebellion was short-
lived, however, as Urcinius, the Roman general charged with defending

the interests of Gallus Caesar in Syria-Palestine, quickly mobilized his troops against the rebels. After a brief period of very fierce fighting, Sepphoris, by all accounts, lay in ruins. Beth She'arim seems also to have been all or partially destroyed at that time (Avigad and Mazar 1978, 233–34). Jerome reports that Tiberias and several towns and villages were also destroyed, with many thousands slaughtered, "even those of an innocent age" *(innoxiam aetatem)* (Donalson 1996, 46). Nothing is known of the fate of Patricius. If the "sort of" revolutionary king survived the fighting, he is not likely to have survived the military occupation that followed the revolt.

The rebellion of 351 was almost certainly sparked by economic distress brought about as a result of Christian-influenced imperial legislation toward the mid-fourth century. Although Theophanes Confessor reports that the rebels "killed a great many aliens, both pagans and Samaritans,"[24] the ecclesiastical histories are noticeably silent regarding any rebel attacks upon Christians or their shrines. Michael Avi-Yonah suggests that the Jewish rebels refrained from attacking Christians in order to "avoid raising the ire of the emperor" (1984, 179). But it seems unlikely that the rebels had any reason to attack civilians at all, only imperial soldiers and mercenaries.

Despite scanty historical sources, a complex and interesting social situation emerges. In response to growing Christian interest in places mentioned in the Bible, bishops of the Byzantine period began promoting a Christian presence in Galilee, transforming places like Capernaum and Nazareth into sacred pilgrimage sites. At the same time, influential bishops from established sees at Caesarea and surrounding areas used their influence with the emperor to isolate Palestinian Jews culturally and economically within their own cities. There is also around this time a shift in Jewish population away from Galilee and into the surrounding hills (Nathanson 1986, 31). A number of Jews economically affected by the new legislation joined in armed rebellion against imperial authority. Their efforts apparently unsupported by Jewish religious leadership, the rebels fought against imperial soldiers but appear not to have attacked Christians or their shrines (Avi-Yonah 1984, 178–79). Church leaders likely witnessed the fighting from a position of relative safety, sitting perhaps somewhat smugly on the sidelines in Acco (Ptolemais) or Caesarea. They watched as the rebels set up their revolutionary government, the "sort of kingship" under Patricius.[25] With the foci of the uprising at Sepphoris and Tiberias threatening the holy sites at Nazareth and Capernaum, the woes of the Gospels no doubt come to mind. Especially attractive is the pronouncement against Capernaum: "And you, Capernaum, will you be exalted to heaven? No, you will be brought down to Hades" (Matt. 11:23a; Luke 10:15), echoing Isaiah's taunt of once glorious, now fallen kings (Isa. 14:13–15):

> You said in your heart,
>> "I will ascend to heaven;
>> I will raise my throne
>>> above the stars of God;
>> I will sit on the mount of assembly
>>> on the heights of Zaphon;
>> I will ascend to the tops of the clouds,
>> I will make myself like the Most High."
>
> But you are brought down to Sheol,
>> to the depths of the Pit. (NRSV)

CONCLUSION

As is often the case in historical reconstruction, all the components of a good story are there, except the necessary smoking gun; thus what is suggested here remains largely circumstantial. Assuming that the Galilean Antichrist legend is no literary fiction, the most reasonable seedbed for its germination is in fourth-century Galilee, not far in time or place from its earliest literary attestation. The rapidly changing social situation brought on by the Christianization of the Roman Empire, fervent interest in biblical sites, and economic hardships from overtaxation enforced by Roman law now charged with anti-Jewish, Christian theological polemic all contributed to the polarization between Christians and Jews, with leadership of the former operating from a theological perspective and a position of advantage. In some parts of the East, Christian attacks against Jews were severe enough to require protective legislation (Nathanson 1986, 29). Did fourth-century Christian leadership in Palestine find an opportunity during the crisis of a short-lived, Galilean revolutionary kingship, perhaps even one with messianic claims, to call to mind the woes and their antiroyal taunting? For as with the Antichrist of Dan legend, the Hebrew Bible was marshaled against another particular social group. The issues that prompted the human events that occurred in mid-fourth-century Galilee were volatile enough to become the stuff of legend, fueled perhaps by the massive earthquake just over a decade later (363 CE) (Russell 1985, 37–60), which may have intensified and reinforced any related cosmic concerns. In any event, this regional, anti-Jewish slander survived long enough to be picked up by the compiler of Pseudo-Methodius (or one of his sources) somewhere in northern Palestine or western Syria; whereupon it was woven into his apocalyptic, anti-Islamic narrative, absorbed by the travelogues of medieval pilgrims, and transmitted to the West.

CHAPTER NOTES

Unless otherwise indicated, all translations are my own. All biblical citations are taken from the New Revised Standard Version.

1. For the full text of this medieval pilgrimage account, see Wright 1969; Hamelius 1987. Authorship of the *Travels* has been questioned; Benjamin Braude suggests that, whoever the writer, "his only journey was to a library" (1996, 135).
2. The process is reciprocal, for once scripture becomes attached to an event, the event itself comes to be understood in light of scripture. One example that comes to mind is the early rabbinic (and Christian) perspective on their Samaritan contemporaries, who were often viewed in light of the Assyrian resettlements of 2 Kings 17 or the priestly expulsions in Nehemiah.
3. Bethsaida-Julias was not located within the borders of Galilee proper but in the region of Gaulanitis just east of the Jordan; however, in discussion of Bethsaida's connection with Chorazin and Capernaum, this technicality will be ignored.
4. For general references to Bethsaida in western medieval pilgrimage accounts, see McNamer 1999, 397–411.The best and most readable treatment of the Antichrist legend is McGinn 1994. The classic *religionsgeschichte* approach to the subject is Bousset 1896.
5. Wilhelm Bousset saw the notion of a human or superhuman incarnation of cosmic evil as being firmly rooted in the Jewish apocalypticism of the Second Temple Period, but as Gregory Jenks has convincingly shown, the Antichrist proper can be so named only with the advent of the Jesus movement; that is, without Christ there is no Antichrist (Jenks 1991). See also McGinn 1994, 3.
6. One might also recall Rev. Jerry Falwell's fairly recent public announcement, made on January 14, 1999, before a congregation of about 1,500 persons at Thomas Road Baptist Church in Kingsport, Tenn., in which he expressed the conviction that the Antichrist is a male Jew living somewhere in the world today. Falwell stated in his televised sermon that the Antichrist will be "a full-grown counterfeit of Jesus Christ. Of course he'll be Jewish."
7. Acre (Akko), the last Crusader outpost, fell to the Arabs in 1291.
8. Wright 1995, 69. *Nascetur Antichristus perditionis filius de tribu Dan qui fuit filius Jacobi genitus de Pala ancille Rachelis. Nascetur Antichristus in Corozaim, nutrietur in Bethsaida, regnabit in Capharnaum. Ingredietur in Iherusalem et sedebit in templo Dei quasi sit Deus.* There is an error in this edition of Wright's book, but a facsimile of the manuscript on p. 70 enables one to see the Latin reading *nutrietur in Bethsaida*, correcting "nurtured in Babylon."
9. McGinn 1979, 70. For the critical edition of the Syriac text of Pseudo-Methodius, along with its English translation, see Martinez 1985.

10. Cited in McGinn 1979, 70. Heraclius (610–41) had led the forces of Byzantium in a monumental victory over the Persians in 630. Upon returning to Constantinople, his son and coruler Constantine, Patriarch Sergius, along with the clergy, the senate, and the people, "received him on the coast of Asia Minor with olive branches and lighted candles, with hymns and acclamations of joy.... Here on 21 March [630] amid great rejoicing, he once more set up the Holy Cross won back from the Persians, and by this solemn act symbolized the victorius conclusion of the first great war of Christendom." Ostrogorsky 1969, 103–4. For a brief time Byzantium exerted control over Syria and Palestine, but in 638 this region was conquered by the Arabs.
11. See Kloppenborg 1987; Catchpole 1993.
12. For the view that the woes may be attributed to Jesus himself, see Kuhn 1995, 243–56.
13. Capernaum (Q 7:2; 10:15), Chorazin (Q10:13), Bethsaida (Q10:13), and Jerusalem (Q 4:1ff.; 11:51; 13:34). Tyre and Sidon are mentioned in Q^3, but are used only rhetorically; Allison 1997, 53.
14. Allison 1997, 53. See also Reed 1995, 17–36.
15. Commodian seems to be one of the first writers to bring the two strands together, a tradition that continues throughout the patristic era.
16. Lower Galilee refers to the topographical depression of the Jordan valley and not southern Galilee.
17. On excavations at Capernaum, see Tzaferis 1989; 1983, 198–204; Laughlin 1993, 54–61.
18. Some scholars claim to have identified tensions with Judaism, ranging from wariness to animosity, reflected in early Christian texts—tensions that are assumed to have arisen in situations of highest frustration. R. J. Bauckham, for example, writes of the second-century Apocalypse of Peter, "It is almost impossible...to imagine its being written outside the immediate context of Bar Kokhba's persecution of Christians" (1985, 287).
19. For discussion of the *minim* from the view that this term refers to Jewish Christians, see Avi-Yonah 1984, 138–45.
20. Yeivin and Navigad 1978, 299–301; Yeivin 1987, 22–36.
21. Cited by Strickert 1999, 369–70 n. 74.
22. Avi-Yonah 1984, 161–76. The new anti-Jewish legislation under Constantius II was directly aimed at keeping Jews separate from Christians and isolating Judaism within a growing imperial Christian presence. A Jew could be put to death for marrying or converting a Christian woman. He could also be put to death by public burning for any attack upon converts to Christianity.
23. 2.11. Cited in Avi-Yonah 1984, 171.
24. *Chronographia*, AM 5843 (351 CE). See Mango and Scott 1997, 67.
25. Aurelius Victor, *Liber De Caesaribus* 42.9–12 (1970). Also Bird 1994, 53, 201 n. 8. Although Patricius is mentioned only by Victor, the revolt was also recorded by others; cf. Sozomen, *Historia ecclesiastica* 4.7; Socrates, *Historia ecclesiastica* 2.33 (Schaff and Wace 1952).

LITERATURE CITED

Alexander, Paul. 1971. Byzantium and the Migration of Literary Works and
    Motifs: The Legend of the Last World Emperor. *Mediaevalia et Humanistica*,
    n.s., 2:47–82.
Allison, Dale C. Jr. 1997. *The Jesus Tradition in Q.* Harrisburg, Penn.: Trinity
    Press International.
Arav, Rami, and Richard A. Freund. 1995. *Bethsaida: A City by the North Shore
    of the Sea of Galilee.* Vol. 1. Kirksville, Mo.: Thomas Jefferson University
    Press.
———. 1999. *Bethsaida: A City by the North Shore of the Sea of Galilee.* Vol. 2.
    Kirksville, Mo.: Truman State University Press.
Aurelius Victor. 1970. *Liber De Caesaribus*, edited by F. Pilchmayer and B.
    Greundel. Leipzig: Teubner.
Avigad, N., and Benjamin Mazar. 1978. Beth She'arim. In *Encyclopedia of
    Archaeological Excavations in the Holy Land*, edited by M. Avi-Yonah and E.
    Stern. Englewood Cliffs, N.J.: Prentice-Hall.
Avi-Yonah, Michael. 1984. *The Jews under Roman and Byzantine Rule: A Political
    History of Palestine from the Bar Kokhba War to the Arab Conquest.* Jerusalem:
    Magnus Press, Hebrew University.
Bauckham, R. J. 1985. The Two Fig Tree Parables in the Apocalypse of Peter.
    Journal of Biblical Literature 104:269-87.
Bird, H. W. 1994. *Aurelius Victor: De Caesaribus.* Liverpool: Liverpool Univer-
    sity Press.
Bousset, Wilhelm. 1896. *Der Antichrist in der Überlieferung des Judentums, des
    Neuen Testament und der alten Kirche: Ein Beitrag zur Auslegung der Apoka-
    lypse.* Göttingen: Vandenhoeck und Ruprecht.
Braude, Benjamin. 1996. Mandeville's Jews among Others. In *Pilgrims and
    Travelers to the Holy Land*, edited by Menachem Mor and Bryan LeBeau.
    Studies in Jewish Civilization 7. Omaha, Neb.: Creighton University Press.
Catchpole, David R. 1993. *The Quest for Q.* Edinburgh: T & T Clark.
Cohen, A., trans. 1939. *Qoheleth Rabbah.* Vol. 8 of *Midrash Rabbah*, edited by
    H. Freedman and M. Simon. London: Soncino Press.
Donalson, Malcolm. 1996. *A Translation of Jerome's Chronicon with Historical
    Commentary.* Lewiston, N.Y.: Mellon University Press.
Emmerson, R. K. 1979. Antichrist as Anti-Saint: The Significance of Abbot
    Adso's Libellus de Antichristo. *American Benedictine Review* 30:179-90.
Fetellus. 1971. *Description of the Holy Land.* Translated by J. MacPherson.
    Library of the Palestinian Pilgrims' Text Society, vol. 5. London, 1895.
    Reprint, New York: AMS Press.
Hamelius, Paul, ed. 1987. *Mandeville's Travels: Translated from the French of Jean
    d'Outremeuse.* English Early Text Society. London: Kegan Paul, Trench,
    Trübner and Co., 1919. Reprint, Millwood, N.Y.: Krause Reprint Co.
Hill, C. E. 1995. Antichrist from the Tribe of Dan. *Journal of Theological Studies*,
    n.s., 46:99-117.

Horsley, Richard. 1996. *Archaeology, History, and Society in Galilee: The Social Context of Jesus and the Rabbis.* Valley Forge, Penn.: Trinity Press International.

Jenks, Gregory. 1991. *The Origins and Development of the Antichrist Myth.* Berlin: Walter de Gruyter.

John of Würzburg. 1971. *Description of the Holy Land.* Translated by A. Stewart. Library of the Palestinian Pilgrims' Text Society, vol. 5. London, 1895. Reprint, New York: AMS Press.

Kloppenborg, John S. 1987. *The Formation of Q.* Studies in Antiquity and Christianity. Philadelphia: Fortress Press.

Koester, Helmut. 1982. *History and Literature of Early Christianity.* Introduction to the New Testament, vol. 2. New York and Berlin: Walter de Gruyter.

———. 1990. *Ancient Christian Gospels: Their History and Development.* Philadelphia: Trinity Press International.

Kuhn, Heinz-Wolfgang. 1995. Bethsaida in the Gospels: The Feeding Story in Luke 9 and the Q Saying in Luke 10. In Arav and Freund 1995.

Laughlin, John C. H. 1993. Capernaum: From Jesus' Time and After. *Biblical Archaeologist* 56:54–61.

Mango, C., and R. Scott, eds. 1997. *The Chronicle of Theophanes Confessor.* Oxford: Clarendon Press.

Martinez, Francisco. 1985. Eastern Christian Apocalyptic in the Early Muslim Period: Pseudo-Methodius and Pseudo-Athanasius. Ph.D. diss., Catholic University of America.

McGinn, Bernard. 1979. *Visions of the End: Apocalyptic Traditions in the Middle Ages.* New York: Columbia University Press.

———. 1994. *Antichrist: Two Thousand Years of the Human Fascination with Evil.* San Francisco: Harper Collins.

McNamer, Elizabeth. 1999. Pilgrim Accounts and the Bethsaida Controversy. In Arav and Freund 1999.

Nathanson, B. G. 1986. Jews, Christians, and the Gallus Revolt in Fourth-Century Palestine. *Biblical Archaeologist* 49:26–36.

Ostrogorsky, George. 1969. *History of the Byzantine State.* Translated by Joan Hussey. New Brunswick: Rutgers University Press.

Pseudo-Beda. 1971. *Anonymous Pilgrims.* Translated by A. Stewart. Library of the Palestinian Pilgrims' Text Society, vol. 6. London, 1895. Reprint, New York: AMS Press.

Reed, Jonathan. 1995. *The Social Map of Q.* In *Conflict and Invention: Literary, Rhetorical, and Social Studies on the Sayings Gospel Q,* edited by John S. Kloppenborg. Valley Forge, Penn.: Trinity Press International.

Russell, Kenneth W. 1985. The Earthquake Chronology of Palestine and Northwest Arabia from the Second through the Mid-Eighth Century A.D. *Bulletin of the American Schools of Oriental Research* 260:37–60.

Savonensus, Phillip Brusserius. 1971. *Account of the Holy Land.* Translated by J. H. Bernard. Library of the Palestinian Pilgrims' Text Society, vol. 6. London, 1895. Reprint, New York: AMS Press.

Schaff, Philip, and Henry Wace, eds. 1973. *Sozomen; Socrates: Ecclesiastical History.* 1952. Reprint, Grand Rapids, Mich.: Wm. B. Eerdmans.

Strickert, Fred. 1999. Destruction of Bethsaida in 1 Esdras 1:11. In Arav and Freund 1999.

Theodorich of Würzburg. 1971. *Description of the Holy Places.* Translated by A. Stewart. Library of the Palestinian Pilgrims' Text Society, vol. 5. London, 1895. Reprint, New York: AMS Press.

Tzaferis, Vassilios. 1983. New Archaeological Evidence on Capernaum. *Biblical Archaeologist* 46:198–204.

———. 1989. *Excavations at Capernaum.* Vol. 1. Winona Lake: Ind.: Eisenbrauns.

Wilson, C. W., ed. 1971. *Pilgrimage of the Russian Abbot Daniel in the Holy Land.* Library of the Palestinian Pilgrims' Text Society, vol. 4. London,1895. Reprint, New York: AMS Press.

Wright, Rosemary Muir. 1995. *Art and Antichrist in Medieval Europe.* Manchester: Manchester University Press.

Wright, Thomas, ed. 1969. *Early Travels in Palestine.* London: Henry G. Bohn, 1848. Reprint, New York: AMS Press.

Yeivin, S. 1987. Ancient Chorazin Comes Back to Life. *Biblical Archaeology Review* 13:22–36.

Yeivin, S., and A. Navigad. 1978. Chorazin. In *Encyclopedia of Archaeological Excavations in the Holy Land,* edited by M. Avi-Yonah and E. Stern. Englewood Cliffs, N.J.: Prentice-Hall.

Contributors

MARK APPOLD received his Th.D. from the University of Tübingen, Germany. He is professor of religion at Truman State University and a Lutheran pastor.

RAMI ARAV earned his Ph.D. at New York University and his M.A. from Tel Aviv University in Israel. As director of excavations and research, Dr. Arav supervises all on-site archaeological work and directs research and publication efforts of the Bethsaida Excavations Project. He is professor of religion and foreign languages at the University of Nebraska at Omaha.

HECTOR AVALOS received his Ph.D. and M.Th. from Harvard University. He is associate professor of religious studies and director of the Latino/a studies program at Iowa State University. His research interests include ancient health care.

RICHARD A. FREUND received his Ph.D. from the Jewish Theological Seminary. He serves as project director and corresponding secretary for the Bethsaida Excavations Project, which he initiated, along with Dr. Arav, during his tenure at the University of Nebraska at Omaha. He is director of the Maurice Greenberg Center for Judaic Studies at the University of Hartford.

JOHN T. GREENE received his Ph.D. from Boston University. He has collaborated with Dr. Rami Arav on the Bethsaida Excavations Project for nearly fifteen years. Dr. Greene is professor of religious studies at Michigan State University. His areas of research are world religions, history of religions, archaeology, ancient Semitic languages, German language and literature, and Sanskrit studies.

RICHARD HESS earned his Ph.D. degree in West Semitic languages and literature from Hebrew Union College. He received his M.Div. and Th.M. degrees from Trinity Evangelical Divinity School. Dr. Hess is professor of Old Testament at Denver Seminary.

HEINZ-WOLFGANG KUHN received his D.Th. from the University of Heidelberg. Dr. Kuhn is professor of New Testament at the University of Munich.

NICOLAE RODDY earned his M.A. in orthodox theology from St. Vladimir's Orthodox Theological Seminary and his Ph.D. in early Judaism and Christianity from the University of Iowa. Dr. Roddy is director for the Bethsaida Excavations Project. He is assistant professor of theology at Creighton University.

MARK D. SMITH earned his Ph.D. in ancient/medieval/Reformation history from the University of California, Santa Barbara, and his M.Div. in church history from Denver Seminary. His primary area of specialization is the Roman Empire. Dr. Smith currently serves as vice president of academic affairs of Albertson College.

FRED STRICKERT received his M.Div. and S.T.M. from Christ Seminary-Seminex, and his Ph.D. from the University of Iowa. Dr. Strickert is professor of religion at Wartburg College.

Index

Livia/Julia, *continued*
"Velleia Livia," 98, **99**, 100, 107,
108
wife of Octavian (Augustus), 97, 156
Luckenbill, Daniel, 80n5

M
Maacah (city), 5, 9, 40n2, 42n18
Maacah (daughter of Absalom), 5, 9
Maacah (daughter of Talmai, wife of
David), 5, 8–9
Maacah (name), occurrences of,
56–57
Maachites, 5
Mandeville, John, *Travels of Sir John
Mandeville*, 273
Maoz, Zvi U., 40n7
maps, medieval and premodern, and
location of Bethsaida, 184–89,
185, **187**, **188**
Martin Jones, Arnold Hugh, 42n20
Mazar, Amihai, 72, 79n1
Mazar, Benjamin, 3, 5, 13, 49
McCown, Chester, 207n4
medical anthropology, 213–31
medicine. *See* health care
Megiddo (Tell el-Mutesellim),
destroyed, 15, 71
Mercator (cartographer), on location
of Bethsaida-Julias, 188–89
Meshorer, Ya'akov, 94, 95, 178n16
Meshoshim River, 184, **185**
Milgrom, Jacob, 25, 26, 29
military campaigns, 11–13, 66
monolatry, and health care, 217–19
moon-god worship, 5, 14, **30**, **35**
Mount Ebal, 27
Mount Hermon, 12

N
Na'aman, Nadav, 13, 43n25
names (personal/geographical)
Akkadian, 52
Amorite, 52–53

at Bethsaida, 54–55; Greek, 143,
147n20; Hebrew, 56
Bronze Age, 50–53
of et-Tell/Bethsaida, xii, 83, 120,
156
Eusebius, *Place-Names in Holy
Scripture,* 256–60
Geshur, 49–62
from Hebrew Bible, 56–57
Hurrian, 53
Iron Age, 53–55
Jericho, 121
Maacah, 56–57
in New Testament, 139
Ptolemy, on Bethsaida, 94, 187–88
Semitic, 52, 53
Tzer (Tzer): of et-Tell, xi, 65
Naveh, Joseph, 54
neo-Assyria. *See* Assyrian empire
Neusner, Jacob, 239
Noth, Martin, 54

O
Odoric dePordenone, *Travels in the
Far East,* 275
onomastica of Bronze and Iron Ages,
49–62

P
Paris, Matthew (cartographer), 185
Parpola, Simo, 216
Paul (Apostle), 137
Pehel. *See* Pella/Pehel
Pekah (king of Israel), 14, 68, 69
Pella/Pehel, 3, 4, 40n5
Penney, Douglas L., 218
Peter (Apostle)
acquainted with tanners, 242
from Bethsaida to Rome, 133–48
confession of, in synoptic Gospels,
150–51
domus ecclesia of Capernaum, 284
as fisherman, 141–42
"Peter-house" at Capernaum,
140–41

Index

Index of Scripture References